ABAP/4: Programming the SAP R/3 System

ABAP/4: Programming the SAP R/3 System

Bernd Matzke

Translated by Audrey Weinland

 Addison-Wesley

Harlow, England • Reading, Massachusetts • Menlo Park, California
New York • Don Mills, Ontario • Amsterdam • Bonn • Sydney • Singapore
Tokyo • Madrid • San Juan • Milan • Mexico City • Seoul • Taipei

First published by Addison-Wesley (Deutschland) GmbH 1996 as *ABAP/4 Die Programmiersprache des SAP-Systems R/3*

Addison Wesley Longman Limited
Edinburgh Gate
Harlow
Essex CM20 2JE
England

and Associated Companies throughout the World.

Cover designed by odB Design & Communication, Reading
Typeset by 42
Typeset in 9.5/12pt Palatino
Printed and bound in the United States of America

First printed 1997

ISBN 0-201-92471-4

British Library Cataloguing-in-Publication Data
A catalogue record for this book is available from the British Library

Contents

Trademark notices

The following are trademarks or registered trademarks of their respective companies:
SAP Aktiengesellschaft; Windows (Microsoft) Corporation; Motif, Open Software
Foundation Inc.; iXOS Software GmbH.

Foreword

The overwhelming success of SAP's R/3 System in German and international industry has led to major changes in the software landscape in the last few years. The result is entirely new tasks for consulting companies who concentrate their efforts on setting up and customizing the R/3 System.

Technically, R/3 is a client/server system that is implemented at three levels. One system holds the database, several application systems execute the applications, and networked PCs display the man/machine interface. The applications themselves are written in the SAP language ABAP/4 and are created and maintained using the ABAP/4 Development Workbench.

Bernd Matzke and other employees of iXOS were naturally immediately fascinated by this development environment. Unfortunately, not much secondary literature was available. Next to SAP's standard training, the only option was to train oneself by trial and error with the R/3 System.

In the tradition of iXOS Software Ltd, and with the support of SAP, Inc., Bernd Matzke has now thankfully written this book, to make the fundamentals of the ABAP/4 programming language accessible to other developers. We hope this will close a gap and contribute to the continued success of the R/3 System.

Hans Strack-Zimmermann
March 1996

1 Introduction

The programming language ABAP/4 is a basic, inseparable part of the SAP R/3 System. Except for the system kernel, which is programmed in C, the entire system, including its development tools and applications, consists of ABAP/4 programs. This insures development that is independent of the operating system. The fact that the development environment is available as a separate product makes the language interesting for non-R/3 users, as well. Programmers who deal with the ABAP/4 language, however, must grow accustomed to several characteristics of this tool that considerably complicate training.

The ABAP/4 language originated in the R/2 System, where a *general report-preparation processor* enabled the creation of print lists using a simple programming language. This language, which was at first used exclusively for reporting, expanded over time into a full-fledged development tool. This is also the origin of the term used today: *Advanced Business Application Language*.

The programming language ABAP/4 was not created by one person or by a small circle of experts around a conference table. Beginning with the first versions in the R/2 System, this language has been and continues to be enhanced. Its development is the responsibility of a large team, although work on individual areas (for example, the type concept, linking to the database, and design of the user interface) is performed relatively independently of the other areas. From version to version, the scope of the language has expanded to include new features. For compatibility reasons, however, it is not (or only in rare cases) possible for outdated elements to be removed. As a result, the scope of the language continues to grow, and the tool itself is becoming more and more complex.

Unlike C or Pascal, the ABAP/4 language is not a programming language that can be implemented universally. Programs created in the R/2 and R/3 Systems are based on certain concepts, for example, the dynpro concept. This concept specifies the structure of an application within relatively narrow limits. The elements of the programming language follow this concept. ABAP/4 consists of statements that have been created specifically for a precisely defined program type with a given functionality and structure. Over the course of time, the programming language has had to become more flexible, especially when the switch was made to graphical user interfaces, and when client/server architecture was implemented. New commands have been created around the existing commands, and new options have been added to existing commands, giving several commands entirely new functionality. Often, a command's option says more about the task of that command than its actual name does. Some of the command variants created this way perform a distinct, sometimes low-level task. For this reason, they are not necessarily of general interest; they are useful only to specialists.

The scope of the ABAP/4 language was never specified by any standard. The language set its own standard. It is therefore not possible, nor does it make sense, to provide an all-encompassing introduction to the syntax of this language. An introduction to ABAP/4 programming must start with programming concepts, because the language is founded on a programming concept that must be understood before many of the commands can be understood.

This book is not meant to be an alternative to SAP's system documentation or training courses. In the course of my own work, I have learned that it is quite difficult for beginners to properly channel the multitude of facts about the R/3 System and the programming language and to filter out the points that are important for their own work. I have therefore tried to fill the gap between general introductions such as the book by Buck-Emden and Galimow [1] and the system documentation, which is very specialized. The main goal of this book is to enable users who have experience in data processing to quickly familiarize themselves with programming in ABAP/4. It is geared especially to those who provide support for SAP systems and to potential application developers.

1.1   About the contents of this book

The development environment has a number of elements and defines several terms. Knowledge of these is very important for understanding the system as a whole. Chapter 2 presents the most important elements of the development system, as well as often-used terms. The chapter does not go into technical details; it explains only the basic tasks of the elements described.

Chapter 3 examines the different program types and their characteristics. In this context, the chapter also presents the ABAP/4 statements that are typically used with these program types. The emphasis here is not on describing the various commands in their entirety, but rather on demonstrating the tasks that the ABAP/4 statements perform in each program. Even with these limitations, the chapter provides enough information about the ABAP/4 commands to enable you to analyze existing standard applications and to write new programs. Chapter 3 consists of five sections. The first section introduces important programming fundamentals, for example, the data concept and the control statements of the ABAP/4 language. The second and third sections discuss the two basic program types, reports and dialog applications. Reports can be expanded into interactive applications through the use of additional language elements. The fourth section presents the dialog concept and the commands used with it. The final section in Chapter 3 describes function modules. These modules allow you to use program code from several other applications.

Creating applications requires other activities besides pure programming. One of these is creating database tables. These tables are Data Dictionary elements, which are described in Chapter 4.

Chapter 5 explores several programming utilities in detail. Particular attention is paid to the Workbench Organizer, which is used for relaying applications and for documenting changes, and to the Online Debugger.

In contrast to Chapter 3, which focuses on programming concepts, Chapter 6 describes the creation of a simple application. It demonstrates how individual components can be combined into working applications.

A quick reference for the current ABAP/4 commands appears in Chapter 8. This reference does not include outdated commands that have since been replaced by other commands. Also absent are various commands designed only for internal use by SAP.

All of the sample programs were developed on a 3.0 system. Many of these examples, however, can also run on other versions of the R/3 software. The text itself contains explicit information regarding versions. All of the screens were captured on a Windows SAP GUI. The essential elements of the manuscript for this book were finalized in January of 1996, shortly before the completion of Release 3.0C. Several minor changes were made in the 3.0C development system after that date. These could no longer be taken into consideration in the book. The changes affect only details, however, such as the revision of some symbols, and the replacement of step loops with table views in several of the development environment's standard tools. So, although there are some minor deviations here and there with regard to the use of various tools, these deviations do not affect the tools' functionality.

1.2 Exercises

A programming language is best learned by analyzing existing programs and practicing creating your own programs. For this reason, you will find exercises scattered throughout the book. In cases where the material taught has a relatively small scope, the exercises are located at the end of the section. Their main purpose is to help you retain the information relayed. Further on, the exercises are dispersed in the text. Examples for the use of new statements sometimes become quite complex, meaning they cannot always be printed in their entirety. In such cases, your task is to write a test environment for the new statements or objects, building on existing knowledge and programs. This should strengthen the knowledge you have gained from previous sections and at the same time increase your confidence and experience in working with the development environment. Even if the text does not explicitly call for it, you should write and test your own programs for all printed program fragments.

1.3 Naming conventions

The SAP system can be configured different ways. Distinctions are made, for example, between SAP development systems (found only at SAP), development systems at partner companies of SAP and customer systems. One of the differences between these systems is the valid name range for development objects (programs, tables and so on). With a few exceptions, the examples in this book are based on the requirements for customer systems. If you attempt to replicate these examples in a system that is configured differently, you will receive messages in several places regarding the violation of naming conventions. You can usually still create the desired objects after you have received the warning. If you encounter difficulties, however, you should turn to the system administrator who is responsible for your system. He or she can provide information about your system's type and the related effects on naming conventions. In many cases, the online help, which you can access by clicking on the *Help* pushbutton in any warning message, can provide assistance.

1.4   Acknowledgments

At this point, I would like to thank everyone who was directly or indirectly involved in producing this book for their help. In particular, I would like to thank SAP and iXOS, who gave me the opportunity to write this book. Special thanks also to the SAP employees who answered my questions with expertise and patience, making it easier for me to delve into the subjects of this book, SAP R/3 and ABAP/4.

Bernd Matzke
Delitzsch, Germany, March 24, 1996

2 The elements of the development environment

An application in the R/3 System that was written in ABAP/4 consists of several different types of elements, called development objects. The actual source code, of course, is one of these, but other elements, such as menus or screens, are also included. Each of these objects performs a specific task in the application, and there are various relationships between them. With a few exceptions, it is necessary to use several types of development objects for every application. As a result, even simple applications require extensive preparation, and they require creating several different, yet coordinated, development objects. This makes ABAP/4 programming very different from programming in traditional, third-generation programming languages such as C or Pascal.

In addition to the development objects, the R/3 System provides some important utilities and tools that play a major role in the system. For this reason, before discussing the elements of an ABAP/4 application in detail, it is important to describe the tasks of the various objects, their characteristics and their relationships to each other, without going into specifics on the ABAP/4 programming language.

2.1 The Data Dictionary

A computer, or rather a program, produces and processes data. Although this data can be temporary in nature, more often it consists of data sets that need to be stored long-term, including when hardware is shut down. One of the most important tasks of an operating system is to manage bulk storage, which usually consists of one or more hard disks. As a result, work with a system's bulk storage is necessarily heavily dependent on the operating system. The user is forced to fiddle around with file names and directory names, which follow different conventions on different systems. Other differences include, for example, the structure of the file system, special file attributes and access methods. Irrespective of this, various relational database systems control specially reserved areas in bulk storage directly, although, again, every system follows its own strategy. This data can only be accessed with the database system. All of these circumstances make it difficult to create applications that are independent of the operating system, let alone develop tools that can be used to create such applications independent of the specific operating system.

The R/3 System does not rely directly on the services of the operating system; instead, it uses a relational database system for the storage of data sets. The database system stores all of the information – not just the actual business data, but also programs, screens, menus and other elements – in table form. To circumvent the problems mentioned above concerning dependency on the operating system, the R/3 System must provide a general, system-independent interface to the data set. This interface is the Data Dictionary.

The Data Dictionary stores all information entirely independent of the platform. Applications – and therefore the programmers – need no longer concern themselves with specific storage locations, drive and directory names or anything like that. Organization based on physical criteria is replaced by an arrangement according to logical viewpoints, such as affiliation to a program, to an object further up in the hierarchy or to a table.

The Data Dictionary is a virtual database whose functionality goes beyond that of typical relational database systems. In particular, it handles the following tasks:

- Creation of a general interface to the database system
- Provision of meta data about the actual database tables
- Provision of general tools for data processing

The Data Dictionary consists of various elements, which are used in different places in an application. For the most part, the elements are maintained independently of each other, but there are certain dependencies to be observed. The most important elements are described in more detail in the sections that follow.

2.1.1   Tables

The central element of a database-oriented application is the data sets that are stored in tables. A data set (also called a tuple) consists of one or more fields; it describes the attributes of a real object (an entity). A table consists of any number of similar data sets.

When implementing a relational database system, whenever possible, you prepare information in such a way as to avoid storing redundant data. This requires appropriate data modeling, followed by the creation of several logically related tables. The set of all related tables is called a database, which is stored in the system's bulk storage. You manage these tables using a relational database system, which usually works with the query language SQL.

In R/3, aside from a few exceptions, the only way to access this database system and the tables of the database is to use the Data Dictionary interface. Since the exceptions can only be used in special cases, and they carry with them a series of disadvantages, they will not be described in detail here. The Data Dictionary can store the data to be processed in a different format in the database than the format in which the user can access it with the interface. The reason for this transformation is that the database systems used are subject to certain limitations concerning the number of tables and fields in those tables. The Data Dictionary minimizes this problem by using special storage methods. This, in turn, has its price: different table types that the programmer cannot treat equally.

For the majority of tables, the Data Dictionary provides a fully transparent interface to the database. This means that all of the fields of a Dictionary table correspond to a field in the real database table. Since the data structure visible in the Dictionary corresponds entirely to the structure of the table created by the database system, these tables are called transparent tables.

The Data Dictionary can handle several other table types in addition to the transparent tables; these, however, will lose importance in the future and should not be used for new development. The capacity limitations of the database systems that were mentioned earlier make it necessary, under certain circumstances, to combine several tables into one. This can be done in two ways. Different tables that are not linked to each other with a common key can be combined in a table pool. The tables contained in this pool are called pooled tables. A table pool is stored in the database as a simple table. The table's data sets contain, in separate fields, the actual key for the data set to be stored, the name of the pooled table and the contents of the data set to be stored. In this way, several logical tables are combined into a single real database table. Although the data structure of each set is lost during the write to the table pool, it is restored during the read by the Data Dictionary. The Data Dictionary uses the meta data mentioned earlier for this.

Occasionally, several tables exist that are linked by a common key. The Data Dictionary can also combine these tables into a single table. Each data set of the real table in the database contains a key and, in a single data field, several data sets of the subsequent table for this key. In this case, too, the data must be prepared by the Data Dictionary during a read or write, because the data structure of the database table does not match the structure stored in the Data Dictionary. The elements created this way are called clusters, and the tables are called cluster tables.

Both table pools and table clusters are stored as tables in the database. Since the actual information must be prepared by the Data Dictionary when it is accessed, these are not transparent tables. Only the structures of the pooled tables and the cluster tables that represent a single logical view of the data are defined in the Data Dictionary. The data is actually stored in bulk storage in a different structure. The Data Dictionary handles the corresponding adjustments itself.

Finally, the Data Dictionary stores structures, also called internal tables. Unfortunately, this latter term is ambiguous. For this reason, the text that follows uses only the term "structure." Structures appear like a table in the Dictionary, but they do not have any data sets in the database. Only the structure of the table is important, that is, the fields it contains and their attributes. The function of a structure in ABAP/4 programs is similar to the function of type definitions in traditional programming languages.

2.1.2   Fields, data elements and domains

A database system stores characteristics (attributes) of an object (entity) that exists in the real world in the fields of data sets. These attributes can be described according to their logical importance to the user; or they can be described according to their technical properties (data type, length and so on).

The first thing you need to gain independence from the system is a general data description that is independent of the database system used. The various database systems can easily have a set of different data types at their disposal that they represent and process internally in completely different ways. These differences might affect, for example, the range of numbers that can be represented, or the format for storing complex data (such as graphics).

The Dictionary provides access to meta data, too. This data is not only of a technical nature; it can also deliver application-related information. Different attributes of an entity may have similar technical properties. Alternatively, different entities may have identical attributes. For example, both the master data record for an employee and the employment contract for that employee contain the employee's personnel number. Both of the fields have the same structure and the same meaning, despite their use in different tables. And yet it is possible to imagine a field with the same format that contains something else, say, an item number. In light of the complexity of the R/3 System, it is desirable to link such information directly to the actual data and not to store it separately, for example in the documentation.

In the SAP system, therefore, considerably more information is stored for field attributes than the relational database system needs for processing the tables. In addition to various technical and application-related entries, this includes valid value ranges for the field, or a reference to a check table. Because such field descriptions can be used more than once, they are managed independently of the database tables. This has the advantage that one can describe fields and their attributes in detail, regardless of their later use. This description is then available in various places at various times, for example, during table maintenance or when writing data entry programs.

Two different elements are always required for the description of a field. Domains form the basic foundation for field descriptions. A domain describes the technical structure of a field, that is, its size and its data type. Every domain is given a unique name. The data elements build on the domains. They contain a reference to a domain, to define the technical attributes, and they supplement this with statements concerning the logical meaning of the data element from the user's point of view. A domain can be used in several data elements; these, in turn, can be used in various database fields.

Data elements and domains exist independently of the actual table, so they can be used in several tables. Before a table can be created in the Data Dictionary, the data elements necessary for its data fields need to be gathered or created.

Practical applications sometimes contain data for which extensive maintenance of domains and data elements is not really justified. Beginning with Release 3.0, it is possible to create table fields with a direct reference to a data type, that is, without a data element and domain. These kinds of fields, however, do not possess the full functionality of fields that reference a data element and are therefore of interest only in special cases. They are not discussed in this book.

The following example shows the connection between the elements described. Imagine a domain with the name NUM4, which is four places long and has the data type NUMC. This domain can accept a text that is four characters long and consists only of numerals.

This domain can serve as a technical description for various data elements. One such data element might be, for example, PLZ, which defines a postal code. This meaning is established in the data element with a descriptive short text. Independent of this, the NUM4 domain could also be used in a different data element, for example PNR, to describe a personnel number.

A table is now created, and the data element PLZ is assigned, as a description, to the field KPLZ, which is to contain the postal code of a customer. With this assignment, all of the attributes of this field are defined at once.

The data element PLZ can also be used in other tables to describe fields that should contain postal codes. These fields can have names other than KPLZ.

The advantage is obvious. Changing all of the postal codes from four places to five places now would not require changing a lot of field descriptions in various tables.

Instead, it would only require the creation of a new domain, NUM5 (five places, type NUMC), and the entry of the new domain in the description of the data element PLZ. The Data Dictionary supports where-used searches for the different objects (domains, fields, tables and so on). In this case, the Data Dictionary would generate a list, in which one could then identify which tables contain fields that use the data element PLZ. Changing the postal code from four places to five places would then simply require changing the contents of these tables (entering the new postal code with a conversion program).

Domains thus correspond roughly to type declarations in the various programming languages (typedef in C/C++, TYPE in Pascal). Traditional programming languages, however, do not have a comparable equivalent to data elements.

In addition to purely describing field attributes, domains also enable automation of several standard checks in applications. For example, the name of a check table or a list of constants may be entered in the description of a domain. When a data set is processed that contains a field based on that domain, an automatic check is performed using various system mechanisms, to see whether the value of the affected table field matches the value from the check table or the list of constants. If there is no match, the data set is rejected. These tests take place automatically; the programmer does not need to write additional code for this.

2.1.3   Views

As previously mentioned, when relational database systems are implemented, the data to be stored is distributed across several tables to avoid redundancies. The related data sets are linked with unique labels. Appropriate statements are needed to establish this link, for example multi-level queries in logically related tables.

To simplify the work, you can create a virtual table that links fields from one or more tables to each other and offers them to the user as a single table. Since this new table does not exist in reality, but is just a special form of presentation, it is called a view. In the SAP system, there are several different types of views for various applications. Database tables can be processed relatively easily using views. Automatically generated maintenance programs handle this. The database view and the customizing view are particularly important for programming your own applications. In addition to these two types of views, the system offers several other views.

Database views

Database views are implemented as true views of the database system, so they can include only transparent tables. They provide a collection of tables. They cannot be edited if they contain fields from more than one table. These kinds of views make it easy to fill tables with data without having to write separate programs.

Customizing views

Customizing views enable editing of data sets, even if several tables are included in the view. When such views are created, the system generates maintenance programs, which can be called and executed with a special transaction. As the name implies, customizing views are used mainly during customizing. Customizing is a process in which an application can be modified to the concrete needs of the user through entry of predefined values in selected tables.

Projection views

Projection views offer a view of a single table, in which fields that are not of interest can be hidden.

Help views

Help views were created for displaying special help information. They have no meaning outside the help system.

Entity views

Entity views are important only for the Enterprise Data Model.

2.1.4   Lock objects

Usually, when you work with a database, the database should be locked against access from other users, since simultaneous write access to the same table can sometimes cause an undefined state.

By calling several functions, you can lock data sets (individually or in groups) against outside access during the processing of a table, and also unlock them. To make it easier to use the locking functions and make changes when the underlying database table changes, the R/3 System uses lock objects. These are managed independently of any specific application. For the programmer, these lock objects appear as input templates, in which the tables and fields to be locked, as well as a locking mechanism, are entered. Once the lock objects have been completely defined, the system uses the information entered to generate two function modules for each menu command. These function modules perform all of the necessary activities for locking or unlocking (releasing) each table or selected data set. These function modules can then be called by all applications that want to process the table.

If the conditions on which a lock was based change, you simply edit the lock object, and the function modules are regenerated. It is usually not necessary to change the source code of the applications that use this lock object or the function modules. In cases where it is still necessary, the generation of a where-used list for each menu command makes executing the changes easier.

2.1.5   Authorizations

Usually, several users from different departments with different tasks work in a single SAP system. This requires using effective mechanisms to prevent unauthorized access. The SAP system provides a very flexible procedure for this, which is based on an explicit authorization check within an application. Before an action is carried out (for example, before the start of a program branch), the authorizations of the user in question are checked. This does not occur automatically; it requires special statements in the program. This procedure is therefore fundamentally different from implicit authorization checks, such as those familiar from network or multi-user operating systems. Those systems usually only monitor access to files, using access privileges such as those for reading, writing, executing or deleting files. SAP authorizations, in contrast, allow you to protect not only tables and individual fields, but also other objects and actions, such as programs, reports, program branches and so on. It is possible, for example, to make the processing and displaying of data as dependent on the existence of the proper authorizations as the processing of a program. Depending on the authorizations of the user, applications can even branch and carry out different activities unbeknown to the user.

The reason for this flexibility is that authorizations are created and managed independently of the object to be protected. The relationship to the object must be explicitly created in the application with an authorization check. The system itself only provides utilities for managing several elements, which you can use to define a user's authorizations.

Dispensing with implicit authorization checks does have a downside, however. It is possible for any programmer to write programs that can access almost all of the tables in a system and manipulate them at will. In productive systems, every user who is allowed to create programs presents a potential security risk. It is therefore important to handle the authorizations in question very carefully.

Authorization checks are based on a simple principle. A user is given authorizations. An authorization is a complex object that contains several authorization fields, which are, in turn, assigned a value. The authorizations are stored in the user's master record. In the program, a special ABAP/4 statement checks if a certain field of the current user's authorization contains a certain value. The result of this check is evaluated explicitly in the program; the check itself does not yet affect the program flow. What specifically should be protected by this authorization is not revealed until the result of the check is evaluated in the program. Only then is the connection between the authorization and the object to be protected established. This means that several actions or data objects can be protected with a single authorization, and that different authorizations can allow access to the same object.

In practice, this type of authorization check requires the use of many individual fields, if truly flexible checks are needed, because a separate authorization field may be required for every object to be protected. For this reason, the fields and authorizations are not allocated individually to the user. Instead, there is a multi-level hierarchy of elements for managing authorizations and allocating them to the user.

The required elements are defined independently of the user. First, an authorization object is created that contains one or more fields (maximum: 10). The authorization objects, in turn, are combined into authorization classes, which contain the objects that belong to an application or a task area. The created objects at first represent only general descriptions, somewhat comparable to the type definitions in procedural programming languages such as C or Pascal. No values have been assigned to the authorization fields yet.

To assign specific privileges to a user, the actual authorizations are derived from an authorization object, again independent of the user. Within each authorization, then, the fields are given concrete values. Each authorization receives a unique name. Any number of authorizations can be derived from one authorization object. These authorizations can be given different field values. Authorizations are similar to instances of a type (the authorization object) in traditional programming languages.

Several authorizations are then combined into a profile, and several such profiles can be combined into a composite profile. Profiles and composite profiles combine logically related authorizations, thereby identifying authorizations as belonging to a certain task area, for example, the authorizations for an asset accountant or a personnel department employee. In order for the authorizations to be uniquely identifiable later, the authorization object is entered in a profile as a general description first, then the actual authorization is entered as a concrete value, as a supplement to the object. It is also possible to combine various authorizations of an object into a single profile. These are then linked with OR in the check.

All of the authorization profiles that the user should have are entered in the user master record. Thus, after the interim steps of composite profile, profile and authorization, the user has authorization fields with values. These values may contain simple yes/no information, but it is also possible to pass on detailed information based on the field value. In the existing authorizations in the SAP system, for example, the value of one field determines whether a user may look into, change, or delete a table. For each of these activities there is a code, whose meaning is revealed only by the authorization check. To simplify documentation, it is possible to store explanations for the possible field values.

2.1.6 Number ranges

In many applications, the key to a table consists of a unique consecutive number, for example a document number or a personnel number. The uniqueness of these numbers must be guaranteed, even when several applications attempt to distribute a number at the same time. For this reason, it is not left to the application to determine this number. Instead, the system provides number ranges. When an application requests a number (by calling special function modules), it is given the next available number from a number range. There can be several number ranges in the system, so each is given a unique name that allows it to be addressed in programs.

2.2   Transactions

Transactions form the core of SAP program processing. They are the smallest unit that can be executed directly by the user. They form a shell around the actual program. Executable applications are not accessible to the user until a transaction has been created for them. Each transaction is identified by a four-character transaction code. The name can contain letters and numbers. These transaction codes can either be entered directly in the input field of the user interface, or be located in the menus.

Transactions are executed by the internal control logic, which is not accessible to the user or the programmer. The control logic monitors the application completely, also, for example, intercepting runtime errors, removing database locks under certain conditions, and automatically recording database changes.

To the user, a transaction in SAP appears as what is commonly thought of as a program. There are very few program types in the SAP system. Every program type also has a special transaction type.

2.2.1   Dialog transactions

Dialog transactions are the transactions used most often. They enable the execution of a dialog program. Such programs are based on one or more screens, which are called *dynpros* in SAP applications. Dynpros provide the only opportunity to carry out a true dialog with the user of a program.

2.2.2   Report transactions

Next to dialog programs, there is another important type of application: the report. In their basic form, reports run without any influence by the user. They produce report lists. In order for the user to be able to start such reports easily from the menu, a special transaction must be created for them, too, linking the transaction code with the report in question.

2.2.3   Parameter transactions

The dialog transactions just mentioned start a dialog application. All of the data must be entered by the user. Often, dialog programs are structured in such a way that the user enters a few values in the first screen, then these values are used to select an object to be edited. All other screens are then used for processing this object.

Take, for example, the transaction SM30, which is used to edit the views mentioned earlier. The name of the view must be entered in the initial screen of this transaction, and an editing type must be selected. In the subsequent screen, the fields of that view are displayed, and the user can edit the data.

To simplify the work of the application user, or to restrict his or her access to certain objects, it is possible to have the program automatically submit the values that would normally be entered manually in the first screen. In this case, the application starts immediately with the subsequent screen, in which a view can be edited. This functionality requires yet another transaction type, the parameter transaction. Parameter transactions start an interactive program and submit default values to the program.

For every parameter transaction, the programmer records the transaction code of the application to be started and the parameters to be submitted. If the same application should be started with different parameters, different parameter transactions are required.

2.2.4   Variant transactions

In dialog applications, communication with the user takes place using the screens (input templates). The screens have a static structure, but the appearance of the screens can be modified at runtime using program statements, for example to hide fields. Variant transactions provide another option for adjusting screens. They allow variants to be created for existing dialog transactions. In these variants, screen fields can be hidden or given default values.

2.2.5   Area menu

There are two ways to call the various transactions. The first is to enter the four-character transaction code directly into the OK field of the user interface. This variant allows the quickest possible access to an application, assuming the user knows the transaction code.

The more elegant method, and the one more in keeping with the graphical user interface, is to call transactions using menus. In an application, menus are stored in what is known as the user interface. These menus call the different functions of an application. In the case of cross-application menus, that is, those that call entire transactions, this variant cannot be used. Instead, area menus must be used. These can be thought of as a special type of transaction.

An area menu has a transaction code that calls it. Its task is simply to display a menu. Transaction codes are, in turn, assigned to the individual menu items. When the user selects a menu item, the corresponding transaction is executed. This may be one of the transactions already mentioned for executing an application, or it may be another area menu.

2.3   Reports

Reports are the second-largest program group next to dialog applications. In their basic form, reports access one or more database tables and display the contents of these tables in a list format. This list can be viewed on the screen or printed out. In contrast to dialog transactions, reports can be processed directly from within the development environment, without additional elements such as screens or user interfaces having to be created first. For this reason, they are also called online applications. Reports are also used as tools for program development and maintenance. For a report to be usable by an end user, it needs to be linked to an application or to a report transaction, as already mentioned.

In principle, you can use almost any ABAP/4 statement in a report. It is even possible to create a report that interacts with the user, although this requires a rather large programming effort, because you need to use special statements and include interactive elements. The programming method is very different from that used to create simple reports without interactive elements. For this reason, reports are divided into standard reports and interactive reports. Reports most closely resemble programs in other programming languages. Since they are easier to create than dialog applications, they are used later in this book to introduce the ABAP/4 programming language.

2.3.1   Selection and parameters

SAP tables and report lists can be very large. The user needs to be able to limit the data set to be processed before the report is executed. It is therefore possible to display a selection screen on which the user can enter values before report execution actually starts. With the help of special statements in the report, this selection screen can accept two basic types of elements: selections and parameters. Using selections, the user can specify complex sets of data, such as a range (from/to) or a group of individual values. With a parameter, in contrast, the user can submit only a single value.

A selection screen is an automatically generated screen. Every report has only one selection screen. The values submitted to the report by the selection screen must be analyzed in the report. They work as filters. Each selection or parameter refers to a field in a table.

To reduce the amount of work involved in entering values in the selection screen, the programmer (and also the user) can save value assignments for a selection screen as report variants. Creating a report variant does not require any programming. Variants are given unique names, and they can be called and executed at any time.

2.3.2   Logical databases

Connections are established between tables in relational databases using primary keys, the result being a multi-level hierarchy of tables. Usually, for a report to analyze data, it must read the contents of several logically dependent tables. To do so, the report must explicitly establish connections between the tables using appropriately formulated queries. In cases where several reports need to access the same data set, the same connections must be established in each report. This costs time and money and requires a high maintenance effort when changes are made to the data structure. To avoid this, SAP uses special programs that can work with several reports at once. These programs are called *logical databases*. They read data from several tables, taking into account the hierarchy and the links. Using special statements, they make the data sets they have read available to the actual report, which then needs only to analyze and perhaps display them. Each report can access only one logical database, but each logical database can be used by several reports. The real database tables can be included in any number of logical databases.

Logical databases are created using a pseudo-graphical screen that shows the hierarchical connection of the individual tables. An ABAP/4 program is generated from this logical hierarchy display, which the developer then edits using the program editor.

2.4   Dialog applications

The interactive manipulation of data takes place in dialog applications. Dialog applications are based on the processing of *dynpros*. A dynpro is a combination of an input screen and program code belonging to the input screen. The user enters data in the screen, and the program code processes this data. A dialog application consists of one or more dynpros. Dialog applications can only be executed using the dialog transactions mentioned earlier.

The dynpros determine only the look of the work area, that is, the number and type of input elements and their behavior. A user interface or status handles other control elements such as menus and pushbuttons.

The link between the dynpro and the program is established by the flow logic. The flow logic is a short piece of source code that calls only modules from the module pool. These modules can be thought of as subroutines. They are called at specifically defined points in time. Some of the modules are executed before the screen is displayed on the monitor, for example modules that perform initialization or dynamic modification of the screen. This event is called PROCESS BEFORE OUTPUT (PBO). A second module group, called PROCESS AFTER INPUT (PAI), is processed after the end of data input. It handles the checking and processing of data. Two other module groups are available for implementing possible entries help. The flow logic is not an ABAP/4 program in the true sense. It uses statements other than those used by normal ABAP/4 programs (to which, for example, the module pool belongs).

When you create a dialog transaction, you assign it the name of a program, called the module pool, in addition to some attributes such as the transaction type and the number of the initial screen. This program has a special form and special contents. Its specific task is to provide screens with the subroutines (modules) they need for their work. The term "module pool" has its origin in this task. The module pool is also responsible for declaring all of the data used. Module pools do not, however, contain constructions comparable to the "main" function in C. They are more like program libraries.

At the beginning of a dialog transaction, the transaction starts the dynpro that was entered as the initial dynpro. This dynpro begins by executing the first group of statements defined in the flow logic. These initialize the screens, for example, filling input fields with values and such. Usually, they also load a user interface for the dnypro, too. Afterwards, the dynpro is executed. Now the user can enter values in the input fields or mark selection fields and check boxes. Various activities can end the dynpro, such as the call of a menu function, the use of special function keys, or the activation of a pushbutton. Ending the dynpro is handled by the second module group, which checks the entered values and transfers them to the database, if necessary.

Every screen has various attributes. These include, among others, the number of a subsequent screen. When one screen ends, it calls its subsequent screen, and when that screen ends, it calls its subsequent screen and so on. New screens continue to be called until the number of a subsequent screen is 0, at which point R/3 returns from the transaction. It is also possible to set the number of the subsequent screen explicitly, to enable branching. And a screen can be set to return to itself, for example to enable continuous data entry, or to re-display incorrect values so that they can be corrected.

2.5   User interface

The computers used as a front end for the R/3 System usually work with graphical user interfaces (for example, Windows or Motif). To a great extent, these systems follow the CUA standard. Use of the R/3 System is therefore relatively independent of the front-end operating system.

A running R/3 System consists of two main parts. One part is the system in the narrow sense, which includes the internal control logic and the ABAP/4 interpreter, among other things. The second part is the application written in ABAP/4 that is being executed at the moment. An ABAP/4 application always operates under the full control of the system kernel, so malfunctions of the application do not endanger the operation of the entire system.

This division of the system into two parts, and its subordination to the elements of the front-end operating system, are mirrored in the design of the system's user interface. The operating system provides several resources, that is, the actual display window and several control elements. The R/3 System's kernel also directly provides and analyzes some additional input elements. The programmer cannot edit these elements at all, or only to a limited extent. The last part, on the other hand, is entirely available for an ABAP/4 application. Figure 2.1 shows the display window of an R/3 application and the names of the various areas of the window. How the user interface really looks depends on the operating system of the front-end computer and the current version of the SAP front end itself, the SAPGUI. These differences only affect the look, however; they do not affect the functionality.

The control elements provided by the operating system are used mainly to move the display screen and to change its size. The toolbar allows communication with the R/3 System's kernel. Several symbols that have the same meaning system-wide appear in the toolbar, as does the command field (sometimes called the OK code field). The icons can be activated or deactivated by the ABAP/4 application. These icons trigger function codes, which directly or indirectly control the ABAP/4 application while it runs. Depending on the application, the respective function codes are either processed by the system (for example: to scroll in a list) or forwarded directly to the application and analyzed there.

The command field is always input-ready. Entries are immediately analyzed by the system kernel. Using special commands, it is possible to do things like cancel a running ABAP/4 application, call a transaction, create a new session (display window), or trigger a low-level function. A symbol next to the input field indicates the presence of a list box, which displays the last entries that were made in the command field. Table 2.1 shows the most important possible entries.

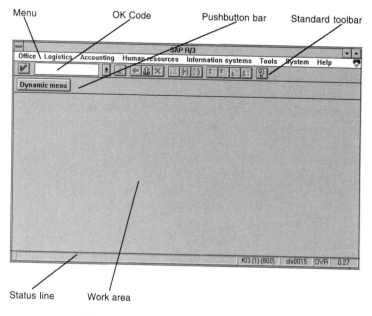

Figure 2.1 User interface of an R/3 application

Table 2.1   Important possible entries for the command field

Entry	Result
xxxx	Calls transaction xxxx. Works only if no other transaction is currently active.
/nxxxx	Cancels the current transaction and starts transaction xxxx.
/oxxxx	Creates a new session (display window) and starts transaction xxxx in the new window.
/n	Cancels the current transaction.
/i	Deletes the current session.
/o	Creates a list of sessions.
/h	Turns on debugger mode.
/$sync	Saves all buffers.
/nend	Logs off.

At the bottom edge of the window is the status bar. The status bar contains several fields, in which the system displays system-related information. The most important field is the first field on the left, where the system displays the short text of messages. Double-clicking on a message in this field displays a popup with the long text of that message.

The programmer can edit without restriction all elements except for the toolbar, the status bar and the elements of the operating system. These elements represent the actual user interface of a transaction. The interface also has two parts: the work area, which is managed by the screen or by a list's output control, and the actual control elements, that is, the menu, the pushbutton bar and the function key assignments. These elements can be edited independently of each other.

Those control elements of an application that the programmer can edit without restriction are called the user interface. A program can contain several variants of the user interface, called statuses. Every status in a program has a unique name. Every user interface, therefore, can be uniquely identified by program name and status name. A status contains the following elements:

- menu
- pushbutton assignments
- function key assignments
- title bar

Because the elements in a status enable the user to control the program flow, it must be clear before the status is processed what should actually happen in the program, that is, which functions the control elements should trigger. An example might be the call of different subsequent screens depending on the menu entry selected or the status of some radio buttons. In the PBO modules, the current status can be set using a special command.

The most important items for controlling the application are function codes. Function codes are identifiers for the various control elements. Every function code that is available in a status must be accessible with a menu item. The menu itself must allow complete control of the application. Function codes are four-character designators that must be unique within a transaction. They are character strings for identifying control elements within the program. Function codes are edited in a list in user interface maintenance, where special attributes and names can be specified for them.

You can assign the most important function codes to function keys, making them immediately accessible. A click with the right mouse button anywhere on the screen displays the most important key assignments in a popup. To trigger a key, or rather its corresponding function code, in this popup, you simply click on it with the mouse. Starting with Release 3.0C, additional key combinations (theoretically a total of 99) are available for assignment with function codes. Some function keys have assignments that are standard across the entire system. Such keys are usually linked to the icons on the toolbar.

Some of the function codes assigned to function keys can also be assigned to additional pushbuttons. Pushbuttons appear underneath the toolbar and enable the quickest possible access with the mouse. Pushbuttons can only be edited through the user interface, that is, the status. They are not the same as the pushbuttons that can be created in a screen in Screen Painter.

2.6   Function modules and dialog modules

Today's R/3 applications exhibit a high degree of complexity. This requires powerful methods for modularizing the source code in an application. It also requires tools that can be used across all applications, such as functions for calendar calculation, or screens for displaying and recording standard data like addresses.

One way to modularize is to structure the application itself with modules and subroutines. Another way is to make use of the two modules that are provided for use across all applications. These modules can be designed and tested independently of any specific application. They cannot, however, run on their own; they must be called by other applications. They have a precisely defined user interface for data exchange; there are no other methods for data transfer. This prevents undesired side effects.

Dialog modules and function modules necessitate an increase in management effort by the system. In the interest of an application's performance, therefore, they are sometimes implemented reluctantly. Skillful division of an application's functionality into function modules, however, enables object-related programming that approaches object-oriented programming in several respects. This method of programming can have a positive effect on the clarity of a program and can simplify future expansion of its functionality.

2.6.1   Dialog modules

Like dialog transactions, dialog modules contain a module pool, screens and a user interface. The modules have an initial screen and can access a status. Dialog modules are therefore programmed similarly to dialog transactions.

2.6.2   Function modules

Function modules make general or cross-application functions available to the programmer. There are no restrictions on the internal functionality of function modules. Although there are appropriate dialog modules for carrying out dialogs, screens can also be called in function modules.

Function modules do not exist in isolation from their environment. Like other elements of SAP applications, function modules are integrated in a hierarchy. Several logically related function modules are combined into a function pool. This function pool is similar to the module pool of a transaction, and the function modules can be compared to the individual modules of a module pool. A function pool contains global data for all of the function modules of that pool. This data is not visible from the outside; it can only be accessed with the function modules. The current values remain intact after a module is exited!

Function modules can be tested independently of the calling program. Test values can be stored and used later for comparison purposes. Because the function modules can only communicate with the calling program over the defined user interface, any error situations that occur are handled by a special exception mechanism, which is also part of the user interface.

2.7   Error handling and message concept

During the processing of a program, unforeseen events may occur that require a reaction on the part of the user. For this reason, ABAP/4 applications can output individual error messages. Using special options of the message-triggering statement, you can influence, within certain boundaries, the display of the message in the application and the reaction required from the user.

The display of a message influences the program flow. For this reason, it is not always a good idea to trigger messages immediately when a special event occurs, for example, if an error is recognized in a function module. Usually, function modules do not trigger an error message, but rather something called an exception. The exception ends the function module and transmits an error code to the calling program, where it must then be analyzed.

2.7.1   Messages

Signaling an error to the user is necessary especially during input checking in the PAI. When an error is recognized, it is necessary to notify the user of the incorrect entry and request a correction. There may also be other instances when the user should be notified of an error. In R/3, this is handled with messages. The triggering of a message can affect the flow logic of the screen; the programmer has little influence over this. Three parameters are required to trigger a message.

R/3 messages are predefined text elements. They consist of a single line of short text and an optional long text that can be several lines long. A three-digit number serves as the message identifier. Message texts can be translated. The system always displays messages in the logon language.

Since the number of messages available, 999, is insufficient for the R/3 System, the messages are assigned to message classes. A message class is identified by a two-character name. It usually contains the messages required for one or more related applications. There are no functional differences between the message classes.

In addition to the message number and message class, a third parameter is required to trigger a message in a program: the message type. This value does not affect the text of the message; it determines only how it is displayed and what influence it has on the flow control of the dynpro.

Messages can be displayed in four different ways. The differences lie in how the messages are displayed and how the application reacts to them. In one variant, for example, the short text is displayed in the status bar. The fields related to the incorrect entry are marked on screen; the cursor appears in the first field to be corrected. In another variant, the message is displayed in its own window, which can be closed only by clicking on a pushbutton. Clicking on another pushbutton in this window causes a second window with more detailed help (the message's long text) to be displayed. After the window is closed, the program continues.

2.7.2   Exceptions

Function modules use exceptions to signal the presence of error situations. These are not necessarily runtime errors. An exception can also be triggered in other circumstances, such as when a function module cannot find a data set. Exactly how an application reacts to an exception depends on the command that causes the exception and the location of its processing. There is only one type of exception, and, unlike messages, it has no variants. On the other hand, there is no limit to the number of exceptions.

When a function module is created, its user interface is defined exactly. This definition of the user interface also includes the identifiers for the exceptions that should be created in the function module. When an exception is created, one of the identifiers is passed to the appropriate exception command as a parameter. If the exception is handled by the function module itself, the identifier appears in the error text.

If exceptions should be handled outside of a function module, the calling program must explicitly relay this information to the function module when it is called. To this end, the identifiers for the possible exceptions are given numerical values. When an exception is created, the corresponding numerical value is placed in a system variable. The calling program can then tell, based on the contents of this variable, whether or not an exception has been triggered and, if so, which exception.

2.8   Input help

The complex structure of the SAP system and the multitude of possible input values make the existence of help for field input a necessity. In certain screen fields, the user can request possible entries help by pressing the F4 function key, clicking on the magnifying glass symbol in the toolbar or clicking on the arrow symbol next to the input field. There are two variants of input help that are implemented most often: one is the selection of a value from a predefined list of values (for example, units of measure); the other is a search for values of which only parts are known or for which only related information is known (for example, the search for a personnel number using a name). Both variants are supported, and there are three principal mechanisms available:

- Use of matchcodes:
  A matchcode is usually used to find the key for a data record when only subordinate values or non-key values are known. Matchcodes do not require any ABAP/4 programming, because they can be created interactively using special Data Dictionary tools.
- Use of PROCESS ON VALUE-REQUEST (POV):
  This is similar to PAI processing and requires the creation of an ABAP/4 program. Using POV allows you to use custom possible entries help.
- Access to a value table or the constant of a domain:
  You can define a foreign key for the fields of a table. This foreign key refers to a field from another table. The field for which the foreign key has been defined may contain only the values that are contained in the other table field, the one referenced by the foreign key. The system can automatically provide possible entries help for these foreign keys. This help is also activated if fixed values have been defined in the domain, instead of a value table. These can also be displayed without foreign key references.

Next to possible entries help, you can also call a general help text for a field with the F1 function key. This help is based on a long text, which can be entered in addition to the short description for many elements in the development environment. Another alternative is to define PROCESS ON HELP-REQUEST (POH) processing, which displays custom help text for an element.

2.8.1 Matchcodes

The term "key" plays a central role in the relational database model. Individual tables are linked together by the contents of key fields. Usually, a key must uniquely identify a data record. In many input screens, the user must enter a key value in order to select a data record for processing. Sometimes, this value (which is often a numeric character string) is not known, but other attributes of the data record to be processed, which are not unique, are known. A personnel department employee cannot know all personnel numbers by heart; he or she will want to search for the data record of an employee using the employee's name. To perform this type of search, you use a matchcode.

From the point of view of the user, a matchcode is a query program that executes predefined searches in a given data set and delivers the value of one particular field out of the data record found. You can define several subqueries in a matchcode that find the desired search term in different ways. Based on the example above, "search for a personnel number," the number could be determined, for example, using the name of the employee, his occupation, his work location or his salary class. From the point of view of the programmer, matchcodes are special views into the data set. They are created independently of the application that will later use them and can be used in a number of applications.

When a matchcode is activated in an application (usually by pressing the F4 function key or clicking on a symbol next to the input field), a list appears that shows the available search possibilities, from which one must be selected. An input screen then appears, in which the search terms are entered. The use of wildcards is possible. Afterwards, the query is started. If data records are found that match the search criteria, these, in turn, are displayed in a list, from which the desired data record, and thus the value to be passed, is selected.

A distinction is made between different types of matchcodes, with regard to the implementation of the program and thus its creation, storage and update. Some matchcodes are stored as tables in the database and are updated whenever database changes occur. Others are not created until they are called explicitly from within a program. One special update runs asynchronously to database changes. This update variant is often used for large data sets that rarely change.

Matchcodes consist of a matchcode object and one or more matchcode IDs. The matchcode object represents a framework that provides those elements (tables and fields) that are later used in the matchcode IDs. Each matchcode ID implements one search variant. Matchcodes are defined interactively in various places; programming in the narrow sense of the word is not required. Every matchcode is given a four-character name.

Accessing matchcodes from screens is very easy, because a matchcode can be entered as an attribute for an input field. In a finished screen, an input field that has been assigned a matchcode is identified by a small triangle in the upper right corner of the input field, as long as the field is not input-ready.

2.8.2 POV event

As an alternative to matchcodes, you can program Process on Value-Request (POV) processing in the flow logic for input fields. This processing phase is an optional part of the flow logic, just like PBO and PAI processing. In the POV section, modules are assigned to individual fields of the screen with the FIELD statement. The syntax corresponds to the syntax for field-related error checks. In the module in question, any statements can be executed that in the end place a value into the corresponding screen field. An interactive report is often called for this purpose.

2.8.3 POH event

As is the case with self-programmed possible entries help, in the Process on Help-Request (POH) processing phase, you can assign to a field a module or a field supplement that contains help for the field. This type of processing is used relatively rarely, because context-sensitive help information can also be provided in other ways.

2.9   System tables and system fields

ABAP/4 programs are executed by the internal flow logic. The flow logic monitors the program and automatically controls some actions. The flow logic stores the information needed for this in several system variables and tables, to which the programmer has access. These can be used, for example, to control the program flow. One of these variables (SY-SUBRC), for example, delivers information about the success of the last ABAP/4 command or function call. This information is needed, for example, to evaluate the success or failure of database selections. Other variables contain the number of the current data record of an internal table, or the number of the data records selected in a search. System variables are predefined. They are automatically available in all applications; you do not have to define them.

When working with screens, the internal control logic creates internal tables that contain information about the screen or some of its elements. For example, there is a predefined internal table called SCREEN, which contains several attributes for every screen field. If this table is edited at PBO time, that is, before the screen is displayed, the modifications affect the input fields of the screen. This allows the programmer to dynamically influence the screen, for example by hiding fields or changing them into pure display fields. This capability is used often.

Many system settings must be available across application boundaries. These settings are stored in database tables. It is often possible to edit the contents of these tables using the menu function *System → Services → Table maintenance*. Such a table must meet several conditions. Its name can be no longer than five characters. When such a table is created in the Data Dictionary, modules for table maintenance must also be generated. These modules enable special transactions to be used. These transactions allow the table to be edited without any programming being necessary.

3 Programming in ABAP/4

A major requirement (though not the only one) for successfully programming your own applications in the R/3 System is knowing the ABAP/4 programming language. ABAP/4 is not a language that can be universally implemented, like C or Pascal, although in practice it has proven to be quite flexible. It was created especially for the SAP system. ABAP/4 is continually being enhanced and adjusted to meet the latest requirements. Sometimes, substantial additions appear between one release and the next. Some elements of the language were designed specifically for particular parts of the development environment or to reflect SAP's philosophy and can be described only in relation to these elements. It is of little use to discuss the programming language in isolation from the SAP environment that surrounds it. Though relevant, a description of all of the ABAP/4 commands, some of which have dozens of parameters and calling options, is less important than basic information about the various elements of an R/3 application. This chapter does not provide a complete description of the ABAP/4 commands. Instead, it describes a selection of the most important statements. Using simple examples, it demonstrates their practical use and their cooperation with other elements of the development environment, and thus the structure of an application. This chapter should not be seen as a reference for the programming language, but rather as a practical introduction to R/3 programming.

The first section provides basic information about the creation of simple programs and the use of data in ABAP/4. Although the type of programs used are *online reports*, these are not reports in the full sense of the word. Rather, they are aids for demonstrating the first couple of statements. Almost all of the statements described here have global importance. Knowledge of these statements is certainly a requirement for understanding all ABAP/4 applications.

In the second section, the focus is on true reports, with their special characteristics. Several ABAP/4 statements can be used only in reports. And reports have a program structure that is entirely different from that of dialog-oriented applications. Aside from describing these special statements, this section strengthens the knowledge gained in the first section about the more general statements presented there.

The third section describes the dynpro concept in detail. It begins by examining the structure of dialog-oriented applications. After that, it presents the statements used to implement this program structure.

It is possible to break up the normally rigid flow of a classic report with interactive language elements. The fourth section deals with these enhancements, which allow you, for example, to branch into details lists or jump to online processing of selected data records.

Function modules and dialog modules are important tools for providing cross-application functionality and for modularizing applications. A separate programming method is

needed for these modules, too. The system provides several predefined function modules
that can be used everywhere. The last section of this chapter introduces function and
dialog modules and shows some examples for use of the function modules provided by
the system.

3.1   Introduction to programming

The term online report was mentioned in Chapter 2. Reports are programs that create an
analysis list, display it on screen, and print it on demand. In their basic form, reports are
not truly interactive. In other words, after being started, reports can create output on the
screen without any additional action on the part of the user.

Since reports are not interactive, they do not need screens, user interfaces, or flow logic.
In their most simple form, reports consist of a single program file. Add to this the fact that
reports can be processed immediately from within the development environment, and it
becomes clear that such reports serve nicely as an introduction to programming and as
demonstrations of the most important ABAP/4 statements.

3.1.1   The first program: Hello World!

Almost all programming manuals start with the same program. Its task consists of writing
a simple line of text to the screen, usually "Hello World!". Practical use of such a program
and the effectiveness of such a program as a tool for teaching the language are, of course,
limited. What is important in this type of introduction is the initial contact with the development environment and the programming tools. Since these are quite complex in R/3, it
makes sense to begin the same way here.

Creating a program

All of the tools required for application development are grouped into what is called a
workbench. The workbench appears as an area menu, which you can access from the R/3
main menu using the menu function *Tools → ABAP/4-Workbench*, and which you can
access from anywhere else using the transaction code S001.

It is easiest to create the programs presented below directly with the ABAP/4 editor.
You can access the editor using the *ABAP/4 Editor* pushbutton or the *Development →
ABAP/4-Editor* menu item. Alternatively, you can use transaction code SE38.

The editor's initial screen (see Figure 3.1) contains an input field for the program name,
as well as several pushbuttons. To create a new program, you enter the desired program
name and click on the *Create* pushbutton.

At this point, it is important to make sure you use a valid program name. The SAP system sometimes automatically generates programs; their names are constructed according
to certain rules. Furthermore, the development environment distinguishes between SAP's
own development systems and customer systems. For each type of system, there are different specifications concerning the name ranges that can be used. For all elements (not
only reports), the development environment checks for adherence to certain naming conventions. In customer systems, the names of new programs must begin with the character

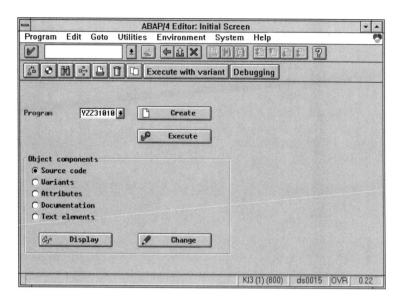

Figure 3.1   ABAP/4 program development initial screen

Y or Z. This ensures that the customer's own developments can be distinguished from SAP's. Accordingly, no objects that begin with those letters may be created in SAP's development systems (at least not without an explicit warning).

To avoid conflicts with automatically generated names, and to enable more than one user to process the demo programs in your system, you should follow several conventions. The format for the names of all of the sample programs in this book is *Yiikknnm*. You should substitute *ii* with your unique initials. This ensures that several users can replicate the examples on the same system. In the book, the initials ZZ are used. The character string *kk* is a place holder for the chapter number (at the second heading level), and *nn* is a number that is incremented within the chapter. For some of the programs presented, you can, and sometime should, create several modifications. These program variants are distinguished by the last character in their name, with the source version always having the character 0. Thus, the first program is given the name YZZ31010.

After you enter the program name in the input field and click on the *Create* pushbutton, the program displays a popup belonging to the Workbench Organizer, which asks for the name of a development class (Figure 3.2).

Development classes are used to group development objects in the R/3 System. Elements that are logically related are assigned to the same development class. This development class also determines if objects can be transported from the current system into other systems or not. In the R/3 System, programs are usually developed in a separate test system. After they have been developed and tested, the programs are then transported to the desired target system by the Workbench Organizer. This topic is discussed in more detail in a later section.

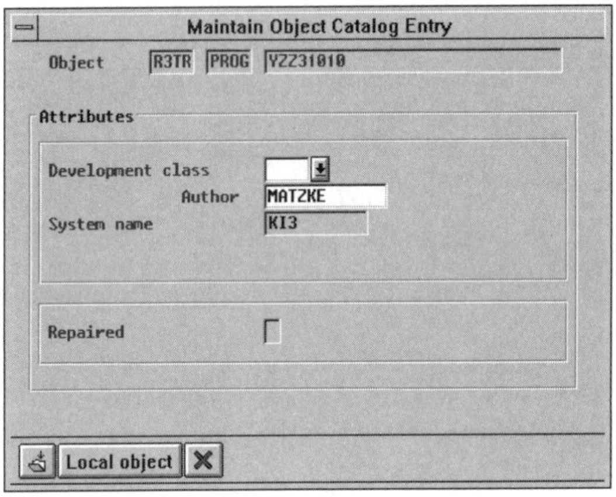

Figure 3.2   Workbench Organizer

To avoid having every little test program or auxiliary program enter official development, you can mark development objects as *local objects*. There is a special button for this in the popup that is displayed. Objects that you declare as local objects are not recorded by the transport system, meaning they cannot be transported to other systems. All demo programs should therefore be declared as local objects. You can close the popup by clicking on the *Local object* button; you do not have to enter any additional information. As you continue programming, this popup will appear for every new object. You should always close the popup in the manner just described. This step will not be described again in this book.

When you create a new program, you do not proceed immediately from the initial screen to the editor. Many of the elements of an application, even a simple report, have a lot of management information. You must enter this information in another screen (Figure 3.3). There are three fields of particular importance; entries are mandatory for these fields. A question mark in the input field indicates that an entry is required for that field. The three fields in questions are the short description of the program, the program type, and the application group to which this program should be assigned.

In the *Title* field, you can enter a short description of the program, for example, "Hello World Program, Version 1." This short description, also called a title, is indispensable in practice, because it appears in addition to the program name in various lists of possible entries and search lists. Because many program names are predefined, and there are so many programs in the SAP system, this title provides the only real clue to the program's function. The title also appears in the automatically generated standard headings of the list that is created by the report.

Chapter 2 mentioned several program types, such as module pools and reports, which are being used here. You determine the program's type in the *Type* field. An entry in this field is mandatory. Reports always have Type 1 (online report). Programs of this type are the only programs that can be processed immediately. You can create other types of programs besides online reports by selecting the appropriate type with the program editor just used (SE38). In practice, however, a different, more powerful tool is normally used. Section 3.3 explores the reasons for this.

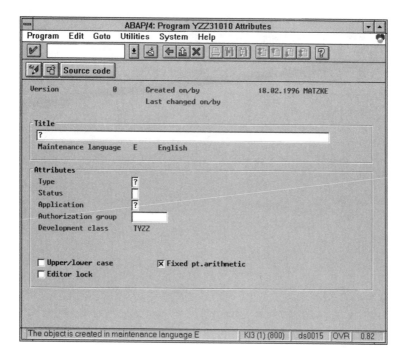

Figure 3.3   Program attributes

The mandatory input field *Application* is required for logical assignment of the program to one of the large application groups. This field has no influence on the operation of the program; it serves mainly to support various search processes. Since the test programs being created here do not belong to any of these groups, you can enter an asterisk (*), to indicate application-spanning reports.

After you have entered values in these three fields, click on the button for saving, or press the F11 function key (Save). After the attributes have been saved, you can finally jump to the actual editor by clicking the *Source code* pushbutton or by selecting the menu function *Goto → Source code*.

The editor displays the program, which currently consists of a single line. For online reports, the system automatically generates a program line that consists of the ABAP/4 keyword REPORT and the program name. Use of the ABAP/4 editor is probably unfamiliar to PC and UNIX users. A brief introduction follows.

The development environment, in a nutshell

You need a basic knowledge of the R/3 System's editor to be able to create and test demo programs. The description presented here, however, does not cover all of the editor's characteristics. It concentrates instead on providing the information required for creating the demo programs. Figure 3.4 shows the editor screen during editing of the first demo program.

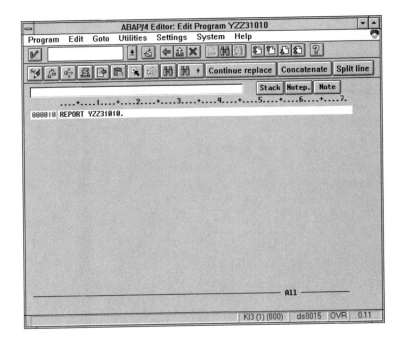

Figure 3.4   The ABAP/4 program editor

Like many other tools in the system, the editor is an ABAP program, which means the editor's user interface is a screen. Since ABAP/4 currently provides only single-line input fields in screens, the editor works in a line-oriented fashion. Wherever possible, however, it takes full advantage of the capabilities of screens. As a result, the R/3 program editor's functionality closely resembles that of more modern, page-oriented editors. It has little in common with the famous/infamous line-oriented editors EDLIN (from early MS-DOS versions) or UNIX-ed.

Beginning with Release 3.0, you can select different modes for the editor by using the *Options* menu item. Only the command mode (the version that was already available in other releases) is used in this book. Figure 3.4 shows the display of this mode of the editor.

The actual work area consists of several lines. Every line is identified by a line number. The system numbers lines automatically, in increments of 10. The length of the input line is restricted to viewable size (72 characters). There is no automatic line wrapping; every input line is edited separately.

When the editor is in change mode, input-ready lines are highlighted in color, the way input-ready fields are highlighted on a screen (default: black text on a white background). In display mode, on the other hand, the text has the same appearance as the labels of a screen (default: black text on a gray background).

Under the pushbutton bar, there is an input field in which you can enter commands called editor commands. These commands are released with the Enter key. Only two of the possible commands are of interest at this point:

i *n*

This editor command causes the editor to add n empty lines after the last line of the program. A newly created program usually consists of a single input-ready line. Often, the first thing you do after starting the editor for a new program is to add empty lines. Later, when you are testing programs, if space becomes tight, you should add new lines. No further mention will be made of this task.

h *keyword*

This editor command calls a hypertext help system, which provides help for the editor (use the keyword "editor") or for ABAP commands. This input field is only available when the editor is in command mode. When the editor is in one of the other modes, you must call special menu functions to use the functions mentioned.

Status information is displayed in the lower right-hand corner of the screen. An example of important status information is the entry mode: insert or overtype.

Pressing the right mouse key displays a menu with the current function key assignments. You can select one of the entries with the mouse, or you can use the appropriate function key. R/3 makes use of up to 24 function keys. Since most PC keyboards only contain 12 function keys, to use the other 12 function keys (from F13 on up) you must combine the Shift key with one of the function keys from F1 to F12. The combination Shift-F1, for example, corresponds to F13. Another way to use the function keys is to press and hold the control key (Ctrl) and enter the two-digit number of the function key. In newer systems (beginning with Release 3.0), you can also access additional functions this way. Some of the most important functions can also be accessed using icons in the pushbutton bar.

You can position the cursor with the mouse or the cursor keys. In the work area, the cursor can be located either in the line number fields or in the actual source code area. Using Tab or Shift-Tab, you can switch back and forth between the program editor's input elements (source code fields, line number fields, pushbuttons). At the moment, there should only be input in the source code area. To edit the program text, you can use the keys listed in Table 3.1.

Table 3.1   Important editor keys

Key	Function
INS	Switches between insert mode and overtype mode.
DEL	Deletes the character to the right of the cursor.
←	Deletes the character to the left of the cursor.
F5	Duplicates the line in which the cursor is located.
Ctrl-63) (before Version 3.0: F14)	Deletes the line in which the cursor is located.
F7 (before Version 3.0: F8)	Splits the line at the cursor position.
F6 (before Version 3.0: F7)	Concatenates the current line and the following line, if there is enough space.

You can save a program by using the menu function *Program → Save w/o check* or the Save icon. The function *Program → Check*, on the other hand, checks a program for syntax errors. You should always run such a check before saving a program. Programs that contain syntax errors should never be saved! Although syntax errors in the demo programs presented here will not cause problems, storing real application programs with syntax errors can lead to the inoperability of entire applications.

ABAP/4 programs make no distinction between upper- and lowercase letters. When you save a program, all letters that are not part of alphanumeric constants or comments are converted to a consistent case. This is either lowercase or uppercase, depending on the setting of the editor. Several other commands, which do not exit the editor but just call internal functions, also perform such a conversion.

Basic structure of a report

The first program consists of two short lines, one of which has already been generated by the system. Compared to other programming languages, this is not much:

```
REPORT YZZ31010.
WRITE 'Hello world! '.
```

In the first line, the keyword REPORT tells the system that the following statements constitute an independent program. (By the way, there is now an alternative statement available, PROGRAM, which is fully equivalent to REPORT.) The second line writes some text to the output window. To create the space necessary to enter the second line, you must either enter the command

```
i 5
```

in the command line, or place the cursor after the last character of the first line and press the F7 function key.

ABAP/4 statements can be entered without formatting, meaning they can stretch across several lines or be indented as desired. This means that the end of an ABAP/4 command must be clearly marked. The ABAP/4 programming language uses a period for this.

After you have entered the two lines, you can execute the short program directly from the editor by using the menu function *Program → Execute*. Assuming no typing mistakes have crept in, the editor screen is replaced by the program output. The result shown in Figure 3.5 should appear. The system reports any syntax errors in the program. Depending on the type of mistake, the system displays either a simple message on the screen, or a popup, from which you can jump directly to the position of the error using certain pushbuttons.

A report does not create screen output by writing directly to the window. Instead, a report writes its output to a buffer, which is not displayed in the output window until the report has been processed in its entirety. In the case of complex reports, this can take quite a while!

Buffering the output makes it possible to scroll lengthy lists as desired on screen after they have been created. The buffer contents, that is, the output list, can also be printed without the report having to contain special statements for this.

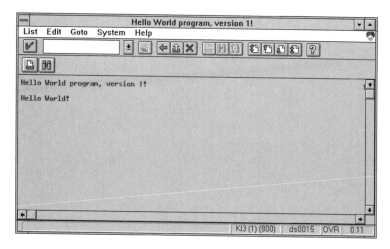

Figure 3.5   Screen output of the first demo program

In addition to the expected "Hello world!" text, the output contains the title of the report and the page number. These elements are automatically generated by the system, since they are usually indispensable on any printout. From the output window of the report, you can return to the editor by pressing the F3 function key or by clicking on the icon with the green arrow.

There are several clauses you can add to the REPORT or PROGRAM statement that affect the appearance of the generated list. You can use the NO STANDARD PAGE HEADING clause now, if you like. It turns off the automatically generated list heading.

Large programs are never clear without comments. In ABAP, there are two ways to mark comments. The first, more noticeable, option is to place an asterisk in the first column of a line. Comments that should not begin in the first column, such as those that should appear on the same line as a command, but after it, begin with a quotation mark. The following lines demonstrate the changes discussed up to this point. Entering the additional characters is good practice for using the editor.

```
*****************************************************
* This program generates a short printout
*****************************************************
REPORT YZZ31010 NO STANDARD PAGE HEADING.
WRITE 'Hello world! '. "Output of a line of text
```

For the examples that follow, you should create a new program. First, save the current program using the menu function *Program → Save w/o check*, then return to the initial screen using *Goto → Back*. You can also do this with the function key sequence F11 and F3, or the corresponding icons in the toolbar. According to the naming conventions described earlier, the name for the new program should be YZZ31020. Create this program the same way you created the first sample program. Insert the following statements into this program one after the other, and test the program after every new command has been added.

Output of a line of text

A single, very simple output statement was used in the first program. The WRITE statement can, however, become very complex, since many options are available for formatting the output line. Many ABAP/4 commands can be called with several parameters. In the case of the WRITE statement, this means that several texts can be written to the output list at the same time with a single statement. A small expansion of the syntax is needed for this, however. You use a colon after the actual keyword to introduce the parameter list; you separate the individual parameters with commas. The colon variant exists for many other commands as well, not just for the WRITE command.

```
WRITE: 'These', 'are', 'several', 'character strings'.
```

Of course, it does not make much sense to specify several hard-coded words as individual parameters. But if you execute this sample program, you will see that the parameters are separated in the output by spaces. The parameter capabilities of the WRITE statement become more interesting when you consider the additional arguments available for formatting output, especially those for positioning parameters. Numeric values preceding the parameter, in the form

```
column(length)parameter
```

cause the parameter to be output in the column specified, in a field of the length entered in parentheses. Both specifications are optional. A leading front slash results in a new line, as shown in the example:

```
WRITE: / 'These',/7'are',/11(7) 'several . . .',/ 'character strings'.
```

In addition to positioning, there are options that enable very powerful editing of the values to be output. For example, you can format the output according to a template, or align it within a column. Describing these options at this point, however, would probably only cause confusion. You can find more information on these options in the chapter about report programming.

Numbered text elements

Modern standard software must be usable in more than one language. Among other things, this means that printouts, error messages, field names on screens and so on, must be easy to translate into other languages. For this reason, it would be unusual to write text elements directly into programs, as was done in the example above. Instead, one would use the text elements that ABAP/4 provides, which are assigned to a program. Text elements are consecutively numbered. The system identifies each text element by the number and the logon language. The logon language is selected by the user when he or she logs on and is stored in a system variable. Translation of text elements into various target languages can take place entirely independently of actual program development.

In the program, text elements are defined by the keyword *TEXT-* combined with a three-digit number. You maintain text elements (and several other translation-relevant elements) in a separate transaction, SE32. You can access this in the development environment using the menu item *Development → Programming environ. → Text elements*. If you call the transaction this way, you must enter in a screen the program for which text elements are to be maintained. You must also mark the *Text symbols* radio button. Only then will the interface of the maintenance tool for text elements appear, as shown in Figure 3.6.

When you are developing a program, it is usually rather tedious to leave the editor, call another transaction to maintain the text elements, then return to the editor. It is also unnecessary. The development environment has a powerful navigation mechanism that allows you to maintain many elements directly from within the editor. You start the navigation mechanism in the source code by double-clicking on the various terms. You can achieve the same result by positioning the cursor on an element and then pressing the F2 function key. The reaction of the editor depends on the element selected. When you click on existing elements such as data fields, names of subroutines and so on, the editor jumps to the place in the source code where this element is defined, or to the tool with which this element can be maintained. If a selected element does not yet exist, the system provides tools to create this element. The navigation mechanism even works across program boundaries!

For a practical demonstration, you first need to create the following program:

```
REPORT YZZ31030.
WRITE / TEXT-001.
WRITE / TEXT-002.
WRITE / TEXT-003.
```

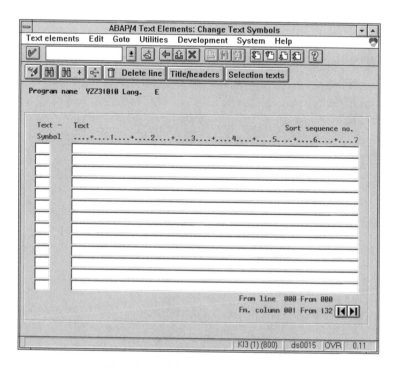

Figure 3.6   Maintenance of text elements

Save the program, then use the mouse to double-click on the character string TEXT-001. The transaction SE32, for maintenance of text elements, is called; you can enter a text for this element. Then store the entry using F11 or the Save icon and return to the editor using F3 or the Back icon (green arrow). Repeat this step for the other two text elements, then test the results by executing the program.

The system always searches for text elements in the logon language. If no translation is available yet in this language, no text can be output. You should avoid such errors whenever possible. Inserting:

```
value(text number)
```

specifies a default value for a numbered text in the program. This default value comes into play only if the text element is not available in the current language. A real statement in a program might read

```
WRITE / 'Date: '(017).
```

Text elements have been left out of the rest of this guide. For the sake of clarity in the source code, texts are incorporated directly in the printed sample programs.

Of course, ABAP/4 also recognizes expressions, which are described in more detail later. It is not possible, however, to use such expressions in the WRITE statement, as is done in other programming languages. A statement like

```
WRITE / 5 + 7.
```

is rejected during the syntax check of a program.

Exercises

1. Practice using the editor. Read the help text concerning the editor in the online help. Test various functions of the editor.

2. Supplement the program with the text elements by adding comments like those in the Hello World program. The text stored in the text element should appear in the comments.

3. Leave the editor and use the menu to call the transaction for maintaining text elements. Change all three texts.

4. Using a menu item, try to copy a program from the program development initial screen (transaction SE38). Change the new program in such a way that the three texts are output with a single WRITE statement. Every text should appear on a separate line and be indented three spaces more than the line preceding it.

5. You can do this exercise only if more than one language is installed on your system. Usually, German and English are always available. Log on in a second language. Execute the program. Change the numbered texts and start the program again.

3.1.2   Data fields and operations

The Hello World program serves as a simple introduction to program development. Of course, a programming language that should be taken seriously needs to be capable of more than just printing out text. It needs to allow flexible handling of all different types of data and to be able to carry out diverse operations on this data.

There are several statements in ABAP/4, each of which can be used to define very specialized data elements with different levels of complexity. In the end, all of these elements are based on simple data fields internal to the program, or on fields with reference to the Data Dictionary (table fields). These have certain similar properties and capabilities, but they also have differences. Table fields have already been discussed in Chapter 2. The following section discusses the fundamental data types and the operations possible with the data in more detail, based on the data fields internal to the program.

Definition of data fields

Like other programming languages, ABAP/4 has the ability to use variables. In ABAP/4, variables are called data fields. Data fields always contain one value of a particular data type. All data fields that are to be used in a program must be defined before their first use. In this definition, you specify the name, type, length, and, in some cases, an initial value. The command for defining fields is called DATA. For simple fields, you use this command in the following form:

DATA *fieldname*.

or

DATA: *field_1, field_2, ..., field_x*.

As with WRITE, you can specify several parameters here, too. The fields defined this way are valid from the point of definition on, throughout the entire program. Field names can be up to 30 characters long. All alphanumeric characters except for the special characters ( ) + . , and : can be used. The name may not, however, consist entirely of numbers. Although the hyphen (-) belongs to the group of permissible characters, it should not be used for field names. It is used in field strings to separate the individual parts of a name. If it were used in data element names, which can also be parts of field strings, this would lead to incomprehensible names. If you need to split individual terms visually in a data field name, it is better to use the underscore _. Examples of valid field names follow:

COUNT
M1
M123
CUSTOMER_NUMBER

The system defines some fields itself. You may not use the names of these fields as field names, either, particularly the field name SPACE and the actual system variables, which all begin with SY- or SYST.

Various ABAP/4 statements use diverse clauses and options. Although you may use the names of these clauses as field names, in certain cases this can lead to unclear statements. Some of the names include, for example, the identifiers TO, INTO, and FROM.

Attributes of data fields

Every table field and data field in an ABAP/4 application has a type, which determines important attributes of the field. Preset data types are shown in Table 3.2. A data type determines how the information stored in the field should be interpreted. In addition, the data type determines the standard length of the data field and its initial value.

Table 3.2   Data types

Data Type	Default length	Valid length	Initial value	Description
C	1	1–65 535	Blank space	Text (character string)
N	1	1–65 535	'0 ... 0'	Numerical character string
T	6	6	'000000'	Time (HHMMSS)
D	8	8	'00000000'	Date (YYYYMMDD)
F	8	8	'0.0'	Floating point number
I	4	4	0	Integer
P	8	1–16	0	Packed number
X	1	1–65 535	X'00'	Hexadecimal

Character string
Character strings can contain any characters. Character strings usually record general information like names, identifiers and so on. Each character is stored in one position in the data field.

Numerical character string
Numerical character strings resemble the character strings just described. However, a numerical character string may contain only numbers. Any other characters that are assigned are simply suppressed. The value is aligned to the right when it is entered; blank spaces are filled with '0'. Numerical character strings are usually used as key values, for example, as order numbers, material numbers or personnel numbers.

Time
This data type records a time in the form of hours, minutes, seconds (HHMMSS), with two places provided for each value. No characters are used to separate the parts. This form of representation without separation characters is used both when a value is assigned and when the value is output with WRITE. Additional formatting during output requires special options in the WRITE command. You should be aware of one particularity when using this data type: when the maximum value of 24 hours is exceeded, no runtime error or other type of warning is generated; instead, counting starts from 0 hours again.

Date
A date field contains a date in the form of year, month, day (YYYYMMDD). The parts of the field are not separated. Using special formatting statements, for example, in conjunction with the WRITE command, you can display the date various ways. If you display the date using WRITE without any additional specifications, the parts are reorganized according to the date variant set in the user profile, which is usually country-specific. Date fields always have a length of eight, to ensure that all information can be recorded. Longer date fields are not necessary; shorter ones could not record an accurate value.

Floating point number

A floating point number is stored in a binary form that cannot be displayed directly. The value is divided into an exponent and a mantissa, for which the basis, of course, is the binary system. This data type is similar to the *float* data type in C or the REAL data type in Pascal. The length of eight places indirectly influences the possible number of places and precision of the value. In ABAP/4, the range of values that can be represented is –1E307 to +1E307. The resolving power (smallest absolute value that can be represented) is 1E–307. It is accurate to about 15 places.

When floating point numbers are output, exponential display is standard. Floating point numbers can be assigned various ways, but the value is always enclosed in apostrophes. In countries where commas are used as decimal points, the comma in a decimal number is represented by a period, as is typical in other programming languages. Some valid values are, for example:

```
'1'
'1.2'
'1.23E2'
'-123E-5'
```

You use floating point numbers when you want to perform calculations that need a large range of values and limited precision is acceptable.

Integer

Integers, too, are stored in binary form, meaning the length of the field does not directly correspond to the number of places that the value has. This data type is somewhat similar to *longint* in C. On the hardware generally used, it is possible to represent a range of values from $-2^{**}31$ to $+2^{**}31$ ($-2\,147\,483\,648$ to $+2\,147\,483\,647$). The data type I is the preferred data type for counter variables, indexes and so on.

Packed number

This data type is used for storing fixed-point numbers. You indicate how many decimal places the data field should have by using the option DECIMALS n in the DATA statement. The default value for DECIMALS is 0! In packed fields, each place (one byte) represents two numbers of the value. An additional number must also be taken into account: this number represents the number of decimal places. A data field of type P and length L, for example, can record values with $L^{*}2-1$ places, without regard to the sign. However, the number of decimal places and, if necessary, a plus or minus sign must be included in the count!

Effective use of packed numbers requires setting the *fixed-point arithmetic* flag in the program attributes. When this flag is set, the number of places is automatically taken into account in both calculations and output. Usually, when a new program is created, this flag is set as the default (see Figure 3.3).

Packed numbers are used for values with a constant number of decimal places, such as prices, quantities and so on. For this reason, the WRITE statement has clauses specifically for fields of type P that work with certain tables of the Data Dictionary. These tables contain entries for special properties of currencies, units of measure and so on. As in floating point numbers, the period serves as a separating character between the integer and the decimal places of the value. Packed numbers may not be written in exponential form during assignments.

Hexadecimal fields
Similar to packed fields, each place in the data element represents two hexadecimal numbers. To assign a hexadecimal value, you must identify it as such with an X, for example X'0D0A'. This type of field is usually important only in special cases.

If nothing is specified when a data field is defined, ABAP/4 creates the data field with type C and a length of 1. Any settings that should deviate from this must be explicitly specified. Length specifications, assuming they are permissible for the data type in question, are enclosed in parentheses and appear immediately after the field name, without a blank space in between:

DATA *field_name(length).*

The keyword TYPE is used for explicitly assigning data types. In the declaration, it appears after the field name and the length specification. The data types you can assign with it are the ones shown in Table 3.2.

DATA *field_name(length)* **TYPE** *data_type.*

Length specification is not possible for all data types; it is permissible only for C, I, N, P and X.
Finally, you can overwrite the initial value with another value during data declaration. You do this with the keyword VALUE. The value is placed in single quotation marks:

DATA *field_name(length)* **TYPE** *data_type* **VALUE** *'field_value'.*

In the final analysis, the purpose of every ABAP/4 program is to edit the contents of database tables. Data fields must often reference table fields. Occasionally, they incorporate the contents of table fields in a program, or they provide data that will later be written to the tables. For this reason, it is desirable for the data fields to have the same attributes as the table fields with which they cooperate. You could manually derive some relevant attributes for a table field from the Data Dictionary, and then take these attributes into account when declaring a data field by entering corresponding length and type specifications. If you did this, however, any subsequent changes to the domain on which the table field is based would lead to deviations between the table field and the data field. You can avoid this by dynamically assigning attributes to a data field at the program's runtime. Using the keyword LIKE, you can give one data field all of the attributes of another field:

DATA *field_name* **LIKE** *field_name.*

The field used as a template can be either a data field internal to the program or a field defined in the Data Dictionary (table field). In the latter case, however, the corresponding table must be declared in the program before its use in the field declaration. You do this with a keyword that will be described later: TABLES.

Several of the clauses already discussed can be used together in definition statements. Of course, type and length specifications and the LIKE clause are mutually exclusive. Some examples of declarations follow:

```
TABLES  : KNA1.
DATA    : IS_CHANGED,
          NAME(10),
          MATNR(8) TYPE N,
          C_OK VALUE 'Y',
          IS_OK LIKE C_OK,
          OK_CODE LIKE SY-TCODE,
          FNAME LIKE KNA1-NAME1 VALUE 'IXOS'.
```

Constants

Until Release 2.2, ABAP/4 did not have true constants. Release 3.0 brings with it extensive expansion of the data concept in ABAP/4. In addition to an improved type concept, this expansion includes the declaration of true constants. Similar to the fields mentioned above, constants are created with the following statement:

CONSTANTS *constant* **VALUE** *value*.

The same naming conventions apply for CONSTANTS as for DATA. The constant's relevant attributes (type, length and so on) can also be determined with LIKE or TYPE, or with explicit length specification using parentheses (). In this statement, too, it is possible to declare several fields at once using a colon.

The type concept

With Release 3.0, ABAP/4's type concept has been expanded to allow the definition of custom data types. Definition of custom types begins with the TYPES statement. The syntax of the complete statement corresponds largely to that of the DATA statement. The difference lies in the fact that fields created with DATA are real elements and can be used immediately for assignments, while data types created with TYPES simply represent a description from which real elements must then still be derived. Custom-created data types mainly ensure a greater degree of security when data is transferred to subroutines. Data types defined with TYPES can be used in other definitions the same way predefined types are used:

```
TYPES: T_NAME(20).
DATA CUSTOMER TYPE T_NAME.
```

Since you can reference already existing fields in type definitions using LIKE, you can also create a type specification for such fields later:

```
TYPES: T_FCODE LIKE SY-TCODE.
```

Names of types are subject to the same rules as names of fields. You can obtain a better overview of the application if you give data types a prefix, for example T_, as shown above. This is not absolutely necessary, however.

Data types and data fields use different name ranges. This means that it is permissible for a type and a field to have identical names. However, this also means that the statement

```
DATA: X1 TYPE A,
      X2 LIKE A.
```

defines two fields with entirely different structures in cases where the field A has a different structure than the type A. Avoiding such misunderstandings is another good reason to mark custom data types as described above.

In addition to defining data types directly, you can create so-called type groups (type pools) in Dictionary maintenance (SE11 transaction). Type pools are source code that may contain only type definitions and constant declarations. You include them in applications using the following statement:

```
TYPE-POOLS type_group.
```

Things to consider regarding output with WRITE

The different data types are handled differently in output with the WRITE command. These differences must be taken into account when formatting a list. The differences to be noted concern the preset output length of the field and the alignment of the value in the output field. Table 3.3 shows the standard attributes.

In many cases, the output length plays less of a role, since the default values usually create usable results. It is mainly in three situations that you need to set the output length:

- Some character string fields become rather long, such as those for identifiers or short textual descriptions. These fields are often shortened.
- For date and time fields, output length is usually increased (to ten or eight), so that the separators are also output correctly. In date and time fields with default output length, there is no room for these characters, meaning that only eight or six characters, respectively, would be output. Note: At the end of this section, there is a demo program for type conversion, and there are exercises.
- For floating point numbers, the length is often restricted, while at the same time the output is formatted to truncate superfluous places after the decimal point.

Table 3.3   Standard format for output with WRITE

Type	Default output length	Alignment
C	field length	left-aligned
D	8	left-aligned
F	22	right-aligned
I	11	right-aligned
N	field length	left-aligned
P	2 * field length, or 2 * field length + 1	right-aligned
T	6	left-aligned
X	2 * field length	left-aligned

Assignments

For a data field to receive a value, a value must be assigned. One assignment method has already been mentioned, that is, use of the VALUE clause during definition. There are other possibilities, as well. At this point, only assignments that fill individual data fields with values will be discussed. Additional assignment variations exist in connection with field strings.

The equal sign is the most often used and most obvious assignment operator. Assignments made using the equal sign closely resemble assignments in other programming languages. The general syntactic description of an assignment is as follows:

```
field = expression.
```

where *expression* can be a constant, a field or a complex expression. The value of the expression is assigned to the specified field. Usually, if the fields in question have different data types, implicit type conversions take place in the process. Of course, the length of the target field is taken into account; the maximum number of places transferred is the number of places the target field can accept. It is also possible to make multiple assignments using the equal sign, as shown here:

```
field_1 = field_2 = expression.
```

These are processed from right to left. The only place where an expression may appear instead of a field is at the very right. An assignment with the MOVE statement, which is functionally equivalent to the equal sign, is reminiscent of assembly programming, which plays a large role in the mainframe-based SAP R/2 System, for example.

MOVE *field_1* **TO** *field_2*.

This statement assigns to one field the value of another field or a value that has been hard-coded in the program. The interesting thing about this variant is that multiple assignments are possible through use of the colon:

```
MOVE: a TO b,
      c TO d,
      e TO f.
```

Finally, the WRITE statement has a special clause that reroutes the output from one field into another field:

WRITE *field_1* **TO** *field-2*.

This statement is interesting because you can specify the field name of the source field indirectly, that is, it does not appear directly in the statement but rather in a third field, which is placed in parentheses in the WRITE statement.

WRITE (*field_1*) **TO** *field_2*.

A short example follows:

```
DATA: NAME(10),
      S1(10) VALUE 'ONE',
      S2(10).
NAME = 'S1'.
WRITE   (NAME) TO S2.
WRITE   / S2.
```

The statement CLEAR resets fields to their initial values. This statement can also process several parameters when used with a colon, for example:

```
CLEAR: NAME, S1, S2.
```

Offset and length specifications

The introductory description of the WRITE statement already demonstrated how the output length of fields can be limited. This is not restricted to output, however. You can also limit the length of fields in other uses, although not for all data types. Fields of data type P, F or I do not have this capability. Due to their internal representation, it only makes sense to access the value of any of these fields as a whole.

Specifying a numerical value in parentheses directly after the field name limits access to a specified number of places. You can also specify an offset, in which case access begins not at the first position of the field in question, but rather shifted by the specified number of places. An offset of 0 corresponds to the first position of a data field, an offset of 1 corresponds to the second position and so on. If one interprets the offset as an index, the index starts in the data field with 0.

Offsets are also entered after the field name. However, an offset is entered before the length specification. It is identified by a preceding plus sign (+). No blank spaces are allowed between the elements! The syntax is as follows:

field+offset(length)

The specifications mentioned here work both for reading data fields and for assigning values to them. At least in assignments, then, you can specify the offset and length dynamically, that is, as the contents of a field, instead of having to specify them as constants. In other cases, for example in output with WRITE, you cannot specify offset and length dynamically in this simple way. The following sample program is provided to help clarify the use of definitions, assignments and offset and length specifications:

```
REPORT YZZ31040.
DATA: S1(4),
      S2(20) VALUE 'In aqua ',
      S3(20) VALUE 'vino veritas.'.
DATA: THREE TYPE I VALUE 3,
      FOUR TYPE I VALUE 4.
* In assignments the length of the data fields is taken
* into account, values that are too long are cut off
S1 = S3.
```

```
WRITE / S1.
WRITE /.

* Position specifications can appear both for the source
* and for the target
S2+8 = S3+5.
WRITE / S2.
WRITE /.

* With a length specification, you can determine
* the area to be replaced exactly,
S2+THREE(FOUR) = S1.
WRITE / S2.
WRITE /.

* because assignments without length restrictions overwrite
* from the starting position to the end
S2+3 = S1.
WRITE / S2.
```

Work with character strings is supported by the STRLEN function. In release versions prior to 3.0, you need this function to link character strings with each other, for example. Beginning with Release 3.0, work with character strings is supported with special statements (see Table 3.4).

Table 3.4   Statements for string processing

Statement	Function
CONCATENATE	links several character strings together
CONDENSE	deletes blank spaces
REPLACE	replaces a character
SHIFT	shifts a character
SPLIT	divides a character string
TRANSLATE	changes the syntax

The following program is an example for working with STRLEN.

```
REPORT YZZ31050.
DATA: S1(30) VALUE 'This is',
      S2(30) VALUE 'a linked sentence.',
      LEN TYPE I.

* STRLEN finds the last character that is not an empty
* space. Important are the spaces between parentheses
* and parameters
LEN = STRLEN( S1 ).
```

```
WRITE: / S1.
WRITE:   / 'LEN:', AT LEN '^', /.
* Addition of 1 to LEN, because of hyphenation
* S1+LEN+1 causes a syntax error!
ADD 1 TO LEN.
S1+LEN = S2.
WRITE: / S1, /.
* All positions of a C field within the length specification
* are always available, outputs use the entire length
S1 = ' '.
WRITE: / S1, '<'.
S1+15 = S2.
WRITE: / S1, '<'.
```

Next to the use of the STRLEN function, this example demonstrates another important characteristic of Char data fields. Although the field S1 only has seven characters in it, the ninth position of the field can be addressed with the statement S1+LEN. In programming languages such as C or Pascal, attempting to address a position outside the actual length of the string would lead to a runtime error. In ABAP/4, in contrast, all assignments are allowed, as long as they are within the valid field length, regardless of the current contents of the field. Even for output, the defined field length is used as the default, not the length of the current value.

Operations

With regard to operations, ABAP/4 distinguishes between those that are executed by operators and those for which there are special statements, called operational statements.

Whenever possible, you should represent arithmetic operations using arithmetic operators. The characters +, −, * and / are available to perform the basic types of calculations. Exponentiation is achieved using **. Integer division is possible using DIV. The arithmetic operator MOD delivers the remainder of a division.

You determine the order of processing in complex expressions with parentheses. As a rule, functions are executed first, then exponentiation, then multiplication and division (including DIV and MOD), and finally addition and subtraction. It is important to note that arithmetic operators and operands must always be separated by blank spaces. Several sample expressions follow:

```
A = 1 + 3.
C = 8 / ( 3 + 1 ).
B = A - C.
D = C+3. "Caution! This is not an addition!
```

ABAP/4 also supports the functions listed in Table 3.5.

Assignments with the equal sign (=) are really a simplified form of ABAP/4 assignments, since these normally begin with an operational keyword. There is also a long form for the assignments described, which begins with an ABAP/4 keyword. The complete syntax for assignments is actually:

COMPUTE *field = expression.*

The keyword COMPUTE, however, is optional and so is never used in practice. Operational statements are an alternative to arithmetic operators. The operational statements are ADD TO, SUBTRACT FROM, MULTIPLY BY, and DIVIDE BY. An example of the use of these statements follows:

```
ADD VALUE TO SUM.
```

A constant or a field must appear after the keywords mentioned; expressions are not processed and result in error messages during the syntax check. There are also several special forms of the statements mentioned. Their use is only interesting in special cases, for example in connection with field strings.

Table 3.5   Mathematical functions

Name	Meaning	Valid data types
EXP	exponential function	F
LOG	natural logarithm	F
SIN	sine function	F
COS	cosine function	F
SQRT	square root	F
DIV	integer division	F
MOD	remainder	F
ACOS	arc cosine	F
ASIN	arc sine	F
TAN	tangent	F
COSH	hyperbolic cosine	F
SINH	hyperbolic sine	F
TANH	hyperbolic tangent	F
LOG10	base 10 logarithm	F
ABS	absolute value	F, I, P
SIGN	sign (–1, 0, 1)	F, I, P
CEIL	smallest integer $>= x$	F, I, P
FLOOR	largest integer $<= x$	F, I, P
TRUNC	integer portion	F, I, P
FRAC	decimal portion	F, I, P

Type conversions

Since there are eight predefined data types, there are 64 possible combinations of types for assignments, and there are 64 different rules for type conversion. ABAP/4 automatically supports just about all conversions imaginable. The rules will not be explained here. They are described in detail in the system's online help. The following ground rules are important:

- The source field must have a value that can be converted into a value of the target field's type. For example, if the source field is of type C and the target field is of type F, the source field must contain the representation of a floating point number.
- System reaction to an insufficient number of places in the target field varies. It ranges from simple truncating, to deleting the contents (filling the target field with *), to producing runtime errors.
- In certain situations, date and time specifications are converted into time intervals (in days or seconds) based on a certain reference time. Conversion in the opposite direction (time interval to date) is also possible. This makes date calculations of the following format possible: date = date + integer.

The following example shows the several type conversions and their results. It can serve as the basis for various experiments. Note that the predominant data types used in ABAP/4 applications are C, N, D and P. This makes type conversions between these types particularly interesting.

```
REPORT YZZ31060.
DATA: S(20),
      N TYPE I,
      D TYPE D,
      X TYPE F.

S = '123'.
N = S.
WRITE: / '1.  CHAR -> INT ', 25(10) S, (20) N.

N = S + 1.
WRITE: / '2.  CHAR -> INT ', 25(10) S, (20) N.

N = S+1.
WRITE: / '3.  CHAR -> INT ', 25(10) S, (20) N.
WRITE /.

S = '123.789'.
X = S.
WRITE: / '4.  CHAR -> FLOAT', 25(10) S,
         (20) X DECIMALS 5 EXPONENT 0.

N = X.
WRITE: / '5.  FLOAT-> INT ',
         25(10) X DECIMALS 5 EXPONENT 0, (20)N.
```

```
WRITE /.
WRITE /.

S = '19900601'.
D = S.
WRITE: / '6.   CHAR -> DATE', 25(10) S, (10) D.

S = '900601'.
D = S.
WRITE: / '7.   CHAR -> DATE', 25(10) S, (10) D.
WRITE /.

D = '19991231'.
S = D.
WRITE: / '8.   DATE -> CHAR', 25(10) D, (10) S.

N = D.
WRITE: / '9.   DATE -> INT', 25(10) D, (10) N.
```

This short program results in the output shown in Figure 3.7. The first three lines demonstrate the assignment of character strings to numerical fields. First, the unchanged character string is assigned to a field of type I. As expected, it is correctly converted to a number. The next assignment demonstrates the use of a character string in a numerical expression. Here, too, the result is a correct conversion into a number, which is then used to evaluate the expression.

The use of character strings in numerical expressions can pose a deceptive trap for the programmer. The third assignment is syntactically correct. However, although its form is identical to that of the previous expression except for the blank spaces, it does not represent a numerical expression. In this case, the contents of the character string, starting with

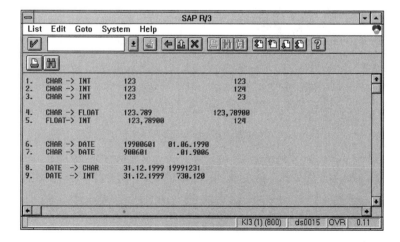

Figure 3.7   Type conversions

offset 1 (that is, starting from the second position), are used in the assignment to the numerical field. This field does not receive the value 124, but rather just 23. In this case, the blank spaces take on added meaning. This type of logical mistake will not be discovered in a syntax check. Sometimes, programmers intentionally make such assignments. In that case, a comment should be added pointing out the fact that the assignment is correct.

In assignment 4, a decimal number represented as a character string is assigned to a floating point number. Note the separators, which are different for the places before the decimal point and the places after the decimal point. Although a printout of the floating point value with WRITE employs a true comma, this must be replaced with a period in the character string representation of the value. The notation

```
S = '123,789'.
X = S.
```

leads to a runtime error, since the character string cannot be interpreted as a number. When a floating point number is assigned to an integer field, places after the decimal point are rounded.

Assignments of character strings to date fields (6) require a particular notation. This notation must be followed even if the assignment is made with a hard-coded constant instead of with a character string field. The date must always be entered in the YYYYMMDD format. Here, too, format during assignment differs from format during output with WRITE. Missing characters in the assignment result in invalid values, as demonstrated in line 7 on the screen. The same is true for time specifications (type T).

The last two assignments demonstrate the conversion of date values to character strings or integer values. In an assignment to a character string, the result is the familiar YYYYMMDD format. The integer value, on the other hand, represents the number of days that have passed since the beginning of time calculation (01.01.0001).

Field strings

Relational database systems combine several individual fields into a single data record. Corresponding constructs have become indispensable in traditional programming languages. ABAP/4 naturally has comparable elements, called field strings here. Field strings are created two different ways. A field string is automatically created for every table used in a program. Field strings or their definitions can also be created explicitly using the keywords DATA or TYPES. In the latter case, supplemental language elements, BEGIN OF and END OF, come into play:

```
DATA: BEGIN OF field_string,
  declarations
END OF field_string.
```

or

```
TYPES: BEGIN OF field_string,
  declarations
END OF field_string.
```

The declarations between BEGIN OF and END OF are declarations introduced by DATA, which has already been described. A sample definition of a field string type in a program could look like this:

```
TYPES: BEGIN OF ADDRESS,
  NAME(20),
  STREET(30),
  CITY(20),
  ZIP(6),
END OF ADDRESS.
```

In field string declarations and definitions, you can reference an existing element (field or field string) using LIKE, or you can reference a type using TYPE, as is possible in the basic form of DATA for simple fields. There are no limitations on the structure of the inserted elements. Field strings can, in turn, contain more field strings:

```
DATA: BEGIN OF INVOICE,
  CUSTOMER TYPE ADDRESS,
  AMOUNT TYPE P DECIMALS 2,
END OF INVOICE.
```

When fields strings are accessed, a distinction is made between access to the field string as a whole and access to the individual fields. To enable the use of an individual field from a field string, a name is built out of the name of the field string and the actual field name, separated by a hyphen. If a field string contains other field strings, the name has more than two parts. Based on the declarations in the examples above, some valid field names would be:

```
INVOICE-AMOUNT
INVOICE-CUSTOMER-CITY
```

The second method of access carries some risk, but is inescapable in certain cases. To ABAP/4, a field string is a single field of type C, whose length is determined by the fields it contains. The length of the field string may be greater than the sum of the lengths of the individual fields, since these might have been aligned with automatically inserted blank spaces. It is therefore possible to access a field string using offset and length specifications regardless of its inner structure. This means that, using offset and length specifications, you can indirectly access fields that you could otherwise not edit. This characteristic also makes it possible to assign a character string to a field string, with the characters of the character string then being distributed among the individual fields. An example of this follows:

```
REPORT YZZ31070.
DATA: BEGIN OF FL,
  C1(2) VALUE '##',
  C2(2) VALUE '##',
  N TYPE I,
END OF FL.
```

```
WRITE: / FL-C1, / FL-C2, / FL-N.
FL = 'ABCDEFGH'.
WRITE: / FL-C1, / FL-C2, / FL-N.
```

In this assignment, all three fields of the field string FL are filled with new values. The assignment to C1 and C2 may be sensible (splitting a field into subfields). However, N also receives a value that depends on the interpretation of the assigned bit pattern according to the data type, and this kind of assignment is definitely undesirable.

It is also possible to use a field string as a whole in assignments from field string to field string or from a field string to an individual field. In these assignments, too, the individual characters are transferred from the source to the target without type conversion, and under certain circumstances they are interpreted there. The only restriction on this kind of field string use is the length of the target field, which is definitely taken into account. Assignments between field strings produce a correct result only if both field strings have the same structure. In ABAP/4 applications, however, there is often a desire to transfer the values of several fields that have identical names between field strings with different structures. In the following program, for example, data from an order and the short text for a product are to be copied into a third field string. In order not to have to write a separate assignment for every individual field, you must use the following statement:

MOVE-CORRESPONDING *source* **TO** *target*.

This statement performs the assignment between fields with the same name in two different field strings:

```
REPORT YZZ31080 NO STANDARD PAGE HEADING.
TYPES T-WERT TYPE P DECIMALS 2.

DATA: BEGIN OF MAT,
  MATNR(10) TYPE N VALUE '1234567890',
  MATBZ(20) VALUE 'Desk Lamp',
  PREIS TYPE T-WERT VALUE '123.45',
END OF MAT.

DATA: BEGIN OF BEST,
  MATNR LIKE MAT-MATNR,
  STCK TYPE I VALUE '2',
  SUMME TYPE T-WERT,
END OF BEST.

DATA: BEGIN OF RECH,
  MATNR LIKE MAT-MATNR,
  MATBZ LIKE MAT-MATBZ,
  STCK LIKE BEST-STCK,
  PREIS LIKE MAT-PREIS,
  SUMME LIKE BEST-SUMME,
END OF RECH.
```

```
MOVE-CORRESPONDING BEST TO RECH.
MOVE-CORRESPONDING MAT TO RECH.
RECH-SUMME = RECH-STCK * RECH-PREIS.

WRITE: / RECH-MATNR, RECH-MATBZ, RECH-PREIS,
          RECH-STCK, RECH-SUMME.
```

Release versions of R/3 software prior to 3.0 do not include this type concept. Referring to existing field strings using LIKE is also not possible in those versions, so the possibilities for creating field strings are limited. In particular, you cannot include substructures as described above. Instead, you must use the following statement:

INCLUDE STRUCTURE *structure_name.*

The INCLUDE statement is a separate statement, which must end with a period. It cannot simply be inserted in the parameter list of the DATA statement. Instead, a separate DATA statement is required for BEGIN OF and END OF, as shown in this example:

```
DATA: BEGIN OF INVOICE.
  INCLUDE STRUCTURE ADR.
DATA: AMOUNT TYPE P DECIMALS 2,
END OF INVOICE.
```

ADR must be either a structure from the Data Dictionary or a program-internal structure defined with DATA. The INCLUDE statement inserts the elements of the structure as individual fields, dissolving the ADR structure. Therefore, field strings from older release versions cannot be repeatedly nested; there is only one field level. The declaration statement shown above is syntactically correct, though somewhat confusing. This is because the field string must be created using two seemingly independent DATA statements. The decisive keywords for the data structure, BEGIN and END, appear in the middle of the statement and could easily be overlooked, especially in complex declaration statements. Such constructs are necessary because of the subsequent expansion of the syntax of ABAP/4; compatibility with older release versions, which was an absolute requirement, prevented a complete overhaul. The price for expanding the language while guaranteeing complete compatibility is often complicated and occasionally misleading syntax. You can minimize the effects of such complicated syntax with clean notation using indents. The following statement is fully compatible with the preceding example, despite the additional (redundant) DATA statement. It is not the DATA statements that play the decisive role in the declaration of field strings. Almost any number of them may be used, even one for every field of the field string. It is the keywords BEGIN OF and END OF that are truly important.

```
DATA: BEGIN OF INVOICE.
  INCLUDE STRUCTURE ADR.
  DATA AMOUNT TYPE P DECIMALS 2.
DATA: END OF INVOICE.
```

Field symbols

Although the procedures for assignment and access that have been described so far allow rather liberal handling of data, they are limited when it comes to solving very general problems. Take the case of dynamic data access. There are subroutines, for example, that must work with data with different structures and cannot use hard-coded field names. For these types of special problems, ABAP/4 provides something called field symbols.

A field symbol bears a distant resemblance to a pointer in C or Pascal. It is assigned a reference to an existing field. From that point on, it is possible to work with the field symbol as though it were the original field. The field symbol also takes on the type of the original field, so that type conversions are performed correctly. You declare field symbols with the statement

FIELD-SYMBOLS *<field_symbol>.*

The angled brackets belong to the name of the field symbol. The ASSIGN statement is responsible for assigning a field to a field symbol. Its structure corresponds somewhat to the MOVE statement:

ASSIGN *field+offset(length)* **TO** *<field_symbol>.*

Indirect assignment of the field is also possible:

ASSIGN *(field)* **TO** *<field_symbol>.*

If there is no explicit length specification, the field symbol copies the field length of the reference field as its length specification. If the reference field is accessed with an offset during assignment, this usually leads to undesired overwriting of other data. To avoid this, you can specify an asterisk (*). This addition keeps field limits from being exceeded during assignments.

```
REPORT YZZ31090.

FIELD-SYMBOLS <FS>.

DATA: BEGIN OF F,
   C1(3),
   C2(2),
   C3(10),
END OF F.

ASSIGN F-C1+2 TO <FS>.
<FS> = '12345'.
WRITE:  / 'field symbol            :', <FS>.
WRITE:  / 'assignment without *   :', F-C1, F-C2, F-C3.

CLEAR F.
ASSIGN F-C1+2(*) TO <FS>.
<FS> = '12345'.
WRITE:  / 'assignment with *      :', F-C1, F-C2, F-C3.
```

In this example, a field symbol is first derived from the field F-C1. Since this field has a length of only three places, only three places are taken into account in the assignment to the field symbol, as demonstrated by the first WRITE statement. Since the field symbol does not begin at the first position of the C1 field, however, the C2 field is also affected by assignments, as demonstrated by the second output. If the addition (*) is used in the derivation of the field symbol, the system determines the available space in C1 and assigns this length to the field symbol. The last output statement shows this quite plainly.

You can use offset and length specifications not only when you link field symbols to fields, but also when you use field symbols. In this case, too, the validity of the values is not checked unless field length monitoring has been turned on with (*), as shown in the example that follows.

```
REPORT YZZ31100.

FIELD-SYMBOLS <FS>.

DATA: BEGIN OF F,
   C1(3) VALUE 'ABC',
   C2(2) VALUE 'DE',
   C3(5) VALUE 'FGHIJ',
END OF F.

ASSIGN F-C1+2 TO <FS>.
<FS>+2 = '12345'.
WRITE:    / F-C1 , F-C2, F-C3.

ASSIGN F-C1+2(*) TO <FS>.
* For now, comment out the following line
<FS>+2 = '12345'. " Runtime error, because <FS> outside the field
```

During definition, the fields of the field string are filled with values to make it easier to recognize the exact position of the later assignments. The field string is first placed on the last position of the C1 field, as in the preceding example. Since assignment to the field list is made with an offset of 2, the last position of C2 is affected by the first assignment. Only one character is allocated to the field string itself. The system knows that the field string can accept a maximum of three characters. Since it is the last position of the field string that is accessed, only one character is transferred. If the (*) addition is used, the system recognizes when attempting to make the assignment that this would lie entirely outside the actual target field C1. In this case, the system generates a runtime error. To be able to test the first part of the program, you will need to comment out the last statement.

Exercises

1. Test the programs presented in this section. Create your own main program for the examples that are incomplete.
2. Test type conversions between various data types. Analyze the behavior when the value range is exceeded.

3. Write a program that fills fields of a predefined type with values and outputs these. Change the output length to values that are smaller than the default and to values that are larger, then evaluate the results.

4. Practice using packed numbers. Watch the rounding behavior and the computation accuracy of interim results.

5. Test date calculation, particularly addition and subtraction between date fields and between date and integer fields. Assign the results to both date and integer fields.

6. Test the output of date and time fields with and without explicitly specifying an output length that is sufficient to represent the value with separators.

3.1.3   Processing dictionary tables

The true task of reports is to analyze tables, which take center stage in this discussion now. The information presented so far provides the necessary foundation for accessing table data.

The TABLES statement

Like all other data elements, tables must be declared in programs before they can be used. You declare a program with the statement

TABLES *table*.

You can also use the colon variation

TABLES: *table_1, table_2, ..., table_n*.

As a prerequisite for a declaration using TABLES, the table must be contained in the Data Dictionary, and it must be active. If it is not, the syntax check before program processing will lead to an error. In addition to tables (in the narrow sense), you can use views to select data. However, the ability to maintain data using views is very limited.

Accessing tables

After a table has been declared, you can edit it using various commands. During editing, the contents of a data record must be transferred from the table to internal program fields or, vice versa, from fields into the table. In the file concept of tradional programming languages, this is handled with explicit read and write statements. Both the file descriptors and the variables that should receive the values must be declared and used in the statements. Files must be opened and closed, and the source and the target must be specified for read and write operations.

In ABAP/4, access to tables is much easier. A declaration using TABLES not only tells the program about the table, but also creates a field string with the name of the table. The field string is automatically given the structure specified in the Data Dictionary for the table in question. You can access it using the statements already described for data fields and field strings. Such field strings always accept only one data record from the table. In SAP terminology, this kind of field string, which is assigned to a table, is called a *header line*, a *work area*, or a *table work area*.

Declaration of a table using TABLES, therefore, results in two different objects with the same name. It is sometimes easy to forget this fact, since ABAP/4 statements, which are relatively simple, almost always have the desired result, even when they are used intuitively. It should be noted that there are statements that process the database table (and only that), and there are other commands that only affect the field string and do not produce any changes in the database table. When a record is read from the database table, the contents of the work area are automatically updated. Changes in the work area, however, such as those resulting from assignments, are not automatically transferred to the database table. This must be done with the appropriate statements.

Database queries

The database systems used in R/3 work in SQL. ABAP/4 provides several statements for accessing the data sets. Collectively, these statements are called Open SQL. The commands are based on standard SQL commands, and most of them have the same name as their SQL counterparts, although there are considerable differences in some of their functions. To a great extent, this also depends on the release version of the SAP system in question. Open SQL does not have the power of fully standard SQL. The desire for system independence forces its command set to be limited to the smallest common denominator between all of the database systems used in R/3.

Reading data records boils down to executing a database query, which you do with the SELECT statement. In its basic form in ABAP/4, this statement requires two additional clauses:

```
SELECT *
FROM table
WHERE condition.
...
ENDSELECT.
```

In the SELECT statement, you specify which table should be read and which data should be selected. Strictly speaking, you could leave out the WHERE clause. But this would cause all of the data records of the table to be read, which is rarely a good idea in practice. The syntax of the SELECT statement is more dependent on the SAP system's release version than is the syntax of other Open SQL statements. A detailed description of this statement appears in a separate section. This section focuses on the relationships instead of the details.

The WHERE clause of the SELECT statement can include one or more comparisons, which can be linked, if necessary, using the arithmetic operators AND and OR. In every comparison, a table field is checked to see whether it fulfills a condition or not. Various kinds of comparisons are possible (numerical comparisons, string checking, pattern checking, checking against a selection table). Similar comparisons are used in several control statements (for example, IF, WHILE, and CHECK), although there are differences between the expressions possible for WHERE clauses and those for other statements. A description of the selection capabilities of the WHERE clause appears at the end of this section.

Open SQL also deviates from standard SQL in the way it handles the data selected. It is well known that SQL works based on sets. SELECT statements always deliver all of the data records that correspond to the search criteria. In the simplest case, the records are simply listed on the screen. In ABAP/4, on the other hand, SELECT statements are loop statements whose end is marked by the keyword ENDSELECT. One loop is executed for every data record of the table that corresponds to the selection criteria.

The following example demonstrates a practical test of the SELECT statement. Please note that the TADIR table is an extremely important system table that you can read but should under no circumstances change. This table is the development environment's "table of contents." One of the things it contains, for example, is an entry for every program. It is these entries (the current user's programs) that the sample program is supposed to retrieve.

```
PROGRAM YZZ31110.

TABLES TADIR.

SELECT * FROM TADIR
WHERE AUTHOR = SY-UNAME
  AND OBJECT = 'PROG'.

    WRITE: /  TADIR-PGMID,
              TADIR-OBJECT,
              TADIR-OBJ_NAME,
              TADIR-AUTHOR.

ENDSELECT.
```

The example above uses two comparison expressions linked with AND. Both of them are pretty much self-explanatory: one checks whether the owner of the program matches the currently logged-on user; the other uses the OBJECT field to filter out all programs.

Since tables in the SAP system have a unique key, it is possible to target a single record using an appropriate formulation of the WHERE clause. In this case, you do not need a SELECT–ENDSELECT loop. Adding the keyword SINGLE to the SELECT statement causes the statement to start only a single search process.

```
SELECT SINGLE *
FROM table
WHERE condition.
```

In this case, the WHERE clause must test the full key. In each comparison to the condition, only a comparison for equality is allowed, which means that only a single record can be found (assuming the key is unique).

As do all other commands of the Open SQL group, SELECT sets the system variable SY-SUBRC to a defined value, thereby signaling whether the command was successful or not. Table 3.6 shows possible values for this variable and the meaning of each value.

The SELECT statement sets other system variables by way of SY-SUBRC. SY-DBCNT is often analyzed in programs. This field contains the number of data records found.

Table 3.6   Values for SY-SUBRC after SELECT

SY-SUBRC	Meaning
0	Search was successful, at least one record found.
4	No record found.
8	Only for SELECT SINGLE. The search term was ambiguous; an arbitrary record of the solution set is returned.

The entire R/3 System is implemented as a client/server application. In practice, this means that the link to the database can span several hierarchically linked computers. Table data may be buffered in the memory of computers known as application servers, if such buffering is allowed for the table in question. Therefore, there is not always direct access to the database. In the case of data sets that are changed often, or queries that are especially critical, this can lead to differences between the results of the SELECT statement and the real data set. If you use the addition

... BYPASSING BUFFER

after the FROM clause, you can force a direct read of the database, sidestepping the buffer. Since direct database access reduces performance, of course, you should use this statement only when justified.

Changing, adding and deleting data records

Before the data sets in a table can be read, they must, of course, be written to it. Statements are also needed for modifying and deleting data records. You add new data records to a table with the command

INSERT *table.*

This causes the contents of the specified work area to be written to the table. Afterwards, the SY-SUBRC field provides information about the success of the command. A value of 0 means that the new record was successfully added; values larger than 0 indicate an error. An INSERT command results in an error, for example, if a data record with the same key already exists. You cannot use INSERT to change the contents of data records that already exist. For this you need to use the command

UPDATE *table.*

This command overwrites an existing data record with the contents of the work area. In contrast to INSERT, the data record to be overwritten must already exist. This statement also affects the contents of the SY-SUBRC field. The key that identifies the data record is taken from the work area.

Like the SQL statement of the same name, the ABAP/4 command has a variant that allows you to change one or more fields of data records that match an entered pattern. The syntax for this is as follows:

UPDATE `table`
SET `assignments`
WHERE `condition`.

In this form, the assignments specified are made in all of the data records that meet the condition. Since it is not always possible to differentiate between inserting and changing, you can also use the command

MODIFY `table`.

This command recognizes on its own whether a new data record should be inserted in the table or an already existing data record should be changed. There is a price for this level of comfort, that is, loss of performance.

All of the commands presented so far (except mass update) work with the header of the table, from which they take, in particular, the key for the data record to be processed. This is also the case in the deletion of data records. A simple

DELETE `table`.

is sufficient to delete the data record, which is identified by the key in the work area. This form of the delete command is useful, for example, when you want to delete some of the records read in a SELECT loop. Similar to mass changes using UPDATE, however, you can perform a mass deletion if the data records to be deleted are selected with a WHERE clause:

DELETE FROM `table`
WHERE `condition`.

The conditions of the WHERE clause correspond to those of the SELECT statement and the UPDATE command.

The changes to the database are not final after a command for database modification has been executed. You can reverse them at any time with

ROLLBACK WORK.

This may be necessary, for example, if one of the write commands ends with an error when writing to several logically interdependent tables. To ensure the consistency of the data, the changes in all tables must be revoked in this case. As a counterpart to ROLL-BACK WORK, of course, there is a command for confirming changes, namely:

COMMIT WORK.

Once this command has been executed, the modifications are no longer reversible. A characteristic of the SAP system related to this should be noted here: at every screen change, that is, at the end of every dynpro, the internal control logic independently executes a COMMIT WORK. One of the things this command does in addition to confirming the changes is delete the internal cursor (data record pointer) of a SELECT statement. For this reason, no screen change may take place between the statements SELECT and DESELECT. This means that in such a loop, you cannot process one after the other, in a single screen, the data records that were read.

In ABAP/4 applications, these commands are usually stored in special parts of the program whose task is to write information to the database, that is, posting. Several special statements and programming techniques have influence on the posting process; these are discussed in a separate section.

The functionality of the Open SQL commands was greatly expanded for Release 3.0 (dynamic specification of table names, aggregate statements in the SELECT statement, cooperation with internal tables). As noted in the introductory remarks for this chapter, however, this expansion of functionality is not the focus here. For more information, please refer to the reference section, the examples and the SAP system's online help.

The following short program fills a table with some data records that are needed as test data for several other programs in this book. Do not execute this program if you have already created data for the example in Chapter 6. When this program starts, the existing contents of the table are erased!

Before you can execute this program, you must create the table. It is not one of the tables delivered as part of the standard SAP system. The section on maintaining Dictionary elements describes how to create data elements, domains and tables.

```
REPORT YZZ31120.
TABLES YZZAKT.

DELETE FROM YZZAKT WHERE NAME LIKE '%'.

YZZAKT-NAME = 'SAP'.
INSERT YZZAKT.

YZZAKT-NAME = 'IXOS'.
INSERT YZZAKT.

YZZAKT-NAME = 'NAGEL & CO'.
INSERT YZZAKT.
COMMIT WORK.

WRITE: / 'Contents after insert'.
SELECT * FROM YZZAKT.
  WRITE: / YZZAKT-NAME, YZZAKT-BRANCHE.
ENDSELECT.

UPDATE YZZAKT
SET BRANCHE = 'S'
WHERE NAME = 'SAP' OR NAME = 'IXOS'.

WRITE: /, /, 'Contents after update'.
SELECT * FROM YZZAKT.
  WRITE: / YZZAKT-NAME, YZZAKT-BRANCHE.
ENDSELECT.

DELETE FROM YZZAKT
WHERE BRANCHE <> 'S'.
```

```
WRITE: /, /, 'Contents after delete'.
SELECT * FROM YZZAKT.
  WRITE: / YZZAYT-NAME, YZZAKT-BRANCHE.
ENDSELECT.
```

The SELECT statement and internal tables

Internal tables are tools for temporary data storage. They are described in more detail in the section that follows. Some of the Open SQL commands work with internal tables. If a SELECT statement should find several data records, these must be either processed in the SELECT–ENDSELECT loop or transferred by the application to an internal table for later processing. The latter option can be handled quite effectively by adding another parameter to the SELECT statement. In the statement

SELECT * FROM *DB-Tab* **INTO TABLE** *Itab*.

or

SELECT * FROM *DB-Tab* **APPENDING TABLE** *Itab*.

the SELECT command writes the data directly to the specified table. In the first statement, the internal table is deleted before data is written to it. In the second statement, the data records are appended to the internal table.

When using the commands INSERT, UPDATE or MODIFY to write data from the application to the database, you can use a similar mechanism to write several records at once. The mechanism you use is the FROM TABLE clause, as shown here:

INSERT *DB-Tab* **FROM TABLE** *Itab*.
UPDATE *DB-Tab* **FROM TABLE** *Itab*.
MODIFY *DB-Tab* **FROM TABLE** *Itab*.

In a deletion, too, the data records to be deleted can be derived from an internal table. In this case, the DELETE statement resembles the statements just mentioned:

DELETE *DB-Tab* **FROM TABLE** *Itab*.

The WHERE clause

The most important of the Open SQL command clauses is the WHERE clause, which determines the selection of the database records. It processes a number of different expressions, which are described in this section. The WHERE clause determines the criteria for selection. It can analyze various expressions. These expressions can be grouped using parentheses and the arithmetic operators AND and OR, and they can also be negated using the arithmetic operator NOT. You can select database records using the following criteria:

- Does a database field match a value or a field?
- Does a database field match any of a set of values or fields?
- Does a database field match a pattern?

- Does a database field match any values or fields in a range (lower and upper limits)?
- Does a database field match any values or fields of a specially constructed internal table (selection)?
- Does a database field match any fields of any internal table (only for SELECT statements)?

You can also declare the condition dynamically (for SELECT statements only).

For direct field-to-field (or value) comparisons, the usual comparison operators are available. You can enter them either as symbols or as two-character operators. Table 3.7 shows the available operators.

Table 3.7   Comparison operators

Operator	Symbol	Meaning
EQ	=	equal to
NE	<> ><	not equal to
LT	<	less than
LE	<=	less than or equal to
GT	>	greater than
GE	>=	greater than or equal to

The following examples refer to one of the tables from the example in Chapter 6. A possible selection expression that lists all stocks whose market rate is higher than a certain value might be:

```
...
WHERE KURS > 250.
...
```

If you do not want to make a one-to-one value comparison, but rather see if a value matches an element from a larger set, you use the statement IN. You specify the sets by placing them in parentheses.

```
...
WHERE BRANCHE IN ('M', 'B', 'V').
...
```

To check against a pattern, you use the LIKE command. There are two characters available for use as wildcards in patterns. You can use the underscore (_) as a wildcard to represent any character, and you can use the percent sign (%) as a wildcard to represent any character string (including an empty one). Pattern checking is only available for alphanumeric values, however. The following statement is an example of this kind of checking:

```
...
WHERE NAME LIKE '%BANK%'.
...
```

From time to time, you might actually want to search for the special characters % and _. For this you need to turn off their special meaning as wildcards. Using the ESCAPE statement, you can define any character to assume the role of one or the other wildcard in the pattern. Since you can select any character as the replacement wildcard, you can tackle even the most complicated situations. Such a statement might read:

```
...
WHERE NAME LIKE '%\_BANK' ESCAPE '\'.
...
```

You use the BETWEEN statement to check against a range with an upper and lower limit. The upper and lower limits are separated by AND:

```
...
WHERE KURS BETWEEN 250 AND 500.
...
```

If you want to select some data records that have entirely different keys, or you want to use dynamic selection, you cannot use the selection criteria already presented. Instead, you need to use what is called a selection table. A selection table has a special structure and can be filled with data easily in a report selection screen. The use of selection tables is described in more detail in a later section. You can perform a check against a selection table simply by entering the name of the selection after the IN statement:

```
...
WHERE NAME IN selection.
...
```

Selection tables are not processed by the database itself. Instead, they are broken down into individual statements by the SAP control logic. Since the database systems restrict the size of SQL statements, this means that the selection table should not be too large. Thus there is a related statement available exclusively for the SELECT statement, FOR ALL ENTRIES, which allows checks against internal tables of any structure. It checks every data record of the database table against all of the entries in the internal table. You do, of course, need to specify which fields should be compared. If you leave this specification out, the WHERE clause checks all of the fields that have the same name. An excerpt from a WHERE clause might look something like this:

```
...
FOR ALL ENTRIES IN I_AUFLISTEN WHERE NAME = I_AUFLISTEN-NAME.
...
```

This command is not available in release versions prior to Release 3.0. Another form of selection that is possible beginning with Release 3.0 involves specifying in an internal table criteria that are formulated dynamically. This table must have a specific structure (only one field, type C, with a length of 72 characters), and it must meet several conditions. In the program, then you execute the check as follows:

```
...
WHERE (internal_table).
...
```

As the examples show, you only need to specify the field name in the WHERE clause; you do not need to specify the table name, because it already appears in the FROM clause. You can, however, store the value against which a table field should be checked in the header line of that table. This results in the following, somewhat confusing statement:

```
YZZAKT-NAME = 'IXOS'.
SELECT * FROM YZZAKT
WHERE NAME = YZZAKT-NAME.
```

To understand this statement, you have to think of the table and the header line as two different objects. First, a value is provided in the header line. The SELECT statement is then processed by the internal control logic of the R/3 System, after which it is sent to the database server. The server receives a statement similar to the following:

```
SELECT * FROM YZZAKT
WHERE NAME = 'IXOS'.
```

So, although at first glance the original statement seems to indicate that the record read from the table will be checked against the NAME field of the YZZAKT table (that is, against itself), this is not the case. Instead, the record is checked against a value stored in the field string YZZAKT. In standard SQL, you can use nested SELECTS or Joins to access fields in other tables whose value changes in each loop iteration. The commands in Open SQL, in contrast, can only process one table at a time, meaning such links are not possible in ABAP/4.

The SELECT statement

In release versions prior to Release 3.0, the SELECT statement used several clauses from the standard SQL command set, although these did not offer nearly the same functionality. Beginning with Release 3.0, these SQL clauses have more support. The clauses described at the beginning of this section, therefore, should be seen as a special form of a more complex SELECT statement in Release 3.0. The syntax of the SELECT statement beginning with Release 3.0 is:

```
SELECT [DISTINCT] field_list, aggregate_expressions
  [INTO field_list | work_area | Itab]
  FROM table
  [WHERE condition]
  [GROUP BY field_list]
  [ORDER BY field_list].
```

The SELECT statement determines if the data set returned should consist of a single record that is completely specified by the key (SINGLE clause) or a set containing any number of data records. It also describes which data fields should be included in the resulting set and whether aggregate functions should be used on those fields. At a minimum, the table to be processed is specified in the obligatory FROM clause.

An aggregate function evaluates the contents of one of the table fields in all of the data records selected. Table 3.8 shows the aggregate functions that are available.

Table 3.8   Aggregate functions

Aggregate function	Description
AVG (field)	average
COUNT (DISTINCT field)	number of different values
COUNT (*)	number of selected data records
MAX (field)	largest value
MIN (field)	smallest value
SUM (field)	sum of the field contents

If you want the data set returned to contain all of the table fields, you use an asterisk instead of a field list. The result is automatically provided in the table header. In all other cases (field list with named fields or aggregate expressions), for every field listed in the SELECT clause or every aggregate expression, you name a data field to accept the result with the INTO clause. The field list of the INTO clause must be enclosed in parentheses. The fields must be separated by commas. The YZZ31110 program, for example, could be implemented as follows:

```
PROGRAM YZZ31130.
TABLES TADIR.
DATA:  PID LIKE TADIR-PGMID,
       OBJ LIKE TADIR-OBJECT,
       NAM LIKE TADIR-OBJ-NAME,
       AUT LIKE TADIR-AUTHOR.

SELECT PGMID OBJECT OBJ-NAME AUTHOR
INTO (PID, OBJ, NAM, AUT)
FROM TADIR
WHERE AUTHOR = SY-UNAME
  AND OBJECT = 'PROG'.

    WRITE: /  PID,
              OBJ,
              NAM,
              AUT.

ENDSELECT.
```

If the SELECT clause field list consists of only an asterisk, a special form of the INTO clause can be used to store the result set in a separate field string or in an internal table.

The data records selected can be prepared in the SELECT statement already, for example using the aggregate functions. It is also possible to suppress duplicate records in the result set using the DISTINCT clause for the SELECT statement, and to combine similar records using GROUP BY. Using GROUP BY, however, requires specifying table fields or aggregate functions in the SELECT statement. Fields from this list are then named with GROUP BY. Data records with the same field contents are combined. This clause is useful particularly when you want to use an aggregate function separately on a group of data records.

```
REPORT YZZ31140.

TABLES TADIR.
DATA: OBJ LIKE TADIR-OBJECT,
      ANZ TYPE I.
SELECT OBJECT COUNT( DISTINCT OBJ_NAME )
INTO (OBJ, ANZ)
FROM TADIR
WHERE AUTHOR = SY-UNAME
GROUP BY OBJECT .
  WRITE: / OBJ,
           ANZ.
ENDSELECT.
```

This short program collects all of the development objects (programs, transactions, screens and so on) created by the current user, but instead of listing them individually, it sums up the number of objects in each group and writes only that number to the screen. All of the fields of the SELECT statement that do not appear in aggregate functions must be listed in the GROUP BY clause. It does not make sense to read fields from the database whose contents are not valid, due to the grouping of data records. For this reason, only aggregate functions should be used on fields that are not contained in the GROUP BY clause.

The final clause that can be used, ORDER BY, allows the output set to be sorted. You can either sort by labels, in ascending order, using the addition PRIMARY KEY, or you can use a field list.

3.1.4 Internal tables

In addition to the various tables managed by the Data Dictionary, there is a second type of table, the internal table. Internal tables do not exist in the database; they exist only in the main memory of the computer. They are therefore not meant to be used for long-term storage of information, but are used in applications for temporary data storage and processing. Internal tables offer the only universal possibility to combine similar data records. ABAP/4 does not have anything like arrays. On the other hand, ABAP/4 provides several commands that allow you to access internal tables through an index, similar to the way you access a single-dimension array.

Internal tables are used for many different reasons. They are often used to buffer the contents of a SELECT statement while an application is running, to improve runtime performance. Internal tables are also used to exchange data with subroutines or function modules. Internal tables also allow you to sort data sets according to various criteria and to compress them.

Definition

You access internal tables similar to the way you access Dictionary tables. The contents of the table itself are hidden from the program; they can be accessed only with a field string, also called a header or work area. Certain commands read a data set from the internal table and make it available in the work area; others insert the contents of the work area into the internal table. For internal tables, too, the header is the only interface between the data set and the application.

Since internal tables are derived only indirectly from Dictionary elements, they lack some information that is stored for database tables only, such as label identification. For this reason, you use other commands for declaration and access (especially data record searches) than those you use with database tables.

The declaration of an internal table is almost exactly the same as the declaration of a field string. The addition of an ABAP/4 keyword turns a simple field string into an internal table:

```
DATA: BEGIN OF Itab OCCURS n.
...declarations
DATA: END OF Itab.
```

The numerical value n indicates how many of the internal table's data records should be stored in main memory. It does not represent an upper limit for the length of the table. Rather, at the time of declaration, an area of memory of that size is reserved in main memory. If the memory area proves to be insufficient, that is, because more records need to be included in the table, part of the table is moved to the hard disk. This, of course, has a negative effect on processing speed, since bulk memory accesses are much slower than read procedures in main memory.

Depending on the release version of the SAP system, you can also use the other declaration variants for field strings to declare internal tables, for example those with TYPE or LIKE:

```
DATA: IAKT LIKE YZZAKT OCCURS 50.
```

It should be noted, however, that internal tables declared in this fashion have one distinction: they possess a header line. This means that to access them, you must specify an additional work area, as described in the next section. This is true also for the declaration variant described next. In addition to being able to declare an internal table directly, you can also create a type statement for an internal table. This type statement then serves as a declaration of the internal table. The TYPES statement for an internal table must meet certain conditions. A two-level definition is required:

```
TYPES:
  BEGIN OF T_FL,
    A(3),
  END OF T_FL,

  T_ITAB TYPE T_FL OCCURS 10.
DATA:
  ITAB1 TYPE T_FL OCCURS 10,
  ITAB2 TYPE T_ITAB.
```

First, the type description T_FL is created for a field string. With this type, an internal table (ITAB1) can be declared immediately. Alternatively, another type (T_ITAB) can be created for an internal table, from which, in turn, an internal table (ITAB2) can then be derived. As already mentioned, neither internal table has a header line.

The only way to process data in an internal table is through the header line or work area just mentioned. Beginning with Release 3.0, however, ABAP/4 allows you to access the entire data portion of an internal table with a special syntax. Currently, the only real use for this is to copy the entire contents of one table into another table. The syntax element used to indicate the data portion of a table is square brackets, which are added to the name of the table. The statement

```
ITAB1[] = ITAB2[].
```

would thus copy the entire contents of the ITAB2 table into ITAB1. The data records are accessed as a whole, that is, without regard to their structure. This form of access was already mentioned in the discussion on field strings. Access with [] makes sense only if the tables' structures correspond to a certain degree.

Writing and deleting in internal tables

One way to fill internal tables, that is, using SELECT ... INTO TABLE, has already been demonstrated. There are also other statements available that enable sentence-by-sentence appending or processing. New data records can be appended to an internal table with

APPEND *Itab*.

or

INSERT *Itab*.

APPEND causes the new data record to be added at the end of the table without regard to sort order. In a program loop over an internal table using LOOP, the INSERT command without an addition inserts a new data record ahead of the current data record. Both statements take the data from the field string Itab and write it to the internal table Itab. If the data should be taken from a field string with a different name, you can use the TO parameter to specify a different work area. In that case, the command is

APPEND *field_string* **TO** *Itab*.

or

INSERT *field_string* **TO** *Itab*.

You can also use the INSERT command outside of LOOP program loops. In that case, however, you must specify the position where the new record should be inserted by using the INDEX clause. INSERT places the new data record ahead of an already existing data record, thereby shifting to the back all of the data records beginning at the position specified.

```
INSERT [field_string TO] Itab INDEX i.
```

Modifying data records in an internal table is somewhat more cumbersome, because internal tables have no true key. While the UPDATE statement for Dictionary tables can easily identify a data record to be modified by its unique key, this is not possible with internal tables. Instead, the data record to be processed must be either implicitly or explicitly specified. In explicit position specification, the data record is identified by the data record number. In this case, the command syntax reads:

```
MODIFY Itab INDEX i.
```

Of course, the index of the data record to be modified must be known in order for this form of specification to work. The search command READ therefore makes the data record number of the data record read available in the system variable SY-TABIX.

If a table is processed in a LOOP program loop, explicit position specification is not necessary. The internal control logic recognizes this special case and uses the data record pointer of the LOOP command for the MODIFY command. In this case, the syntax of the MODIFY statement is simpler:

```
MODIFY Itab.
```

With the addition of FROM, the MODIFY statement can also retrieve the data to be written from another field string. Deletion of internal tables is similar to deletion of database tables. A simple

```
DELETE Itab.
```

deletes the current record in a LOOP program loop. Using an index specification, you can target any record of an internal table for deletion:

```
DELETE Itab INDEX i.
```

The next and final variant of the WRITE command has some risk associated with its use. With the additions TO and INDEX, the WRITE command can write directly to an internal table. The general syntax for this statement is as follows:

```
WRITE field_string TO Itab INDEX i.
```

The field string is directly written to the internal table record that is named after INDEX. The effect of this command generally corresponds to that of MODIFY with an index specification.

What is interesting about this command is that assignment of a field string is not mandatory. Since ABAP/4 treats a data record of an internal table the same way it treats a field string, that is, like a data field of type CHAR, it is possible to write any value to any place in the internal table using offset and length specifications. This effect is reflected more accurately in the following, more exact, syntax description of this WRITE variant:

```
WRITE value TO Itab+offset(length) INDEX i.
```

There are dangers inherent in this form of usage, of course. Under certain circumstances, a single error in a direct write to an internal table can make the entire data set unusable, since correct analyses are no longer possible.

Reading in internal tables

Internal tables are accessed quite frequently. Large programs often load all of the data they need into internal tables, then work mainly with these. For one thing, this minimizes the effects of some programming problems. It also dramatically improves runtime performance. Since the R/3 System as a whole requires considerable resources, the runtime performance of applications is of major importance.

There are two ways to access the data records of internal tables. One way is to run a loop over the internal table. This loop works similar to the way a SELECT ... ENDSELECT statement works for database tables. The second possibility, comparable to SELECT SINGLE, is to access a single data record.

To search for an individual data record, you use the READ command, which has two principal variants. In the first variant, READ searches for a data record in the internal table using one or more search terms. In this variant, in turn, there are two ways to pass the search terms to the command.

The first way to pass search terms to the READ command is to use the header record, which is required for data exchange anyhow. You enter the search terms in the header line of the internal table, and afterwards you call the READ command with the name of the internal table. The command searches for the first data record whose field contents match those of the header line. Only alphanumeric fields whose contents do not consist entirely of blank spaces are considered in the comparison. If the READ command finds such a data record, it fills the header line with the data record and gives values to several system variables. If no data record is found, the header record remains unchanged. If several data records in the internal table fit the search pattern, only the first one is returned.

Before you can enter search terms in the header line, this must, of course, be emptied. Otherwise, the already existing values would be used in the search. The following command is usually used to empty the header line:

```
MOVE SPACE TO Itab.
```

This command fills the entire header with blank spaces. In a program, a complete call might look something like this:

```
MOVE SPACE TO IAKT.
IAKT-NAME = 'DAIMLER'.
READ TABLE IAKT.
IF SY-SUBRC = 0.
*   Process data record, for example:
    WRITE: / IAKT-NAME, IAKT-BRANCHE.
ELSE.
*   Output error message or other actions
ENDIF.
```

You can also specify the fields for which you want to search directly in the call of the READ command, in the following form:

```
key_field = value
```

Key specifications are not limited to one; you can enter several in a row. In order to tell the command that the search terms are being passed as parameters, you need the addition WITH KEY. Another way to formulate the example above would thus be:

```
READ TABLE IAKT WITH KEY NAME = 'IXOS'.
IF SY-SUBRC = 0.
...
```

The importance of the WITH KEY variant lies in another clause that allows the execution of a time-saving binary search. Use of this clause requires that the internal table be sorted in ascending order, according to the field or the order of the fields in which you want to search. If the internal table with stock values, which has already been used several times in this chapter, were sorted by stock, you could start this type of search with the command

```
READ TABLE IAKT WITH KEY NAME = 'IXOS' BINARY SEARCH.
```

Sorting a table just so you can use this form of access is not worth it, since the sort will always take longer than the subsequent reading of the table. However, if attention is paid to the order of an internal table when it is created, a binary search like this can result in considerable performance benefits.

The second variant of the READ command dispenses with searching by key and instead accesses the desired record with an index. The syntax is as follows:

```
READ TABLE Itab INDEX i.
```

In addition to allowing a targeted search for a data record, this also makes sequential processing of an entire internal table possible. This is done using a LOOP program loop:

```
LOOP AT Itab.
...
ENDLOOP.
```

The LOOP commands are executed once for every data record. The data is always made available in the respective header record. You can use several clauses to restrict the range of data records over which the program loop should run. FROM and TO allow you to specify an index range; WHERE lets you specify a selection, similar to the way you can with Open SQL commands. In this case, the LOOP command reads

```
LOOP AT Itab FROM start TO end.
...
ENDLOOP.
```

or

```
LOOP AT Itab
WHERE condition.
...
ENDLOOP.
```

Sorting and combining

In addition to the commands described so far, there are several more commands, or variants of existing commands, which affect the order of the records in the internal table. To sort according to a different field or a list of fields, you must use the SORT command. Specifying the name of an internal table is mandatory. You name the fields that you want the table sorted by with the BY clause. The sort order is determined by the parameters ASCENDING and DESCENDING. If you do not specify a field list with BY, the SORT command builds the key out of all of the alphanumerical fields of the data record. Sorting is quite time-intensive, so it is used sparingly.

The APPEND command recognizes a clause called SORTED BY. This command does more than just ensure that new records are inserted in a defined order. It has the following effects:

- The internal table is sorted in descending (!) order according to the field named.
- Only the number of records specified in the OCCURS parameter are stored in the table. In this special case, therefore, the OCCURS parameter is a true size specification.

This statement is only useful, of course, if all of the data records are written to the internal table in this way.

The COLLECT statement is a somewhat more specialized and therefore seldom-used statement that automatically combines several data records. This statement checks if a record already exists with the same contents in all alphanumeric fields as the record to be inserted. If such a record is found, the numeric fields of the two records are summed, and the existing record is updated with the sums. If no such record exists, the new record is appended.

3.1.5   Control statements

The commands discussed up to this point have been relatively simple commands for data processing. These commands are processed sequentially; you cannot influence the program flow with them. ABAP/4 also has several statements you can use for program branching or cyclical repetitions. The principles underlying the use of these statements should be familiar to those with programming knowledge, so an extensive discussion is unnecessary here.

IF

An IF statement branches into a yes (IF) branch or an optional no (ELSE) branch, depending on the result of the evaluation of a complex condition. These conditions are described in a separate section, because they are also used in several other statements. The two alternative control sections are constructed with the statements IF and ELSE, or ELSE and ENDIF.

You can link the ELSE branch of an IF statement to an ELSEIF command by using an additional IF statement.

Examples of the use of these statements are as follows:

```
IF A < B.
  WRITE / 'A is smaller than B'.
ELSEIF A > B.
  WRITE / 'A is greater than B'.
ELSE.
  WRITE / 'A is equal to B'.
ENDIF.
```

WHILE

You use the WHILE statement to build loops; the system runs through a loop as many times as a condition is met. The complete syntax of the WHILE statement is as follows:

```
WHILE condition.
*  statements
ENDWHILE.
```

CASE

In a CASE statement, the contents of a field are compared to several patterns. Each pattern has statements allocated to it; if the field matches the pattern, these statements are executed. If the contents of the field do not match any of the patterns, an optional alternative branch is executed. The syntax is as follows:

```
CASE field.
  WHEN pattern_1.
    statement sequence 1
  WHEN pattern_2.
    statement sequence 2
  WHEN pattern_x.
    statement sequence x
  WHEN OTHERS.
    alternative statements
  ENDCASE.
```

A CASE statement may contain only one WHEN OTHERS branch.

DO

The DO statement has two variants. In one form, it constructs an infinite loop, which can be exited only with an explicit EXIT statement.

```
DO.
*  statements
ENDDO.
```

In its second form, you can use the DO loop as a simple substitute for a FOR loop, which does not exist in ABAP/4. A parameter specifies how many times the loop should be performed:

```
DO n TIMES.
* statements
ENDDO.
```

The SY-INDEX system variable tracks the number of loop iterations within the DO loop.

EXIT, CONTINUE, and CHECK

As mentioned earlier, DO loops must be exited with EXIT. If called inside a loop (including LOOP, WHILE, SELECT), this command causes the loop to end. If called outside of a loop but inside a modularization unit (FORM, MODULE, FUNCTION, AT), on the other hand, this command causes the unit to be exited.

Many reports contain no subordinate modularization units. In this case, an EXIT causes report generation to end and the report list to be output.

Using the CONTINUE statement makes sense only inside loops. This statement causes the system to terminate the current loop iteration and jump to the beginning of the loop. The loop condition is evaluated again, and the next iteration of the loop is carried out. The statement

```
CHECK condition.
```

represents a shortened form of the following sequence of statements:

```
IF NOT condition.
   CONTINUE.
ENDIF.
```

The CHECK statement ends one loop iteration and begins the next one. It is often used in SELECT loops in reports to analyze selections.

Conditions

The logical conditions that can be evaluated by the commands described above most closely resemble the conditions that were presented in the description of the WHERE clause.

The simplest variant of a condition construction is the comparison of a field to a value or to another field. The operators you use for this are the same operators used in the WHERE clause. With these operators, you can compare not only numerical values, but also fields of all data types. You can even compare values of different types; such comparisons, of course, require type conversions, whose effects you must consider when formulating the expression.

In a comparison, of course, the different data types are handled individually. A comparison of character strings is based on alphabetical order. The two character strings are compared character-by-character; the first different character that is encountered determines the outcome of the comparison. In a comparison of date fields, the earlier date has a greater value; in a comparison of time specifications, the later time specification has a greater value.

There are several other comparison operators available for character strings. Table 3.9 lists these operators. They are used in the following form:

`c1 operator c2`

The function descriptions in Table 3.9 are based on this same sequence of operands.

Table 3.9   Operators for string comparisons

Operator	Description
CO	contains only C1 contains only the characters of C2
CN	contains not only C1 contains not only the characters of C2
CA	contains any C1 contains at least one character of C2
NA	not any C1 does not contain any characters of C2
CS	contains string C1 contains C2
NS	no string C1 does not contain C2
CP	contains pattern C1 matches the pattern in C2
NP	no pattern C1 does not match the pattern in C2

One note about the operators CP and NP: their effect is similar to that of the WHERE comparison using LIKE. However, the wildcards differ. In contrast to LIKE, in CP and NP the asterisk character (*) represents any pattern, and the plus character (+) represents any character.

Table 3.10 shows several other possible comparisons, some of which have already been described in connection with the WHERE clause.

Table 3.10   Additional comparisons

Function	Description
BETWEEN ... AND	range specification
IS INITIAL	field equals initial value
IS SPACE	field equals SPACE
IN	contained in the selection table

For hexadecimal fields with a length of 1, bit-by-bit comparisons are also possible. These comparisons differ somewhat from traditional bit comparisons in other programming languages. The operators are used in the following form:

```
f1 operator f2
```

where f1 is the field to be checked and f2 is the bit pattern. Table 3.11 shows the three bit operators that can be used.

Table 3.11   Bit operators

Operator	Description
O (One)	true if f1 contains 1s in the same positions in which f2 also contains 1s
Z (Zero)	true if f1 contains 0s in the same positions in which f2 contains 1s
M (Mixed)	true if f1 contains a 1 in at least one of the positions identified in f2 and a 0 in at least one of the positions identified in f2

3.1.6   Subroutines

Large programs demand modularization. It helps keep the source code clearer, and it allows you to reuse program sections. The simplest way to divide a program is to use subroutines. The subroutines used in ABAP/4 are much like the procedures used in Pascal. They can receive parameters, but they do not return a function value.

Definition

You define a subroutine with the following statement:

```
FORM subroutine.
* statements
ENDFORM.
```

Because of the name of the statement itself, FORM, these kinds of subroutines are also called form routines in SAP terminology, or simply forms. The name of the form may be up to 30 characters long. It may begin with numbers and even special characters, but in practice it is best to follow the same naming conventions as field names. This means that subroutine names should begin with a letter and be as descriptive as possible, and the only special character they should contain is an underscore (_).

The FORM definition is followed by the subroutine statements, with the ENDFORM statement bringing up the rear. In principle, you can use any statement in a form routine that can appear in the main program. The only limitation concerns additional modularization: form routines may not contain other statements for program modularization, that is, they may not contain events or additional subroutine declarations. Declaring local data in subroutines, on the other hand, is entirely possible.

A potential trap awaits the programmer in subroutine declaration in reports. There are other statements used for modularization, in addition to subroutines, for example events. The statement block associated with such statements is not explicitly closed. Instead, it ends at another modularization statement or at the end of the program. It may be the case, then, that a FORM statement ends the statement block of a preceding event. These relationships are easy to overlook. The trap lies in the fact that the PROGRAM and REPORT statements work a lot like the as-yet-undescribed START-OF-SELECTION event. A report's statements will only be executed if they appear after a START-OF-SELECTION statement or immediately after PROGRAM or REPORT. If you define a subroutine at the beginning of a report, any of the report's statements that appear after ENDFORM will not be executed unless a START-OF-SELECTION statement appears after ENDFORM. For this reason, you should define subroutines at the end of the program.

Subroutine calls

You call a subroutine with the command

PERFORM *subroutine* ... .

You can include fields or tables of the current program as current parameters. There are two additional keywords you use to identify these. If you want to include internal tables, you use the TABLES statement:

PERFORM *subroutine* **TABLES** *Itab1 Itab2* ... .

Fields and field strings, on the other hand, you pass with USING:

PERFORM *subroutine* **USING** *param_1 param_2* ... .

You can also call subroutines across program boundaries. This is known as an external call, or, in SAP terminology, an external perform. For this type of call, you enter the name of the foreign program or module pool after the name of the form routine.

PERFORM *subroutine(program)* ... .

Another variant is the IN PROGRAM addition to the PERFORM statement, which also makes dynamic transfer of routine and program names possible. You either list both names directly in the statement, or enter fields enclosed in parentheses:

PERFORM *subroutine* **IN PROGRAM** *program* ... .

or

PERFORM (*subroutine*) **IN PROGRAM** (*program*) ... .

Parameters

Subroutines can have parameters passed to them. A limited type check is performed in the process. Any of the data types described up to this point (except database tables) can be used as parameters, that is, individual fields, field strings, and internal tables. When parameters are passed, it is also possible to determine whether they are value parameters or reference parameters. The latter kind allow values to be returned to the calling program.

Now let's turn to the syntax. You enter the list of formal parameters in the FORM statement after the USING keyword. These are names for fields that are only accessible inside the form routine. You separate the formal parameters with blank spaces.

FORM *name* **USING** *f_param_1 f_param_2* ... *f_param_x.*

When you call a subroutine with PERFORM, you specify current parameters, which are then assigned to the formal parameters according to the sequence in the parameter list. All formal parameters that are defined solely with USING are reference parameters. Changes to the values of the formal parameters also affect the current parameters of the calling program. The formal parameter points to the same area of memory as the current parameter.

Passing values like this can have undesirable side effects, for example if values are assigned to formal parameters even though the current parameters are not supposed to change. This may not necessarily happen in the same routine, either. Often, a subroutine calls other subroutines and passes on the formal parameters. In such cases, it is difficult to identify the source of a formal parameter; side effects can no longer be anticipated. This is one reason why value parameters are used in addition to reference parameters. Value parameters are copies of the current parameters. Assignments affect the formal parameter, but not the current parameter. The syntax for this type of call is a bit longer:

FORM *name* **USING VALUE**(*f_param_1*) **VALUE**(*f_param_2*) ... .

Finally, there is also a somewhat inconsistent mixture of value and reference parameters, which is probably unique in this form. The syntax resembles the syntax for the definition of value parameters:

FORM *name* **CHANGING VALUE**(*f_param_1*) **VALUE**(*f_param_2*) ... .

Usually, these parameters are reference parameters, which make it possible to pass values to the current parameters. No values are passed, however, until the ENDFORM statement is reached. If the subroutine terminates abnormally with an error message (MESSAGE statement), the contents of the current parameters remain unchanged. Subroutines terminated with EXIT, however, jump to the ENDFORM statement, causing the values to be passed.

You use the statements mentioned so far, USING and CHANGING, to pass simple fields or field strings, with field strings being treated like simple, unstructured CHAR fields in the subroutine. The correct type is passed along internally for simple fields only. Here is one example:

```
REPORT YZZ31150.
DATA: BEGIN OF FL,
   N TYPE I,
   C(10),
END OF FL.

DATA I TYPE I.

FL-N = 123.
FL-C = 'abc'.
I    = 12345.

PERFORM X USING FL I.

FORM X USING F1 F2.
DATA:    T,
         L TYPE I.
```

```
    WRITE F1-N.    "Leads to a syntax error!
                   "Delete after first syntax check!

    WRITE / F1 .
    DESCRIBE FIELD F1 TYPE T.
    DESCRIBE FIELD F1 LENGTH L.
    WRITE: / T , L, / .

    WRITE / F2.
    DESCRIBE FIELD F2 TYPE T.
    DESCRIBE FIELD F2 LENGTH L.
    WRITE: / T , L .
ENDFORM.
```

It is possible to derive the data type of the second parameter correctly. But the structure of the field string is not known inside the form routine, so the attempt to access one of its elements results in an error message during the syntax check. The corresponding statement must therefore be commented out or deleted.

It is possible to access the field string as a whole, as shown by an additional statement of the subroutine. This leads to an undesired result, however: the (binary) content of an integer field is interpreted and output as a character string. The problems demonstrated here can, of course, be avoided. When passing field strings, you can include structure information. You do this with the optional keyword STRUCTURE, which you enter after the parameter:

FORM ... *formal_parameter* **STRUCTURE** *structure_specification.*

You can use the name of a Dictionary structure (table or structure), the name of an internal table, or the name of a field string as the structure specification. No check is performed, however, to see if the formal parameter really possesses this structure, because it is exactly this information that is not accessible. If it were accessible, the STRUCTURE statement would not be necessary. The only things checked are the length of the formal parameter and the length of the structure. The parameter must be at least as long as the structure. Otherwise, it would be possible to use elements of the structure to access data areas that no longer belong to the formal parameter. You could expand the form routine from the last example as follows, to enable access to the individual elements of the field string:

```
FORM X USING F1 STRUCTURE FL F2.
...
    WRITE: / F1-N, F1-C.
```

Incorrect field lengths in structure specifications are recognized by the ABAP/4 interpreter's syntax check. The error is recognized when a program is checked in the development environment, or before it is processed the first time. When field strings are defined, the control logic sometimes inserts filler fields, to align fields to word boundaries. These filler fields are taken into account when the length is checked. Occasionally, then, the sum of a structure's field lengths is greater than the sum of the field lengths of the formal parameter's actual components. It is not the sum of the field lengths that is checked, but rather the actual amount of space needed in main memory.

As already mentioned, Release 3.0 makes user-defined types available, which you define with the TYPES statement. You can use these kinds of data types, too, to tell a subroutine about the inner structure of a formal parameter. To do so, you substitute the keyword STRUCTURE with TYPE.

FORM ... *formal_parameter* **TYPE** *data_type*.

The specification of a type makes several wider-ranging data checks possible. Instead of just comparing length, the control logic checks every component of a formal parameter to see if its length and its elementary data type correspond to the respective element of the type description. It does not, however, check whether the names of the components match. An example follows:

```
REPORT YZZ31160.

TYPES:

BEGIN OF T1,
  A,B,C,
END OF T1,

BEGIN OF T2,
  E,F,G,
END OF T2,

BEGIN OF T3,
  H(3),
END OF T3.

DATA A TYPE T1.

PERFORM F1 USING A.    "OK
PERFORM F2 USING A.    "OK
PERFORM F3 USING A.    "Type error

FORM F1 USING F TYPE T1.
ENDFORM.

FORM F2 USING F TYPE T2.
ENDFORM.

FORM F3 USING F TYPE T3.
ENDFORM.
```

This program consists entirely of declarations; it has no functionality whatsoever, so it does not need to be processed. What is of interest here is the syntax check for the program. All three of the declared types have the same total length. If the STRUCTURE statement were used instead of TYPE in all three subroutines, the program would be syntactically correct. The type check, however, which is more exact, recognizes that the length of the first component in the F3 form routine differs, causing a syntax error:

```
In PERFORM "F3", the actual parameter "A" is incompatible with the formal
parameter "F".
```

Because of the intensive checking, you should use the TYPE statement whenever possible in connection with preceding type declarations made with TYPES to describe the formal parameters of form routines in more detail.

In addition to passing fields and field strings, you can pass internal tables to form routines as parameters. In this case, however, it is not possible to distinguish between value parameters and reference parameters; internal tables are always passed as references. Changes to the table's contents remain in effect after the subroutine is exited. To identify a table as a formal parameter, you use the keyword TABLES:

FORM ... **TABLES** *Itab1 Itab2* ... .

The TABLES statement must appear before any USING or CHANGING statements. Of course, you can also give tables a structure. And you pass this structure using the STRUCTURE or TYPE statement, as is done in the case of field strings.

```
REPORT YZZ31170.

TYPES:
  BEGIN OF F_TAB,
    NUMBER TYPE I,
  END OF F_TAB,

  T_TAB TYPE F_TAB OCCURS 10.

DATA:   FL TYPE F_TAB,
        ITAB TYPE T_TAB.

PERFORM FILLTAB TABLES ITAB USING 3.

LOOP AT ITAB INTO FL.
  WRITE / FL_NUMBER.
ENDLOOP.

FORM FILLTAB TABLES  P_TAB TYPE T_TAB
             USING   P_NUMBER TYPE I.
  DO 10 TIMES.
    P_TAB_NUMBER = P_NUMBER.
    APPEND P_TAB.
    P_NUMBER = P_NUMBER + 1.
  ENDDO.
ENDFORM.
```

Local data

Local data elements can be declared in subroutines. These are only valid inside the subroutine. All of the statements described up to this point can be used for such a declaration. The elements created this way are only valid in the respective subroutine. If you create a field in a subroutine that has the same name as a global field, the local field is the one that is valid in the subroutine. The global field is not affected by the actions in the subroutine. You can still access from within the subroutine all of the global fields for which no local fields exist with the same name. When the routine is exited, the contents of local fields created with DATA or CONSTANTS are lost. These fields are created and initialized again every time the routine is called. In addition to declaring data that is completely local, you can protect a global field against unintentional changes by using the following statement:

LOCAL *field*.

or

LOCAL: *field1, field2, ... field_n*.

It only makes sense to use this statement after a FORM statement. The LOCAL statement causes the contents of the field or fields to be saved immediately after the routine is started and to be recreated after the routine ends. Since more powerful means for creating local data exist now, the LOCAL statement is no longer current and is used only in rare cases.

Release 3.0 has introduced a new declaration statement with which you can create fields in subroutines that have local visibility but static validity (that is, the value remains intact after the subroutine is exited). These fields can only be accessed inside the subroutine. You create these kinds of fields with the statement

STATICS *field_name* ... .

As with the DATA statement, you can create fields, field strings and internal tables. The following example demonstrates the difference between normal fields and static fields.

```
REPORT YZZ31180.

DO 10 TIMES.
   PERFORM FSTAT.
ENDDO.

FORM FSTAT.
DATA      N1 TYPE I.
STATICS   N2 TYPE I.
   WRITE: / N1, N2.
   ADD 1 TO N1.
   ADD 1 TO N2.
ENDFORM.
```

3.1.7 Macros

Some of the statements already described require a lot of coding work, especially those for declaring internal tables and such. You can reduce the amount of work necessary by using so-called macros. A macro is a statement block with a name that can contain several place holders. The macros are called in the program, and current parameters are passed. When an application is generated, the macros are dissolved, that is, the macro calls are replaced by the complete source code. You define a macro with the following statements:

```
DEFINE macro.
* statements
END-OF-DEFINITION.
```

In the statements, you can use the characters &1 through &9 as place holders. Here is an example of a macro and its later use:

```
DEFINE DEFITAB.
  DATA: BEGIN OF &1 OCCURS &3.
    INCLUDE STRUCTURE &2.
  DATA: END OF &1.
END-OF-DEFINITION.
...
DEFITAB I_AKT YZZAKT 5.
DEFITAB I_PRICE YZZKURS 30.
```

The DEFITAB macro simplifies the declaration of an internal table derived from a Dictionary table or a Dictionary structure. When you use this macro, you need only enter the three variable parameters in the source code.

3.1.8   Data exchange between applications

Every application in ABAP/4, that is, every transaction and every function group (which will be described later), presides over its own data area in main memory. The data stored there is not easily accessible to all applications. In many cases, however, it is desirable for applications to share data. Sharing data is of interest, for example, when external subroutine calls are made to help routines from other reports. When programming applications, there are three ways a programmer can use data stored in main memory across program boundaries. The variant used depends on the type of program and the linking of the applications in question.

Common part

One possibility is to create a so-called common part with a special variant of the DATA statement. You use this variant for data exchange between applications that are linked to each other by external subroutine calls. A common part can contain any number of data declarations. A program may contain several such areas, which must then be given unique names. If just one common part is used, no name is necessary.

```
DATA: BEGIN OF COMMON PART name,
* declarations
END OF COMMON PART.
```

The shared data area must be created in both programs with the identical name and the identical structure. The easiest way to do this is to put the declaration of such an area in a separate file. You give the file the program type I for *Include program*, and you link it to all of the applications involved with the statement

```
INCLUDE filename.
```

GET/SET parameter

GET/SET parameters are used to retain individual values across application boundaries and, more importantly, to pass these automatically to input fields in screens. GET/SET parameters are given a three-character identifier. These identifiers are defined in the system table TPARA, which you can maintain with the SM31 transaction. You can fill a parameter in a program with a value, usually the contents of a field, using the statement

SET PARAMETER ID *parameter_name* **FIELD** *field_name*.

The contents of the parameter remain intact until the user logs off of the system. The parameter's contents can be read from main memory and assigned to a field with the following statement:

GET PARAMETER ID *parameter_name* **FIELD** *field_name*.

You can also assign such a parameter to the individual fields when creating a screen, and activate the Get mechanism or the Set mechanism independent of each other. The values are then passed automatically. This variant is explained in more detail in the section on dialog applications.

Global memory

You can call various elements (transactions, function modules and dialog modules) from a report or dialog application using the CALL command. These elements then operate like subroutines. In an application chain that has been invoked with CALL, field contents or internal tables can be placed into a global memory space with the following command:

EXPORT *element* **TO MEMORY.**

The data can be read from the memory space with

IMPORT *element* **FROM MEMORY.**

The EXPORT command is a command that overwrites; it does not append to the contents of the memory space. You can get around this limitation by giving the elements you place in the memory space a name. You do this by entering the following clause:

... ID *name*

The nameless variant and the elements with names can be used together. The memory space is released when the first-level element of the applications linked with CALL is exited.

3.2   Standard reports

The online programs presented up to this point let you explore some of the ABAP/4 commands. These examples were not, however, 100% reports in the narrow sense of the word, even if they selected data from a database table. In the R/3 System, the term report indicates a special program type with a rather narrowly defined task. Reports read, analyze, and display data from one or more tables. The ABAP/4 programming language was not developed as a universal language, but as a tool for developing the R/3 System. For this reason, it contains several commands whose functionality is tailored to list programming statements. To be able to use these statements effectively, and for the R/3 System's internal logic to be able to support list generation, a manner of programming tailored to their characteristics is necessary. The preceding section introduced several commands with global importance; the section that follows deals specifically with requirements for report programming and the statements needed for it. In keeping with the goal of this book, which is to concentrate on explaining concepts and relationships in the ABAP/4 programming language, this section begins with those commands that shed light on a report's structure and method of operation. Other commands, which are helpful but not absolutely necessary for the function of a report, are located at the end of this section.

In the beginning, reports were not interactive, but as development of the R/3 System and the ABAP/4 programming language continued, their value was enhanced with some very specialized statements. These allow the programmer to recognize some of the actions a user can take in a report (for example, pressing a function key) and to give these actions their own program functions. Now that reports can have interactive capabilities, they are often divided into non-interactive (standard) reports and interactive reports. Although the latter are just a special kind of the former, they are described in a separate section because of the new statements and the change in programming method associated with them.

3.2.1 Editing data

Extensive lists are usually divided into sections using partition headings and subtotals. Often, the data in a list is from several tables that were linked together by labels. So, in some cases, different data records or data record groups require different action with the data. ABAP/4 has several functions that let you program typical data editing activities quickly and very easily.

Pooling

When you process a table using a LOOP program loop, you can make the program activities dependent on changes to the contents of a table field. You cannot, however, use the WHERE clause in the LOOP statement to do this.

Data records in which the field in question has a value that does not change are combined into groups, for which common statements are executed. The program sections related to a group can be executed before or after the group. The statements for group processing are as follows:

```
AT NEW field.
...
ENDAT.
```

or

```
AT END OF field.
...
ENDAT.
```

The statements in the AT–ENDAT block are executed when the value of a specified field or a field further to the left in the field string's structure changes. To specify whether the command block should be executed when the first record or the last record of a cohesive group is read, you can use the option NEW or the option END OF, respectively. The LOOP statement knows the name of the table to be processed, so you only need to enter the actual field names (without table names) in the AT statements inside the LOOP program loop. This also means that AT commands can only be used on the table named in the LOOP statement. The following commands work independent of field names:

AT FIRST.

...

ENDAT.

and

AT LAST.

...

ENDAT.

They allow you to execute commands immediately after either the start of the first iteration of the LOOP program loop, or after the end of the last loop iteration.

Despite similarities in syntax, pooling statements are not events, which are described later. They are not jump targets to which the internal control logic jumps when certain events occur; they are simply symbols for more complex operations. You could imitate the effect of these commands by temporarily storing a data record and comparing it with the current data record in an IF statement. This is why the pooling commands are not called by the control logic; instead, they insert themselves in the command sequence in the LOOP program loop. You should take this into consideration when you position these statements in connection with output statements. You should also be aware that the data set may need to be sorted. Of course, the statements for pooling only work correctly if the data records that should appear in a group in the list are read one after the other.

The pooling statements and their peculiarities are described in more detail for the following two programs. In the first version, all of the data records for a set of sales statistics are output, with a subset being created for every employee. In this case, the internal table required for this work is filled directly with data. In practice, of course, a read from a database table would take place.

```
REPORT YZZ32010 NO STANDARD PAGE HEADING.

* internal table for demo
DATA: BEGIN OF SALES OCCURS 10,
   NAME(20),
   DATE TYPE D,
   TURNOVER TYPE I,
END OF SALES.

* fill the table with 6 data records
SALES-NAME = 'MEIER'.
SALES-DATE = '19950703'.
```

```
SALES-TURNOVER = 300.
APPEND SALES.

SALES-NAME = 'MEIER'.
SALES-DATE = '19950703'.
SALES-TURNOVER = 200.
APPEND SALES.

SALES-NAME = 'MEIER'.
SALES-DATE = '19950704'.
SALES-TURNOVER = 100.
APPEND SALES.

SALES-NAME = 'LEHMANN'.
SALES-DATE = '19950704'.
SALES-TURNOVER = 110.
APPEND SALES.

SALES-NAME = 'LEHMANN'.
SALES-DATE = '19950704'.
SALES-TURNOVER = 220.
APPEND SALES.

SALES-NAME = 'LEHMANN'.
SALES-DATE = '19950705'.
SALES-TURNOVER = 330.
APPEND SALES.

* loop in internal table
LOOP AT SALES.

* output a heading in the first loop iteration
AT FIRST.
  WRITE: / 'Date', 19 'Turnover', / .
ENDAT.

* partition heading for every new name
AT NEW NAME.
  WRITE: / SALES-NAME.
  WRITE: / '============================='.
ENDAT.

* output a data record
WRITE: /(10) SALES-DATE, SALES-TURNOVER.

* output subtotal
AT END OF NAME.
  SUM.
  WRITE: / '============================='.
  WRITE: / 'Subtotal:', 12 SALES-TURNOVER, /.
ENDAT.
```

```
* in the last loop iteration, output total
AT LAST.
  SUM.
  WRITE: /, /,  'Total:' , 12 SALES-TURNOVER.
  WRITE: /, /10 '*** END ***'.
ENDAT.

ENDLOOP.
```

The demo program processes the internal table, which it has just created and filled, in a loop. In the first loop iteration, identifiable by the AT FIRST, the application creates a modest table heading. This is just to demonstrate the AT FIRST command. In full-scale reports, table headings and page headings are created a different way. Following the AT FIRST command, the AT NEW NAME command analyzes a potential change of group and creates a partition heading using the name of the sales associate. The contents of the data record that are of interest can be output after that.

It is absolutely necessary to ensure that the AT and WRITE commands appear in the correct order. The partition heading must be created before the actual data records are output. If the AT FIRST and WRITE commands were switched in the example above, the data record would appear first in the list, followed by the partition heading.

A new statement, SUM, appears in the AT END OF command. This statement totals all of the numerical fields of the data records of the group in question and displays them in the table header. After the SUM statement, the TRADE-SALES field contains the sum of all of a sales associate's sales. The AT END OF statement is also dependent on the order of statements in the program. This statement must appear after the data record output. Figure 3.8 shows the report list that this program creates.

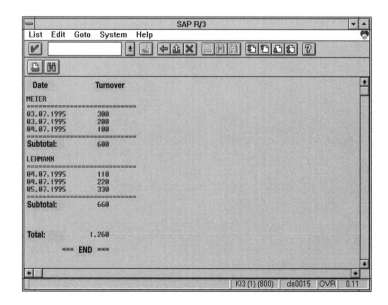

Figure 3.8   Output of the YZZ32010 demo program

When the field contents change, not only the field named in the AT statement, but all of the fields to the left of it cause a change of group. You can test this by pooling according to the DATE field instead of the NAME field in the first pooling demo program. Although the third and fourth data records do not have different dates, the field further left in the data structure, NAME, causes a change of group. Both the structure and the sorting of the internal table must be tailored exactly to the analysis that will take place later. This is particularly important when AT statements are nested. A short example follows: pooling is to be done according to name, and data records in a group that have the same date are to be combined. The following listing shows only the new LOOP program loop; the rest of the program does not need to be changed. You can copy YZZ32010 and simply make a few modifications in the LOOP statement.

```
REPORT YZZ32020.
...
LOOP AT SALES.
   AT NEW DATE.
     AT NEW NAME.
        WRITE: / SALES-NAME.
        WRITE: / '============================='.
     ENDAT.
   ENDAT.
   AT END OF DATE.
     SUM.
     WRITE: /(10) SALES-DATE, SALES-TURNOVER.
     AT END OF NAME.
        SUM.
        WRITE: / '============================='.
        WRITE: / 'Total:', 12 SALES-TURNOVER, /.
     ENDAT.
   ENDAT.
ENDLOOP.
```

The outer AT statements must refer to the field with the lowest value, in this case DATE, so that every change of group is recognized. It is then possible to determine in the date group change whether a change of group also occurred for the NAME field. If the name were used as the criteria for a change of group in the outer AT statement, the system would check for a change in date only if a change in name occurred. Data records with identical dates would then not be combined.

Individual data records can no longer be output, because only one total record is to be displayed for every date. The WRITE statement behind AT END OF DATE does not refer to a specific data record of the table; instead, the header record handled by SUM is used. Since SUM processes only numerical fields, however, the date field contents are correct. Figure 3.9 shows the modified program's output.

What is interesting about this example, aside from the nested AT statements, is the use of the SUM command. Without additional specifications, it summarizes all of the sales for

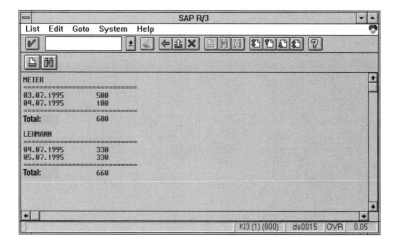

Figure 3.9   List with combined records

one date behind AT END OF DATE. In contrast, all of the sales of the sales associate in question are taken into account behind AT END OF NAME. The SUM command has a close relationship to the AT commands. What this example also indirectly demonstrates is that SUM, for example, is a very complex command that can only recognize which data records to total based on the source code and the AT statements.

EXTRACT data sets

Often, in list generation, you want the individual lines of a listing to appear in an order that is different than the order specified by the table's primary key. Often, data from several tables go into a single output line. A practical, but somewhat simplified, example: all of the invoices for a certain time period (invoice header and all line items) are to be output in a list, sorted by vendor and invoice number. The list is to contain a partition heading and subtotals for every vendor and invoice. The data query is relatively simple. The system performs a search in the table with the document headers for the invoices from the desired time period. It searches for the individual document lines using the invoice number, and it searches for the entries for the vendor using the vendor number. The primary criterion for the organization of the list is the vendor, but the data structure specifies the invoice number as the main attribute. The desired list can therefore not be output immediately; it must first be prepared with the help of an internal table. One could imagine the following pseudo-code:

```
DATA: ITAB OCCURS 1000,
   VENDNR,
   VENDNAME,
   INVNR,
   INVDAT,
   TYPNR,
```

```
   TYPDESC,
   QUANT,
   UNITPRICE,
   TOTAL,
END OF ITAB.

SELECT FROM INVHEAD WHERE DATE IN timeperiod.
   SELECT SINGLE * FROM VENDOR WHERE VENDNUM = INVHEAD-VENDNUM.
   SELECT FROM INVITEM WHERE INVNUM = INVHEAD-INVNUM.
      MOVE ... . " Fill the internal table.
   ENDSELECT.
ENDSELECT.

SORT ITAB.

LOOP AT ITAB.

   AT NEW INVNR.
      AT NEW VENDNR.
         " Output vendor data
      ENDAT.
         " Output invoice header
   ENDAT.

   " Output line item

   AT END OF ... .
      ...
   ENDAT.

ENDLOOP.
```

In addition to internal tables, ABAP/4 can use another variant for such data combinations, namely EXTRACT data sets. These are somewhat less flexible to use, but they require less effort to code. These days, they are used less frequently than internal tables. Using EXTRACT data sets takes some getting used to and requires a more detailed explanation.

Each report can manage exactly one EXTRACT data set. For this reason, the data set is not given a name; it is used implicitly when special commands are implemented. The following steps are necessary:

1. First you name one or more field groups to be inserted in the data set. You need only declare the names of these field groups. You can select any names desired, as long as they meet the restrictions for identifiers. Although a HEADER field group is not automatically created by the system, it has a predefined meaning if it is created in a report. Because its meaning is predefined, usually this field group is always included.

2. In the second step, you assign any desired data or table fields to the field groups. A field group thus becomes a symbol for one or more fields. It is no longer comparable to a field string, because access to its elements is not possible (or does not lead to the desired result).

3. Data analysis is next. Whenever all of the fields belonging to a field group are filled with correct values, the field group, along with all of the fields assigned to it, can be sent to the extract data area. The contents of the fields contained in the HEADER field group are automatically sent along. For this reason, this field group usually includes all labels.

4. After the data set has been built, it can be sorted. All of the fields of the HEADER field group are taken into consideration. After sorting, no additional values can be included in the data set.

5. Sorting is followed by a final analysis. This analysis runs like the analysis of an internal table. In particular, the pooling statements mentioned earlier are available. After an analysis, again, no more values can be included in the extract data set.

For each of these steps, there are new commands or variations of commands that have already been described. These commands are described in the sections that follow, in the order of the steps.

Declaration of field groups

Declaring field groups involves declaring their names. The statement for this is correspondingly simple:

FIELD-GROUPS: *field_group_1*, *field_group_2*, ... *field_group_n*.

This syntax description shows the colon variant because the declaration of an individual field group, though possible, rarely makes sense. Of course, you can also use this statement without the colon, to declare a single field group.

Assigning fields to field groups

To assign fields to a field group, you use a special variant of the INSERT command.

INSERT *field_list* **INTO** *field_group*.

In the field list (not field string!), you list all of the fields to be included in the field group. You separate the individual field names with blank spaces. INSERT also has a colon variant, which you can use to make assignments to several field groups in an INSERT statement:

INSERT: *field_list_1* **INTO** *field_group_1*,
        field_list_2 **INTO** *field_group_2*,
        ...
        field_list_n **INTO** *field_group_n*.

Although the INSERT command is used here, this is not quite data manipulation. No data is inserted in the field group, only pointers to the fields or field names!

Filling the data set

The current contents of the fields that were assigned to the field group with INSERT are transferred into the data set with the statement

EXTRACT *field_group*.

If there is a HEADER field group, its fields are automatically transferred, as well. An EXTRACT command creates a data record in the data set. The fields of the field groups that were not listed in the EXTRACT command remain empty.

Like many other commands, EXTRACT can process several parameters when used with a colon:

EXTRACT: *field_group_1*, *field_group_2*, ... *field_group_n*.

Sorting the data set
In its simplest variation, sorting occurs when you specify:

SORT.

If you do not specify a name, the command automatically references the extract data set. There are several options you can use to influence the sort order and the fields to use for sorting. The selected fields, however, must all belong to the HEADER field group.

If any of the fields according to which the sort is being done are empty, these fields or data records appear at the top of the sort order. The order of data records that have the same sort term is indeterminate!

Analyzing the data set
Extract data sets are processed by LOOP–ENDLOOP program loops.

LOOP.

   ...

ENDLOOP.

As is the case with SORT, no name appears after LOOP. This indicates that the internal data set should be processed. The fields sent to the data set using EXTRACT appear one after another inside the loop. The contents of each data record in the extract set are transferred back into the original fields and can be analyzed there. Only those fields are changed for which there is data in the extract set. All other field contents remain unchanged! This characteristic makes it necessary to test the validity of data using special statements. You use the statements for field group creation for this.

Pooling and field group referencing
The normal statements that were described earlier, for example, AT FIRST and AT NEW, are available for pooling. They reference the data fields.

When you use the following statement:

AT *field_group*.

   ...

ENDAT.

execution of the statements in the block becomes dependent on whether or not the current data record was created with an EXTRACT statement for exactly this field group.

A variant exists that also makes the execution depend on whether or not the data record following the current record corresponds to an explicitly specified second field group.

AT *field_group_1* **WITH** *field_group_2*.

...

ENDAT.

This allows you to hide header records that have no subsequent records, for example.

An example follows, to demonstrate these rather theoretical explanations. In contrast to other demo programs, line numbers have been included here, to simplify references. The data set used for analysis is created in the example and appears in internal tables, making this example different from pseudo-code presented earlier. However, the focus in this example is not on reading data from tables, but on analyzing it with the help of an extract data set.

```
 1   REPORT YZZ32030.
 2
 3   DATA NUM TYPE I.
 4
 5   DATA: BEGIN OF LIEF OCCURS 10,
 6     LNUM(4) TYPE N,
 7     NAME(20),
 8   END OF LIEF.
 9
10   DATA: BEGIN OF RECH OCCURS 10,
11     RECHNR(4) TYPE N,
12     LNUM LIKE LIEF-LNUM,
13   END OF RECH.
14
15   DATA: BEGIN OF RECHZEIL OCCURS 10,
16     RECHNR LIKE RECH-RECHNR,
17     ARTIKEL(20),
18   END OF RECHZEIL.
19
20   LIEF-LNUM   = '1'.   LIEF-NAME = 'iXOS'. APPEND LIEF.
21
22   LIEF-LNUM   = '2'.   LIEF-NAME = 'SAP'.  APPEND LIEF.
23
24   RECH-RECHNR = '123'. RECH-LNUM = '1'.    APPEND RECH.
25
26   RECH-RECHNR = '234'. RECH-LNUM = '2'.    APPEND RECH.
27
28   RECH-RECHNR = '345'. RECH-LNUM   = '1'.  APPEND RECH.
29
30   RECHZEIL-RECHNR  = '234'. RECHZEIL-ARTIKEL = 'SAP R/3'.
31   APPEND RECHZEIL.
32
33   RECHZEIL-RECHNR  = '123'. RECHZEIL-ARTIKEL = 'Informix'.
34   APPEND RECHZEIL.
```

```
35
36   RECHZEIL-RECHNR  = '123'. RECHZEIL-ARTIKEL = 'Archiv-Link'.
37   APPEND RECHZEIL.
38
39   RECHZEIL-RECHNR  = '123'. RECHZEIL-ARTIKEL = 'Indios'.
40   APPEND RECHZEIL.
41
42   RECHZEIL-RECHNR  = '345'. RECHZEIL-ARTIKEL = 'Archiv-Link'.
43   APPEND RECHZEIL.
44
45   FIELD-GROUPS: HEADER, LIEFERANT, ARTIKEL.
46
47   INSERT: LIEF-LNUM RECH-RECHNR NUM INTO HEADER,
48           LIEF-NAME                 INTO LIEFERANT,
49           RECHZEIL-ARTIKEL          INTO ARTIKEL.
50
51   LOOP AT RECH.
52
53     MOVE SPACE TO LIEF.
54     LIEF-LNUM = RECH-LNUM.
55     READ TABLE LIEF.
56     IF SY-SUBRC = 0.
57
58       EXTRACT LIEFERANT.
59       LOOP AT RECHZEIL WHERE RECHNR = RECH-RECHNR.
60         EXTRACT ARTIKEL.
61         ADD 1 TO NUM.
62       ENDLOOP.
63
64     ENDIF.
65
66   ENDLOOP.
67
68   CLEAR: LIEF, RECH, RECHZEIL, NUM.
69
70   LOOP.
71     WRITE: / LIEF-LNUM, RECH-RECHNR,
72              NUM,       LIEF-NAME,
73              RECHZEIL-ARTIKEL.
74
75   CLEAR: LIEF, RECH, RECHZEIL, NUM.
76
77   ENDLOOP.
78
79   SORT.
```

```
 80
 81   LOOP.
 82
 83     AT LIEFERANT WITH ARTIKEL.
 84       AT NEW LIEF-LNUM.
 85         WRITE: /,   'Lieferant:', LIEF-NAME.
 86       ENDAT.
 87     ENDAT.
 88
 89
 90     AT NEW RECH-RECHNR.
 91       WRITE: / RECH-RECHNR.
 92     ENDAT.
 93
 94     WRITE: /5 RECHZEIL-ARTIKEL.
 95
 96     AT END OF RECH-RECHNR.
 97       WRITE: /.
 98     ENDAT.
 99
100    CLEAR: LIEF-LNUM,  RECH-RECHNR,
101           LIEF-NAME,  RECHZEIL-ARTIKEL.
102
103   ENDLOOP.
```

In the example, lines 3 to 43 take care of declaring all of the fields and internal tables and filling them with data. The contents of these tables correspond somewhat to the problem discussed in the example's introduction. This section of the program does not contain any new statements. In line 45, three field groups are declared: HEADER, LIEFERANT (vendor) and ARTIKEL (product). In lines 47 to 49, these are linked to data fields or table fields. The fields for the vendor number (LIEF-LNUM) and the invoice number (RECH-RECHNR) are included in the HEADER field group, whose contents are needed for sorting the data set. Furthermore, a count is started to ensure the orderly sequence of the individual data records in the list.

After this preparation, construction of the data set can begin. Two nested LOOP program loops and a READ statement in lines 51 to 66 simulate the SELECT statements of the pseudo-code. The outer loop processes all invoice (RECH) headers. A READ statement searches for vendor (LIEFERANT) data for each invoice header (RECHZEIL). If such data exists, line 58 places the contents of the fields belonging to the LIEFERANT (vendor) field group in the extract data set. The fields of the HEADER field group are automatically included in the transfer. The statements in lines 59 to 62 read the individual line items of each invoice and place these in the extract set, too, as separate data records.

The effects of lines 68 to 77 show the structure of the extract set and the contents of the individual data records. First, the data fields are initialized. Subsequently, the data set is read with a LOOP program loop, and the contents of the pertinent fields are output.

Because only those fields that are actually contained in the data set are updated in the LOOP program loop, the data fields are initialized in every loop iteration. This is the only way to show which data is contained in each of the extract set's data records. This section of the program serves only to demonstrate the data set.

Actual analysis of the data begins in line 79 with the sorting of the data records. A large loop in lines 81 to 103 then finally lists the sorted data set. The AT statement in line 83 ensures that only LIEFERANT (vendor) data records that are followed by an ARTIKEL (product) data record are processed. Whenever this is the case, the subsequent AT statement checks if a header must be output for the vendor and, if so, it creates one. All of the other statements are easy to understand. In the case of a new invoice number, the new number is also displayed; afterwards all of the line items of this invoice are listed. At the end of every invoice, the report creates a blank line.

Exercises

1. Create your own report for the second group change example, then execute it.

2. In the first sample report for group change, change the order of the AT FIRST and WRITE statements. Execute the report and analyze the results.

3. Rewrite the first example so that the date instead of the name is used for pooling.

4. In the second example, change the order of the AT statements. Analyze the results.

5. In the EXTRACT command example, remove the NUM field (line 47) from the field group declaration. Compare the results with those of the original program.

6. In the EXTRACT command example, remove the CLEAR statement in the first loop (line 75). Compare the contents of the field string to the contents that result when the CLEAR statement is used.

7. In the EXTRACT command example, remove line 26. This results in a vendor without a delivery. What happens?

3.2.2 Event concept in standard reporting

The ABAP/4 programming language is event-controlled. When the system's internal flow logic processes programs, be they reports or interactive applications, it distinguishes between various events, such as the end of input in a screen, or recognizes certain events such as when the end of a page is reached in a list. There is a series of different types of events. The programmer can (but does not have to) assign certain program code to the events. At first glance, event control seems to resemble programming with graphical interfaces like Windows in its approach. Upon closer inspection, however, there are considerable differences in the implementation of event control. Prior Windows knowledge is of little use in this case.

Events are linked to program code using so-called event statements. When an event occurs in an application, the control logic searches in the program for an event belonging to this event statement and processes the program code that follows this statement. The end of the program, another event statement, or the definition of a subroutine (that is, the statement FORM) constitutes the end of the statement block.

In SAP documentation, the pooling statements described earlier are mentioned in relationship to actual event statements. However, despite almost identical syntax, there are essential differences in their functionality. For this reason, the two types of statements are handled separately here.

You can assign event statements precisely to specific sections or divisions of an application. In standard reporting, there are several events that are addressed by certain events mainly during output to the list and processing of the selection screen. The simplest events, and the most often used, are:

`TOP-OF-PAGE.`

and

`END-OF-PAGE.`

As the names imply, these events, or rather the corresponding statements, are executed when a new page begins or when a page ends. This is how you insert headings and footers in the list.

A report can cooperate with elements known as logical databases. These are elements that retrieve data in one or more tables, taking into consideration any links between the tables, and transmit the data they read to the actual report in a defined sequence. The report itself then takes over just the analysis and output of the data, which is provided by the logical database. Logical databases are discussed in a separate section because of the complexity of the topic. The reports used up to this point did not use logical databases. The following event is triggered immediately when a program starts, before the first record of a logical database is read:

`START-OF-SELECTION.`

After the last data record is read, the following event is triggered:

`END-OF-SELECTION.`

If the report is not meant to work with a logical database, the START-OF-SELECTION event, if explicitly entered, effectively becomes the beginning of the actual main section of the report. If an application contains the START-OF-SELECTION event, the statements that begin at REPORT or PROGRAM are executed first, then the statements that begin at the explicit start statement are executed. In programs that do not use a logical database, you use a START-OF-SELECTION statement mainly to separate the "main program" from the statements for additional events, for example, TOP-OF-PAGE.

3.2.3   Selections and parameters

The SAP system is meant to process very large sets of data. The number of data records in a table can sometimes exceed one million. Without tools for selecting particular data records, lists with such a large number of entries are practically worthless. The selection tool itself, the SELECT statement, has already been presented. But this statement needs parameters in its WHERE clause that the report cannot simply request from the user, because it has no interaction capabilities. The solution is the selection screen, an automatically generated input screen in which users can enter their own selection criteria. Figure 3.10 shows an example of such a selection screen from the development environment's info system.

The programmer determines which input fields should appear on the selection screen using two special statements in the report's source code. The internal control logic then creates the selection screen without any more help from the programmer and processes it before the report is executed. The appearance of the selection screen can be changed, within certain limits. This is done with special commands in connection with events.

You can store queries that are often used with the same selection parameters as variants, which you can call again later. The system makes this utility available automatically: no programming effort is required.

Use of the selection screen requires some explanation. First, you enter the desired search terms in the various input fields. Then, using the menu function *Goto → Variants → Save as variant*, you save the current contents of the selection screen as a variant with a unique name. All of the variants stored this way can be accessed later with the menu function *Goto → Variants → Get ...* or the pushbutton with the same name.

The report is executed only if execution is explicitly requested by command. There are three menu functions available for this request: *Program → Execute, Program → Execute + print, and Program → Exec. in background*. The first two functions are also accessible with the icons in the pushbutton bar. The first icon resembles the icon for Enter. The two icons do not have identical meanings, however.

A word about creating the examples that follow. You can execute simple reports without having to save the current version of the source code. In the case of reports that have a selection screen, however, this can sometimes lead to abnormal termination of the program. It is therefore always best to save the source code after you make changes, before testing the program.

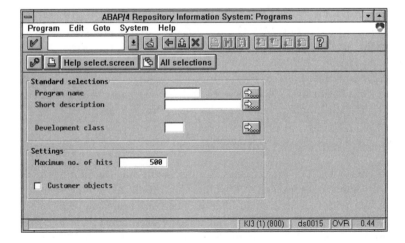

Figure 3.10   Selection screen of a report

Parameters

The easiest way to pass a value to a report is to use parameters. You create a parameter in a report with the statement

PARAMETERS *parameter_name*.

By using a colon, you can declare several parameters at once. A parameter appears on the selection screen as a simple input field (see Figure 3.10, maximum number of hits) in which a value can be entered. The name of a parameter must meet the same requirements as the name of a data field. In addition, it may be no more than eight characters long. Within a report, a parameter can be used like a simple data field. Put another way, a parameter is a data field on an input screen that can be filled with a value by the user of a report before the report is executed.

As described earlier, fields have several attributes, such as type and length. Naturally, parameters must also have such attributes, since in reports they are just data fields. You can define these attributes using various clauses for the PARAMETERS statement. If these clauses are missing, a parameter of type C and length 1 is created, similar to DATA. The easiest and most often used clause is the LIKE clause, which is used to reference an existing field:

PARAMETERS *parameter_name* **LIKE** *data_field*.

Table fields are often used as reference fields, which makes it easy to analyze the parameter later. If so-called foreign key dependencies have been maintained for the table field, possible entries help using F4 and a value check are automatically available. In addition to referencing a field using LIKE, you can reference a predefined or self-declaring data type:

PARAMETERS *parameter_name* **TYPE** *type_identifier*.

There are no restrictions with regard to data type, but if you specify the packed number data type (P), you must also specify the number of decimal places. A special clause is available for this case:

PARAMETERS *parameter_name* **TYPE P DECIMALS** *decimal_places*.

For some parameters, it can make sense to set default values. When you declare the parameter, you pass these using the DEFAULT clause, for example:

PARAMETERS ... DEFAULT '*'.

You can make it mandatory for a user to enter a value in a parameter field by using the OBLIGATORY clause.

PARAMETERS *parameter_name* ... **OBLIGATORY.**

Graphical interfaces recognize more than just alphanumeric input fields. They also recognize check boxes and radio buttons. The former are fields that can be marked (with a check mark) individually, independent of each other. Using check boxes, for example, you can mark several entries in a list. Radio buttons, on the other hand, are combined into groups. In each group, only one of the radio buttons can be marked. Radio buttons allow you to choose from a set of objects.

You can also create these kinds of fields in selection screens. For check boxes, you use the variant:

PARAMETERS *parameter_name* **AS CHECKBOX**.

For radio buttons, you use

PARAMETERS *parameter_name* **RADIOBUTTON GROUP** *group*.

In the latter case, you must specify an identical group name for all of the fields that belong together. After data entry on a selection screen, marked fields contain an "X", while the other fields contain a blank space. The example that follows demonstrates the declaration of several parameters. You can execute this example. After execution starts, the parameter screen appears, in which you can enter values. Afterwards, you select the menu function *Program → Execute*. This ends input on the parameter screen and executes the actual report. The report displays the contents of all of the parameters. The START-OF-SELECTION statement is described later.

```
REPORT YZZ32040 NO STANDARD PAGE HEADING.
TABLES: KNA1.
DATA M_FIELD.

PARAMETERS P1.
PARAMETERS P2 LIKE KNA1-NAME1.
PARAMETERS P3 TYPE P DECIMALS 2.
PARAMETERS P4 LIKE M_FIELD OBLIGATORY.

PARAMETERS: C1 AS CHECKBOX,
            C2 AS CHECKBOX,
            C3 AS CHECKBOX.

PARAMETERS: R1 RADIOBUTTON GROUP G1,
            R2 RADIOBUTTON GROUP G1,
            R3 RADIOBUTTON GROUP G1.

START-OF-SELECTION.
   WRITE: / 'P1:', P1.
   WRITE: / 'P2:', P2.
   WRITE: / 'P3:', P3.
   WRITE: / 'P4:', P4.

   WRITE: /.
   WRITE: / 'Checkbox    :', C1, C2, C3.
   WRITE: /.
   WRITE: / 'Radiobutton:', R1, R2, R3.
```

Selections

ABAP/4 provides selection tables, in addition to simple parameters. Selection tables are internal tables with a predefined structure (see Table 3.12).

Table 3.12   Structure of selection tables

Field	Task
SIGN	Indicates whether selected data records are included in the results set (I) or should be excluded from it (E).
OPTION	Comparison operator (EQ, NE, CP, NP, GE, LT, LE, GT)
LOW	Wildcard or lower limit of a range
HIGH	Upper limit of a range

The selection table is filled through the selection screen with one or more individual wildcards or range specifications. The internal control logic provides the functionality for this; no programming effort is necessary. The system provides only two input fields for a selection table on the selection screen. Clicking on the button next to the second input field causes an additional screen to appear, in which you can create more data records for the selection table, or a popup, depending on the release version. Figure 3.11 shows the popup for the first selection from Figure 3.10. In this popup, you can enter search terms as individual values or as range specifications.

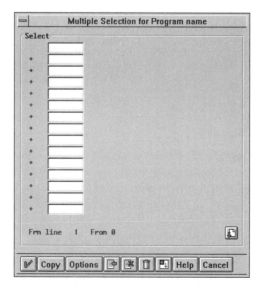

Figure 3.11   Selection table processing

Clicking on the *Copy* pushbutton copies the values into the selection table. The *Options* pushbutton calls another dialog, in which you can select another comparison operator for an entry in the selection table. You create selections similar to the way you create parameters. The declaration statement is as follows:

```
SELECT-OPTIONS selection FOR data_field.
```

Selection names have the same length restriction: a maximum of eight characters. The mandatory reference to a data field determines several of the attributes of the input fields on the selection screen, for example the length. If the database field is three characters long, the input field on the selection screen is also only three characters long. When an entry is confirmed, the system also checks whether the values or wildcards have the same data type as the referenced field. In selections linked to a field of type N (numerical character string), for example, only the permissible numerical characters may be entered. All other characters cause the system to generate an error message. The CHECK statement, which will be described shortly, also provides a kind of shorthand for the analysis of a selection table, in which the field from the declaration statement is always checked.

It is not always possible or sensible to allow the user to fill selection tables. For example, you can optimize the performance of SELECT statements using selection tables, since selection tables enable quite detailed preselection of data records by the database. For this, you could have the program itself create and fill the selection tables in an application, without a selection screen having to be created. In dialog applications, this would not be possible as such. You declare a selection table using the following statement:

```
RANGES selection_table FOR data_field.
```

This creates a table with the default structure. You fill the table using the usual statements for internal tables, that is, mainly APPEND.

Analysis of parameters and selections

Selections and parameters are used mostly to pass search terms to the report. These must, of course, be analyzed in the report during data record selection. There are essentially two methods for doing this:

- Incorporation in the WHERE clause

- Use in the CHECK statement

The CHECK statement has already been mentioned. It enables the analysis of parameters or selections in any loops. These loops can, but need not, be SELECT–ENDSELECT loops. In terms of performance, however, it is much more beneficial to perform checks directly in the SELECT statement, instead of within the loop with CHECK.

If a selection has been derived from a database field with LIKE, a form of shorthand can be used for the condition description. The statement

```
CHECK selection.
```

automatically creates the reference to the database field in a SELECT loop. This corresponds to the long form:

CHECK *database_field* **IN** *selection*.

Parameters can be used in direct comparisons using various comparison operators (see IF statement):

CHECK *table_field* **=** *parameter*.

They can, however, also appear in a WHERE clause. They are used there just like other fields or hard-coded constants. Since search patterns that can also contain wildcards are usually entered in parameters, the only thing that can seriously be considered a comparison operator is the LIKE statement. This statement expects the percent character (%) and the underscore character (_) as wildcards, but the wildcards usually entered by the user are the asterisk (*) and the plus sign (+). Before a parameter is used in the WHERE clause, then, the wildcards "*" and "+" must be replaced with "%" and "_". ABAP/4 provides the TRANSLATE statement for this. The syntax for this statement is as follows:

TRANSLATE *character_string* **USING** *wildcard_string*.

The TRANSLATE statement replaces characters in a character string according to the wildcard string. In the wildcard string, the characters to be replaced and the new characters appear one after the other, in pairs. To replace the wildcards in a parameter, you need the following statement:

TRANSLATE *parameter* **USING** '*%+_'.

For the wildcards of the selection table, which you can check in the WHERE clause using the IN statement, such a transformation is not necessary.

A system limitation in the use of selection tables should be noted here. The system's internal flow logic uses the contents of the selection table to build a true SQL Select statement that consists of several individual conditions. This statement may not exceed a certain size (currently about 8 Kbytes). The number of data records in a selection table is therefore limited, at least theoretically. Use of selection tables offers significantly better performance in comparison to checks using CHECK in a SELECT–ENDSELECT loop, since fewer data records must be selected in the database and transported over the network. The following example demonstrates the two most important methods for analyzing parameters and selections.

```
PROGRAM YZZ32050.
TABLES TADIR.

PARAMETERS P_AUTHOR LIKE TADIR-AUTHOR.
SELECT-OPTIONS S_NAME FOR TADIR-OBJ_NAME.

TRANSLATE P_AUTHOR USING '*%+_'.

SELECT * FROM TADIR
WHERE AUTHOR LIKE P_AUTHOR.
  CHECK S_NAME.
  WRITE: / TADIR-PGMID, TADIR-OBJ_NAME.
ENDSELECT.
```

This program begins by selecting, with a SELECT statement, all of the programs by programmers whose name matches the pattern in the P_AUTHOR parameter. It then checks these individually, to see if they fall within the name range specified by the selection table. Note that there should definitely be an entry in the parameter for the name. If the field remains empty, the SELECT statement will find no data records. As a practical matter, then, the parameter should be marked as OBLIGATORY or given a default value with DEFAULT.

Of course, you could place both checks in the SELECT statement or implement them using CHECK. This can significantly affect runtime behavior. And the comparison conditions must also be reformulated for this. The listing that follows shows a second variant of the same program:

```
PROGRAM YZZ32060.
TABLES TADIR.

PARAMETERS P_AUTHOR LIKE TADIR-AUTHOR.
SELECT-OPTIONS S_NAME FOR TADIR-OBJ_NAME.

SELECT * FROM TADIR
WHERE OBJ_NAME IN S_NAME.
  CHECK TADIR-AUTHOR CP P_AUTHOR .
  WRITE: / TADIR-PGMID, TADIR-OBJ_NAME.
ENDSELECT.
```

In addition to alphanumeric input, parameters can also provide check boxes and radio buttons. In this case, the parameters receive either a blank space or an "X". Such parameters cannot, of course, be used directly for database selection; instead, they are analyzed in control statements like IF or CASE to modify program flow.

Editing the selection screen

The examples presented up to this point show that the individual parameters and selections appear in the order of their declaration, each on an individual line on the selection screen. The program-internal name of the parameter or selection serves as its identifier.

Several statements let you influence the appearance of the selection screen. For one thing, you can assign explanatory text to the selections and parameters. You maintain this text with the same transaction you use to create numbered text elements, transaction SE32. You can reach this transaction, for example, from the editor using the menu function *Goto → Text elements*, letting you create the text while editing the program. Text created this way can also be translated, resulting in multi-lingual selection screens.

Additional commands allow you to influence the order of the fields on the screen. You use different variants of the SELECTION-SCREEN command to design the selection screen. The two commands

```
SELECTION-SCREEN BEGIN OF LINE.
...
SELECTION-SCREEN END OF LINE.
```

form a statement block, in which line feed is turned off. All of the parameters declared in this block appear in a single line. Selections may not be declared in such a block. To align horizontally the input fields in a line, you set the output position for a subsequent parameter declaration using

```
SELECTION-SCREEN POSITION pos.
```

in the block mentioned above. A parameter must be declared immediately after such a statement, of course. In this type of positioning, however, the identifiers are lost. For this reason, there is a different variant of the SELECTION-SCREEN command that allows you to place text in selection screens. The command is as follows:

```
SELECTION-SCREEN COMMENT format text.
```

Two variants are possible for format specification. The first involves length and output column specifications, as already described for WRITE. The second variant involves the symbols POS_LOW and POS_HIGH, which specify the positions in which the low field and the high field of a selection are to be displayed.

The text can also be defined two ways. One way is to use a numbered text element (not selection text!) to represent the text. You maintain the text element's value using the methods already described. It is static; no modifications are possible at runtime. The second way is to specify a field name, which, however, may have a maximum of only eight characters in this case. This field is automatically declared by the SELECTION-SCREEN statement.

At runtime, the text field must be given a value before the selection screen is displayed. This is only possible using selection-screen-related events. This type of statement is therefore demonstrated in the next section.

You can break up large selection screens with blank lines or rules. To insert n blank lines, use

```
SELECTION-SCREEN SKIP n.
```

If you do not specify a number of blank lines, the default value of 1 is used. In contrast, the statement

```
SELECTION-SCREEN ULINE format.
```

inserts a line. The format specification corresponds to that used for SELECTION-SCREEN COMMENT. The following example demonstrates several simple statements for designing the selection screen. It has no functionality, that is, it does not produce an output list.

```
REPORT YZZ32070.

SELECTION-SCREEN SKIP.

SELECTION-SCREEN BEGIN OF LINE.
   SELECTION-SCREEN COMMENT 5(10) T1.
   SELECTION-SCREEN POSITION 20.
   PARAMETERS C1 AS CHECKBOX.

   SELECTION-SCREEN POSITION 40.
   PARAMETERS C2 AS CHECKBOX.
```

```
SELECTION-SCREEN POSITION 60.
PARAMETERS C3 AS CHECKBOX.

SELECTION-SCREEN END OF LINE.

SELECTION-SCREEN ULINE.

SELECTION-SCREEN BEGIN OF LINE.
  SELECTION-SCREEN COMMENT 5(15) T2.
  SELECTION-SCREEN POSITION POS_LOW.
  PARAMETERS R1 RADIOBUTTON GROUP G1.

  SELECTION-SCREEN POSITION POS_HIGH.
  PARAMETERS R2 RADIOBUTTON GROUP G1.

SELECTION-SCREEN END OF LINE.

INITIALIZATION.
  T1 = 'Checkbox'.
  T2 = 'Radio Button'.
```

Another possibility for designing the screen is to combine fields into groups. You can separate groups using frames. Both groups and frames can be nested; currently up to five layers are possible. The dimensions of the frames are automatically set by the system. Special events (see the next section) make it possible to execute activities specifically for a single group of parameters or selections. You create groups with the commands

SELECTION-SCREEN BEGIN OF BLOCK *block_name.*

and

SELECTION-SCREEN END OF BLOCK *block_name.*

These two commands pool the enclosed parameters or selections. The clause

... WITH FRAME

used with the BEGIN OF BLOCK statement creates a frame. To insert a title, you use

... WITH TITLE *title.*

The title is created the same way as a comment, that is, using either a numbered text element or an automatically created data element. The next listing shows a simple example of this.

```
REPORT YZZ32080.

SELECTION-SCREEN BEGIN OF BLOCK A WITH FRAME.

  SELECTION-SCREEN BEGIN OF BLOCK B WITH FRAME TITLE T1.
    PARAMETERS P1.
  SELECTION-SCREEN END OF BLOCK B.

  SELECTION-SCREEN BEGIN OF BLOCK C WITH FRAME TITLE T2.
```

```
     PARAMETERS:  R1 RADIOBUTTON GROUP G1,
                  R2 RADIOBUTTON GROUP G1.
   SELECTION-SCREEN END OF BLOCK C.

SELECTION-SCREEN END OF BLOCK A.

INITIALIZATION.
   T1 = 'Group B'.
   T2 = 'Group C'.
```

In addition to the usual input elements, a selection screen can also have pushbuttons. Using special events, you can determine which pushbutton has been selected on the selection screen. Different program branches can then be executed in the report, based on the pushbutton selected. For example, many repair programs allow a test run in which changes to be executed are displayed but not yet executed. The selection screen provides two pushbuttons for this: *Test* and *Change*.

There are two different methods for creating pushbuttons. You can insert up to two additional pushbuttons in the actual pushbutton bar with the following statement:

SELECTION-SCREEN FUNCTION KEY *n*.

where *n* is the number 1 or 2. When these pushbuttons are activated, they generate the function code FC01 or FC02. The next section demonstrates how these function codes are analyzed. The additional function codes and their analysis must be accompanied by the declaration of a Dictionary structure in the report:

```
TABLES SSCRFIELDS.
```

This structure is used for communication between the selection screen and the surrounding program. In the case of the pushbuttons, in the initialization section, the text for the two pushbuttons is assigned to the fields SSCRFIELDS-FUNCTXT_01 and SSCRFIELDS-FUNCTXT_02.

In the second method, you can create any number of pushbuttons on the selection screen using the following command:

SELECTION-SCREEN PUSHBUTTON *format name* **USER-COMMAND** *command*.

The format corresponds to the format already described for the COMMENT clause. It determines the position and width of the pushbutton. You give the pushbutton a text with the *name* parameter. The procedure described for COMMENT also covers this, that is, you use either a numbered text element or a data element filled at initialization. The function code to be triggered by the pushbutton is a four-character, alphanumeric identifier. It is passed to the statement in the *command* parameter and should be entered without apostrophes.

One of the features of a selection screen is that it is only displayed if at least one parameter or selection has been defined. You cannot create a selection screen that consists only of pushbuttons.

The following example shows the creation of both types of pushbuttons. The mandatory parameter serves to display the function code that is triggered by the pushbutton. This example also leads into the problematic nature of events for selection screens, two of which are used here without further explanation.

```
REPORT YZZ32090.
TABLES SSCRFIELDS.

PARAMETERS P1 LIKE SSCRFIELDS-UCOMM.

SELECTION-SCREEN SKIP 3.

SELECTION-SCREEN FUNCTION KEY 1.
SELECTION-SCREEN FUNCTION KEY 2.

SELECTION-SCREEN PUSHBUTTON  5(15) PB1 USER-COMMAND 0001.
SELECTION-SCREEN PUSHBUTTON 25(15) PB2 USER-COMMAND 0002.
SELECTION-SCREEN PUSHBUTTON 45(15) PB3 USER-COMMAND 0003.

INITIALIZATION.
   SSCRFIELDS-FUNCTXT_01 = 'Button 1'.
   SSCRFIELDS-FUNCTXT_02 = 'Button 2'.
   PB1 = 'Button 3'.
   PB2 = 'Button 4'.
   PB3 = 'Button 5'.

AT SELECTION-SCREEN.
   P1 = SSCRFIELDS-UCOMM.
```

Events for selection screens

The selection screens presented up to this point were processed by the system's control logic. The control logic ensures, for example, that the default values stored in variants are transferred to the parameters and selections if the user calls a report with one of those variants. The programmer can influence this process.

When the selection screen is created and edited, the system generates three events. These enable the programmer to execute individual statements, using corresponding event statements. These events are INITIALIZATION, AT SELECTION-SCREEN OUTPUT and AT SELECTION-SCREEN.

The INITIALIZATION event is the first event processed when the report starts. It is processed after the selection screen has been created and filled with default values from the PARAMETERS statements, meaning these can be overwritten at this point. Since values from variants are not transferred until after INITIALIZATION, they then overwrite the defaults. The INITIALIZATION event is triggered only once for every program call.

The AT SELECTION-SCREEN OUTPUT event is triggered immediately preceding display of the selection screen. The control logic makes no other modifications to the selection screen between this event and editing of the selection screen by the user. Values can thus be overwritten again, or the selection screen can be otherwise modified, for example by hiding fields and so on. The AT SELECTION-SCREEN OUTPUT event is inseparably linked to selection screen editing. It is always processed before the selection screen is ready for editing. It is not possible to display the selection screen without triggering this event.

After the user has finished editing the selection screen, the control logic processes the AT SELECTION-SCREEN event. In the related statements, input values can be tested for validity, for example. If an error message is triggered with the MESSAGE statement in this event, the selection screen is reprocessed, and the selections and parameters become input-ready again. Of course, the AT SELECTION-SCREEN OUTPUT event is processed beforehand.

The AT SELECTION-SCREEN statement has several variants. These variants reference selected elements of the selection screen (individual input fields or groups). You can also use variants of this statement to implement possible entries help for fields and display help information. Programming this kind of context-sensitive help and input help requires some knowledge of dialog programming, however, which is not discussed until the next section. In any case, selection screen processing starts again after the statements have been executed. The following example builds on the block definition program (YZZ32080). The following statements are simply added to that program:

```
AT SELECTION-SCREEN ON P1.
  IF P1 > 'H'.
    MESSAGE ID 'YZ' TYPE 'E' NUMBER '000'.
  ENDIF.

AT SELECTION-SCREEN ON BLOCK C.
  IF R2 <> 'X'.
    MESSAGE ID 'YZ' TYPE 'E' NUMBER '000'.
  ENDIF.

START-OF-SELECTION.
  WRITE: / 'Parameter      :', P1.
  WRITE: / 'Radiobutton 1:', R1.
  WRITE: / 'Radiobutton 2:', R2.
```

The MESSAGE statement triggers a message. The message concept is discussed in more detail in the section on dialog programming. We will just note here that the MESSAGE statement can terminate program and dialog processing. It also displays text in the status bar. In the example, an arbitrary message is used to terminate selection screen processing. None of the information in the status bar is linked to the example; it is purely coincidental. Most likely, only the output "E:EYZ000" will appear.

The two checks in the example only demonstrate the principle; they do not serve any practical purpose. The first event checks whether a value was entered in the P1 parameter that is greater than the letter "H". In this case, the MESSAGE statement is executed, and the selection screen is processed again. Only the parameter is input-ready, however; the two radio buttons are grayed out and cannot be selected. Aside from the first time the selection screen is processed, the only time either of the two radio buttons can be selected is if a character smaller than "H" has been entered in the P1 parameter. The second event affects the C block, that is, the block with the two radio buttons. In this case, it is mandatory that the second button be marked, otherwise the program will not continue. Because the event is linked to the block, only the two radio buttons are input-ready on the selection screen; the parameter is inactive.

Exercises

1. Change the YZZ32050 or YZZ32060 program so that the checks are either both implemented in the SELECT statement or both implemented with the CHECK command.
   Note the runtime behavior.
2. In the programs with field grouping, change the order of the pooling statements, then
   analyze the results.
3. Create your own text for parameters and selections.
4. Modify the YZZ32080 program as described in the text (parameter-related AT
   SELECTION-SCREEN ON statements), then test the program. Modify the program
   again by replacing the parameter-related AT SELECTION-SCREEN ON statements
   with a combined check at the general AT SELECTION-SCREEN event. Analyze the
   results.

3.2.4   Editing output

In the examples presented so far, data has already been output to the screen and formatted to a limited extent. In full-fledged reports and their output lists, you can use more
extensive variants for editing individual lines for output. These simplify programming
and can increase the clarity of screen output with the use of colored design elements. To
format output lines, you use the WRITE and FORMAT commands. In addition to formatting
individual lines, you can use other commands to set global defaults such as page length
and width. None of these commands are very important with respect to the functionality
of a report. They are, however, indispensable for giving an output list a professional look.
To test the statements that follow, please create a program called YZZ32100.

Parameters for page layout

The system uses standard values for the measurements of a list (length and width of a
page). The width of the list is based on the width of the current window; page length is
not limited. The list therefore consists of a single page. You can, however, also define
custom defaults using two options of the REPORT statement:

```
... LINE-SIZE characters ...
... LINE-COUNT lines(footers) ...
```

In the LINE-COUNT option, you can enter an optional specification for footer lines that
should be left blank. If you do not enter a specification for footer lines, a default value of
0 is used. Enter the numbers directly, that is, not enclosed in apostrophes. No matter what
page length has been set, the list's header and title are always displayed at the upper edge
of the page, independent of their current position in the list. This is also the case when the
list is printed on paper. So, even if no specific page length has been set for a list, a correct
page heading always appears. Specification of a page length mainly ensures correct page
numbering. In the case of unlimited page length, all printed pages receive the same page
number. You can avoid this situation by using the following command to manually
trigger form feeds:

NEW-PAGE.

This command has several options that allow you to change the length and width of the new page, as well as turn on and off titles and headings, which are generated as a standard. The format of individual pages within a report can thus vary. There are two methods for defining the title and heading of a list. There are default values for titles and headings, which you can edit by using the SE32 transaction (ABAP/4 text elements) or by selecting the menu function *Goto → Text elements* from the editor. This transaction was used earlier to edit numbered text elements. In addition to numbered texts, you can edit titles and headings using this transaction. To do so, you simply mark *Titles and headers* in the initial screen of the transaction.

The default consists of three different elements: the title, the header line (list header), and the column header (see Figure 3.12). All three elements are called text elements. Despite the similar name, they have nothing to do with numbered texts.

The title is displayed in the title line of the window. It cannot be turned on or off. The title is the same as the report's short description, which is entered in the screen with the program attributes. Both types of input refer to the same object; changes made to the title when the text element is maintained correspond to changes in a program's short description.

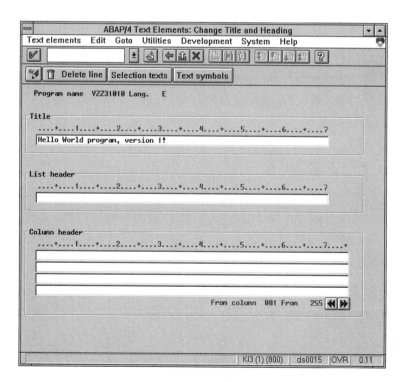

Figure 3.12   Maintenance of a list's text elements

The next element is the list header. It appears in the list's header line, together with the date and the page number. You can display or hide the header line using the NEW-PAGE command options WITH-TITLE and NO-TITLE. Although these options contain the word TITLE, they do not refer to the title just discussed, but to the header line.

With the third text element, the column header, you can declare up to four lines for column headers in addition to the general header line. You can turn the column header on or off, independent of the header line, using the WITH-HEADING clause and the NO-HEADING clause, respectively.

As an alternative to using standard elements, you can create a custom page heading in a report with the TOP-OF-PAGE event. Both the header line and the column headers must be output in this page heading. If you create a custom heading with this event, you must, of course, turn off output of the standard page heading. You can do this either with the statement

```
NEW-PAGE NO-TITLE NO-HEADING.
```

or, more simply, with

REPORT *name* **NO STANDARD PAGE HEADING.**

You can change the REPORT statement defaults easily in a report by using NEW-PAGE with the appropriate options. The NEW-PAGE command does not execute a form feed unless there was truly output to the page beforehand. It is not possible to create blank pages using NEW-PAGE. Note, however, that although no blank pages are generated, the options (for example, NO-TITLE) nevertheless take effect.

As an alternative to using the report's short description as a window title, you can insert the title of a program in an application with the statement

SET TITLEBAR *title_identifier*.

It is possible to record so-called titles for a program. These resemble numbered texts, but are edited using entirely different tools. The title identifier in this case is not a number, but a three-character string. You maintain titles using either the functions of the Workbench (which has not yet been described) or the double-click mechanism already demonstrated for numbered texts, which is easier. First you enter a syntactically correct SET TITLEBAR statement in the source code, for example:

```
SET TITLEBAR 'T01'.
```

Then you position the cursor on that line and press the F2 function key, or you double-click the title identifier with the mouse. Following a possible confirmation prompt, the system displays a popup window (Figure 3.13) in which you can maintain the title. Like numbered texts, these titles are translated and are therefore available in the logon language.

The titles created this way have nothing to do with the titles of text element maintenance. They are entirely independent elements that can be used as an alternative to standard titles. The title identifier can be passed to the SET TITLEBAR statement either as a direct value, as described above, or as the contents of a field.

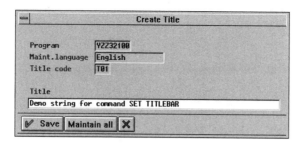

Figure 3.13   Editing of a title

Lists to be output to a printer often need a margin. Depending on the printer used, this may or may not be created by the printer itself. You can start printing at a specific position using the statement

SET MARGIN *column line*.

Specifying the line is optional. You can specify both values as direct values or as fields.

Lists may be up to 255 characters wide. In order for such a list to be viewable on the screen, it must be scrollable with the scroll bars of the Windows window. To make orientation easier for the user, you may want to leave certain help values in the left-hand margin, for example a line number, a reference number or a key term. To fix a column in place, you use the command

SET LEFT SCROLL-BOUNDARY.

This fixes in place the columns up to the current write position. When the image is scrolled horizontally, these do not move; they remain at the left edge of the screen. You can also determine the number of columns to be fixed in place independent of the write position, using the following clause:

SET LEFT SCROLL-BOUNDARY COLUMN *column*.

It is also possible to fix individual lines in place, for example, the lines of a table heading. To do so, you use the command

NEW-LINE NO SCROLLING.

This ensures that the next line that is output is not scrolled horizontally. The standard list header is automatically output with this option.

Positioning

The first demo programs already presented one of the methods for positioning screen output. There are, however, several other commands you can use as an alternative to WRITE in connection with formatting specifications. Before describing these commands, this section describes the WRITE command in more detail. You can give any field to be output a format specification, which has a maximum of three parts: a line feed character,

an output position and an output length. You enter these specifications in the following
form, in front of the value to be output:

/position(length)

The slash is the symbol for line feed. All three of the format specification elements are
optional. The values for position and length can be passed either as direct values or as
fields. In the latter case, however, the whole construct must begin with the prefix AT. The
following program section demonstrates several correct statements:

```
...
DATA: P TYPE I.

WRITE:  'ABC'.
WRITE: / 'DEF'.
WRITE: /4 'GHI'.
WRITE: 8(2) 'JKL'.

P = 8.
WRITE: AT /P 'MNO'.
...
```

If no output length is specified, the default output length for the applicable data type is
used. If the field to be output is empty, the line feed character has no effect, as shown in
the following example:

```
...
DATA: C.

WRITE: / 'START'.
WRITE: /C.
WRITE: /C.
WRITE: / 'END'.
```

This situation only occurs, however, if the line feed character appears in the format specification for a field. If it is used as an independent character, that is, in a separate WRITE
statement without a field specification, or at least as an independent element in such a
statement, a line feed is always generated:

```
DATA: C.

WRITE: / 'START'.
WRITE: /.
WRITE: /, C.
WRITE: / 'END'.
```

Note that even if the field to be output is empty, you can force blank lines to be output by
using the statement

SET BLANK LINES ON.

This statement remains in effect until it is turned off with

SET BLANK LINES OFF.

A reliable way to create blank lines is to use the command

SKIP.

In this form, the command inserts a blank line in the text. With an additional parameter, you can specify the number of blank lines to be inserted:

SKIP *number*.

One last variant positions the cursor on a particular line on the page, allowing you to jump forwards and backwards within the current page. The line count begins with 1:

SKIP TO LINE *line_number*.

You can set the position within a line for a subsequent output with WRITE to the column specified using the following statement:

POSITION *column*.

In lists, values should usually be aligned precisely with the column headers, or, in multi-line lists, with another data field. Changes in the header thus require fixing all the other position specifications. It is easier to use another option of the WRITE command. Using

WRITE *value* **UNDER** *field*.

you can position a value to be output in exactly the same column in which the field was output. The field name must be entered the same way as when it is to be output itself. This is particularly important if numbered texts with default values are referenced. The following program, a modification of YZZ32060, shows several variations of the UNDER option.

```
PROGRAM YZZ32110.
TABLES TADIR.

PARAMETERS P_AUTHOR LIKE TADIR-AUTHOR DEFAULT '*' .
SELECT-OPTIONS S_NAME FOR TADIR-OBJ_NAME.

WRITE: 'Object type', 20 'Name:'(001), 40 TEXT-002.
* create numbered text 002 as 'Program author'!

SELECT * FROM TADIR
WHERE OBJ_NAME IN S_NAME.
  CHECK TADIR-AUTHOR CP P_AUTHOR .

  WRITE: / TADIR-PGMID    UNDER 'Object type',
           TADIR-OBJ_NAME UNDER 'Name'(001),
           TADIR-AUTHOR   UNDER TEXT-002.
ENDSELECT.
```

The UNDER clause covers positioning within the line only. It does not generate a line feed. If the line feed is missing, the texts that are referenced might be overwritten by the new values, since the output occurs on the same line.

The following commands can also be used for positioning:

BACK.

and

RESERVE *n* **LINES**.

If there are not at least *n* lines free on the current page, the second statement executes a form feed. This statement usually appears in front of linked outputs that are several lines long or in front of a partition heading output. In those cases, it ensures indirectly that at least a few data lines follow a header on the current page. The BACK statement sets the output position either to the first line of a page or, if the RESERVE statement is used, to the first line that is output after RESERVE.

Formatting

The WRITE command handles not only output and positioning of values, but also formatting. There are several options available for this, which have not yet been discussed. You enter these after the value to be output. This gives the WRITE statement the following form:

WRITE *format value formatting_option*.

Most of the formatting options (see Table 3.13) need just a short description. More detailed explanations are necessary for only a few options.

Table 3.13   Formatting options for WRITE

Option	Effect
NO-ZERO	Leading zeros preceding numbers are replaced by blank spaces. If the content is equal to 0, only blank spaces are output.
NO-SIGN	No plus or minus sign is output.
NO-GAP	No separating space is output after the value.
DD/MM/YYYY	Date fields are edited and output according to the pattern.
MM/DD/YYYY	
DD/MM/YY	
MM/DD/YY	
DDMMYY	
MMDDYY	
CURRENCY currency	The field is edited according to the currency specifications. These specifications are set in Customizing. The TCURX table plays a major role in this.
DECIMALS n	Output with n decimal places.

Table 3.13 continued   Formatting options for WRITE

Option	Effect
ROUND n	For data type P only. The decimal point is shifted n places to the left (n > 0) or to the right (n < 0). The value is then output without decimal places.
UNIT	Similar to CURRENCY. The value is edited according to the specifications in a unit table (T006).
EXPONENT n	For floating point numbers only. The number is output as an exponential number, using the exponent specified.
USING EDIT MASK template	The value is edited according to a template.
USING NO EDIT MASK	The conversion set in the Dictionary is not executed.
LEFT-JUSTIFIED	The value is aligned to the left in the output field.
CENTERED	The value is centered in the output field.
RIGHT-JUSTIFIED	The value is aligned to the right in the output field.
AS SYMBOL	The field contents are interpreted as a symbol name and are output as such.
attributes	Controls the attributes (color, intensity) of a field using the same statements as FORMAT.

The two USING options require some explanation. In the first variant (USING EDIT MASK), you specify a template whose characters are mixed with those of the value to be output. The template may contain the characters listed in Table 3.14. The template itself must be specified as a character string, that is, it must be enclosed in single quotes.

Table 3.14 Characters in output templates

Template characters	Effect
_ (underscore)	Represents one character of the value to be output.
V	Plus or minus sign.
LL (at the beginning of the template)	Insert left-aligned.
RR (at the beginning of the template)	Insert right-aligned.
==xxxxx	Conversion of the value with the routine CONVERSION_EXIT_xxxxx_OUTPUT
all other characters	Separators that are mixed with the characters of the value.

Some examples follow to demonstrate the effects of the individual template characters. In the program that follows, for clarity's sake, the output created appears as a comment under the output statement.

```
REPORT YZZ32120
DATA:  W1(4)      VALUE 'ABCD',
       W2(8)      VALUE '12345678',
       W3 TYPE I VALUE '-12345'.

WRITE /(20) W1 USING EDIT MASK 'LL:_____:'.
* :ABCD               :

WRITE /(20) W1 USING EDIT MASK 'RR:_____:'.
* :            ABCD:

WRITE /(20) W2 USING EDIT MASK ':__-__-__-____:'.
* :12-34-56-78  :

WRITE /(20) W2 USING EDIT MASK 'RR:__-__-__-____:'.
* :   -12-34-5678:

WRITE /(20) W3 USING EDIT MASK 'RR:V_____:'.
* :-          12345:
```

For all domains, you can set in the Data Dictionary the five-character name of a conversion routine, also called a conversion exit. Using this identifier, the system builds the names of two function modules called CONVERSION_EXIT_xxxxx_OUTPUT and CONVERSION_EXIT_xxxxx_INPUT.

When a value is transported from an input field into the actual data field, the CONVERSION_EXIT_xxxxx_INPUT routine is automatically called. When the field is output, CONVERSION_EXIT_xxxxx_OUTPUT is called. In these routines, the field contents can be converted as desired. Using the template characters ==xxxxx, you can call any desired conversion function for the value. You might want to do this, for example, if the field to be output has not been derived from a Dictionary field.

If a conversion is already provided in the Dictionary for the field's underlying domain, you can turn this conversion off with the option USING NO EDIT MASK.

The R/3 System contains several tables for currencies and units of measure in which information is stored during customizing, such as the number of places after the decimal point, conversion factors and so on. You can use the CURRENCY and UNIT options to format the values to be output according to the specifications in these tables.

Screen attributes

Lists are much clearer if particularly important elements are highlighted visually. In the R/3 System, this can be done using various highlights and color. You can use a maximum of eight colors in lists. You access these colors with a number or a predefined identifier. The SAP Style Guide recommends certain colors for certain elements of a list. The names of the predefined identifiers are based on this recommendation for implementation (see Table 3.15). It is advisable to follow these recommendations. They fulfill their purpose only if all of the lists in the system are designed according to uniform guidelines.

Table 3.15   Colors in lists (line background)

Number	Identifier	Use	Color
OFF	BACKGROUND	background	GUI-dependent
1	COL_HEADING	headings	gray-blue
2	COL_NORMAL	list body	light gray
3	COL_TOTAL	totals	yellow
4	COL_KEY	key columns	green
5	COL_POSITIVE	positive threshold value	green
6	COL_NEGATIVE	negative threshold value	red
7	COL_GROUP	group levels	violet

You can set the colors, as well as several other attributes, with the command

FORMAT `attribute_1 attribute_2 ... attribute_n.`

They become effective with the next WRITE statement. An event, that is, the start of an event statement, resets the attributes to their default values. When the event is exited, however, they become effective again. Attributes that are set in a TOP-OF-PAGE block, for example, are only valid in that block.

You set the colors using the statement

FORMAT COLOR `color.`

The color is either one of the numbers listed in Table 3.15 or one of the predefined identifiers. The color number can also be passed dynamically, that is, as a field value. Such indirect assignments are also possible for other commands, as already demonstrated with the dynamic specification of a field name in the WRITE TO statement. In that case, the field containing the field name had to be entered in parentheses. The SELECT statement, too, allows a similar value transfer for the table name. Unfortunately, the FORMAT statement handles dynamic value specification differently:

FORMAT COLOR = `field.`

In this case, the field is a data field of type I. The field contains one of the color numbers. In addition to the color, you can also set the highlight intensity, using the INTENSIFIED and INTENSIFIED OFF clauses. The INVERSE and INVERSE OFF clauses switch the background and foreground colors. In this case, too, you can specify the option in question (ON or OFF) dynamically. If the contents of the field are equal to 0, this is interpreted as OFF. All other values are interpreted as ON.

The FORMAT command options described here can also be used in the WRITE statement, where they determine the output attributes of an individual field. The following program demonstrates several variants of this command.

```
REPORT YZZ32130 NO STANDARD PAGE HEADING.
DATA N TYPE I VALUE 0.

DO 8 TIMES.
   WRITE: / 'Color: ' NO-GAP COLOR = N ,
            N COLOR = N,
            'Color: ' NO-GAP COLOR = N INTENSIFIED OFF,
            N COLOR = N INTENSIFIED OFF,
            'Color: ' NO-GAP COLOR = N INVERSE ON,
            N COLOR = N INVERSE ON.
   ADD 1 TO N.
ENDDO.
```

Exercises

1. Add several statements for output formatting to the programs YZZ32010 and YZZ32020, for example, to highlight partition headings or total lines with color.

2. Set custom headings for any reports.

3. Write a report that creates enough output lines with any content. Test the commands for explicit specification of page length and page width.

4. Add column headings to the YZZ32100 report. Test the commands for fixing lines and columns in place.

3.2.5   Logical databases

The preceding sections have indicated that selecting the data needed for a report can take a lot of time. Often, several tables form a hierarchy. Every report must take into account these hierarchical dependencies when selecting data by using appropriately nested SELECT statements or similar constructs. If several reports access the same data for similar analyses and must always observe the same dependencies, identical or nearly identical queries are used again and again. You can reduce the programming effort related to this considerably by using so-called logical databases.

Task and structure

A logical database is a type of add-on program for traditional reports. It performs selections in several logically linked files and provides the data records read to the actual report. The report receives the data records in the correct order and must simply analyze and display them. Preparation of the data records by the logical database and reading of the data records in the actual report are accomplished with the command pair PUT and GET, with GET being an event.

A logical database is a rather complicated structure. It has three essential elements:

• Structure (table hierarchy)

• Selections

• Database program

The structure determines the hierarchy of the tables. You maintain it using a pseudo-graphical editor (see Figure 3.14). Starting from a root, you assign the subordinate tables one by one. The hierarchy is not an object that can be used directly. It simply represents the tables included in the logical database and their interdependencies. Based on this hierarchy, the system automatically creates a fundamental framework for the other two parts.

As the name already implies, the selections are a series of SELECT-OPTIONS statements. A separate SELECT-OPTIONS statement is generated for each of the labels of all of the logical database's tables. The system stores these statements in an Include file, which, in turn, is included in the database program. The programmer can process this file as desired, inserting selections or parameters for additional fields, or deleting existing selections. The following program section shows the not-yet-processed selections generated by the system for the logical database in Figure 3.14. You need to give the required selections a name, and you must remove the comment characters to activate the statement. Question marks appear in the source code in the places that need to be edited.

```
* _____ *

* INCLUDE DBYAKSEL
* It will be automatically included...
* _____ *

* ...
* SELECT-OPTIONS:  ?             FOR YZZAKT-NAME.

* Parameter for matchcode selection (DD-structure MCPARAMS):
* PARAMETERS p_mc AS MATCHCODE STRUCTURE FOR TABLE YZZAKT.
* SELECT-OPTIONS:  ?             FOR YZZB-BRANCHE.
* SELECT-OPTIONS:
*                 ?             FOR YZZBT-SPRACHE,
*                 ?             FOR YZZBT-BRANCHE.
* SELECT-OPTIONS:
*                 ?             FOR YZZKURS-NAME,
*                 ?             FOR YZZKURS-DATUM.
```

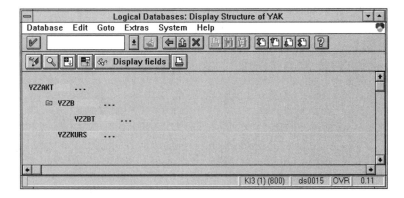

Figure 3.14   Example of a logical database

The database program is the actual main program of the logical database. After generation, it contains several empty subroutines, or subroutines consisting only of comments and therefore nonoperational, as well as SELECT statements for every table of the logical database. A WHERE clause is generated for each SELECT statement, although these are inactive due to automatically inserted comment characters. The programmer must modify the WHERE clauses to suit his or her purpose. The programmer could, for example, insert the selections from the Include shown above, assuming some were defined there. In the SELECT statement, the current data record is sent to the report with the PUT command. This statement is the only one that is not commented out. This ensures that even without any added programming in the selection and the database program, data records (in this case all of them) are transferred to the calling report.

The system takes into account in the generated WHERE clauses the dependencies prescribed by the structure of the logical database. When a subordinate table is read, labels of the superordinate table are referenced, as demonstrated in the following section of a database program.

```
*    _____    *
* Call event GET YZZAKT
*    _____    *
FORM PUT_YZZAKT.
   SELECT * FROM YZZAKT
*            INTO TABLE ?
*            WHERE NAME      = ?.
      PUT YZZAKT.
   ENDSELECT.
ENDFORM.                               "PUT_YZZAKT

...

*    _____    *
* Call event GET YZZKURS
*    _____    *
FORM PUT_YZZKURS.
   SELECT * FROM YZZKURS.
*            INTO TABLE ?
            WHERE NAME      = YZZAKT-NAME
*            AND DATUM      = ?.
      PUT YZZKURS.
   ENDSELECT.
ENDFORM.                               "PUT_YZZKURS
```

The system automatically calls the subroutines identified by the names INIT, PBO, and PAI for the events related to the selection screen, which have already been discussed (INITIALIZATION, AT SELECTION-SCREEN, AT SELECTION-SCREEN OUTPUT).

Logical databases are not objects that can be used in and of themselves. They can only be used in connection with a report. When you create a new report, you can enter the name of a logical database in the attribute screen. The name has two parts. You enter the actual name of the logical database in a two-character field, and the abbreviation for the logical database's application group in another, single-character field. No additional direct references to the database are necessary.

You must declare all of the tables from which data is to be read in the report itself with the TABLES statement. You can then define the processing of a data record in the report with the event

GET `table.`

Both the PUT statement and the GET statement are events. They work together in a relatively complicated way. The database program always takes control, never the report. The database program first executes the PUT statement for the table highest in the hierarchy. After the data record has been read, the GET event is processed for the appropriate table. At this point, the data record could, for example, be output. After the GET event, the database program executes all of the PUT subroutines belonging to the next table in the hierarchy, assuming that GET processing has been programmed in the report for these tables. When the subroutines are called, any dependencies are taken into account, even across several levels. Even if a report analyzes only a table that is very low in the hierarchy, all of the tables between the root and the table to be analyzed are read.

In the form described here, the GET event for a superordinate table is always called before the GET event of the subordinate tables. Using the clause

GET `table` **LATE.**

you mark GET events that should not be processed until all subordinate tables have been processed. This makes it possible to write analyses related to the subordinate tables in the list. Only one GET and one GET LATE event are allowed in a report.

Creating and including

You call the processing of a logical database from the CASE menu with the menu function *Development* → *Programming environ.* → *Logical databases*. The transaction code is SE36.

In the first screen of this transaction, you specify the three-character name of the logical database. The first two characters represent the actual database name; the last character represents the application to which the logical database belongs. These characters later constitute a part of the names of automatically generated programs. You should specify all three characters. Spaces in the program names created by the system will cause hard-to-locate syntax errors later.

After you enter the name, you can create the database with the *Create* pushbutton. A logical database has several components, such as the structure, the selection and the database program. You can select these components in a selection window using different radio buttons. Two pushbuttons then allow you to change or display the selected component for already existing databases. Furthermore, you can check a database for errors or copy it. With the latter function, you can choose one of the already existing logical databases, copy it with a new name, then modify it to meet specific needs.

Structure

Immediately after a new database has been created, the transaction requests the name of the node. On the subsequent screen, the structure of the database is displayed graphically as a tree, with both the table name and the descriptive short text visible in the display. Using several pushbuttons, you can add new nodes to the tree and replace existing ones with other table names. Of course, deleting nodes and entire sub-trees is also possible.

Each table may appear only once in the structure. To make the access path to a specific table more visible, you can display it in the uppermost line of the work area by choosing *Edit → Sub-tree → Display*. The graphic consists only of those table names that stretch from the root to the previously selected node. From the selected node on down, the sub-tree is displayed in more detail. Double-clicking on the node in the access path makes this the selected node, that is, shortens the displayed access path and expands the tree display in the work area.

To simplify work, you can display the selected table's field list at any time. It provides a brief overview of the table's fields, their data types and their short descriptions. Labels are marked. After the database is set up, you can use the menu function *Database → Exit* or the corresponding symbol in the toolbar to end editing. R/3 then displays a message asking if the changes should be saved or not.

Selections

In the basic screen of the SE36 transaction, you mark the element *Selections* and activate the *Change* pushbutton. The system then displays the Include with the selections for editing. Here, you must now create all of the required selections. You must remove several comment characters and enter names for the required selections. Usually, you must then still create descriptive texts for the selections. You do this using the tool for text element maintenance, as was done for the selections already described.

Report program

You create a report program as previously described. In the attributes screen, in addition to the attributes used to this point, you enter the name of the logical database. Note that here you enter this name across two input fields (name and application). The link between the report and the logical database is only visible through the attributes. There are no statements in the report that point out the logical database.

You declare the tables to be analyzed in the report itself. Selections and all of the statements related to them do not belong here, however. After this, you can write the flow logic for the individual tables. A short example might look like this:

```
REPORT YZZ32140.
TABLES: YZZAKT, YZZKURS.

GET YZZAKT.
   WRITE: / YZZAKT-NAME.
   WRITE: / '==============='.

GET YZZKURS.
   WRITE: /YZZKURS-DATUM, YZZKURS-KURS.
```

```
GET YZZAKT LATE.
  WRITE: /, /.
```

This program produces sensible output only when both tables, YZZAKT and YZZKURS, have been filled with sensible values. For this reason, you cannot test this table until you have either programmed and processed the example in Chapter 6, or filled the two tables with test data in a report you have written yourself. Be sure to delete the test data before you execute the sample program in Chapter 6.

3.3   Dialog applications

3.3.1   A simple way in

The functionality of reports is not extensive enough to create full-fledged, interactive applications. The SAP system provides dialog applications for this. As is the case with reports, there is a basic, predefined structure for applications, to which the available ABAP/4 commands adhere. Dialog applications are largely based on the use of screens, which SAP calls dynpros. The basic concept for dialog applications is therefore also called the dynpro concept.

Several characteristics of this concept have already been touched on in the section on report selection screens. Selection screens employ some of the mechanisms of screens; but program-related implementation is completely different for true dialog applications. It is more complicated to program, but in return it provides more extensive application functionality.

Dialog applications provide the user with all of the input and control elements available in modern graphical interfaces. These elements can be divided into two large groups. The first includes elements that enable the editing of data, that is, edit fields and such. These elements are included in the screen. The second group contains all of the elements with which the user can trigger a function. These include, for example, menus, push-buttons and icons. Within ABAP/4 applications, these elements are grouped under the term *interface*. The term " interface" cannot, therefore, be used to mean the whole user interface, that is, the screen. It covers the named elements only; it does not include the elements of the actual screen. Unfortunately, the screen itself consists of several parts, one of which is the visible screen. Occasionally, this visible element of the screen is called the screen interface or visual interface of the screen, which can lead to confusion. For this reason, the term *fullscreen* is very often used for the screen.

All dialog elements must be linked to elements of the program to create the desired functionality in the application. When a menu item is selected, the desired subroutine should be executed, the values should be transferred from the input elements into the data fields, and so on. Program code is also required, in addition to the screen and the interface. While a report consists, in the simplest case, of a single program file that can be processed directly, a dialog program includes the following elements:

- One or more input screens (dynpros)
- One or more interfaces
- ABAP/4 statements

There is a big difference between the execution of reports and the execution of dialog applications, which makes it difficult for users of traditional procedural programming languages to make the switch. A report has one program section that is somewhat comparable to the main program in traditional languages. Usually, this is the section in which data is read and output, that is, the section after the START-OF-SELECTION event. The actual program activities take place in this section. All other events resemble subroutines, even if they are not executed directly but are executed through events and event statements. They perform auxiliary tasks. They have certain similarities to programs written in procedural languages. The preceding section intentionally exploited these similarities to simplify the introduction to the ABAP/4 programming language.

A dialog application does not have such a program kernel. The only thing to be found in the source code is a set of so-called modules, which are a type of subroutine. The actual program file is therefore called a module pool. The module pool is vaguely comparable to a library, which makes a series of auxiliary routines available. Sequential processing of the statements in the module pool is not possible, nor does it make sense. Nevertheless, the name of the module pool is also the name of the application.

Screens play the deciding role in the control of program flow. A screen has, among other things, two very important parts: the visible work area (the fullscreen) with the input elements, and the flow logic. When a dialog application is processed, it is screens that are called, not programs or subroutines. It is these screens that execute individual modules from the module pool. Screens and module pools are therefore inseparably linked. The module pool is used by several of an application's screens. Screens are identified by the name of the module pool and the number of the screen.

Dialog applications must be linked to a transaction; the application is then called using the name of this transaction. The name of the module pool and the number of the first screen to be executed are passed to this transaction. Creating and testing a dialog application requires the following steps:

- Creating a module pool

- Declaring global data

- Creating the user interface(s)

- Creating the dynpros (see Section 2.4), i.e. the screens with their flow logic

- Programming the modules

- Creation of a transaction

Similar to the preceding section, the section that follows is designed to provide educational information concerning dialog-oriented applications. The first two subsections describe the editing of a very simple dialog application. This application serves the following purposes only: it introduces important elements of a dialog application, demonstrates the creation and editing of one, and identifies relationships. Beyond that, it serves no practical purpose! In terms of meaning, then, this application is comparable to the "Hello World" program. The next subsection describes the different elements in more detail. The end of this section contains a description of the update concept.

Creating a simple, dialog-oriented application requires considerably more effort than writing the "Hello World" program. You cannot test the application until you have created several parts of it. Relationships do not become visible until the number of connected facts reaches a critical mass. For this reason, the most important elements of the dialog application are to be created first; the application's functionality will be restricted to that which is absolutely necessary. If you replicate the examples in your system, please note that all of the elements should be created as local, private objects.

The first dialog application, like the first report, simply displays the character string "Hello World!" This requires creating at least one screen and one module pool.

Creating a module pool

Since screens are assigned to a module pool (that is, the module pool must exist before the screen is created), you begin programming a dialog application by creating a module pool. In principle, you could create it, like a report, with the program editor used up to this point (the SE38 transaction). On the other hand, there is another tool, the Object Browser, which offers considerably more comfort. Not only can you manage all of an application's sub-objects with the Object Browser, you can also create development objects, in which case several of the objects' attributes are set automatically, according to the application. For example, when a module pool is created, the Browser takes into consideration a sub-division into several Include files. You can access this tool from the main menu of the development environment, using the menu function *Overview* → *Object Browser* or the *Object Browser* pushbutton. For expedited calling, you can use the SE80 transaction. In Release 2.2 and earlier versions, the Object Browser was called the Workbench. In Release 3.0, however, the term "Workbench" is used to mean the entire development interface, which contains all of the tools and resources for creating ABAP/4 programs. Please note this difference in names depending on the release version.

On the Object Browser's initial screen, you enter the name of the module pool in the *Program* input field in the *Object list* box. You should give this first program the name SAP-MYZZ1. You also need to mark the appropriate radio button. Figure 3.15 shows the initial screen of the Object Browser at this point in time. The SAP system's naming conventions will not be discussed here. Please note, however, that in your system you should replace the letters ZZ with your own initials.

Afterwards, click on the *Display* pushbutton. Assuming that the module pool does not yet exist, the system creates a query similar to the one shown in Figure 3.16. Confirm this with *Yes*. Another popup appears. It contains, in addition to the name of the program to be created, another check box for something called a Top Include. Module pools should always contain this Include. It is used for the declaration of global data. Mark the check box, then click on *Continue*, or, more precisely, on the corresponding icon, which is the green check mark.

Now a third popup appears, in which you must enter the name of the Top Include. Use the name MYZZ1TOP, which is the name automatically suggested by the system. After you confirm your entries, the familiar initial screen of the program editor appears, ready for entry of the program's attributes.

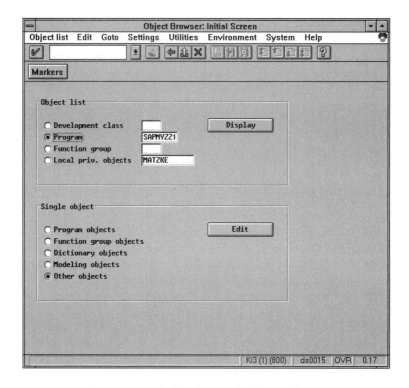

Figure 3.15   The initial screen of the Object Browser

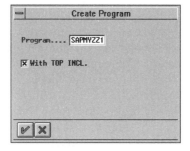

Figure 3.16   Creating a module pool

The program type contains the default entry "M" for module pool. Just as you would for reports, enter a short description and the application abbreviation, then save the attributes. Using the *Source code* pushbutton, you can now edit the source code directly. After the jump into the editor, the following source code appears:

```
*&--------------------------------------------------------*
*& Include MYZZ1TOP          Modul-Pool           SAPMYZZ1 *
*&                                                         *
*&--------------------------------------------------------*

PROGRAM SAPMYZZ1.
```

The editor jumps immediately into the Top Include, not into the actual module pool. You will notice that the PROGRAM statement appears in the Include. The actual module pool consists only of several INCLUDE statements. You do not yet need to edit the source code at this point. You can exit the editor. When you do so, you do not return directly to the initial screen. Instead, you first land in the Browser's element list or object list. This list is the center of the Object Browser. It contains all of the elements that belong to the application. Figure 3.17 shows the object list after the module pool has been created, which is still rather modest. The elements are grouped according to type. Double-clicking on the name of a group turns the element list for that group on or off. Double-clicking on an element brings up the tool for editing that element and loads the element to be edited into the tool.

The first screen

After the module pool has been created, you can create a preliminary version of the screen. You edit screens using the Screen Painter. This tool is accessible from the interface of the development environment (not from the Object Browser) with the menu function *Development → Screen Painter*. Alternatively, you can use a pushbutton, but this is only visible if the window is large enough. The transaction code for calling the Screen Painter directly is SE51. In addition to making a direct Screen Painter call, you can also create a screen directly from the object list of the Browser.

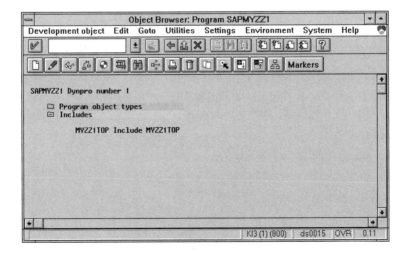

Figure 3.17   The Browser's object list

The object list of the Browser contains all of the elements of the current program. Since only the module pool and an Include have been created so far, the list is relatively short. Place the cursor on the name field of the module pool and call the menu function *Development object* → *Create*. A popup appears (Figure 3.18) in which you can mark an object. In the input field beside the radio button, you enter the name of the respective object to be created. In this example, you want to give the screen the number 9100.

After you click on the *Create* pushbutton or its icon, a screen appears in which you record the important attributes for the screen. Figure 3.19 shows this input screen. As was done for all other elements handled up to this point, you need to record a short description. Mark the *Normal* radio button for screen type, if this has not already been automatically marked by the system. You do not need to change any other fields.

Save the values in this screen. Clicking on the *Fullscreen* pushbutton or choosing the menu function *Goto* → *Fullscreen Editor* takes you to where you can edit the visual interface of the screen. At first, a blank screen appears, divided into individual lines (see Figure 3.20).

Later, you will place all of the input elements in the work area provided here. For this first test, it is enough to put the cursor in the middle of the screen and enter some text. This could be "Hello World!" like in the first practice program. Then save the screen and generate it with the menu function *Screen* → *Generate*. Screens must be regenerated after every change, otherwise the changes will not take effect. This applies to both changes to the fullscreen and changes to the flow logic.

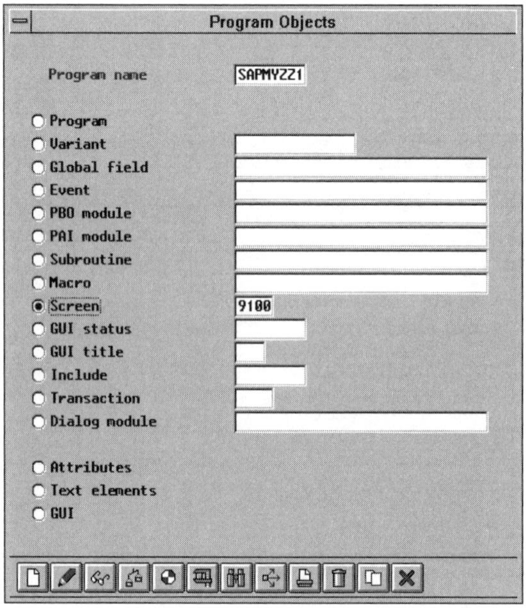

Figure 3.18   Creating a development object

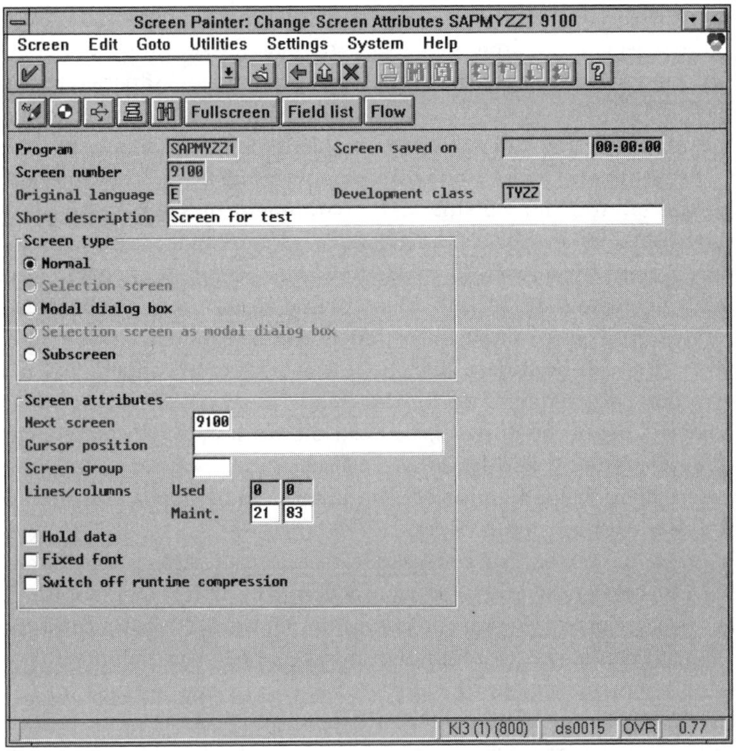

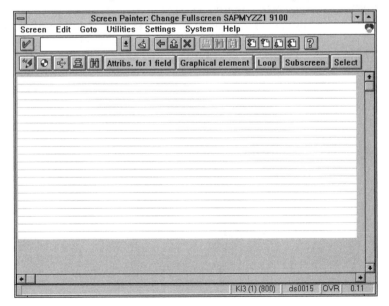

Figure 3.19   Attributes screen for screens

Figure 3.20   Fullscreen editor

You can now end screen editing and return to the Browser's object list. You can test the screen from the object list. To do so, place the cursor on the screen's number and then start the test by clicking on the icon or choosing the menu function. If necessary, you may first need to open the *Screens* group by double-clicking on the folder icon. A popup with coordinates appears, which you can confirm without changing the values by pressing Enter. The screen then appears. It does not contain any input fields, only the static text that you entered earlier. You can exit the test environment by clicking on any icon or the corresponding function key (for example, F3).

The application is now already in a state in which it could be executed. The only thing still required is to create a transaction. Many dialog applications can be called with more than one transaction. They evaluate the transaction code to determine how the application should behave. You can perform a realistic test of such applications only if you call the correct transaction, which must therefore be created early on.

From the object list of the Browser, you can call up transaction maintenance, just like the Screen Painter, using the function *Development object → Create*. The popup in which you must select the development object and enter a name appears again. For the demo application, use the transaction code YZZ1.

After you enter the transaction code, you can start its creation by clicking on the *Create* pushbutton. You must now enter the transaction type in another popup. The default, *Dialog transaction*, is correct, so you can confirm it. Figure 3.21 shows the popup.

Of course, you can also call transaction maintenance from the general development interface using the menu function *Development → Other tools → Transactions*. The transaction code for calling transaction maintenance directly is SE93.

After confirming the transaction type, you must record certain specifications for the transaction in another popup (Figure 3.22). These include a title (any desired), the name of the module pool (SAPMYZZ1), and the number of the first screen to be called (9100).

After you have entered the specifications and saved them, you can execute this first dialog application by entering the transaction code in the OK field. Since the initial screen of transaction maintenance is still active at this point, to do this you must enter /nYZZ1 in

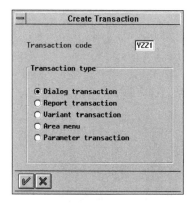

Figure 3.21   Selecting the transaction type

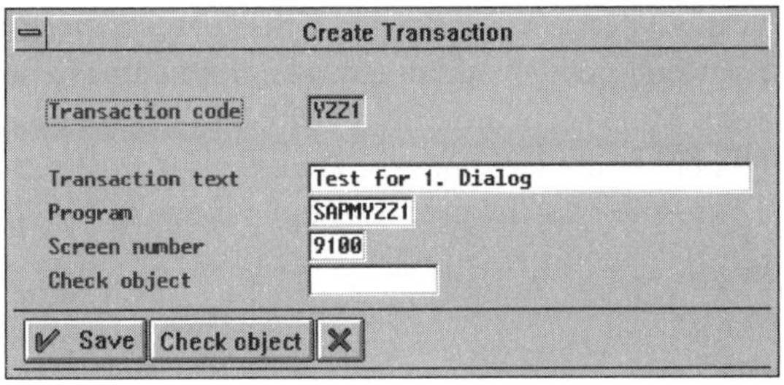

Figure 3.22 Transaction data

the OK field and press Enter. This terminates the current transaction and starts a new one. The screen, which was already seen in the test environment, appears again. Note, however, that all of the icons except the icon for Enter are grayed out. The only way you can end the application is to enter /n in the OK field. The reason for this lies in the screen's attributes. For every screen, a subsequent screen can be specified in the attributes. When the system finishes processing one screen, it calls the subsequent screen. When you create a new screen, the screen's own number is used as the subsequent screen. The screen therefore keeps calling itself. For this reason, you cannot end the application in the usual way.

Expanding the functionality

The application just created does not yet have any functionality. It does not even contain any input fields for processing data. No data is read or displayed, let alone written to the database. It is not even possible to end the application in a normal fashion. What follows is the incorporation of several additional elements in the existing application. In particular, a table will be read and displayed. Furthermore, a menu will make proper ending of the application possible.

Data declarations

For the most part, dialog applications process data records from tables. Of course, the tables to be processed must be declared in the program. You do this, as you do with reports, using the following statement:

TABLES: KNA1.

The declaration is recorded in the Top Include MYZZ1TOP. The KNA1 table is one of the standard SAP tables. This means it is delivered by SAP and processed by the common applications. It is therefore important to ensure that in your own experiments you do not under any circumstances change the contents of this table. This could lead to inconsistencies in data in the system. If you find later that you also want to write data to tables, you should use a custom table to do so.

There are various ways to select the Top Include for processing. At the moment, you have two choices. You can display the list of Include files by double-clicking on the *Includes* group identifier in the object list, if it is not already displayed. Another double-click on the name of the Include file MYZZ1TOP starts the editor for this file. When you edit development objects with the Object Browser, these are at first only in display mode. For this reason, you must first activate change mode, then enter the declaration.

The second way to edit the Top Include involves the module pool. You double-click on the name of the module pool in the Workbench. This starts the ABAP/4 editor, not directly for the Include at first, but rather for the module pool, whose current source code is shown in the following listing.

```
*&---------------------------------------------------------*
*& Modul-Pool       SAPMYZZ1                               *
*&                                                         *
*&---------------------------------------------------------*
*&                                                         *
*&                                                         *
*&---------------------------------------------------------*

INCLUDE MYZZ1TOP.                        "global Data

*  INCLUDE MYZZ1O01.                     "PBO-Modules

*  INCLUDE MYZZ1I01.                     "PAI-Modules

*  INCLUDE MYZZ1F01.                     "FORM-Routines
*
```

At the moment, the module pool consists only of a few comments and the INCLUDE statement for the Top Include. When you double-click on the name of the Include file in the source code, this file is loaded into the editor.

All of the elements in the user interface (menu) and screen with which the user can trigger functions, that is, menu items, pushbuttons and so on, have an identifier, which is also called a function code or OK code.

When one of these elements is selected, the corresponding function code is automatically placed in a specific screen field. If the function code should be analyzed in the program, that specific screen field must be linked to a data field. This screen field is automatically created by the system, so it is available in all screens immediately after its creation. The programmer cannot delete it. The only activity that the programmer can carry out on this screen field is a data field assignment. This data field must therefore also be declared. Function codes are four-character strings, whose processing requires a type C field with a length of 4. Usually, this field is derived from SY-UCOMM. Since this data field is needed for function codes in every dialog application, and it always performs the same task, a few field names have become quasi-standard. These are, for example, OK_CODE, FCODE and, in disregard of the naming conventions recommended by SAP for field names, OK-CODE. In this case, the hyphen in the field name is not so bad, because it is very unlikely that this field will be used in field strings. In the example, you should call the field FCPDE. You also need the following declaration in the Top Include, in addition to the table declaration:

```
DATA: FCODE LIKE SY-UCOMM.
```

After you enter both declarations, you can save the file and return to the Browser's object list.

Release 2.2

In Release 2.2, the Object Browser operates somewhat differently. Up to and including this release, it was called the Workbench. The object list does not contain a separate group for Includes. Instead, after you double-click on the name of the module pool, a popup appears that contains, among other things, the list of Includes and the main program (this is the module pool's program file). It makes no difference whether you now use the name of the Top Include directly or first jump to the main program and then jump to the Include file from there.

Screen painter

After declaring the most important data fields in the module pool, you can now edit the screen. You should give it several input fields that correspond to the structure of the database table just declared. Double-click on the *Screens* group in the object list to open the screen for editing, then double-click on the screen number, 9100, to load the screen. The flow logic of the screen appears, which does not need to be edited yet. To reach the fullscreen editor, click on the *Fullscreen* pushbutton. As you did when you edited the Top Include, you must explicitly activate change mode here.

For the screen, every complete character string in the fullscreen is a field, regardless of which characters it contains. This field is included in a field list. Various attributes then determine how the field will appear in the screen. It is possible, for example, to display it as a field that can be edited, as a pure display field without an editing function, as a check box or radio button, or simply as text. This last variation was used in the first version of the screen. Section 3.3.2 goes into more detail about the different attributes and the various incarnations of fields.

You can set and change the attributes in various ways. One of the methods involves manually editing the field list. You can also assign attributes with the menu function *Edit → Attributes*. This calls a popup for the field identified by the cursor location. All of the field's attributes are displayed in this popup, and most of them can be changed there, too. Certain editing functions, for example converting a field into a graphical element, also affect some attributes. These attributes can only be set by that particular editing function. The final method consists of assigning attributes using a special tool that supports the creation of screen fields.

This tool can create screen fields and link them to data fields that have already been declared in the module pool, or to table fields from the Data Dictionary, all in one move. It also ensures that additional fields with the corresponding descriptions are created for input fields. You do not normally edit the fullscreen manually to create screen fields and assign individual attributes to them without a compelling reason. Generally, you use the insertion tool described next.

The field currently contained in the 9100 screen was used in the first demonstration. You can remove it in the fullscreen editor using the menu function *Edit → Edit lines → Delete line*. Now call the insertion tool with *Goto → Dict./program fields*. A popup appears, in which you must enter several specifications to more closely identify the fields to be inserted. In the *Table/field* name input field, enter the name of the table for whose fields you want to create input elements in the screen, in this case KNA1. Of the five radio buttons after *Key word*, mark *Average*. Each of a table's fields is based on a data element in the Dictionary. You can allocate three keywords and a heading to this data element to describe the application-related meaning of the data element. You can use one of these short texts on the screen to identify the input field. At runtime, the screen loads the corresponding text from the Dictionary and displays it. This text is maintained in the Dictionary in various languages and is read by the screen in the logon language of the user. If the keywords for a data element have been translated, the screen is automatically multi-lingual, assuming the input fields were created with reference to the Dictionary fields. Although this is not the only way to create multi-lingual screens, it is the easiest way.

In addition to the keyword, of course, you need the actual input field, at least in this example. In SAP terminology, input fields are also called *templates*. For this reason, mark the *Yes* radio button after Templates. Figure 3.23 shows the popup with the entries described.

When you click on the *Get from Dict.* pushbutton, all of the selected table's fields are listed. A check box in front of each field name allows you to mark the table fields to be copied. You can scroll the selection list with a scroll bar. In the list, mark the fields KUNNR, NAME1, NAME2, ORT01 and ORT02 by clicking on the check boxes. The first field is at the beginning of the table; to reach the others you must scroll the list.

You now copy the selected table fields into the screen by clicking on the *Transfer* pushbutton. The popup disappears, and the fullscreen editor work area reappears. You insert the previously selected fields there by positioning the cursor (using the mouse or the cursor keys) and confirming the location (by double-clicking with the mouse or pressing the F2 function key). Figure 3.24 shows the fullscreen at this point. Both the labels, that is, the identifiers, and the templates for the input fields, represented by a series of underscores, are inserted.

The field templates are aligned according to the maximum length of the labels (15 characters for the middle label). Thus the actual length of the keyword can be anywhere between 1 and the respective maximum length, without negatively influencing the appearance of the screen.

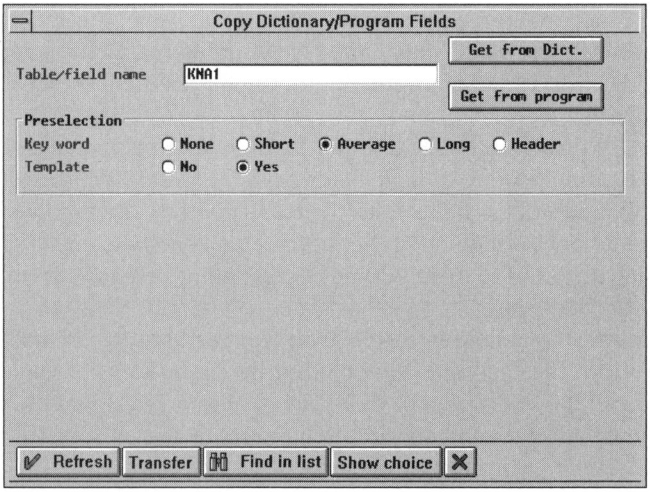

Figure 3.23   Copying fields from the Data Dictionary

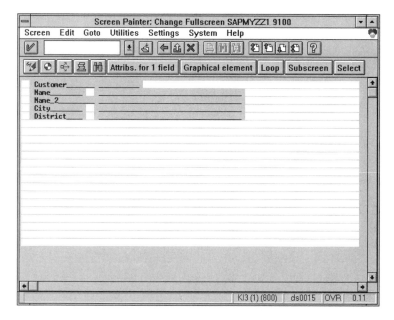

Figure 3.24   Fullscreen with Dictionary fields inserted

More specific details of the screen fields are visible in the field list. You can access this list at various points during screen editing by using the menu function *Goto → Field list views → Field types,* or by using a pushbutton. A look at this field list (Figure 3.25) shows that two screen fields have been created for every table field. Both screen fields

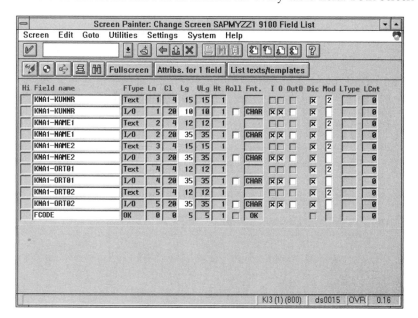

Figure 3.25   Field list of the screen

reference a table field, but they display it differently because of the different attributes. All field names have been entered automatically. Only the last field, which receives the screen's function code, is not yet linked to a data field. Since analysis of function codes is to be demonstrated in this section, as well, you can use this opportunity to enter the already declared FCODE field as the data field for the last screen field.

Afterwards, you save and generate the screen. You can then call up the test environment again from the initial Screen Painter screen. It shows the new screen with the five input fields. Starting the application using transaction code YZZ1 is not yet worth it, since there has been no change in functionality for the screen yet.

Release 2.2

While the insertion tool is also available in Release 2.2, it is somewhat more difficult to use. When the possible entries help starts, a divided screen appears. In the upper half is a list from which you can later select the fields to be inserted. This list is filled after you enter the name of the table to be edited in the input field in the list header.

The lower half of the screen displays a section of the Screen Painter. You can move this section with the scroll bars. This is where you position the selected fields later.

After you have entered a table name in the input field, the field list is filled, and you can click on an entry to mark it. The *Choose/enter* pushbutton displays additional specifications for this field, such as the three labels from the data element and the default field template. The field list is divided vertically to display these values. So the screen now consists of three windows, as shown in Figure 3.26.

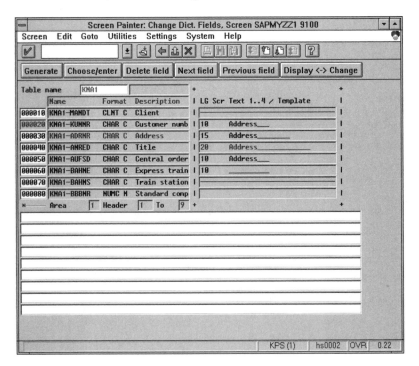

Figure 3.26   Possible entries help in Release 2.2

The process for inserting fields is as follows. First, you mark a field in the field list and click on the *Choose/enter* pushbutton. In the detail window, you can now click on the entry to be inserted, that is, either one of the identifiers or the field template, then click on the pushbutton again to activate the entry. Next, you place the cursor in the spot on the sub-section of the screen editor where the new element should be inserted. Clicking on the *Choose/enter* pushbutton a third time now inserts the previously selected element. You repeat this process for each of the elements to be inserted, usually in the order identifier – field template for all database fields. Accurate positioning is somewhat complicated with this tool. It is therefore better to correct the positioning in the fullscreen editor.

Menus and function keys

The next step towards a functioning application is the creation of a user interface. It is only through elements of the user interface that the user can communicate actively with the application. There is only one user interface in an application, which is not identified more precisely because of the obvious link to the application. However, the user interface contains one or more statuses. A screen can set several statuses during different phases of processing, but one status can also be used in several successive screens.

Each of these statuses contains certain forms for menus and function key layout. The status is thus identified by the name of the application, that is, the name of the module pool, and an identifier that is unique in the application and has a maximum of eight characters. A status, like the screen and the transaction, can also be created from the object list. You should give the status the name STAT1. The tool for status maintenance is the Menu Painter. To call the Menu Painter, select the menu function *Development* → *Menu Painter* from the main menu of the development interface, or use a function key or the SE41 transaction code.

Several changes regarding user interface maintenance became effective in Release 3.0C. These were not fully available in the R/3 System used to create the sample programs when this book was written. The following explanations therefore describe user interface maintenance for release versions up to 3.0B. Some notes are included at the end regarding the procedure in 3.0C.

You start status editing by clicking on the *Create* pushbutton or the corresponding icon. In a popup (Figure 3.27), enter the short text (any desired text) for the status and the status type. Select *Screen* as the status type, since you want this status to work with a screen.

After you confirm the entry, the work area for the status appears. This screen is quite large, because it contains all of the elements of a status: the menu, the function key layout, the toolbar and the pushbutton layout.

Figure 3.28 shows the most essential section. Several areas on the screen are displayed in white. These are input fields in which values can be entered. The upper area is used for defining menus; the lower area is used for assigning function codes to function keys. The line in the middle defines the pushbutton bar and the icons.

The area for function keys consists of two parts. Some of them can be used as desired; recommendations exist for the use of others. The function keys of this latter group have already been assigned icons, which are displayed instead of the function key text in the pushbutton bar, assuming the appropriate function code is inserted in the pushbutton line.

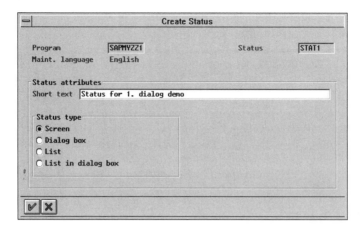

Figure 3.27   Popup for defining the status attributes

Status editing can be time-consuming and require a lot of work. For this application, however, a few functions will suffice. Their implementation will allow a comprehensive overview of the Menu Painter functionality. The status to be created should have the following characteristics:

- Activation of the icon (red plus sign), the function key (F12), and a menu function (*Edit* → *Cancel*) for canceling the application.

- Definition of two application-related menu functions and the corresponding pushbuttons.

The design of this status does not follow the requirements of the SAP Style Guide in all points; nevertheless, it creates a functional status that is fully sufficient for this demo application. The steps that follow lead to the results shown in Figure 3.28. The individual steps, or rather the elements to be edited, are numbered consecutively in this figure.

Some preparatory work is necessary. Double-clicking on *Display standards* in the upper left corner of the screen (which changes it to *Hide standards*) (1) fills the empty input fields for menu entries with default values. In the uppermost input field (menu bar), enter a simple text (2). Overwrite the identifier for the first menu, which is automatically filled with *<Object>* by the system, with some custom text, for example "Demo" (3). In this menu, you will later create the two individual menu functions.

Now press the function key for the *Cancel* function. The system designates the F12 function key as a default for this function. This function key is automatically linked to the corresponding icon. When a function code is assigned to the icon, the icon and the corresponding function key are both activated. You can choose any function code desired. Remember, however, that the function codes must be analyzed later in the program. This is a lot easier if the function code indicates the intended purpose. In the case of function keys that have a default meaning that is identical across the entire system, you can use the number of the function key as the function code, in this case FT12. Enter this character string in the four-character column (4) in the function code area.

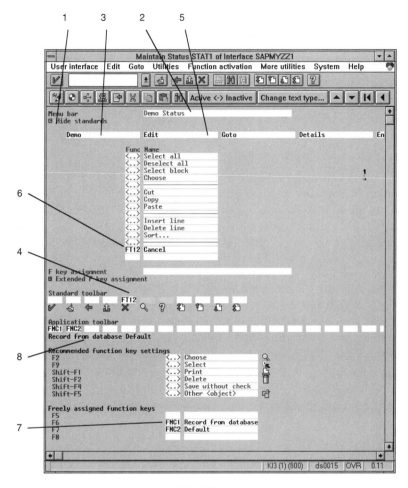

Figure 3.28   Editing a status

Double-clicking on the *Edit* menu (5) opens that menu. Here, too, there is a series of defaults, one of which is *Cancel*. This menu function also receives the function code FT12 (6). The term *Cancel* has a purely informative nature. The Menu Painter does not automatically check the assignment of function codes to the identifiers of menu items. It is entirely possible that several entries with different function codes, but with identical identifiers, exist, or that identical function codes with different identifiers exist. Such mistakes are rarely discovered, and then only with a special checking tool in the Menu Painter. Therefore, some care is in order when assigning function codes.

Now you create the two individual function codes. To do so, open the *Demo* menu by double-clicking on the heading (3). Overwrite the first two menu items with the function codes FNC1 and FNC2 and the following texts: *Record from database* and *Default*, respectively. Afterwards, assign the F6 and F7 function keys to these two function codes. To do so, enter the function code in the four-character column right after the identifiers F6 and F7 (7). These two keys are used because no defaults exist for them. Finally, enter the function codes in the first two fields of the pushbutton bar (8). Pushbuttons can only be created for function codes that can also be accessed with a function key.

For the F12 function key, you first created the icon assignment, then the menu item. For the individual functions, you worked in the opposite order. Both variations are possible. However, since there should be a menu item for every function, you can avoid errors if you first create the menu item, then the function key and pushbutton layouts.

Now all that is left to do is to set a function type that differs from the default for the FT12 function code. This function type is needed later, in the flow logic, to execute certain modules. This relationship is described in the section on flow logic. Call up function code editing from the status work area using *Goto → Function list*. All of the function codes that are used in the user interface's various statuses appear in this list. For the FT12 function code, enter type "E", for Exit code, in the *Type* column.

At this point, a remark about older release versions is necessary. Function types have not always been available as an additional attribute for function codes. Previously, instead of the function type, the first letter of the function code determined how it would be handled by the system. All function codes beginning with "E" were automatically Exit function codes! Some older documentation mentions that Exit function codes must start with the letter "E". In Release 2.2 and 3.0, this is not necessary.

Direct assignment of function codes to symbols is also new in Release 3.0. Older versions of the Menu Painter offer only one input method for the 24 function keys and, if necessary, the Enter key. The assignment of function codes to function keys at the same time activates the corresponding icon in the toolbar. Table 3.19 (see page 187) shows the assignment of function keys to icons.

Functionality

The user interface, or rather the status, was the final dialog application element missing. Now you can program the modules for the flow logic. This is the only way to give the application the desired functionality. To link the screen with program code, you call the screen's modules in the flow logic. You must create these modules in the module pool and fill them with source code. To edit the flow logic, call the Screen Painter; double-clicking on the screen number in the Object Browser list is the easiest way. The flow logic for a new screen consists of only three lines at first.

```
PROCESS BEFORE OUTPUT.
*
PROCESS AFTER INPUT.
```

These two statements are events. They are called before or after the screen is called. Upon first glance, the flow logic appears to be a normal ABAP/4 program. This is an illusion, however. There are only a few special statements that may be used in the flow logic. They are considerably different from those in normal ABAP/4 programs. You will only use one of them at first anyway.

What can also cause problems is that the flow logic editor works somewhat differently than the ABAP/4 program editor. Some of the function key layouts are different, with the differences depending on the actual release version.

You now insert three module calls into the flow logic, which results in the following source code:

```
PROCESS BEFORE OUTPUT.
  MODULE D9100_SET_STATUS.

*

PROCESS AFTER INPUT.
  MODULE D9100_EXIT AT EXIT-COMMAND.
  MODULE D9100_FCODE.
```

At this point, save and generate the flow logic, and thus the screen. Without generation, the module calls would appear in the screen's flow logic, but they would not be recognized during processing of the screen and would therefore not be executed. This mistake is relatively difficult to uncover, since the statements look correct in the source code.

All three modules perform basic tasks. For this reason, they appear in just about every screen, sometimes with nearly identical names. In the module D9100_SET_STATUS, the STAT1 status is loaded. This makes the menu functions and function keys created there available in the screen. The D9100_EXIT module is responsible for processing all function codes that have the function type E. These are called Exit function codes. All other function codes are analyzed in the D9100_FCODE module. The reason for splitting the function code analysis will become clear later, in the discussion on field checking.

Module names can be up to 20 characters long, otherwise the same recommendations apply as for the names of subroutines or fields. Note, however, that there are several (unwritten) naming recommendations. A module pool often contains modules for several screens. To increase clarity and promote consistent naming of modules, many developers begin the name of a module with the screen number and append the actual identifier. For example, if there are several screens in which a different status is set, you need several SET_STATUS modules, all of which must be given unique names. By using the screen numbers, you can create unique module names without losing meaning. It is not unusual to combine similar functions for several screens in one module and, in this module, to select the actual functions to be executed based on the number of the current screen, which is contained in the system variable SY-DYNNR. Common use of modules can, however, lead to rather complex and confusing programs. Such modules also make screen-related documentation more complicated.

After you have incorporated the module calls in the flow logic, you must of course still create the related source code in the module pool. Since the flow logic editor, like the general ABAP/4 editor, has a rather easy-to-use navigation mechanism, it is not necessary to exit the Screen Painter and change to the program editor. Double-clicking on the name of the module is enough to start the ABAP/4 editor for the module pool. The system recognizes that the module to be edited does not yet exist and asks if it should be created. You enter the name of the program file where the module should be created in another popup. In this popup, all of the module pool's Include files are displayed in a list, from which you can select. You can also enter a new name in the input field. The system displays a default value in this field, which you can overwrite. The system then automatically creates the Include file with that name and links it to the module pool with an INCLUDE statement.

The names of the Include files for modules are put together the same way as Top Includes. This means that only the last three places are available. Of these three characters, the first should indicate the event to which the module belongs. For PBO modules, use the letter O, and for PAI modules, the letter I. The last two places are often filled with the first two characters of the screen number, but consecutive numbering is also possible. In this example, create the Include MYZZ1O91 for the PBO module by entering this name in the popup as the name of a new Include. Figure 3.29 shows the popup.

After you confirm the name, the Object Browser creates the Include file. It also creates the module's shell (MODULE and ENDMODULE statements) and adds several comments to the source code. The Browser then starts the ABAP/4 editor for the Include file and gives the programmer the automatically generated source code for further editing. You add only one line to the module:

```
*&---------------------------------------------------------------------*
*&---------------------------------------------------------------------*
*&       Module D9100_SET_STATUS OUTPUT
*&---------------------------------------------------------------------*
*&       text                                                          *
*&---------------------------------------------------------------------*
MODULE D9100_SET_STATUS OUTPUT.
    SET PF-STATUS 'STAT1'.              "insert
ENDMODULE.                             "D9100_SET_STATUS OUTPUT
```

This application loads the previously defined status, making the menus and other elements defined there available for this screen. The SET PF-STATUS statement expects the name of the status as a parameter, which must be entered as a character string constant, that is, enclosed in single quotes. The name of the status must also be specified in capital letters.

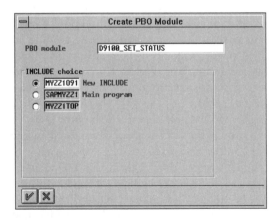

Figure 3.29   Selecting an Include file for the PBO module

The system automatically appends the term OUTPUT to the module name. Modules must be assigned to a unique section of screen processing in their declaration. When executing a module, the system searches only among the modules of the current processing section. PBO modules are identified with the OUTPUT clause. The PAI modules are either not identified at all or are identified by the INPUT clause in their declaration. Two modules with the same name can therefore exist in a single module pool, if one of them has the clause OUTPUT. In the interest of clear program code, however, it is a good idea to avoid this situation.

The function codes must, of course, be analyzed in the PAI section of the flow logic after screen processing. This occurs in the two other modules, which are created in the MYZZ1I91 Include as just described. The following listing shows the source code of the two modules, this time without the generated comments.

```
MODULE D9100_EXIT INPUT.

  CASE FCODE.
  WHEN 'FT12'.
    SET SCREEN 0.
    LEAVE SCREEN.
  ENDCASE.

ENDMODULE.                    " D9100_EXIT INPUT
```

Usually, several function codes are analyzed in one screen. This is most easily accomplished using a CASE statement. Although this example contains only one Exit function code, a CASE statement is entered in the Exit module. It is easy to expand the statement, in case more Exit codes must be accommodated later. The statement to be executed for the FT12 function code is quite simple. The number of the subsequent screen is set with SET SCREEN 0. The parameter 0 has a special function here. It means that the application is to be exited. The application is not actually exited until the LEAVE SCREEN command. This statement ends processing of the current screen and calls the screen that was set as the subsequent screen.

```
MODULE D9100_FCODE INPUT.

  CASE FCODE.
    WHEN 'FNC1'.
      SELECT * FROM KNA1
      WHERE KUNNR = KNA1-KUNNR.
        EXIT.
      ENDSELECT.
      IF SY_SUBRC <> 0.
        CLEAR KNA1.
      ENDIF.

    WHEN 'FNC2'.
      KNA1-KUNNR = '123456'.
      KNA1-NAME1 = 'iXOS'.
```

```
      KNA1-NAME2 = 'Application Software Co.'.
      KNA1-ORT01 = 'Leipzig'.
      KNA1-ORT02 = ''.
   ENDCASE.

ENDMODULE.                                " D9100_FCODE INPUT
```

The two application-related function codes are analyzed in the D9100_FCODE module. One of them fills the table header with several values that are hard-coded in the program. The other one, in contrast, reads the database table based on the customer number entered in the screen and fills the rest of the fields if a suitable data record is found. Both functions have no practical use; they only demonstrate the analysis of different function codes. In real applications, actions such as saving data or branching to other screens would take place here. After you have programmed the modules, you can test the application again by calling the YZZ1 transaction. If the KNA1 table in the client to which you have logged on contains data, you can display this data now by entering the customer number and clicking on the *Record from database* pushbutton.

In practice, data records are checked before being written to the database. In addition to some checks that are automatically performed by the system, there are, of course custom-programmed checks that can or must be performed. If these checks encounter an error, the incorrect entries in the screen fields must be corrected, meaning that processing of the screen starts from the beginning again.

The field checks in a screen can be carried out according to the fields. This means that a separate check routine can be created for every field or group of logically related fields. Field(s) and check routine are linked together in the flow logic with a particular statement. If a check routine triggers an error message, the only input fields on the screen that are input-ready are those linked to the check routine. The cursor appears in the first field to be edited. This procedure increases clarity and prevents new mistakes due to unintentional overwriting of correct values. In addition, field checks can be made dependent on whether the contents of a field were processed at all. This saves unnecessary checking and improves the performance of an application.

The check routine principle is quite easily demonstrated in the demo application. First, insert an additional statement in the PAI part of the flow logic:

```
PROCESS AFTER INPUT.
   MODULE D9100_EXIT AT EXIT-COMMAND.
   FIELD KNA1-KUNNR MODULE D9100_CHECK.        "new
   MODULE D9100_FCODE.
```

Afterwards, save and generate the flow logic. Double-click on the character string D9100_CHECK to create the missing module in the MYZZ1I91 Include. An error message is output without any further checking in the module. The syntax and possible parameters for the MESSAGE command are described in more detail in the next section.

```
MODULE D9100_CHECK INPUT.
MESSAGE ID 'YZ' TYPE 'E' NUMBER 1.
ENDMODULE.                               " D9100_CHECK INPUT
```

After entering the source code, you can test the application again. The F12 function key or the Terminate icon ends the application as usual. When you click on one of the two pushbuttons for the other function codes or select the corresponding menu function, the program performs the field check before analyzing the function code. This definitely triggers an error, which starts the processing of that screen from the beginning again. The function codes FNC1 and FNC2 never take effect, since the module for their analysis is no longer executed. Since the module for field checking has been linked only to the field for the customer number, only this field is input-ready again. You can end the application, as usual, with FT12.

This example illustrates why the function codes are divided into two groups and analyzed separately. Certain activities such as saving data and branching into other screens should only take place if the entries in the screen are correct. Other functions such as terminating, however, must be possible anytime, especially in the case of incorrect entries. The easiest way to meet these requirements is to have Exit function codes analyzed before the field checks are executed, and all other function codes afterwards. If an Exit function code in the Exit module does not lead to termination of processing, all of the other modules are executed. This makes it possible to save the contents of a screen, if necessary, even if certain Exit function codes end screen processing.

3.3.2   The screen in detail

The cornerstone of all dialog applications is the screen. The input elements seen on the screen's fullscreen follow the SAA / CUA standard. Many more elements are possible than just the edit field used up to this point. Their operation can also be modified with a series of attributes. The flow logic and the various modules use statements that are tailored specifically for the screen concept. This information is the focus of this section.

Screen types

In its basic form, the screen takes up the entire work area. In certain cases, for example, when additional information needs to be displayed, popup screens make more sense. Selection screens are also screens, but the system processes them somewhat differently than normal screens. There are five different types of screens, only three of which can actually be edited. The other two are automatically generated by the system.

Normal
All of the demo applications presented so far create screens of this type. When executed, the screens take up the entire work area. Their flow logic can and must be edited by the user. Normal screens are processed one after the other. The order of processing is determined by the *Next screen* attribute or by statements in the flow logic (SET SCREEN ..., LEAVE ...). The processing of these screens is thus similar to the sequential processing of a program's statements.

Selection screen
The system automatically generates a selection screen when a report with parameters or selections is processed for the first time, or if such a report is generated with a menu

function. Selection screens are given the default number 1000. You can load such screens into the Screen Painter, but you may under no circumstances change them. Selection screens have a flow logic, but it contains modules that are analyzed directly by the system. These modules are not true ABAP/4 program code. Changes to the flow logic in most cases lead to failure of the report!

Modal dialog box

Certain flow logic statements let you deviate from the usual sequential processing of a series of screens and call any screen as a sort of subroutine. The command for this is CALL SCREEN. If screens called in this fashion end with the subsequent screen 0, the whole program does not end; instead, there is simply a return to the calling screen.

Special clauses for this command allow you to display such screens as popups. In this case, the calling screen is not replaced by the new screen; rather, the new one is displayed in a separate window. Entries can only be made in this window. The application menu and the OK field do not work. The popup reacts only to function keys and pushbuttons that have been defined in the current status. The pushbuttons are displayed in a popup at the bottom of the window. If a screen is to be called as a popup, it must be given the screen type *Modal dialog box*.

Selection screen as modal dialog box

This type of screen is available starting with Release 3.0. Like basic selection screens, screens of this type are automatically generated and should not be manually edited.

Subscreen

In addition to popups, which take control entirely when called, you can create so-called subscreens. These are screens that can be dynamically incorporated in another screen at runtime. They cannot run independently. Such subscreens must satisfy certain requirements. They may not process any Exit function codes, and they may not contain any fields for receiving function codes. Subscreens may also not influence the current user interface (status). Subscreens are called in the flow logic of a superordinate screen with a special command. More detailed explanation of these screens accompanies the description of flow logic commands.

Field types in the screen

During screen layout, elements for data input and output are created in the fullscreen. These elements are called screen fields. When you edit the screen in the pseudo-graphical Screen Painter, the fields are displayed as groups of different alphanumeric characters. These characters are place holders. You can create the fields manually by entering the characters in the fullscreen or by using various utilities. The fields' characteristics are determined by the field type and various attributes. The programmer can determine the field type and some of the attributes when laying out the screen. Several special attributes, however, are preset automatically by tools in the Screen Painter and cannot be edited by the programmer.

The field types that can be used on the screen fall into two large groups: those with processing functionality and those that are used only for the display of information or for the graphical layout of the screen. A representative field type from each of these groups was presented in the second phase of demo development. Each of these groups contains a basic element from which all of the other elements in the group are derived.

This section begins by describing all of the field types and how they are created. Then it describes the attributes with which the field characteristics can be modified. Since a concrete example makes absorbing this information easier, all practical explanations will refer to the screen in Figure 3.30.

An input field usually consists of two elements: a field name, that is, an identifier (or, in SAP terminology, a label) and the field template, the actual input area. Both appear on the screen. The label is a text element that the program user cannot change. The field template, on the other hand, represents the actual input field in which the edit process takes place. In order for the edited value to be available in the program, it must, of course, be linked to a data field. This data field then automatically determines several characteristics of the input field.

The fullscreen editor always identifies fields, no matter what type, with a colored block that is set apart from the background. Such a block can no longer be edited directly character by character; it can only be edited using various functions of the fullscreen editor. The fullscreen editor itself is a screen. This means that manual entries (for example, when you create a field manually) are not recognized and analyzed until PAI processing is

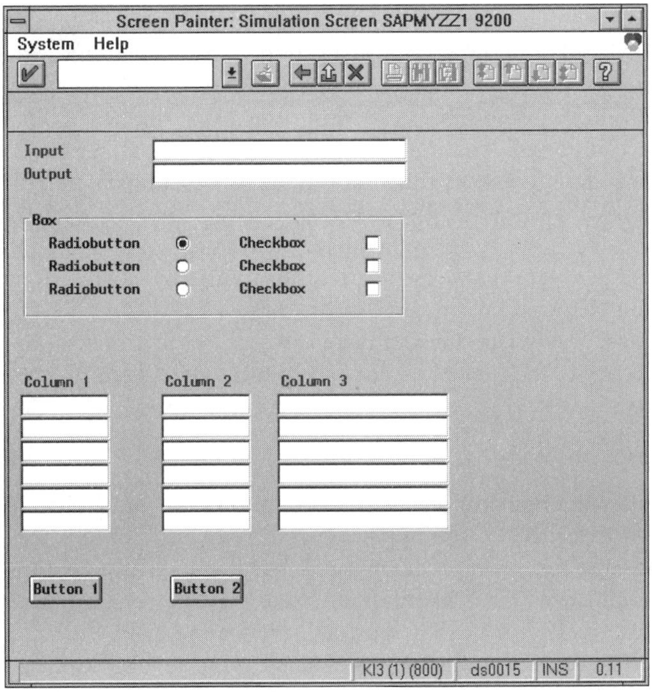

Figure 3.30   Elements of a screen

executed for the fullscreen editor's own screen. This occurs when you select a menu function or pushbutton, or when you press the Enter key. Only then, for example, is a character string converted into a real screen field.

Label (keyword)

Labels are static text elements in the screen work area. They are used to display general information or the field identifiers for input fields. You usually create labels with the insertion tool (menu function *Dict./program fields*). This automatically gives them a reference to the Dictionary. The text is taken from the description of a data element in the Data Dictionary. Exactly which text is copied from the Dictionary is determined by the *Modified* attribute. Inserting a Dictionary field using the possible entries help determines which key text should be copied.

It is also possible to create labels without a Dictionary reference. To do so, you enter the desired text directly in the screen. This procedure results in increased translation time and effort. Whenever possible, you should avoid this variant, since alternatives are available (field templates without input capability with two-dimensional display).

Template (input/output field)

For the actual input fields, you must create something called field templates. Since input fields are used to input or output data, these fields must reference a Dictionary field or at least a program-internal field, for data transfer. For this reason, you usually create them using the possible entries help just mentioned.

Field templates are represented in the fullscreen editor by some special characters. Each character in the place holder represents an input field character. The underscore serves as a standard place holder. Other characters symbolize certain characteristics of the screen field. A question mark in the first position indicates that the field is a mandatory input field. All other characters, regardless of their exact position, serve as templates. This means that in this exact position, this exact character must be entered. The system automatically performs a check when the screen is processed in an application. When a field is created with the insertion program, a default field template is created that consists only of underscores. If template characters are to be inserted, this must be done in the *Field text* field in the attributes popup.

Field templates can contain any characters, except in the first position, which the user must then enter exactly the same way. For example, if the field template consists of the following characters

___-___/___

the user must, after entering any desired three characters, enter a hyphen (-), and after three more characters, a slash (/). The application's control logic checks for correct input in mandatory fields and for the input of template characters. Incorrect entries are recognized, and the user is notified with a printout in the status bar. The cursor is automatically placed in the (first) incorrect field. If existing data is displayed in a field with template characters, the screen logic fills the template's non-fixed characters one after another with the characters of the data field, so that no data is lost. With the template shown above, a field with the contents 123456789 would be displayed as 123-456/789 and would be stored that way.

You can also create field templates manually by entering the template characters in the screen. A field template may begin with an underscore or a question mark. A question mark makes the field a mandatory input field. You can also insert template characters directly. The character string is editable on screen until the moment you select a fullscreen editor function or press the Enter key. It is only then that the fullscreen editor recognizes it and converts it into a real screen field. You must then set all of the field's other attributes in an attributes popup or in one of the various field list processing variants. In particular, you must set the link to a data field.

Radio buttons
Radio buttons are input elements that can accept only yes/no information. A radio button is either selected or not selected. Radio buttons are combined into groups. Only one radio button in a group can be marked. A group is not the same as a surrounding box. Rather, it is a form of combining that is internal in the dynpro and is not recognizable visually. You can, however, enhance the togetherness of the fields by adding a surrounding box, although this is not functionally necessary.

Every radio button has a data element. If the radio button is selected, the corresponding data element contains an X, otherwise it contains a blank space. The data element is therefore typically a type C data element with a length of 1.

You cannot create radio buttons directly. For every radio button, you must first create a field template and link it to a data field. Then you need to align the fields correctly. To do this, you place the cursor on the upper left screen field in the group of combined fields. It does not matter if this is a label or a field template. Then you click on the *Graphical element* pushbutton.

The fullscreen editor then changes the view. You use this new view to edit so-called graphic elements, which, among other things, include radio buttons. In this new view, you can only edit elements using the various functions; you can no longer edit them by making entries in the fullscreen.

The field in which you placed the cursor is highlighted in color. Now you place the cursor on the lower right corner of the radio button group. Clicking on the *Mark end of block* pushbutton then combines all of the elements into a block, to which the function that follows refers. This next function consists of clicking on the *Radio Buttons* pushbutton. It converts all of the field templates in the marked area into radio buttons. These are represented in the fullscreen editor by a corresponding symbol (see Figure 3.31).

The fullscreen editor view, or more precisely the status, that is, the available functions, changes again after the radio buttons are created. The radio buttons must still be combined into a group, to ensure that only one of the fields can be marked at a time. To access the function for this, you click on the *Define graph. group* pushbutton. It affects all of the fields contained in the block just marked.

The radio buttons do not necessarily have to appear directly under each other. You can also organize them into several columns or insert blank lines between the individual fields. You do not have to convert all fields together into radio buttons; you can also do this field by field. The fullscreen editor does require, however, that you exit the tool for graphic elements after every definition of a graphic element. After you have defined all of the radio buttons, you must then create the graphic group. To do this, you place the

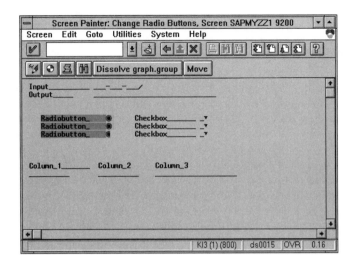

Figure 3.31   Editing of graphic elements

cursor on the element in the upper left-hand corner and click on the *Graphical element* pushbutton to call the tool for editing graphic elements. Since the cursor is already located on a graphic element, the function for group definition is immediately available. You now place the cursor in the lower right-hand corner, enclosing in a rectangle all of the fields that you want included in the group. You then create the group by clicking on the appropriate pushbutton.

To ungroup radio buttons or to change a radio button back into a field template, you need only place the cursor on the element in question and click on the *Graphical element* pushbutton again. In the next fullscreen editor screen, only the functions that are available for the marked element appear for use. Thus, the fullscreen editor works in a context-sensitive, or object-oriented, manner. To reverse a characteristic (grouping or radio button), you use *Dissolve graph. group* or *Delete graphic*, respectively.

Check boxes
Check boxes are similar to radio buttons, except that they are not interdependent. The user can mark as many check boxes as desired in a screen. It is therefore not necessary to combine check boxes into a group. Check boxes, like radio buttons, must be linked to a data element. Check boxes have the same requirements for their properties as radio buttons. For every check box that is marked, an X is entered in the data element.

You create check boxes the same way you create radio buttons, except you use the *Check Boxes* pushbutton instead of *Radio Buttons*. In the fullscreen editor, check boxes are distinguished from radio buttons by their icon, which is a small square with diagonals.

Box
A group box serves only to set visual boundaries for fields; it has no functionality of its own. You can create a group box in a screen only in connection with a screen field, and this field may not be an input field. This means that both key fields and field templates for

which the *Input field* attribute was deselected can serve as the basis for a group box. Using field templates makes it possible to set the group box heading dynamically in the program.

To create a group box, you must first create a screen field. This field may reference a Dictionary field. If the field should be a key field, it is simple to copy a (static) identifier from the Dictionary. If it is not possible to copy an appropriate text from the Dictionary, you can also create the key field for the group box manually by entering the desired identifier in the fullscreen editor. When you position the field, you need to make sure that the upper left corner of the group box is created directly to the left of the screen field. Headings in group box header lines are always left-aligned; other alignments are not possible.

If the field already exists, position the cursor on the field and click on the *Graphical element* pushbutton. In the next screen, you can begin group box creation by clicking on the *Box* pushbutton. The status changes again, as is immediately visible in the changed pushbutton bar. Now mark the lower right-hand corner of the group box by positioning the cursor, then press the pushbutton for *Mark box end* or double-click with the mouse. The group box may not touch any other screen fields or intersect them. The fullscreen editor recognizes such errors and rejects them.

In the fullscreen editor, the group box's horizontal lines are marked with the tilde (~), while vertical lines are marked with different-colored fields.

Pushbuttons
In addition to the pushbuttons in the user interface's pushbutton bar, you can create similar control elements in the screen. The function codes triggered by screen pushbuttons are fully equivalent to those of the user interface. Like frames, screen pushbuttons are based on an existing field. This field can be either a label or a field template with no input capability. The latter kind allows you to set the text displayed in the pushbutton dynamically.

Pushbutton creation is similar to the creation of elements already described. You create an appropriate screen field, place the cursor on this field, and then click on the *Graphical element* pushbutton. In the next screen, the *Pushbuttons* pushbutton is then available for turning the field into a pushbutton. In the fullscreen editor's general screen, you must then still assign a function code and a function type to the pushbutton.

Pushbuttons can be linked to icons. You can insert an icon in addition to text, or you can give a pushbutton just an icon and no text. Some of the popups in the development environment, for example the one in Figure 3.29, make use of this feature.

When assigning icons, you must take into consideration the screen field's type. For labels, you can assign an icon directly in the attributes popup using the *Icon Name* attribute. The possible entries help for this attribute offers for selection all of the valid icons and their identifiers. The procedure for field templates is more time-consuming.

Subscreen
Subscreens were already mentioned in the discussion on screen attributes. This type of screen can be incorporated in another screen dynamically as an Include at the application's runtime. The superordinate screen must reserve a special area for the subscreen's screen. For simplicity's sake, this area is also called a subscreen. Several such subscreens can be incorporated in a single screen. Each of them receives a unique identifier that is up

to 10 characters long. Subscreens make it possible to easily insert the user's functions into standard SAP programs, assuming these programs allow expansion using subscreen incorporation at all.

To create a subscreen area, you position the cursor in the upper left-hand corner of the area that you want to incorporate. You then click on the *Subscreen* pushbutton or choose the menu function *Edit → Subscreen*. In a popup, the Screen Painter asks for the name of the subscreen area. You can select any name desired. After you confirm your entry, the Screen Painter fills the maximum available space in the screen with a block that consists of dots and is highlighted in color. You position the cursor at the desired end of the subscreen (lower right-hand corner). You then confirm the size of the subscreen by clicking on the *Mark end of area* pushbutton, double-clicking with the mouse or choosing the menu function *Edit → Mark subscreen end*.

Loops

The screen elements described so far are meant for processing a single data record at a time. This has a negative effect on the ergonomics and speed of an application. Loops make it possible to process several of a table's data records simultaneously. Loops require certain statements in the runtime logic. The program's handling of loops is the focus of the following section.

A loop consists of a number of blocks, each of which can consists of several lines with several elements (screen fields). To create a loop, you first create one of these blocks in the fullscreen editor. This block is the template for the structure of the loop, which consists of multiple repetitions of this block. After creating the block, you position the cursor on the field that is uppermost and farthest to the left, then click on the *Loop* pushbutton. The fullscreen editor switches into another editing mode, in which you mark the end of the template block, that is, the field that is lowermost and furthest to the right in the block to be repeated, by double clicking on the desired lower right corner or positioning the cursor and clicking on *Mark loop block end*. The Screen Painter automatically creates a copy of the marked block directly underneath it. Both the template block and the copy are highlighted in a separate color. The fullscreen editor remains in loop editing mode, but makes a new status available with several new functions. Figure 3.32 shows the development user interface at this point.

When a loop is first created, it is created as a so-called fixed loop. A fixed loop is always displayed in the finished screen with as many fields as have been defined in the fullscreen editor. Since the Screen Painter first creates a loop consisting of only two blocks, you can extend the loop area to the current cursor position. You do this by positioning the cursor on the desired end line and then clicking on the *Mark end of loop* pushbutton.

There is another pushbutton, or menu function, that lets you convert a fixed loop into a variable loop. When the screen size changes, the number of visible lines adjusts itself to the current window size. Distances to other screen fields remain intact when the number of lines changes. What matters here is the distance of these fields from the loop area in the fullscreen editor. If another field is inserted two lines below a variable loop, the two lines under the loop will remain empty, even if the window size changes. If a group box is placed around a variable loop, the size of the box changes with the size of the loop.

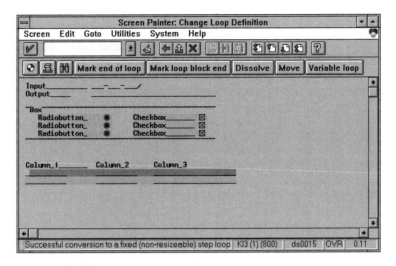

Figure 3.32   Editing loops in the fullscreen editor

There is a peculiarity that should be noted in connection with the positioning of labels for a loop. If the labels are located inside the loop block with the field templates, they are automatically repeated in every subsequent block. This often complicates the screen. It is therefore possible to position labels outside the actual loop in the form of a table heading. In this case, the labels and field templates are located in different screen areas, which is not allowed by the Screen Painter. An error message to this effect appears when the screen is generated. In this instance, you can access the reference table for the labels using a second table name, which consists of the actual table name preceded by an asterisk (*). You need to specify this table in the declaration part of the application, too, that is,

```
TABLES: *KNA1, KNA1.
```

You can copy the labels and the field templates into the screen using two separate calls to the insertion tool. But you can also change the field name manually in the field list.

Table control
Beginning with Release 3.0, features known as table controls (see Figure 3.33) simplify the display and processing of data in screens. Currently, there is only one table control variant, called *Table view*. This is a modern variant of step loops. Table views offer a table work area that, unlike a loop, does not consist of individual screen fields that are visually distinct, but rather appears as a self-contained object. The use of table views requires special statements in the runtime logic that resemble those for step loops.

You create a table view, similar to a loop, by clicking on a pushbutton or choosing the menu function *Edit → Table Control*. After calling this function, you record the name of the table view in a popup. In the module pool, you must later create a field that has the same name and the TABLEVIEW type, using the CONTROLS statement.

After assigning the name for the table view, you edit it in a specific screen. You set the size of the table view by double-clicking on any desired spot in the screen. You insert the

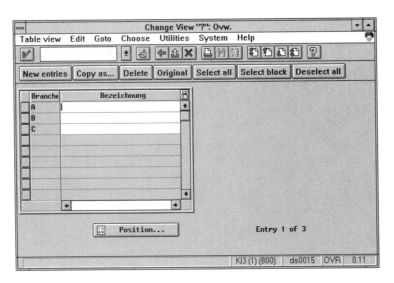

Figure 3.33   Screen with a table view

fields to be displayed in this area by clicking on the *TC fields* pushbutton. A popup appears
in which you must enter the field names. In this popup, you can use the possible entries
help for screens for Dictionary fields by clicking on a pushbutton.

Icons
Beginning with Release 3.0, it is possible to use icons in screens, too. Note that the term
icon here does not mean the same thing as symbol. The SAP system uses both icons and
symbols. These are two different elements! At this point, only icons will be discussed,
since only they can be used in screens.

Icons can only be assigned in certain non-input fields. This includes labels, output
fields, and pushbuttons. You make assignments to labels in the attributes popup. The system provides an appropriate field there, with possible entries help. This assignment is static, meaning it cannot be changed at runtime.

Dynamic assignment of icons is possible in field templates, in which the *Input field*
attribute must be deselected. Two actions are required for this. In the screen, you should
mark the *With icon* attribute for the field in question. This is not absolutely required, but
it helps the Screen Painter calculate the field's output length accurately. The second step
consists of assigning the icon to the field. You cannot assign the name of the icon directly.
Instead, the function module ICON_CREATE converts the name of the icon into a special
character string, which you assign to the data element. A function module, to put it
simply, is a special subroutine. Function modules are discussed in more detail later.
Several parameters that influence the appearance of the display field must be passed to
the module mentioned. You can pass several optional parameters to the function module
mentioned in order to influence some of the icon's display options.

Attributes of screen fields

If you place the cursor on a screen field, you can display and maintain the field attributes by choosing the menu function *Edit → Attributes* or clicking on the pushbutton of the same name. The attributes appear in a popup, as seen in Figure 3.34.

Not every attribute can be maintained for each of the field types described below. You will find more specific information about this in the description of the field types. The attributes are described as an introduction here. In Release 3.0, the attributes popup is divided into five sections. The upper section contains input or display fields for the general attributes. The middle section of the screen consists of three columns with logically related attributes. At the bottom of the popup are two fields that belong to the Dictionary group but do not fit in that column due to their length.

Field type

The field type provides information about the type of field and about its appearance on the finished screen. You cannot set or change it in the popup. A newly created field is at first either a label (an identifier) or a field template (input field). You can change the field type using the Screen Painter tools; this also changes the appearance of the input element.

Field name

Most screen fields must be linked to a data or table field for data transfer to be possible. The name of this field is stored in this attribute. You can change it in the popup.

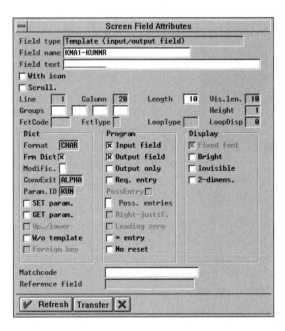

Figure 3.34 Popup for maintaining the attributes of a screen field

Field text
The contents of this field depend on the field type. For screen fields with an input or output function, the place holder found in the fullscreen editor appears here. For input fields, this usually consists of underscores (_). Often, however, the place holder contains wildcards. For details, see the description of field types.

For fields that do not allow direct input (for example, labels, frames, pushbuttons), the field text corresponds to the identifier later visible in the screen.

With icon
Starting with Release 3.0, icons can be used in screens. These icons can be set statically as an attribute of a screen field (see *Icon name*), but they can also be displayed dynamically in output fields. For this, you create an output field and mark the *With icon* field. In the PBO module, a function module then derives an identifier for the icon, based on the icon name. This identifier is then assigned to the data field that works with the output field of the screen. The icon then appears in the screen instead of the identifier.

Icon name
Fields of a certain type (pushbuttons and labels) can be supplemented with an icon or can consist of only an icon. For these fields, the *Icon name* input field is active. Using the possible entries help key, you can determine which icon names are available.

Quick info
If the mouse pointer pauses briefly on an icon, a descriptive text appears directly under the icon in a field highlighted in color. You enter this text in the *Quick info* field. When you select an icon, a default value is placed in this field, which you can overwrite.

Scroll.
For input fields that are not based on certain Dictionary data types (TIMS, DATS, QUAN, CURR, DEC, INT1 or INT2), you can choose a visible length for the input field that is smaller than the total length. This is only possible if you mark the *Scroll* field. When the field contents are processed, the contents are scrolled when the left or right field margin is reached.

Line, Column
These two fields contain the coordinates for the screen field. You can change these coordinates only by moving the field to the fullscreen editor. In the attributes popup, these fields are purely display fields.

Length, Vis.len.
The defined length of a screen field indicates the maximum number of characters this field can accept and process. For input fields, the screen field's defined length must concur with the length of the corresponding data field, otherwise the contents of the data field are cut off. This may be desirable in certain cases, for example if numbers should be entered with a maximum number of places that is smaller than the maximum possible value. When screen fields are created with the fullscreen editor's possible entries help, the defined length is copied from the underlying data element.

The visual length is the width of the field that is visible on the screen. This usually corresponds to the defined length. Beginning with Release 3.0, scrollable fields are possible. If the *Scroll* attribute is set, you can select a visual length that is smaller than the defined length. During editing, the field contents are scrolled when the left or right boundary is reached.

Height
This output field represents the height of the screen element in question.

Groups
In the internal description of a screen field, four fields are maintained that have the names GROUP1 through GROUP4. These fields and their contents are analyzed during the dynamic layout of a screen. You can use the four input fields of the *Groups* attribute to enter any values in these four fields. They do not have a direct effect on the display of the field on the screen; they are just a kind of classification. Several detailed examples follow for dynamic editing of screens.

FctCode, FctType
You can define pushbuttons not only in the user interface status, but also in screens. Each of these must, of course, also have a function code, which in turn identifies a function type. For screen pushbuttons, you can set both values in the attributes popup. The values are not compared to the user interface function list! This creates a dangerous situation, since you could create identical function codes with different function types. Since the function type is not displayed during debugging of an application, seemingly inexplicable abnormalities may crop up when the function code is analyzed.

LoopType, LoopDisp
To simplify editing of mass data, it is possible to edit several data records of a table simultaneously in one screen. You do this with a particular input element called a loop. This loop can have one of two different types, which provide information about the number of input lines in the loop. Loops with the type *Fix* have a fixed number of lines, independent of the size of the window. This number is visible in the *LoopDisp* field. You can change the number of lines only by editing the loop in the fullscreen. In loops with the type *Variable*, the number of loop lines is adjusted to the size of the window. Although the number of loop lines from the fullscreen editor still appears in the *LoopDisp* field, this has no effect on the screen display.

Format
This display field contains the data format of the data field to which the screen field has been linked. In the case of fields with a Dictionary reference, the data type is set automatically. If the linked data element is a program-internal field without a Dictionary reference, you must enter the data type here. To do so, you should use the possible entries help (F4), since not all data types are permissible in screens.

Frm Dict
With this check box, you specify whether all of the information for this screen field should be copied from the corresponding Dictionary field. In the case of field templates, for example, this affects the length; in the case of labels, this affects the field text.

Modific.
Using the possible entries help, you can copy various key texts from the Dictionary. You can also modify these pieces of text afterwards. This attribute indicates whether any (and if so, which) of the three key texts are used in unchanged or in modified form. The possible entries help for this field shows all of the available values.

ConvExit
Conversion routines can be activated during input or output of fields. These are stored in the system in the form of function modules. These function modules have the names CONVERSION_EXIT_xxxxx_INPUT and CONVERSION_EXIT_xxxxx_OUTPUT. Because of their predefined structure, only five characters are required to identify them. You can enter these in the *ConvExit* field.

Param. ID, SET param., GET param.
Parameters are data elements that cross transaction boundaries. They can be filled and read with the statements GET PARAMETER and SET PARAMETER. The use of the ABAP/4 statements is not necessary for screen fields. You release the data transfer with the SET parameter flag or the GET parameter flag. This allows you, for example, to automatically use important labels as default values in screens.

Up./lower
If this field is marked, upper- and lowercase letters are taken over unchanged. If the field is not marked, they are converted to uppercase letters. This may be a good idea for labels, to ensure a consistently clear format.

W/o template
Some characters, such as the question mark (?) and the exclamation point (!), have a special meaning in input fields. With this flag, you can turn off analysis of these characters, so that they can be entered just like other characters.

Foreign key
For every field for which a foreign key check has been defined in the Dictionary, inputs are also checked against the check tables, regardless of possible field checks in the flow logic. This type of checking must be turned on with this flag. If no automatic foreign key checking is desired, you can deactivate this flag.

Reference field
This attribute is only filled for currency or unit-of-measure fields. It contains a field name in which the currency or unit key is contained at runtime. This screen field is displayed according to the attributes of the currency or the unit of measure. In the case of Dictionary fields, the reference field is assigned to the table field directly.

Input field
Entered values are transferred from the screen field into the data element only if this flag is marked. In the case of key texts, this flag is deselected anyway. In the case of field

templates, it can be deactivated. The field is then inactive. This state is recognizable by the different background color of the field. The field's frame, however, remains intact.

Output field
If this flag is marked, a data transport takes place from the data element to the screen field. If this flag is not activated, the contents of the corresponding data element are not displayed. Transfer from the screen field to the data element after screen processing is not affected by this flag.

Output only
This flag is useful only for field templates. It causes the field contents to be output in the form of a label, that is, without the surrounding frame that field templates normally have. Such fields can be used to display text dynamically.

Req. entry
You can identify input fields that must always receive a value (such as labels) as mandatory input fields. After analyzing the Exit module, the screen's internal control logic checks whether the contents of the fields so identified are unequal to the initial value. If there are one or more such fields without values, a standard error message is displayed, and processing of the screen starts over.

PossEntry
This field provides information about whether value help is available for the field in question. The field serves for information only; it cannot be changed. Value or possible entries help can be created in various ways, for example with foreign key relationships, matchcodes or special statements in the runtime logic of the screen.

Poss. entries
With this attribute, you determine if existing value help should be active for this field or not. In addition, the value of this attribute has influence on when the value help symbol should be displayed next to the field. Table 3.16 shows the possible entries.

Table 3.16   Range of values for the value help key attribute

Value	Value help status	Symbol for value help visible
SPACE	value help active	when cursor in field
0	value help turned off	
1	value help active	when cursor in field
2	value help active	always

Right-justif.
The contents of the field are displayed right-aligned. Aside from numerical fields, this applies only to output fields.

Leading zero
Right-aligned numerical values in field templates are given leading zeros.

* entry
The use of this attribute is outdated. In input fields with this attribute, an asterisk (*) can be entered in the first position. In this case, a PAI module identified by a special clause is called for this field.

No reset
If the user enters an exclamation point (!) in the first position of an input field, the field is initialized in the screen after data input ends, that is, no value is transferred. You can turn this mechanism off by setting the *No reset* attribute, making it possible to enter an exclamation point in the first position of a field, too.

Matchcode
Matchcodes are special possible entries help that allow you to search for key values using non-key values. Matchcodes are generated in separate maintenance programs. They are given four-character names. If the name of a matchcode is entered in this attribute, it is possible to call up the matchcode for the screen field in question using the F4 key. The existence of a matchcode is identified in the screen field by a small, colored triangle in the upper right-hand corner.

Beginning with Release 3.0, the name of the matchcode can also be passed dynamically at runtime. In this case, the name of the field, preceded by a colon, appears in the *Matchcode* attribute. At runtime, in the PBO part of the screen, the field is filled with the name of the matchcode to be used.

Fixed font
With this field, you can cause pieces of text to be output in monospaced type in certain circumstances. This means that every character is printed with the same width.

Bright
When activated, the field is made to stand out with a different color or highlight.

Invisible
This attribute is used for fields with a password function. In fields with this attribute, input and output are not visible; instead, asterisks are displayed in the field. An example of such a field is the field for entering a password during logon to the R/3 System.

2-dimens.
Field templates and pushbuttons in the screen are displayed so they appear three-dimensional. You can turn off this function with this flag.

Processing logic

Calling of the program modules from the module pool takes place in the flow logic of a screen. The statements contained there determine the functionality of the screen. The flow logic consists of several sections, which are processed at certain points. These events are defined by four different event statements. These statements are:

- PROCESS BEFORE OUTPUT.
- PROCESS AFTER INPUT.
- PROCESS ON HELP-REQUEST.
- PROCESS ON VALUE-REQUEST.

One does not encounter all four events in every flow logic. The last two are relatively rare, since powerful mechanisms for possible entries help and support are already provided by the system. The first two statements, on the other hand, are found in almost every screen. They are therefore automatically written into the flow logic when a new screen is created.

The modules called in the different sections perform only certain actions that make sense there. Several of the actions are mentioned in the discussion that follows. Concrete programming, however, is not described in more detail until the section on module pools.

In the flow logic, certain statements are used that resemble ABAP/4 commands but are not identical to them. In principle, the commands have only one task: to call modules from the module pool. For this reason, there are only a few different commands for the flow logic. Just like ABAP/4 statements, you can modify the operation of flow logic commands with several parameters. Even if several of the commands described below bring to mind ABAP/4 commands, they have nothing in common with them except for their names. In this section, the term command refers to flow logic commands, which are sometimes also called screen commands.

The FIELD statement
In the PAI portion of a screen, you can trigger field-related activities with the FIELD statement. The commands entered in connection with FIELD then only refer to the field recorded behind FIELD. The basic form of the command is as follows:

```
FIELD: field_name.
```

In this form, the command only causes the field to be addressed, so it is useful only in a CHAIN–ENCHAIN chain. If no clauses follow, you can address several fields by using the colon variant:

```
FIELD: field_name_1, field_name_2, ... field_name_n.
```

More important is the linking of the FIELD statement to the MODULE statement in the following form:

```
FIELD field_name MODULE module_name.
```

The module is called. If an error message is created in the module, only the field specified in the FIELD statement becomes input-ready again. Other clauses, which belong to the MODULE statement and are described there, allow you to make processing of the module dependent on certain prerequisites.

A second variant of the FIELD statement makes a direct test of a field against a table possible, without having to write a separate module for that. It is as follows:

FIELD *field_name* **SELECT** ...

The SELECT statement is also available as an independent statement. It is therefore described separately. In connection with FIELD, when an error message is triggered in the SELECT statement, only the specified field is input-ready.

The last variant of the FIELD statement can be used only for fields of type CHAR and NUMC. It checks the field against a list of values recorded directly in the source code:

FIELD *field_name* **VALUES** (*value_list*).

The value list, which must be enclosed in parentheses, consists of one or more individual values. These must be enclosed in single quotes and separated by commas. You can use the NOT operator to identify a non-permissible value, and you can use BETWEEN AND or NOT BETWEEN AND to identify valid and invalid ranges.

Several of the described clauses can be used in a single FIELD statement. In this case, they must appear in the following form:

```
FIELD field_name :  VALUES ...  ,
                    MODULE ...  ,
                    ...            .
```

The MODULE statement

You call modules from the module pool with the following statement:

MODULE *module_name*.

This statement can be used for all four events. There are several clauses for this statement with which you can influence the operation. The clause

... AT EXIT-COMMAND.

which was already demonstrated in an example, causes the module to be called only when a type E function code is triggered. This clause is therefore only useful in the PAI portion of the flow logic. The typical activities triggered by an Exit function code involve exiting the screen. For this reason, only one statement with this clause makes sense per screen. It should also be the first statement of the PAI event.

All other clauses can only be implemented if the module is called in a field assignment in connection with the FIELD command. The available clauses and their effects are shown in Table 3.17.

Table 3.17   Clauses for the MODULE screen command

Clause	Effect
ON INPUT	Processing takes place only if the applicable field contains a value that is unequal to the initial value.
ON CHAIN-INPUT	Processing takes place only if at least one field in the chain contains a value that is unequal to the initial value (only useful in CHAIN chains).

Table 3.17 continued   Clauses for the MODULE screen command

Clause	Effect
ON REQUEST	Processing takes place only if an entry was made in the applicable field.
ON CHAIN-REQUEST	Processing takes place only if an entry was made in at least one of the fields of the chain (only useful in CHAIN chains).
.ON*-INPUT	Processing takes place only if an asterisk (*) has been entered in the applicable field, and the field has the asterisk input attribute.
AT CURSOR-SELECTION	Processing takes place only if a selection was made using a double-click or the F2 function key.

The CHAIN ... ENDCHAIN statements
These two commands form a frame. They usually surround a FIELD statement for several fields and one or more corresponding MODULE calls. These commands are linked by the CHAIN statement to a processing block or a processing chain. If an error message is triggered within the chain, all of the fields addressed with FIELD in the chain become input-ready again. This behavior is useful, for example, if a user must enter several key-words or other interdependent values in a screen. An error can then no longer be clearly attributed to a particular field. A sample CHAIN statement might look like this:

```
CHAIN.
   FIELD:  INVOICE-AMOUNT,
           INVOICE-PAYTYPE,
           INVOICE-CURRENCY.
   MODULE  CHECK_PAYTYPE ON CHAIN-REQUEST.
ENDCHAIN.
```

The CHECK_PAYTYPE module checks if a payment with the entered amount may be set-tled in the desired way (check, cash, credit card). For example, payments with credit cards should not fall below a threshold amount that depends on the currency. An error can also crop up if an incorrect payment type, an incorrect currency or an incorrect amount has been entered by mistake. For this reason, all three fields must be input-ready again. This can only be accomplished with a CHAIN statement. Although several fields can be recorded behind FIELD, if a module is called directly in the FIELD statement, the system only makes the last field in the field list input-ready again in the case of an error.

The SELECT statement
A special form of the SELECT statement is available within the flow logic. In the PBO section, this statement allows a data record to be read from a table and provided in a screen. In the PAI section, the statement is used to check values from the screen against a table. This screen command is rarely usable in new development these days. It can eas-ily be replaced by a module; there are easier-to-use variants of the SELECT statement available.

The basic form of the flow logic SELECT statement is as follows:

```
SELECT * FROM   table
   WHERE table_field = input_field ...
```

Several selection requirements may be specified in the WHERE clause, although only an equals-test is possible. The only operator allowed is the equal sign. Any fields from the current program can be used in the WHERE clause; the fields are not restricted to the fields of the current screen. It is therefore possible to make the selection depend on values recorded in other screens. For example, one could query labels in one screen and read a data record in the PBO section of the subsequent screens based on these labels. To do this, you would need to place the contents of the data record read in the header line of the table. You do this with the clause

```
... INTO table_name
```

It can only be transferred into the header of a Dictionary table; the screen fields must be directly linked to the table fields. Without the INTO clause, the SELECT statement would find the data record, but it could not prepare it for additional processing. This behavior is useful, for example, in the PAI section in relation to checks.

The result of the SELECT statement can affect the subsequent program flow. The only method for influencing the program flow within the flow logic consists of sending messages. There are two clauses for this that can be made to depend on the result of the search procedure. The clause

```
WHENEVER NOT FOUND
   SEND ERRORMESSAGE number WITH value_list.
```

sends an error message if the data selection was not successful. You can also use FOUND instead of NOT FOUND to trigger the error message if a record already exists. With the WARNING clause instead of the ERRORMESSAGE clause, you can change the hard error message (processing of the screen from the beginning) into a warning. A warning does not restart screen processing. After the warning is confirmed with the Enter key (or a corresponding symbol), processing of the screen continues.

It is not absolutely necessary to send an individual error message. The system generates a standard error message if there is no WHENEVER clause and data selection was not successful. This behavior is usually undesirable in the PBO section. SELECT statements in the PBO section therefore usually send a warning if the data record could not be found.

The SELECT statement can, as already mentioned for the FIELD command, be used as a clause for this statement. In this case, the field linked to FIELD becomes input-ready again, if the SELECT statement creates an error message. If several fields should become input-ready again, SELECT should be used with a FIELD statement for several fields in a CHAIN chain. The following three examples are typical for the use of the SELECT statement.

1. Search for a data record in the PBO section:

```
PROCESS BEFORE OUTPUT.
...
SELECT * FROM KNA1
```

```
WHERE KUNNR = KNA1-KUNNR
WHENEVER NOT FOUND
   SEND WARNING 123 WITH KNA1-KUNNR.
```

2. Checking of a single field in the PAI section with a standard message:

```
FIELD KNA1-KUNNR SELECT * FROM KNA1
   WHERE KUNNR = KNA1-KUNNR.
```

3. SELECT in a CHAIN chain:

```
CHAIN.
   FIELD: INVOICE-PAYTYPE
          INVOICE-CURRENCY.
   SELECT * FROM ZULZART
     WHERE PAYTYPE = INVOICE-PAYTYPE
       AND CURRENCY = INVOICE-CURRENCY
     WHENEVER NOT FOUND
       SEND ERRORMESSAGE 345.
ENDCHAIN
```

The LOOP and ENDLOOP statements

Loops were already mentioned in the section on visual elements of the screens. They enable processing of several data records in one screen. Since the individual blocks of a loop represent copies of a template block and therefore contain identical field names, it is not possible to address the fields of these blocks directly. For this reason, a special statement is needed for processing the individual blocks in the loop areas of a screen.

The two statements LOOP and ENDLOOP in the flow logic form a loop in which all of the blocks of the loop area in the screen are processed once. During this event, the fields of the current block can be addressed by their field names. Field content processing, of course, must be done in a module that is called in the LOOP program loop.

You need such a loop for the PAI event, to fill the screen fields with data, and for the PBO event, to check data and, if necessary, write data to the database table. If there is no LOOP–ENDLOOP program loop, generation of a screen with a step loop area causes an error message. A simple flow logic for a screen with a loop area might look something like this:

```
PROCESS BEFORE OUTPUT.
...
  LOOP.
    MODULE INIT_LINE.
  ENDLOOP.
*
PROCESS AFTER INPUT.
...
  LOOP.
    MODULE PROCESS_LINE.
  ENDLOOP.
```

With these statements, for example, you could record several invoice line items in a screen and write them to a database table in the PROCESS_LINE module.

If you want to be able to page through large data sets using a loop, there are several additional tasks to perform. The LOOP statement in its basic form, as presented above, supports only the data transport from and to the loop block of the screen. If this block represents only a section of a larger data set, the programmer must handle the management of this section and ensure correct data transport. In particular, he or she must record values that may have changed and determine the data area to be output in dependence on the paging function (page down, page up, home, end). There are two simple and thus often-used methods for programming such a paging or scrolling function. Both are based on the use of internal tables, since these allow simple, index-controlled access to data records. The data records to be processed are placed in an internal table before screen execution and are written from the internal table back to the database after screen processing ends.

The first variant uses the basic form of the LOOP statement, as already presented in a short program section. It is based on an index that is managed separately from the actual LOOP statement. Paging is possible in an internal table using the function keys F21 through F24.

A demonstration of this procedure requires the creation of a complete application with a screen, flow logic, a user interface and a transaction. You can either create a new application using the demo application in this section as a template (fullscreen and flow logic must be empty here), or you can modify the demo application. The first of these two methods is preferable. Give the program you create the name SAPMYZZ2.

First, declare the following data fields in the declaration portion of the module pool:

```
DATA: BEGIN OF ITAB OCCURS 20,
  Z TYPE I,
END OF ITAB.

DATA: FCODE LIKE SY-UCOMM,
      ITAB_OFFSET LIKE SY-TABIX,
      TABLEN TYPE I,
      I TYPE I,
      DYNPRO_ZEILEN LIKE SY-TFILL.
```

After you have defined the global data (*Dynpro Zeilen* means screen lines), you must generate the program. Generation is not required for the program to function, but it is necessary so that the insertion tool can find the program-internal data fields when it subsequently processes the screen. The screen is then processed. Enter the screen's own screen number as the subsequent screen to ensure that the application functions correctly. The screen must always call itself. In the fullscreen, create a loop area with about five blocks. Each of the loop lines should contain just one input field without a label. The fields are based on the ITAB-Z field. When you use the possible entries help (*Goto* → *Dict./program fields*), enter the field name ITAB-Z and click on the *Get from program* pushbutton. Now change the step loop into a variable loop. To do so, position the cursor on the first line of the loop, then call the menu function *Edit* → *Loop* and, in the next screen, *Edit* → *Convert loop* → *Variable loop*.

After you finish editing in the fullscreen, you must link the screen's OK field to the FCODE data field (enter it in the field list). After the fullscreen is edited, you create the flow logic:

```
PROCESS BEFORE OUTPUT.
  MODULE INIT.

  LOOP.
    MODULE READ_ITAB.
  ENDLOOP.
*
PROCESS AFTER INPUT.
  MODULE EXIT AT EXIT-COMMAND.
  LOOP.
    MODULE CHANGE_ITAB.
  ENDLOOP.

  MODULE FCODE.
```

You can now generate the screen. You use the navigation mechanism (double-click on the module name) to create the modules. The source code for the modules is shown in the following listing:

```
MODULE INIT OUTPUT.

  SET PF-STATUS 'STAT1'.

  DESCRIBE TABLE ITAB  LINES TABLEN.
  IF TABLEN = 0.
    DO 20 TIMES.
        ITAB-Z  = ITAB-Z  + 1.
        APPEND ITAB.
    ENDDO.
    TABLEN = 20.
    ITAB_OFFSET = 1.
  ENDIF.

ENDMODULE.
```

The INIT module performs two tasks. First it loads the STAT1 status. You need to create this status, too (or change it if you are modifying the demo application). Link the function keys F21 through F24 to the function codes FT21 through FT24 (beginning with Release 3.0C, the corresponding paging icons from the toolbar, which correspond to the virtual function keys V80 through V83). These function keys are usually used for scrolling functions. Later in the application, depending on the release version, they can be triggered with the four icons that appear all the way to the right in the toolbar, with the function keys Shift-F9 through Shift-F12, or with the PgUp, PgDn, Ctrl-PgUp and Ctrl-PgDn keys. In addition, you must link the F12 function key to the FT12 function code, which you must give function type "E". This makes it possible to end the application in an orderly fashion.

The second task of the module consists of initializing the internal table. Its length is limited to 20 lines. This is enough for a demonstration. If necessary, of course, you can select a greater length. The table may be initialized only when the application is processed the first time. You can use the length of the table as an indicator for this. You need to give the data record pointer ITAB_OFFSET and a help field, TABLEN, correct values in this section, as well.

The second module is called in the LOOP statement. When a screen LOOP program loop is executed, the system counts the number of iterations in the SY-STEPL field. This number therefore equals the number of the current loop block in the screen. You can derive the table line to be displayed from the starting value ITAB_OFFSET and the number of the loop block. Since you linked the screen field directly to the table field, the flow logic transfers the value of the table field automatically into the screen. The help field I is required because the READ statement expects a value as an index. It cannot process any expressions.

```
MODULE READ_ITAB OUTPUT.
   DYNPRO_ZEILEN = SY-LOOPC.
   I = ITAB_OFFSET + SY-STEPL - 1.
   READ TABLE ITAB INDEX I.
ENDMODULE.
```

The assignment to the DYNPRO_ZEILEN field is not necessary for the module's function. It just saves the number of loop blocks currently displayed in the screen for later analysis in the FCODE module. The contents of the SY-LOOPC system field are only current within the LOOP program loop! It is therefore absolutely necessary to store it in a program-internal field. The modules that follow belong to PAI processing.

```
MODULE EXIT INPUT.
   SET SCREEN 0.
   LEAVE SCREEN.
ENDMODULE.

MODULE CHANGE_ITAB INPUT.
   I = ITAB_OFFSET + SY-STEPL - 1.
   MODIFY ITAB INDEX I.
ENDMODULE.
```

In the CHANGE_ITAB module, the contents of the screen field are transferred into the internal table. You derive the record to be changed, just like in READ_ITAB, using the specification of an offset and the loop counter of the LOOP statement.

```
MODULE FCODE INPUT.

   CASE FCODE.
      WHEN 'FT21'.
         ITAB_OFFSET = 1.

      WHEN 'FT22'.
         ITAB_OFFSET = ITAB_OFFSET - DYNPRO_ZEILEN.
```

```
      WHEN 'FT23'.
         ITAB_OFFSET = ITAB_OFFSET + DYNPRO_ZEILEN.

      WHEN 'FT24'.
         ITAB_OFFSET = TABLEN - DYNPRO_ZEILEN + 1.

   ENDCASE.

   I = TABLEN - DYNPRO_ZEILEN + 1.
   IF ITAB_OFFSET > I.
     ITAB_OFFSET = I.
   ENDIF.

   IF ITAB_OFFSET < 1.
     ITAB_OFFSET = 1.
   ENDIF.

ENDMODULE.
```

The FCODE module in this example only analyzes the function codes for scrolling. Based on this function code and some global values, the starting value ITAB_OFFSET is recalculated. The display of the lines selected this way then occurs in the READ_ITAB module.

For testing, you should select the window size so that about five step loop lines are displayed. You can change the internal table's data fields as desired in the screen. Presetting with numbers is just for orientation purposes. The internal table is used in this example only because such tables can be read relatively easily with the index. The program structure would easily allow data to be read from other sources, for example database tables, based on the unique index. In practice, however, one rarely makes use of this capability, because working with internal tables improves the application's runtime behavior. The advantage of this variant is that you can analyze the concrete action based on the function code. Depending on the function desired, you can execute other commands together with scrolling through the data set. You could, for example, read just a portion of the database table into the internal table and read additional data only if necessary.

If all of the data to be processed is available in its entirety in an internal table, you can use a special form of the LOOP statement that requires less programming. You can specify the table to be processed directly in the LOOP statement. You must also define a so-called cursor and use it in the PBO section. In the PAI section, on the other hand, the CURSOR clause is not necessary.

```
LOOP AT internal_table CURSOR cursor.
   ...
ENDLOOP.
```

In this form, the LOOP statement inserts a vertical scroll bar into the screen. This scroll bar allows the internal table to be scrolled in the loop area. The communication between the scroll bar and the LOOP statement takes place automatically; the programmer does not need to create or analyze a function code. The function keys F21 through F24 and the icons in the toolbar should not be given function codes, as this could lead to undesirable side effects with the scroll bar.

The cursor serves as a data record pointer. It must be derived from the SY-INDEX field. In the LOOP statements, it receives the index of the data record currently being processed; outside the LOOP statement, it receives the index of the first data record displayed in the loop. The value of this field can be dynamically set in the program. This, like activation of the scroll bar, causes movement through the list.

It is much easier to design an application with the LOOP AT ITAB statement, since you can avoid the analysis of the function code and the calculation of the data record index. An example is presented for this, too; it is based on the preceding demo application. You can modify it or create a new application.

The first change affects the status. It should now contain only the F12 function key with the function code FT12, which you can use to end the application. You can erase (or not create) the assignment to the function keys F21 through F24. This makes the flow logic just a bit simpler.

```
PROCESS BEFORE OUTPUT.
  MODULE INIT.
  LOOP AT ITAB CURSOR I.
  ENDLOOP.

*
PROCESS AFTER INPUT.
  MODULE EXIT AT EXIT-COMMAND.
  LOOP AT ITAB.
    MODULE CHANGE_ITAB.
  ENDLOOP.
```

Real simplification is possible in the modules. You can leave out all of the help fields for calculating indexes. This makes the declaration portion much shorter.

```
DATA: BEGIN OF ITAB OCCURS 20,
  Z TYPE I,
END OF ITAB.

DATA: FCODE LIKE SY-UCOMM,
        I LIKE SY-INDEX.
```

The INIT module can, of course, also be simplified, since only the internal table must be filled.

```
MODULE INIT OUTPUT.
DATA TABLEN TYPE I.

  SET PF-STATUS 'STAT1'.

  DESCRIBE TABLE ITAB  LINES TABLEN.
  IF TABLEN = 0.
    DO 20 TIMES.
      ITAB-Z  = ITAB-Z  + 1.
```

```
      APPEND ITAB.
   ENDDO.
 ENDIF.

ENDMODULE.
```

The flow logic's LOOP statement automatically reads the record from the internal table and performs the transfer into the screen fields. The READ_ITAB module is therefore superfluous. You can take the EXIT module over from the preceding example unchanged. You need not analyze any function codes besides FT12, so you can leave out the FCODE module. The remaining module, CHANGE_ITAB, is still needed, but it can also be simplified:

```
MODULE CHANGE_ITAB INPUT.
   MODIFY ITAB INDEX I.
ENDMODULE.
```

The I cursor always contains the correct data record number, not just the line number in the screen. The cursor can therefore be used immediately to write a data record back into the internal table.

The LOOP statement for an internal table can also process the following clauses, in addition to the CURSOR clause:

FROM *start*

and

TO *end*

The fields START and END must also be derived from SY-INDEX. You must provide them dynamically in the program; directly entered values are not permissible. The specifications restrict the scroll area to the data records between the two limits. If one of the values is missing, the first or last data record is assumed to be the limit.

The only thing that happens in the LOOP statements is data transfer. If internal tables are to be processed, you can sometimes use additional function codes to process a selected data record from a screen, for example to insert new records or delete existing records. From the user's point of view, these actions are especially easy if the data record to be edited on the screen is identified by the position of the cursor, and no marking of fields or other such action is necessary. Programming such functions requires determining inside the PAI module but outside the LOOP program loop in which loop block the cursor is positioned, then determining from this specification the index of the data record. You can easily determine the loop block number with the statement

GET CURSOR LINE *line*.

This statement places the number of the current loop block in the field specified as the parameter. It should be noted that a loop block on the screen can consist of several lines. The GET statement calculates the same value for all lines of a block!

To derive the final data record number, you take the loop block number thus determined, combine it with the number of the first data record displayed in the loop

(ITAB_OFFSET in the first example, or the value of the loop cursor I in the second example) and subtract 1.

The GET CURSOR statement has several options, which also deliver useful results if the screen cursor is not located in a loop but in a simple screen field. In addition to the return parameter, the statement also delivers, in the system variable SY-SUBRC, the information about whether the screen cursor is located in a loop area (SY-SUBRC = 0) or not (SY-SUBRC = 4).

Using the statement is quite simple. The last example serves as the starting point. In the status, link the function key F2 to the function code FT02. You want this function code to insert a new record in front of the data record where the screen cursor is located, and fill the record with a value (line number + 100). You only need to write an FCODE module to analyze the function code, and incorporate this module in the flow logic.

```
MODULE FCODE INPUT.
DATA CL TYPE I.

  CASE FCODE.
    WHEN 'FT02'.
      GET CURSOR LINE CL.
      IF SY-SUBRC = 0.
        CL = CL + I - 1.
        ITAB-Z = CL + 100.
        INSERT ITAB INDEX CL.
      ENDIF.

  ENDCASE.

ENDMODULE
```

In addition to maintaining internal tables, another variant of LOOP can cooperate directly with database tables. The syntax for this variant of the LOOP statement is as follows:

```
LOOP AT Dictionary-table.
ENDLOOP.
```

This statement carries out a series of actions in the background. It has considerably more functionality than its similarity to the basic form of the LOOP statement would lead one to believe. This variant of the LOOP statement assumes the existence of a specially structured screen. In addition to the actual loop area, whose input fields you link to the header line of the database table, a second input area must exist in the screen for the table's key fields. You also link these input fields to the database table, but you use the asterisk variant of the name. You do not have to declare the tables with the TABLES statement.

The typical flow logic consists of just a few lines:

```
PROCESS BEFORE OUTPUT.
  LOOP AT Dictionary-table.
  ENDLOOP.
```

```
*
PROCESS AFTER INPUT.
  LOOP AT Dictionary-table.
    MODIFY Dictionary-table.
  ENDLOOP.
```

The PBO LOOP command fills the loop blocks with the first data records of the table. In the PAI loop, the contents of the loop block are written back into the table. For once, no module is required for this. In loops in Dictionary tables (and only there), you can use a screen variant of the MODIFY command.

The hidden functions of this LOOP statement affect paging in the table. Pressing the Enter key causes the system to read the contents of the input fields based on the * table. The system searches for these values in the database table. If such a record exists, it becomes the first record in the loop area. If no such record exists, the system places the record that is next closest to the search pattern in the first loop block. If the fields for the search pattern are empty, the flow logic pages down one screen.

LOOP program loops in a database table are rarely used in custom programs, since you can use other programming methods that are much easier to use to create applications. Until Release 2.2, this form of LOOP statement was used mainly in automatically generated maintenance programs. For certain tables, something called *Table maintenance* may be allowed in the Data Dictionary. Using a certain menu function (create table screen), the Dictionary creates a program and a screen that satisfies the requirements listed above. These programs can be called indirectly with the SM31 transaction or the function *System → Services → Table maintenance*. The transaction mentioned asks the user for the name of a table, then calls the applicable maintenance screen. This simple data maintenance capability is often used in the editing of various system tables and in Customizing. It is not at all unusual to further edit the general table maintenance modules manually after they have been created. If the table screens are regenerated, however, these additions are lost. In contrast to the usual naming conventions, the created module pools begin with the three letters MST, followed by the name of the table. Since the name of a module pool may be no more than eight characters long, such a maintenance program can only be created for tables whose names have a maximum of five characters.

Beginning with Release 3.0, other tools are available for table maintenance that generate considerably more complex maintenance programs. In these programs, the variant of the LOOP statement just described no longer has any relevance.

Another variant of the LOOP statement is required for processing table views. A global data object with a unique name exists for every table view. Similar to step loops, the flow logic's LOOP statement runs through the individual lines of a table view. The basic form of this statement, which must be called in this form in both the PBO section and the PAI section, is as follows:

```
LOOP WITH CONTROL table_view.
  MODULE ... .
ENDLOOP.
```

For every line of the table view, a module is called in which the individual fields of the table line can be processed (filled or analyzed). The fields are accessible through their field names, as in loops.

In this simple form, the table view's fields must be filled manually with values. This task is simplified by another variant of the LOOP statement that works with internal tables. For the PBO event, the following statement is required:

```
LOOP AT Itab WITH CONTROL table_view CURSOR cursor.
ENDLOOP.
```

It is not necessary to fill the lines of the table view manually. At the PAI event, on the other hand, the validity of the data must be tested in a special module, and the internal table must, if necessary, be updated. For every line, the data is placed in the table header line.

```
LOOP AT Itab.
   MODULE ... .
ENDLOOP.
```

The CALL SUBSCREEN statement

The term subscreen has already been explained. It is a special screen type. In order to insert a subscreen into an existing screen at runtime, the existing screen must contain a subscreen area that is identified by a unique name. At runtime, you insert a subscreen screen into another screen with the following statement:

```
CALL SUBSCREEN area_name INCLUDING program_name screen_number.
```

This statement must, of course, appear in the PBO section of the flow logic. The area name is the name of the subscreen area as recorded in the Screen Painter. It appears in the statement directly, that is, without quotation marks. The two other parameters, *program_name* and *screen_number*, identify the subscreen screen. Either they must appear in the statement as character strings, that is, enclosed in single quotes, or data fields must be used that contain the desired values. The use of fields makes true dynamic calling of subscreens possible.

Another, somewhat simpler, statement is necessary in the PAI section of the superordinate screen:

```
CALL SUBSCREEN area_name.
```

When a subscreen screen is called with CALL, a part of its flow logic is executed. If the CALL command appears in the PBO section, only the PBO modules are executed, of course. The CALL statement in the PAI section of the superordinate screen executes the PAI modules of the embedded screen.

Embedded screens may neither change the user interface of the calling screen nor process the function code. In the field list of the subscreen screens, no data element may be assigned to the field for transferring the function code. So it is mainly field checks that are done in the flow logic of a subscreen screen.

Context-sensitive help and possible entries help

The term possible entries help has already been mentioned in the description of the screen field attributes. For every input field on the screen, you can display the available values using various mechanisms. Two of the help possibilities (implicit possible entries help and matchcodes) are based on Dictionary elements and are described there. These elements mostly take advantage of dependencies between tables that are defined in the Dictionary, called foreign keys. The possibilities for their use are numerous, but in certain cases the functionality they offer is insufficient. In those cases, you can write custom possible entries help for every screen field. You do this by calling a corresponding module at the PROCESS ON VALUE-REQUEST event. The call resembles the call of a field check:

```
PROCESS ON VALUE-REQUEST.
  FIELD KNA1-KUNNR MODULE VALUES_KUNNR.
```

This statement ensures that the symbol for possible entries help appears in the screen next to the customer number input field. Clicking on this symbol with the mouse is the same as pressing the F4 key. When this key is pressed, the application processes only the statements after the PROCESS ON VALUE-REQUEST event. If the field in which the screen cursor was located at that moment is linked to a module with the FIELD statement, this module is processed. There are no restrictions on the contents of this module. A value is determined somehow and placed in the screen field at the end of the module. As a simple test, to shed some light on this principle, you can incorporate the flow logic addition above and the following module into the sample application SAPMYZZ1.

```
MODULE VAL_KUNNR INPUT.
  KNA1-KUNNR = '9876'.
ENDMODULE.
```

When such possible entries help exists for a field, any other possible entries help that may exist for this field (foreign key or matchcode) no longer works.

Context-sensitive help, which is called with the F1 function key, works like value help. You can record, in addition to the four labels of different lengths and the short description, another piece of detailed documentation for data elements in the Dictionary. Pressing the F1 key displays this documentation in a popup, assuming it exists. If it does not exist, the short description appears.

In cases where the documentation is not informative enough, or if you want help text to be displayed for fields that have no Dictionary reference, you must use the self-programmed help function. Its usage differs from that of possible entries help in its event and the required functionality of the module. This capability is rarely used in practice.

After custom input or possible entries help modules are executed, processing of the screen starts from the beginning with the PBO event. The PAI event is not processed.

3.3.3 The user interface

Every application, whether a report or a dialog application, has exactly one user interface with control elements. Several so-called statuses are combined in one user interface. Every status represents an independent instance of the user interface and its elements. It has at its disposal the function codes and the control elements for triggering these. You use the Menu Painter to edit the user interface or status. You access this tool from the main menu of the development environment *(Development → Menu Painter)*, from the object list of the

Object Browser, or from the navigation mechanism of the program editor. Like with other elements, it is enough to enter the name of a status in a program and double-click on this name with the mouse. This loads the Menu Painter for the desired status. The transaction code for this tool is SE41.

The Menu Painter's scope of functionality is limited because of its limited task area. In principle, this consists only of creating control elements and function codes and assigning them to each other. Despite the Menu Painter's rather complex user interface, it is relatively simple to use. In user interface maintenance, you can work in either a status-oriented or an element-oriented fashion. Status-oriented means that all of the elements of a status are available at the same time in one work interface. Element-oriented means that the menus or the function key layouts for all of the statuses of a user interface can be displayed and edited together. Beyond this, several elements (function codes, titles) in the user interface are global, although they can also be maintained from the work interface of a status.

The user interface types

A status does not exist in isolation, but is always used from within a screen or a report. For this reason, you must enter a status type when you create a new status. Currently, there are four different types.

Screen
This status type provides a user interface for normal screens. It contains all three groups of control elements, that is, a menu, function keys, and pushbuttons.

Dialog box
Screens of the type *Modal dialog box* can be executed as popups. Such popups do not have a menu; they can only be used with function keys and pushbuttons. For such screens, you create a status with the type *Dialog box*, which does not have a menu.

List
Reports also have a user interface. If this is not set explicitly, the system uses a default user interface with certain function codes that are required for list processing. If you want to change this user interface, you must give the status the type *List*. Such a status is at first no different visually from the *Screen* type. However, certain Menu Painter functions let you fill a newly created status with default values. Screens and lists have different defaults. Some of the default function codes for lists are processed directly by the system. Since they trigger basic functions (for example, list scrolling), they should always be available. This is most easily ensured if the status has the type *List* and is filled with the default values.

List in dialog box
Lists, too, can be displayed in popups. This capability is used relatively rarely, especially in connection with interactive elements of a report. The necessary status does not have a menu.

Function codes

Function codes are four-character identifiers. They are assigned to control elements. When the control element is used, the function code is passed to the application. The passing method is different in reports than in dialog applications. The function codes of all of the statuses of a user interface are contained in a common list. In order to prevent all function codes from being triggerable in all statuses, you can activate or deactivate a function code separately in each status.

You can choose the four-character identifiers for function codes as desired. Two restrictions should be noted, however. In older release versions, function codes that begin with the letter E are automatically treated as Exit function codes. If possible, you should avoid this letter as the first character of normal function codes. The second exception involves the letter P, again in the first position of an identifier. For certain statuses, the system creates defaults that contain many function codes beginning with P (for example, PICK, P+, P++, etc.). Such function codes are analyzed by the system itself. Double definitions could unintentionally distort the expected functionality of the application. You can easily avoid such problems by avoiding the letter P. For this reason, you select function codes of the form FTxx for the function keys in the introductory example.

A function code has several attributes. The most important are the function type, the text type, the text and a fastpath. The function type determines how the function code is handled by the system. The text type and the text influence the display of the function text in the menu items and pushbuttons. The fastpath defines a key that allows the function code to be selected directly in an open pulldown menu. You can edit all of these attributes in the function list (see Figure 3.35).

For every function code, the function list first displays the text or texts that are available. You can assign a function code a different text in every status. You maintain the function type in an input field in the list. Table 3.18 shows the available function types.

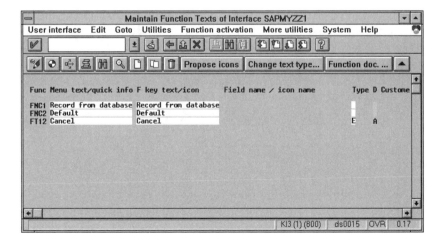

Figure 3.35   Menu Painter function list

Table 3.18   Function types

Function type	Meaning
blank space	preset, normal function code
X	normal function code
E	Exit command (analysis by an AT EXIT-COMMAND module)
T	starting of a transaction
S	system function

The effects of the default function type (blank space or X) have already been demon-strated. Such function codes end input in a screen and start the PAI section. Exit function codes work in a similar fashion. Only they start the processing of PAI modules that have the AT EXIT-COMMAND clause. They do not perform automatic screen checks (for example, for mandatory input fields) in the process.

If you want to trigger a direct jump to another transaction, you use function type T. The function code is then evaluated as the identifier of the transaction to be started. Again, no checks are performed. If the function type S has any importance, it is in an application's test phase. This function type triggers system functions, including, for example, turning on the debugger. For this, the system function's identification letter is used as the function code. In practical applications, only the function types for normal functions and for Exit functions are really important.

You can record two pieces of text for every function code. One of these is only used in the menu; the other is used for function keys and pushbuttons. There are two input fields available in the function list for these pieces of text. Until Release 2.2, these texts have a purely static nature. Beginning with Release 3.0, you can specify a text type in addition to the two pieces of text. There is a pushbutton, *Change text/txt type*, in the function list and a menu function with the same name in the *More utilities* menu for this. With this attribute, you can choose between three options: static text, dynamic text and icon (see Figure 3.36).

Figure 3.36   Selection of a text type for a function code

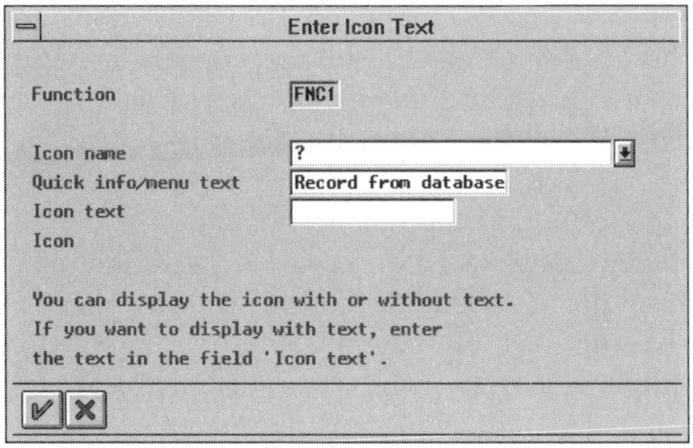

Figure 3.37   *Assignment of an icon to a function code*

A dynamic text is passed to the status in a data field. After you select the appropriate text type, the Menu Painter asks you to specify the corresponding field name in another popup. Before the status is called, the field is filled with the desired text in the program. In this variant, however, no distinction is possible between menu text and pushbutton text.

You can define up to 20 pushbuttons in a status. However, if these are filled with text, they cannot all fit in the pushbutton bar. The *Icon* text type lets you display icons instead of text in the pushbuttons. When you select this option, the system asks you to define an icon in a popup (Figure 3.37).

In this popup, you first record the name of the icon. Possible entries help is available for this field, offering all of the icons for selection. Figure 3.38 shows a section of this selection list.

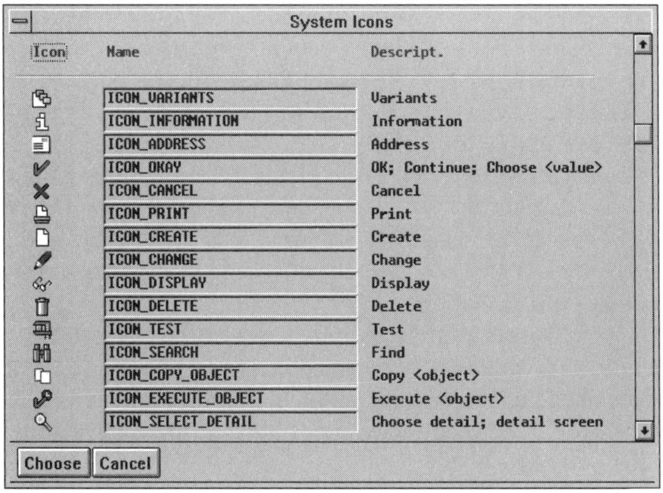

Figure 3.38   *Possible entries help for icons*

Since the icon is displayed as an icon only in the pushbutton bar, not in the menu, you must also record an additional menu text. This text appears in the menu and as a so-called quick info in a small window under the pushbutton. This quick info does not become active unless the mouse pointer pauses briefly (about two seconds) over the pushbutton. In another field, *Icon text*, you can enter a text that should appear with the icon in the pushbutton. Unlike the menu text, this text is optional.

If you have specified dynamic text for a pushbutton, the identifier for an icon may also appear in the corresponding data field at runtime. It then appears instead of or together with the actual pushbutton text. The identifier for an icon must be determined with a specific function module, whose use will be demonstrated later. Dynamic assignment of icons has one disadvantage. The icon identifier is analyzed only when the pushbutton is displayed, not when the menu items are displayed. So, if a function code that has dynamic text is used in the menu as well as in the pushbutton bar, any icon that may have been assigned will be correctly displayed only in the pushbutton. In the menu, only the icon identifier, a cryptic character string, will appear.

The menu itself can also be accessed with the keyboard. To speed up selection, individual letters in the menu items are underlined. A menu item marked this way can be selected with the key combination <ALT>-letter key. With this so-called fastpath, you determine in the Menu Painter which letters should be used for accelerated selection in each menu. Although a column for fastpath appears in the function list, you can edit it only in a certain screen. You call this screen from the function list with *Goto → Further options → Fastpath*. A pushbutton is also available in this screen with which you can display valid values.

Most of the functions and tools described here are accessible not only from the function list, but also from other places in the Menu Painter. A complete description of the Menu Painter's menu structure would go too far here, however.

You assign function codes to control elements in the work interface of the Menu Painter, where there are two input fields, one for menu items and one for function keys. In one of the input fields, you enter the function code, in the other the relevant text. When you enter a function code that does not yet exist in the function list, it is automatically created. When you press the Enter key, the Menu Painter fills all of the text fields with the function code texts, assuming such texts exist. You can enter any missing text later, either in the work interface or in the function list.

Each function code can be activated or deactivated for a particular status. You use the menu functions *Function activation → In current status* and *Function activation → In several statuses* for this. The first of these menu functions displays a list of all of the function keys of the user interface for a status (see Figure 3.39). Using check boxes, you can release the function code in that status or lock it.

The second function creates a similar popup, in which you can set the activation status for an individual function code in all of the current user interface's statuses. Using the language elements available in ABAP/4, it is often easier to create several identical statuses that differ only in their function code activation state than to deactivate the function codes dynamically in the program.

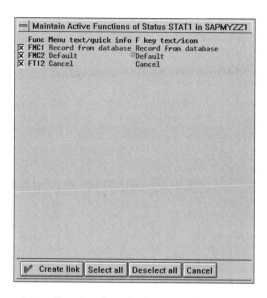

Figure 3.39   Changing the activation status for function codes

Control elements

Function codes are triggered by the use of one of the control elements in the user interface.
Control elements are assigned to one of four groups:

- Menu
- Toolbar
- Pushbutton bar
- Function keys

The contents of the toolbar are preset; they cannot be changed. However, you can activate
all of the icons except the Enter key as desired. You do this by assigning function codes to
either certain function keys or the icons, depending on the release version. You can edit
the three other types of control elements in the Menu Painter. In addition to the general
view shown in Figure 3.28, there are also functions for editing individual groups.

You create a control element by entering a function code and, for new function codes,
a text, in one of the input fields provided for this purpose. Defaults are available for every
status type; you can enter them in the status with a double-click on the relevant text element. Already existing entries are not overwritten in this process. You call up the defaults
separately for menus and function keys. The defaults correspond to the recommendations
of the SAP Style Guide. Whenever possible, you should modify the default to create custom
statuses, to ensure consistency in the user interface across the entire system.

Menus

The menu consists of the menu bar and the pulldown menus. The items in the menu bar can point only to pulldown menus. The items in the pulldown menus, on the other hand, can either accept function codes or activate additional pulldown menus. Up to three levels of pulldown menus are possible.

At first only the menu bar is displayed in the work interface. You can assign a short description to the menu bar that facilitates orientation when using the element-oriented work method. This description is optional. As suggested in the guidelines, you fill the input fields of the menu bar and the pulldown menus manually with the names of the menus. The default for menus fills the first item in the menu bar with the <*Object*> place holder. You must replace this place holder with the name of the object that should be edited in the application to be created.

Double-clicking on an item in the menu bar opens the applicable pulldown menu. To create a menu item that triggers a function code, you fill the first column of the menu element with the function code. If the function code in question is new, you should enter an identifier in the second column. You can insert a separating line in a pulldown menu using the menu function *Edit → Insert → Separator line*. If you want a menu item to open a subordinate pulldown menu instead of triggering a function code, you leave the column with the function code empty. You just enter the identifier of the new menu in the second column. Double-clicking on this item then opens the new menu. At the program's run-time, items in pulldown menus that point to additional menus are identified by a small triangle pointing to the right. You can delete elements with another menu function, *Edit → Delete entry*.

Because the Menu Painter's work interface is also a screen, items are not analyzed until the PAI section of the current screen, that is, of the Menu Painter, is executed. This happens when you press the Enter key, choose a menu function or press a function key. At that moment, all of the newly created function codes are supplemented with the available identifiers from the function list. In the case of new function codes for which no identifier exists yet, the Menu Painter asks you to enter the corresponding text in a popup.

Function keys

To speed up the selection of important functions, the system makes so-called *function keys* available. These are keys (for example, function keys) or key combinations (for example, Control key + alphanumeric key) that can trigger function codes directly. In SAP terminology, the term function key does not refer only to the specific function keys on the keyboard (usually F1 through F12), but rather to all keys that can trigger a function code. Beginning with Release 3.0, there are 99 function keys available.

The available function keys are divided into four groups. The first are function keys that have a predefined meaning system-wide. These keys (F1, F4, and F10) are recognized and analyzed by the system. They do not require any function codes and are always active. If you nevertheless assign a function code to them, for example through an incorrect entry, these keys no longer trigger their usual, system-controlled functions.

The second group contains keys that correspond to certain icons in the toolbar. Such keys also trigger the same functions system-wide. However, it is the responsibility of the programmer to assign a function code and implement the actual functionality. The assignment of icons to keys is predefined. For this reason, the Menu Painter does not offer those function keys for editing. Instead, for the preset functions, it also provides the toolbar for editing, in which you assign a function code to these functions and thus immediately to one of the preset keys. You activate these functions by assigning a function code to the icon.

Table 3.19 shows the keys of both groups discussed so far, along with their normal assignments.

Table 3.19   Function keys with predefined meanings

Function key	Icon	Meaning	Function code required
F1	question mark	context-sensitive help	no
F3	green arrow	back	yes
F4	magnifying glass	possible entries help	no
F10, ALT	no icon	activate menu bar	no
F11	yellow folder	save	yes
F12	red plus sign	cancel	yes
F15	yellow arrow	exit	yes
F21, Ctrl-PgUp	double up-arrow	back to the first page	sometimes
F22, PgUp	single up-arrow	one page back	sometimes
F23, PgDn	single down-arrow	one page forward	sometimes
F24, Ctrl-PgDn	double down-arrow	forward to the last page	sometimes

The third group consists of function keys for which SAP recommends a specific use, for example delete or select. You assign these function keys directly to the function code. For some of the keys, predefined icons exist that appear in the pushbutton bar if the function code is assigned to a pushbutton.

The last group contains function keys that can be used as desired. You edit these just like the function keys in the third group. In the standard case, a total of 24 function keys are provided. By double-clicking on the *Extended F key assignment* field, you can increase the number of function keys available.

To ensure that the user interface can be designed independent of the actual front end, the new Menu Painter works internally with so-called virtual function keys only. In a special table, these are mapped to the actual keys that are available in the front end in question. Regardless of the assignment of virtual keys to real keys, the function code of a virtual key can be triggered with the key combination *Control-nn*, where nn is the two-digit number of the virtual key. At the moment, this capability is undocumented.

Table 3.20 shows all of the virtual keys reserved for certain functions and the actual keys assigned to them in Windows 3.x.

Table 3.20   Predefined key assignments for virtual function keys

Virtual key	Function	Actual key in Windows
V3	back	F3
V4	possible entries	F4
V10	menu bar	F10
V11	save/post	F11, Ctrl-S
V12	cancel	F12, ESC
V13	print	Shift-F1, Ctrl-P
V14	delete	Shift-F2
V15	exit	Shift-F3
V70	execute	Ctrl-E
V71	search	Ctrl-F
V72	mark all	Ctrl-A
V73	delete all marks	Ctrl-D
V74	create	Ctrl-N
V75	change	Ctrl-O
V76	cut	Shift-Del
V77	copy	Ctrl-Ins
V78	paste	Shift-Ins
V79	undo	Alt-Backspace
V80	first page (home)	Ctrl-PgUp
V81	previous page	PgUp
V82	next page	PgDn
V83	last page (end)	Ctrl-PgDn
V84	continue search	Ctrl-G
V85	display	Ctrl-R
V86 through V99	reserved	

In its basic state, the Menu Painter displays only the first 24 function keys in this list. All others are available only after you double-click on the small icon next to *Extended F key assignment*. In this list, the assignment to an actual key is displayed for every function key. Since this depends on the front end, you can select the actual front end by double-clicking on a certain field. This changes the key identifiers in the Menu Painter. It is not possible to assign function codes to virtual keys directly by number (V1 through V99).

In the finished application, pressing on the right mouse key displays a popup menu in which the available function keys appear and can be selected with a mouse click.

You edit all entries for function keys that can or must be given a function code the same way you edit menu items. When assigning function codes, you should heed the recommendation to use only those function codes for function keys that are also available in the menu. It should always be possible to use all of an application with the menu.

Some of the function keys correspond to icons in the toolbar. All of the others can be defined as pushbuttons, as long as they have been given a function code. To do this, you enter either the number of the function key (Release 2.2 and earlier) or the function code (Release 3.0) in the elements of the pushbutton bar. At the program's runtime, the pushbuttons appear in a separate area below the toolbar. If no pushbuttons have been defined, or if all of the function codes for pushbuttons are inactive in a status, this area is not displayed.

Some of the function keys can automatically be given function codes by the defaults (norms). This depends on the status type. In particular, this applies to the statuses for list display. These function codes are then also analyzed by the system. Though changes are possible, they would make it unnecessarily difficult for the user to edit lists.

In older release versions, the Enter key was an exception among the keys with special meaning. It did not have a function code. When it was used, the screen field receiving the function code was not changed. Beginning with Release 3.0, you can assign a function code to the Enter key, too. On the one hand, this is good for creating clearly structured, readable programs. On the other hand, undesired side effects may crop up if older applications are expanded or this capability is used carelessly.

Release 2.2
In release versions up to and including Release 2.2, the only function keys available are the F1 through F12 keys and the combinations of these keys with the Shift key. The combinations correspond to the function keys F13 through F24. In the Menu Painter, therefore, 24 function keys can be given function codes. In the lower part of the work area, the Menu Painter provides 24 input fields for the function keys F1 through F24. You edit these function keys in a two-part list. Several input fields of the function key list always appear highlighted in color. These function keys are keys whose meaning is preset system-wide. These keys correspond to icons in the toolbar. Some of the icons (all except Enter, general help and possible entries help) are active only if a function code has been assigned to the corresponding function. Figure 3.40 shows the old Menu Painter.

Title list

In addition to control elements, you can also maintain so-called titles in user interface maintenance. A title is a one-line text that can appear in the window's title bar at the program's runtime. A user interface can have several titles, which are identified by a three-character identifier. The title list is not part of a specific status; it applies to the whole user interface.

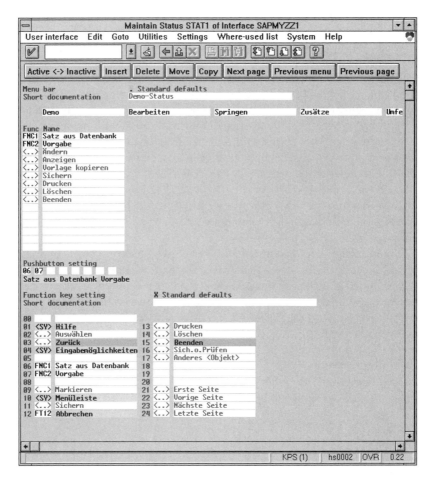

Figure 3.40   Menu Painter in Release 2.2

3.3.4   Typical actions in the module pool

A module pool makes the program modules for one or more screens available. In addition, global data is declared in the module pool. Theoretically, all of the source code could be contained in a single file. In the editor, however, it is much easier to handle shorter files. For this reason, it is normal, though not mandatory, to split module pools into several Include files. There are six essential sections, which are formed by six Include files or groups of Include files. For each file group, recommendations exist for the names of the Include files.

- Data declaration
- PBO modules for processing before screen display
- Modules for processing after screen display

- Include files for subroutines (forms)
- Modules for help (F1)
- Modules for possible entries help (F4)

The actual module pool only incorporates the various INCLUDE statements; often it no longer contains any source code. The program header required for every program is stored in one of the Includes, the Top Include, for simplicity's sake. This must therefore always appear at the beginning of the source code. This special role is reflected by the name of the Include, which ends with TOP.

Module pool names always begin with SAPM. The next letter should identify the application group for which the module pool is designed, for example F for Financial Accounting. Just like for reports, the two letters Y and Z are designated for customer development; all other letters are reserved for SAP use. The last three letters actually identify the module pool. In the previous example, the initials and a running number, that is, ZZ1, were used, as was the case for the reports.

Similar conventions apply to the names of the Include files. They start with the last five characters of the module pool name, MYZZ1 in the example. A letter follows, indicating the type of elements in the Include. An O stands for files that contain a PBO module. An I, on the other hand, indicates Includes with PAI modules. Files with subroutines, that is, form routines, receive an F. The last two characters distinguish between the individual files of a group.

These conventions do not necessarily have to be followed. As a minimum, you can select the last three characters as you choose, since the first five characters already ensure a unique assignment to the module pool. The names hardly express the functionality of the application. But this is not necessary anyway. The Browser in the Workbench, which has not yet been discussed, guarantees an overview of the program code.

This section will describe important actions in dialog applications and the ABAP/4 commands required to execute them. Although these commands are explained in connection with dialog applications, this does not mean that they may only be used there. Some of the statements can be used in reports.

Setting the user interface

A screen must almost always be linked to a user interface status so that the user can trigger program activities. You create this link with the command

```
SET PF-STATUS status.
```

The name of the status is up to eight characters long. It must be entered in capital letters and enclosed in single quotes. After a status has been set, it remains active until a new status is set or until a default status is called using

```
SET PF-STATUS SPACE.
```

This default status is also active if no status has been set. In applications, a status can be changed any number of times, even in the same screen. The name of the current status appears in the system field SY-PFKEY.

A status can be set not only in screens, but also in reports. Different defaults exist for the two types of programs. When you create a status, you must already specify if it is meant for a screen or a report.

Occasionally, you may want some function codes to be temporarily deactivated in a status. If a screen allows record-by-record paging in a data set, for example, with the functions *Next record* and *Previous record*, it makes sense to turn off one of the two functions at the beginning or the end of the data set. Even in cases where there are no authorizations for certain functions (for example, deleting), these functions should be deactivated, so that unauthorized users cannot even call them. You could solve this problem using various different statuses, of course, but the programming and management effort required would be rather extensive. It is also possible to deactivate function codes at runtime in a status, without having to change the status. The menu items of the deactivated function codes continue to appear in the menu, but they are grayed out and cannot be selected.

You deactivate function codes with the EXCLUDING parameter of the SET PF-STATUS command. Either a single function code or an internal table that can contain any number of function codes may appear after this clause. This table must have the following structure:

```
DATA: BEGIN OF FCODE_TAB OCCURS 5,
   FCODE LIKE SY-UCOMM,
END OF FCODE_TAB.
```

Some examples of the expanded command call, which you can test in the previously presented demo applications, are:

```
SET PF-STATUS 'STAT1' EXCLUDING 'FNC1'.
```

or

```
REFRESH FCODE_TAB.
FCODE_TAB-FCODE = 'FNC1'.
APPEND FCODE_TAB.
FCODE_TAB-FCODE = 'FNC2'.
APPEND FCODE_TAB.
SET PF-STATUS 'STAT1' EXCLUDING FCODE_TAB.
```

The last example requires that the internal table FCODE_TAB be created in the module pool's global data. A status is usually set for the PBO event. In rare cases, it might make sense to set a new status that depends on the current function code or to modify the existing one. For the sake of clarity, you should do this only in exceptional cases.

Setting titles

Every window has a title bar. You set this title, too, at the PBO event, using the following statement:

SET TITLEBAR *title*.

You specify the title with a three-character identifier. In the program, the identifier must be enclosed in single quotes. It can therefore easily be confused with a constant. If no title exists when the command is processed, the system uses a default.

You maintain the titles in the Menu Painter. It is easiest, however, to call the title main-tenance tool using the navigation mechanism when you are entering the source code. First, you enter the correct identifier, then you double-click on this identifier.

A title can contain up to nine place holders for parameters. These consist either of only the ampersand character (&) or of this character and a consecutive number between 1 and 9. When you set this title, you can pass the values to be inserted after the WITH clause.

SET TITLEBAR *title* **WITH** *parameter_1 ... parameter_9.*

Numbered place holders are replaced by the parameter in the corresponding position in the command. Unnumbered place holders, on the other hand, are assigned to the parameters of the SET command sequentially, starting from the left. If no parameter is available for a place holder, blank spaces are entered. If an ampersand (&) is supposed to appear in the title, it must be entered double in title maintenance (&&).

In addition to displaying the final title in the window on the screen, the system also places it in the system field SY-TITLE.

Changing field attributes

In the Screen Painter, you preset attributes for the screen fields. Some of these attributes can be dynamically changed at runtime. For example, it is possible to remove the input authorization for some fields, that is, to turn them into pure display fields, or to delete the fields entirely from the screen. This way, a screen can be adjusted to the actual authorizations of the user or to certain properties of the data record to be processed with relatively little programming effort.

Dynamic modifications also take place at the PBO event. A special variant of the LOOP statement (the ABAP/4 statement, not the screen statement of the same name) allows you to edit all screen fields. When a screen is executed, important, relevant data for every field template (key fields are ignored) is placed in the internal table SCREEN. This table has the structure shown in Table 3.21.

Table 3.21   Table for screen fields

Field name	Length	Type	Content/effect	Editing sensible
SCREEN-NAME	30	C	field name	
SCREEN-GROUP1	3	C	valuation of the modification group 1	
SCREEN-GROUP2	3	C	valuation of the modification group 2	
SCREEN-GROUP3	3	C	valuation of the modification group 3	
SCREEN-GROUP4	3	C	valuation of the modification group 4	
SCREEN-REQUIRED	1	C	mandatory input	X
SCREEN-INPUT	1	C	input readiness	X
SCREEN-OUTPUT	1	C	field is displayed	X

Table 3.21 continued   Table for screen fields

Field name	Length	Type	Content/effect	Editing sensible
SCREEN-INTENSIFIED	1	C	highlighted display	X
SCREEN-INVISIBLE	1	C	password entry	X
SCREEN-LENGTH	1	X	length (hexadecimal!)	X
SCREEN-ACTIVE	1	C	1 = field appears in screen	X
			0 = field does not appear in screen, overwrites all other attributes	
SCREEN-DISPLAY_3D	1	C	3D display	X
SCREEN-VALUE_HELP	1	C	possible entries help exists	
SCREEN-REQUEST	1	C	entry follows	

In the LOOP program loop, you can change several attributes and write them back to the SCREEN table using the MODIFY command. This is not useful for all attributes, since some only deliver information about certain attributes of a field. A preliminary example:

```
LOOP AT SCREEN.
  SCREEN-INPUT = '0'.
  MODIFY SCREEN.
ENDLOOP.
```

These statements remove the input readiness from all fields of the screen. The character zero (0) serves as the identifier for a turned-off attribute. Attributes are turned on with the character 1.

If you want to make modifications to only a few fields, you can request the field name in the LOOP program loop. The name corresponds to the name of the field as it can be found in the fullscreen or the screen's field list.

```
LOOP AT SCREEN.
  IF SCREEN-NAME = 'KNA1-KUNNR'.
    SCREEN-INVISIBLE = '1'.
    MODIFY SCREEN.
  ENDIF.
ENDLOOP.
```

If you need to modify a larger number of screen fields, you can use modification groups. For every screen field, you can maintain four attributes in the fullscreen editor, called modification group 1 through 4. You can enter any three-character string in each of the four fields. You can choose these values as desired; there are no restrictions or checks. These are simply four additional identifiers for the field. Later, you can determine the contents of these attributes using the four fields SCREEN-GROUP1 through 4. Let us assume that a screen contains several fields that should always be hidden together, for example because the current user should not see these fields. In the fullscreen editor, you set the modification group 1 to the value '001' for these fields. You then hide the fields using the statements

```
LOOP AT SCREEN.
  IF SCREEN-GROUP1 = '001'.
    SCREEN-ACTIVE = '0'.
    MODIFY SCREEN.
  ENDIF.
ENDLOOP.
```

Of course, you can choose the modification group and the value for this attribute as desired. Often, such modifications are carried out in dependence on the transaction code. In addition to a transaction for maintaining data, there is often one for purely displaying data. For example, all of the tools used so far have such a display mode. The initial screen provides separate menu functions or pushbuttons for displaying and changing. The transaction code can be found in the system field SY-TCODE.

Another way to modify the appearance of screen fields before the screen is displayed is to use icons. You place a special identifier in the data field that is linked to the screen field. The system recognizes this as a reference to an icon and replaces it with the icon when the field is output. The screen field may only have output attributes. This mechanism also works in connection with dynamic text for function codes. To determine the identifier for an icon, you call a specific function module. It expects the name of an icon as the input parameter. The return value consists of a certain character string that is recognized by the screen as a reference to an icon. If necessary, the icon can appear together with text. You can also define text for a quick info.

You can easily test the dynamic creation of icons and the function module needed for this by declaring a global data field (P1) that is sufficiently long and incorporating this data field in the fullscreen of the screen. Give it the attributes *Output field* and *With icon*. You must deactivate the automatically set *Input field* attribute! The length of the field and the output length anticipated in the screen conform to the type of icon and the text to be output, among other things. The data field must also be able to receive the actual text and the text for the quick info, in addition to the icon identifier.

You usually assign the icon to the screen field in a PBO module. Very often, screens have at their disposal a module in which all modifications to the user interface are performed. In the example at the beginning of this section, the D9100_SET_STATUS module was created. For the first test, you can have the icon assignment take place in this module. The following listing shows the use of the function module mentioned. You can take the icon names, for example, from the possible entries help of the corresponding field in the Screen Painter attributes popup.

```
...
CALL FUNCTION 'ICON_CREATE'
  EXPORTING
    NAME                    = 'ICON_GREEN_LIGHT'
```

```
    TEXT                      = 'Icon text'
    INFO                      = 'Quick info'
    ADD_STDINF                = 'X'
IMPORTING
    RESULT                    = P1
EXCEPTIONS
    ICON_NOT_FOUND            = 01
    OUTPUTFIELD_TOO_SHORT     = 02.
...
```

Recognizing data changes

In almost every screen, there is at least one function code available for immediately leaving the screen. If data has already been entered, it is a good idea to inform the user before leaving the screen about the possible loss of data. The system enters an X in the system field SY-DATAR (Data Received) if values have been edited in the screen. This is the only way to recognize a data change in EXIT modules. The transfer of data from screen fields to program-internal fields does not take place until after the EXIT module. Saving data is therefore not possible in the EXIT module! If this should become necessary, screen processing is not allowed to end in the EXIT module. The sample application presented in Chapter 6 demonstrates in detail how such cases should be handled.

Another way to note data changes consists of using a global flag. In the processing logic, a FIELD statement that combines all of the fields of the screen sets the flag:

```
* Flow logic
PROCESS AFTER INPUT.
...
  FIELD: ... "Include all screen fields in the FIELD statement
    MODULE DATA_CHANGED ON REQUEST.
...
* Module pool
MODULE DATA_CHANGED.
  FLG_DATA_CHANGED = 'X'.
ENDMODULE.
```

The flag is reset when the screen is filled with new data. In contrast to SY-DATAR, however, it is not effective if termination occurs immediately when the screen is first processed.

Program branching from screens

Various other elements can be started from a screen. This branching usually happens in the PAI section. But calls of other programs or program portions are also possible and useful in the PROCESS ON VALUE-REQUEST section. The following branching possibilities exist:

- Continuation with another screen
- Execution of a report
- Start of a different transaction

There are two commands for calling other elements, LEAVE and CALL, both of which have their own variants. LEAVE executes a final jump to another element without automatic return to the calling spot, whereas you can return from the elements called with CALL to the calling spot by using certain return statements. A description of the LEAVE command variants follows.

You need at least two commands to call a screen. First, you set the number of the screen to be called using

SET SCREEN *screen_number.*

You can leave out this command only if the number of the new screen has already been set as the subsequent screen in the current screen. You make the jump to the new screen using

LEAVE SCREEN.

Starting with Release 3.0, you can use these two statements together, as follows:

LEAVE TO SCREEN *screen_number.*

This type of branching is final. It should not be mistaken for a subroutine call; after the called screen is ended, there is no automatic return to the calling screen. Jumping to screen 0 has a special function. It ends the application. You can achieve this same function using

LEAVE PROGRAM.

To jump to another transaction, you use

LEAVE TO TRANSACTION *transaction_code.*

You must enter the transaction code in capital letters, enclosed in single quotes. You can give this statement an optional clause:

... AND SKIP FIRST SCREEN.

The effect of this clause is to suppress display of the initial screen of the called transaction. The flow logic of the first screen is correctly processed. The fields of this screen must be filled automatically, either by GET/SET parameters in connection with corresponding attributes in the screen, or by statements in the PBO modules. As long as all of the mandatory input fields have been filled correctly, the user is not given an opportunity to input data. Processing immediately continues with the PAI modules. The current function code is that for Enter (blank space). Using this form of the statement and skipping data input in the first screen make sense only if the called transaction has a certain structure. This is discussed in more detail at the end of this section.

In addition to calling other screens and transactions, you can call reports. You do not use the LEAVE statement for this, but rather

SUBMIT *report.*

About 20 different clauses are available for this command that allow you to give the report defaults for everything from the format of the output list to printing and archiving. Most of these clauses are only interesting in specific cases. Only five are of interest at this point. The clause

`... AND RETURN.`

causes a return to the calling program after the report is executed. This continues at the spot after the SUBMIT statement. The report starts immediately, without any selection screen that may be present having to be processed first. The user has no opportunity to restrict the data set to be searched by the report. However, the programmer can ensure that the report is given parameters and selections anyway. The simplest way is to name a variant using

`... USING SELECTION-SET` *variant_name*

Furthermore, you can pass presets for parameters and selections to the report using

`... WITH` *parameter* `...`

or

`... WITH SELECTION-TABLE` *selection*

If the user should still be able to edit the selection screen, you can use

`... VIA SELECTION-SCREEN`

This causes the selection screen to be processed. If default values have been set for parameters and selections by the calling application using WITH, the user can change the passed suggested values on the selection screen before executing the report.

The operation of the CALL statement is similar to that of the LEAVE command. However, it executes the called application as a subprocess; after the called application ends, the calling application is continued at the interruption point. Use of this command is especially widespread for calling popups in screens. In the work you have done so far, you have already encountered many popups, mostly for input of individual values or for confirmation of certain activities. All of these popups were called with a variant of the CALL command. In addition to several other variants, three CALL commands allow jumps to other applications or elements.

In the following command, the specified transaction is called as a subprocess, that is, as a sort of subroutine:

`CALL TRANSACTION` *transaction_code.*

As with LEAVE TO TRANSACTION, you can skip the first screen by adding the following clause, if all of the mandatory input fields are filled with valid values:

`... AND SKIP FIRST SCREEN`

In the called transaction, all of the commands that would usually end this transaction in a normal fashion (for example, LEAVE TRANSACTION, LEAVE TO SCREEN 0) instead return to the calling application.

You can use CALL to call individual screens from the same application, not just transactions. You use the following statement for this:

`CALL SCREEN` *screen_number.*

In the called screen, the statement LEAVE TO SCREEN 0 now no longer ends the entire application, but returns to the calling point. In the basic form of the command, the new screen occupies the entire work area, meaning it replaces the old one entirely. The called screen should be a normal screen.

A popup is a screen for which the screen type *Modal dialog box* is marked in the attributes, instead of *Normal*. The call requires specification of the position at which the popup should appear. You specify this position relative to the current screen:

CALL SCREEN *screen_number* **STARTING AT** *line column*.

In this form of the call, the system ensures that the size of the popup corresponds to the surface area actually occupied in this screen. Very long popups whose length would exceed the space available on the screen are automatically limited to the screen height or width and are given a scroll bar. But this can only be a temporary solution. Therefore, if necessary, you can also specify the end position explicitly. This only makes sense, however, if you have also specified a start position.

CALL SCREEN *screen_number* **STARTING AT** *line column*
                                     ENDING AT *line column*

The system handles popups somewhat differently than basic screens. The pushbutton bar is moved to the lower edge of the popup. Menus, the toolbar and the OK field are not accessible. Only the function key layout can be displayed with the right mouse key. In screens that should be processed as popups, all of the important fields must be placed on function keys.

You can only call screens from the same application using CALL SCREEN. If screens of a general nature were needed in several applications, this would lead to an unacceptable amount of programming effort. Such screens are therefore programmed as so-called dialog modules, which can be called from any application. Dialog modules are described in detail in another section. Only calls of such modules will be demonstrated here:

CALL DIALOG *dialog_module*.

Since these dialog modules do not belong to the current application, they also cannot access its data fields. For data to be passed to the dialog module or returned from it, you must specify the fields involved in the call. You do this separately for export parameters and import parameters. Export parameters are the elements that are passed to the module:

... **EXPORTING** *D_field_1* **FROM** *P_Field_1* ... *D_field_n* **FROM** *G_field_n*.

Dialog modules have a defined user interface. In this user interface, all of the parameters are presented for which values can be assigned or from which values can be read. With the FROM clause, a value from the current program (P_field ...) is assigned to one of the values of the user interface (D_field ...). If the names of the fields happen to be identical in the calling program and the dialog module, the FROM clause can be left out. Then the only field you still need to specify is the name of the field to be exported. The procedure for returning values is similar. With the following clause, you can return data to elements of the calling program using the parameters of the dialog module:

... **IMPORTING** *D_field_1* **TO** *P_field_1* ... *D_field_n* **TO** *G_field_n*.

With regard to identical names, the same simplification is possible here as for EXPORTING.

A dialog module does not have to consist of just a single screen. Within a dialog module, you can branch to other screens. For this reason, the AND SKIP FIRST SCREEN clause may also be used for the CALL DIALOG statement.

Until now, the assumption was made that a strong separation exists between reports and dialog applications. This strict differentiation can be overcome in select cases. The design of screens can be influenced dynamically only in a relatively limited fashion. For some application cases, screens are therefore not flexible enough to display and process values. In these cases, list processing is used, which can also be embedded directly in screen processing using the statements described below. One example of this is match-codes, which display lists in some of their popups, from which the user can select an entry. Even the Object Browser, which you have already used (or, more precisely, its object list), is based on list processing. In dialog processing, you can turn on list-oriented operation temporarily with the statement

```
LEAVE TO LIST-PROCESSING.
```

You can now execute all of the commands that are only allowed in list processing (for example, WRITE). The list is displayed on the screen after the screen in which the list was built has been exited, not at the same time the list is created. Reports, too, are not displayed until they have been completely processed. In the usual processing of a screen, the screen is automatically exited after every PAI section. Depending on the operation of the *Next screen* attribute, processing of the current screen starts from the beginning. This procedure is sufficient to display the list at first. In certain cases, however, a LEAVE SCREEN may be necessary; this is not allowed to appear until after the last statement for building the list.

If the standard function codes provided for this kind of processing are available in list processing, pressing F3, F12 or F15, or selecting the corresponding menu functions, should be enough to return to dialog processing. The simplest way to make these function codes available is to set the predefined status for list processing. You can do this very easily with the statement

```
SET PF-STATUS ' '.
```

Since the specified status does not exist, the system uses the default status that belongs to list processing. The system intercepts the default function codes and processes them.

In many cases, this status cannot be used, since an entirely different application functionality in comparison to normal reporting is supposed to be implemented. In these cases, it is necessary to analyze the function codes themselves and return to dialog processing with the command

```
LEAVE LIST-PROCESSING.
```

When list processing ends, the PBO section of the screen that called list processing is started. You can deviate from this default with the statement

LEAVE TO LIST-PROCESSING AND RETURN TO SCREEN *screen_number*.

After list processing ends, the program jumps to the specified screen. Screen number 0 causes the application to end.

After the command LEAVE TO LIST-PROCESSING, function code analysis no longer proceeds with a screen's flow logic, in the manner familiar from screens, but with the event for reports or internally in the system. The events must be entered directly in the module pool.

The following example illustrates the embedding of list processing in a screen. Further down in the text, you will find only the relevant section of the module pool. You can create the surrounding application yourself using the examples at the beginning of this chapter. In the screen status, make three pushbuttons available that trigger the function codes FNC1, FNC2 and FNC3. Assign these function codes to the function keys F6 through F8. In order to be able to end the application, of course, you must make the F12 function key available as the Exit function key, as previously described. However, you should assign the function code PF12 to this function key, although custom function codes should actually not begin with the letter P. Please note that this function code must be an Exit code, and that the screen must have an Exit module. Use the screen's own screen number as the subsequent screen.

The screen should have only one module in the PBO section and two modules in the PAI section of the flow logic. In the PBO section, set the status described above. The PAI section has two modules, the familiar Exit module and the following PAI module for analyzing the function code:

```
MODULE FCODE INPUT.

  CASE FCODE.

    WHEN 'FNC1'.
      LEAVE TO LIST-PROCESSING.
      NEW-PAGE NO-TITLE NO-HEADING.
      SET PF-STATUS ' '.
      WRITE / 'Embedded list processing'.
      WRITE 'with default status for reports'.
      WRITE / 'Exit with F3 or something similar.'.

    WHEN 'FNC2'.
      LEAVE TO LIST-PROCESSING.
      NEW-PAGE NO-TITLE NO-HEADING.
      WRITE / 'Embedded list processing,'.
      WRITE 'Status of the screen still valid'.
      WRITE / 'Exit with function key F12 or 3rd pushbutton'.
  ENDCASE.
ENDMODULE.
```

Manually enter the following two events and the corresponding statement blocks in the same program file where you create the FCODE module.

```
AT USER-COMMAND.
  IF SY-UCOMM = 'FNC3'.
    LEAVE LIST-PROCESSING.
  ENDIF.
```

```
AT PF12.
  LEAVE LIST-PROCESSING.
```

The function code FNC1 displays the first list. After list processing is turned on, the default title and the list heading are turned off. The command NEW-PAGE handles this. It does not create a form feed in this case, since there were no outputs to the list before the command was called. It only serves to turn off the title and heading here. An empty character string serves as the identifier for the status to be set. There is no such status, so the default status for list processing goes into effect. The functions made available by this status are analyzed by the system itself; additional programming effort is not required. The list can easily be printed, since printing is part of the standard functionality of a report.

In the second list creation, triggered by function code FNC2, no new status is set. Therefore, the status of the screen remains available. Ending list processing with the F3 function key is no longer possible, since the report does not automatically analyze the function codes of the screen's user interface. This must be done using the various events for list processing, which must be programmed individually. Two of these events immediately follow the module, as an example of this method of programming. The AT USER-COMMAND event triggers the start of any function code not to be processed by the system. In the example, this happens when all three pushbuttons are used. Only in the case of the third pushbutton, however, does an additional query lead to the end of list processing. This functionality is used here to demonstrate this event only; in practical applications, other statements could be executed here.

All of the function keys that have been given a function code in the form PFn, where n is the number of the function key, trigger an AT PFn event. This event, too, can be used to end list processing.

In this example, the screen is displayed to enable selection between the two different lists. In addition to the task of calling list processing, it also has other functionality. In real applications, such a selection is usually not required. In this case, the screen only creates the framework that makes it possible to insert list processing in a dialog application. In order to retain the modular character of the screen within the application, dialog processing and list processing should be separated. In a screen where list processing is performed, there is usually no dialog processing. This is not an absolute requirement, but just some advice that comes from experience. Applications structured this way are easier to program and maintain than applications that combine several functions in one screen. Display of the dialog screen is not necessary in such cases; in fact, it is disruptive. In the ABAP/4 command record, there is a statement that makes it possible to skip the dialog in a screen and immediately execute PAI processing. This statement is as follows:

```
SUPPRESS DIALOG.
```

This statement can be demonstrated using the last example, which is easy to change. In the PBO section of the screen, only one module is required, to execute the statement just presented: SUPPRESS DIALOG. Since the actual dialog is skipped, a function code can also be triggered. So you also only need one module in the PAI section of the screen, to create the list.

```
MODULE FCODE INPUT.

  LEAVE TO LIST-PROCESSING AND RETURN TO SCREEN 0.
  NEW-PAGE NO-TITLE NO-HEADING.
  SET PF-STATUS ' '.
  WRITE / 'Embedded list processing'.
  WRITE 'with default status for reports'.
  WRITE / 'End with F3 or something similar.'.

ENDMODULE.
```

No function code analysis takes place in the screen's flow logic, since function codes cannot be created without a dialog. Without the AND RETURN TO SCREEN 0 clause for the LEAVE statement, the screen would be executed again after exiting list processing, since after the end of list processing, the PBO section of the calling screen is always executed again. Ending the screen is therefore only possible with the clause mentioned. Depending on how the 9100 screen is called, this clause either ends the entire application or, if screen 9100 was called with the CALL SCREEN statement, returns to a different screen. In most cases, the latter variant is recommended for incorporating a list in a dialog application.

In the real world, processing of events in the list very often requires programming additional functionality using list events. These events are described in the section on interactive reporting.

Checking authorizations

The branching methods just described execute specific functions. In many cases, not every user should be allowed to execute all of the available applications. Sometimes, distinctions are made with regard to the way data is accessed. Often, the group of users allowed to change data is smaller than the group of users allowed to display data. You must use explicit authorization checks to implement authorization for access to data and programs. As a prerequisite for this, you must store so-called authorizations in the user master record. These authorizations represent instances of something called an authorization object.

Creating authorization objects and authorizations is covered in Chapter 5. To understand the description of the checks, you need only know the following: an authorization object is a template (type description) for an authorization. Such an object contains up to 10 authorization fields. You can derive any number of authorizations from one authorization object and assign separate values to their fields. You store the authorizations and their actual field values in a user master record. When checking an authorization, however, you must specify the authorization object to be checked. The system then determines which actual authorizations derived from this object the current user possesses and checks against the field values contained in these authorizations. To program authorization checks, you need only have some knowledge of the authorization objects and the fields contained in them. If new authorization objects are needed for an application, it is the responsibility of the programmer to create and document these. The system administrator cannot create any authorizations for the users without documentation. He or she needs to know which fields from which objects must be assigned values to allow access to certain data or program branches.

You check an authorization in a program using the following statement:

```
AUTHORITY-CHECK OBJECT authorization_object
   ID authorization_field_1 FIELD check_value_1

   ...

   ID authorization_field_x DUMMY

   ...

   ID authorization_field_10 FIELD check_value_10.
```

All of the values can be passed either as constants enclosed in single quotes or as fields with the corresponding contents. The statement first determines the authorization of the current user based on the authorization object specified. This authorization contains one or more authorization fields whose names are entered after the ID clause. These fields contain one or more values or range specifications. Now the system checks if the check value (field or constant) entered in the statement is contained in the authorization field. If several fields are contained in one authorization object, the individual check results are linked with AND. A user may possess several authorizations that have been derived from the same object. In this case, the check results are linked with OR, field by field. If an authorization field should not be checked, you use the DUMMY clause instead of the FIELD clause.

The AUTHORITY-CHECK command returns the check result in the system field SY-SUBRC. You can distinguish between different check results. Table 3.22 shows the possible return values.

Table 3.22   Values returned by authorization check

Return value	Meaning
0	authorization exists
4	authorization does not exist
8	number of parameters too large
12	no expression (authorization) exists for the desired object in the user master
24	authorization fields do not exist in the authorization object
28, 32, 36	authorizations corrupted in the user master

It is the responsibility of the programmer to analyze the check result. The command only delivers the return value; it does not lead to automatic program termination or anything like that if the outcome of the check is negative. Since you can program the reaction of the application to a non-existing authorization as desired, this kind of authorization check is very flexible.

A small example follows to illustrate the use of the authorization check. Let us assume that the opportunity is offered in an application to display additional information in a screen for the data record currently being processed. This could happen, for example, with a popup called using a pushbutton. The OK-CODE module would contain statements resembling the following listing:

```
CASE OK-CODE.
  WHEN 'DETA'.
    CALL SCREEN 210.
  ...
ENDCASE.
```

An authorization check must take place before the popup is called. You need an authorization object for this, whose field(s) are used to grant the actual authorizations. You should call this object Y_ZZDEMO, and it should contain the field YPOPUP. If an authorization check were now executed before the CALL SCREEN command, it might look something like this:

```
CASE OK-CODE.
  WHEN 'DETA'.
    AUTHORITY-CHECK OBJECT 'Y_ZZDEMO'
      ID 'YPOPUP' FIELD 'X'.
    IF SY-SUBRC = 0.
      CALL SCREEN 210.
    ELSE.
      MESSAGE E999.
*       You do not have authorization for this function.
    ENDIF.
  ...
ENDCASE.
```

The authorization check delivers the return code 0 only if the YPOPUP field in the authorization derived from Y_ZZDEMO is filled with a value or pattern that matches the check value. Since in this case the lock is only supposed to be turned on or off, one would probably always release the authorization by entering an X.

The authorization check could, however, also proceed differently. It is rather time-consuming to maintain a separate authorization for every user and to set or delete the flag in this authorization. Authorization checking also allows another procedure. The names of the users authorized to call the additional function, for example, could also appear in the authorization field. Then there would be only one, easy-to-maintain authorization for all of the potential users. The number of users to be entered in the authorization field represents a limitation for the use of this kind of authorization check, however, meaning that this variant for granting authorizations is suitable only for a small group of users. You only need to modify the check a little in the program:

```
CASE OK-CODE.
  WHEN 'DETA'.
    AUTHORITY-CHECK OBJECT 'Y_ZZDEMO'
      ID 'YPOPUP' FIELD SY-UNAME.
      IF SY-SUBRC = 0.
```

```
    CALL SCREEN 210.
      ELSE.
    MESSAGE E999.
*     You do not have authorization for this function.
  ENDIF.
 ...
ENDCASE.
```

In this variant of the check, an asterisk in the authorization field would release the additional function for all of the users, since it functions as a wildcard.

Messages

Messages serve two functions. In almost all cases, they influence the program flow, usually by causing processing of the current screen or selection screen to start from the beginning again. They also give the user information that points out an error.

In a narrower sense, messages are special, numbered text elements. They are identified by two fields, the message class (two characters long, alphanumeric) and the message number (three characters long, numeric). For every message, you can record a more extensive long text in addition to the one-line short text. The message text may contain up to four wildcards (&), which are handled similar to the way they are handled for title elements, as described earlier. The place holders in messages, too, can be indexed (&1 through &4). You maintain messages using the SE91 transaction or by choosing the menu function *Development → Programming environ.→ Messages*.

You send a message in an application with the command

MESSAGE ID *class* **TYPE** *type* **NUMBER** *number.*

All three parameters must appear in single quotes. In addition to the message class and the message number, you also need to specify the message type in this command. There are several system-internal defaults for this type, so, in contrast to the message text and the message class, you do not have to maintain it. It is not an attribute of certain messages in the way, for example, that a function code can be assigned to a function type. Instead, a message type is more of a code letter that specifies how the message should be handled by the system. The message type influences the program flow and the message's form of display. Table 3.23 shows the message types possible.

Table 3.23   Message types

Type	Identifier	Display	Result
I	info	popup	program continuation after confirmation (pushbutton or Enter key)
W	warning	status bar	continuation of processing after Enter key
E	error	status bar	restart of screen processing
A	abend	popup	termination of the transaction
S	success	status bar	display of text only

The message type most often used is type E. It displays the short text of the message in the status bar and causes processing of the screen to restart. It is used to point out incorrect entries in a screen. In dialog applications, a message is always triggered in a module or in subroutines that have been called from a module. When processing of a screen is restarted due to a message, only those fields are input-ready that were linked to the error-causing module with the FIELD statement.

Somewhat less severe in its effects is the message type W. Like type E, it also appears in the status bar and points out an error. However, processing of the screen can continue after the warning is confirmed with the Enter key. Type I, which displays the message in a separate popup instead of in the status bar, works in a similar fashion.

Message type S just displays a message in the status bar. Since it does not influence the program flow, it does not appear until after the current screen is processed, in the status bar of the subsequent screen. Messages of type S are usually used to inform the user of the successful completion of a command, for example "Record saved."

Message type A is an exception. It terminates the current transaction. This message type is used to stop continued work in cases of serious problems, for example inconsistencies in the data set. Again, the message short text is displayed in the status bar.

If a message short text is displayed in the status bar, double clicking on the text displays the long text in a popup. For type I, a pushbutton is available for this in the popup.

In addition to the long form of the MESSAGE command, there is also a somewhat easier-to-use short form, as follows:

MESSAGE *tnnn(kk)*.

where t represents the message type, nnn the message number, and kk the message class. The type and number appear without separating characters and without quotation marks. The message class must be enclosed in parentheses, which also follow the message number without any separating characters. You can leave out the specification of the message class if a default is set for the entire application in the PROGRAM or REPORT statement with the clause

... MESSAGE-ID *kk.*

The name of the message class may not appear in single quotes here. The message class must be specified in the program only if a class other than the default class should be used.

If you want the place holders in the message mentioned earlier to be filled with values at runtime, you pass these to the MESSAGE command with the following clause:

... WITH *value1 value2 value3 value4.*

Locking concept and posting concept

SAP applications are multi-user applications. This means that at any point in time several users could try to access the same data record simultaneously. Read access is not a problem. However, to ensure the consistency of data, one must prevent several users from editing a data record at the same time. For this reason, you can lock individual data records or entire groups of data records in an application against foreign access. In practice, you would lock a data record immediately after reading and not release it until after writing to the database. If other users attempt to lock an already locked data record or to overwrite a locked data record, the commands lead to an error that is passed by the system field SY-SUBRC.

Locking and releasing (unlocking) data records is not done directly with special ABAP/4 commands; instead, it is done by calling automatically generated function modules. These function modules, in turn, are based on the definition of a so-called lock object, which belongs to the Dictionary objects and is described in Chapter 4. The typical statements for dialog applications discussed in this section, however, include the call of these function modules and the analysis of the return values. The following excerpt of a real program shows the statement for locking a group of data records:

```
...
CALL FUNCTION 'ENQUEUE_EFMHICTR'
  EXPORTING
    FIKRS = G_FIKRS
  EXCEPTIONS
    FOREIGN_LOCK   = 1
    SYSTEM_FAILURE = 2.

CASE SY-SUBRC.
  WHEN 1.
    MESSAGE E645.  " already locked
  WHEN 2.
    MESSAGE A523.  " System error during lock request
ENDCASE.
```

Actual writing of data records takes place, of course, with the already described commands for database work, for example, MODIFY and UPDATE. Several procedures exist, however, that can improve the performance and the clarity of a program. You can, for example, move write procedures to subroutines and call these routines with the clause

... ON COMMIT.

Subroutines called this way are not executed until the application calls the statement COMMIT WORK, which is used to confirm database changes. You cannot, however, pass parameters to the subroutine. The data to be written must therefore be available globally.

The call or execution of function modules can also be made dependent on the COMMIT WORK command. To this end, you give the function module the clause

... IN UPDATE TASK.

Function modules given this clause must have certain attributes. These attributes control, for example, the type of execution, which can be asynchronous to the program flow in the case of very large postings. You will find more on this kind of function module call in Section 3.5.

3.3.5 Discussion

The commands presented in this section and the relationships described explain how a screen operates. This knowledge alone, however, is not enough to allow you to create usable applications. The screen concept and some of the commands mentioned require that when you develop an application, you follow a programming structure and several unwritten (SAP-internal) rules. Many applications in the SAP system follow a relatively simple basic form. Sometimes, this basic structure is modified quite extensively, without being entirely abandoned. Although you may decide not to observe these principles, you pay the cost for this freedom of application design with a complicated program structure and costly maintenance. Newcomers to ABAP/4 should at first heed the following rules. The basic ideas in application development are as follows.

- You use a dialog application (and thus a transaction) to process an object or to perform a task that cannot be broken down any further. This does not mean, of course, that you only process a table. However, if an application (for example, SE38) processes the source code of a report, then it does not directly process any other elements such as text elements or messages. There are separate transactions for that.

- A transaction is completely independent. No program-related prerequisites are allowed for the call of a transaction.

- Despite their independence, transactions should be considered modules of the whole system. In particular, you should design them in such a way that they can also be called from within other applications. An example is the maintenance of text elements using a separate transaction or from within SE38. Since no parameters can be passed when a transaction is called from a program (CALL TRANSACTION), many dialog applications have several transaction codes, which decide, for example, whether an object is to be created, edited, deleted or displayed in a program.

- A dialog application often has two parts, each of which consists of at least one screen. In the first part (in the first screen, the initial screen), input of the key fields determines the actual object to be processed. In the subsequent screens, the selected object is then processed. The fields of the initial screen are usually linked with GET/SET parameters. When the application is called from another transaction, the global parameters are filled and the initial screen of the called transaction is suppressed with ... AND SKIP FIRST SCREEN. This way, a predefined object can be processed by the user without input of key values.

- When planning an application, the what and when should be the primary focus, not the how. The pure functionality of an application is relatively easily expanded by adding to the flow logic of the screens. Changing the program structure, on the other hand, is often complicated and leads to undesirable side effects.

- When implementing functionality, you should take the properties of both parts of the flow logic into consideration. The PBO section performs initializations of the data and the screen. The PAI section, in contrast, handles the actual checking and analysis of the data.

3.4   Interactive reports

The reports discussed in Section 3.2 allow you to call several standard functions with the menu, for example character string searching or list printing. This simple form of list processing does not offer true interactivity. Some simple additions that fit seamlessly into the concept discussed so far let you expand simple reports into interactive list processing, which can react to certain events triggered by the user. With the help of these additional language elements, for example, you can program the following functionality:

- Selection of a data record from a list and return of the information to a calling program (example: matchcode)
- Branching to subordinate lists with additional information
- Flexible representation of data structures or hierarchical lists (example: Object Browser)
- Entry of values and subsequent processing in the report (example: expansion level in various error lists, such as those of the Workbench Organizer)
- Implementation of hypertext applications

You need to perform up to four steps to add interactive elements to a report:

- Create a user interface with separate function codes.
- Link this user interface to the report.
- Intercept custom function codes with events.
- Program the individual functionality.

The following section will explain these steps in more detail and provide examples for practical use.

3.4.1   Events in interactive reports

In addition to the events already described, there are three groups of events that are important for interactive reporting, to recognize and process the user's actions. Each of these events is processed with a separate event statement.

Double-clicking with the mouse or pressing the F2 key triggers an event, which is recognized by the event statement

```
AT LINE-SELECTION.
```

Using several system fields or the HIDE statement (which will be described later), you can gather information about the line that has been selected. This event is used quite often. It also works in connection with the standard user interface for reports, meaning no additional function code needs to be created.

The following statement handles all of the function codes that are not automatically processed by the system:

```
AT USER-COMMAND.
```

This event is a generalized form of AT LINE-SELECTION. At this event, you fill all of the system fields using the F2 key or double-clicking, like you do when selecting a list line. In addition, you put the function code for the selected function in the SY-UCOMM field. It is processed in the event's statement block similar to the way a dialog application's function code is processed in the OK-CODE module. The line where the cursor was placed is used as the current line.

The advantage of the AT USER-COMMAND event over AT LINE-SELECTION is that you can execute several different actions for the current line. If you create a custom user interface with the Menu Painter and call it in the report, separate function codes are available that can be analyzed with AT USER-COMMAND.

The event

AT PFxx**.**

plays a special role. If you give one of the function keys the function code PFxx, where xx is the number of the function key, AT PFxx is processed instead of AT USER-COMMAND. Since function codes should really not begin with the letter P, this statement is suitable mainly for test purposes. You must modify the user interface to use this event, as well.

3.4.2   The user interface for lists

The R/3 System automatically provides a user interface with a separate status for reports. If the programmer of a report does not set a different status, the system uses the default status. The system automatically analyzes the function codes created in this status. Tables 3.24 through 3.26 show all of the function codes processed by the system, organized according to logical points of view. Not all of these function codes are available in all statuses. The system first analyzes the function codes, during which it processes events for some function codes, which then enable individual analysis.

Table 3.24   Function codes for list processing: jump to other program sections

Function code	Function	Function key provided
%CH	heading maintenance	
%EX	exit	F15
%GD	graphic	
%PC	save the list in the front end system	
%SC	search for character string	
%SL	jump to Office menu	
%ST	reporting tree	
BACK	back	F3
FSET	set of values	
RSET	variants	

Table 3.24 continued   Function codes for list processing: jump to other program sections

Function code	Function	Function key provided
LEAV	exit	
ONLI	start program (from selection screen)	
RW	one list level back	F12

Table 3.25   Function codes for list processing: moving around in the list

Function code	Function	Function key provided	Event
P	first page		
P+	one page down	F23	
P++	jump to end of list	F24	
P-	one page up	F22	
P--	jump to beginning of list	F21	
PFnn	function key PFnn pressed	Fn	AT PFnn
PICK	select line	F2	AT LINE-SELECTION
PL++	jump to last line of current section		
PL+n	jump down n lines		
PL--	jump to first line of current section		
PL-n	jump up n lines		
PP+(n)	jump down one (n) section(s)		
PP++	jump to beginning of last page		
PP-(n)	jump up one (n) section(s)		
PP--	jump to beginning of list		
PPn	jump to beginning of section n		
PRI	print list	F13	
PS++	jump to last column of list		
PS+n	jump n columns to the right		
PS--	jump to first column of list		
PS-n	jump n columns to the left		
PSnn	jump to column n		

Table 3.26   Function codes for list processing: selection screen

Function code	Function	Function key provided
ALLS	selections	Ctrl-B
DBAC	back	
DCAN	cancel	
DELA	delete all data records or lines	
DELS	delete single data record or line	F14, Ctrl-14
DSAV	copy	
DYNS	dynamic selection	F16
E	back	F3
ECAN	cancel	F12
ENDE	exit	F15, Ctrl-15
FC01	user function 1	F19
FC02	user function 2	F20
FEWS	selected selections	Ctrl-D
FSET	complex selection	
GET	get variant	F17
GOON	continue	
JOBS	place in job	
NFIE	new field selection	
ONLI	execute	F8
OPTI	selection options	F2
PRIN	execute + print	F13, Ctrl-13
SAVE	save as variant	
SCRH	selection screen help	
SJOB	execute in background	F9
SPOS	save as variant	F11
VATT	attribute	
VBAC	back	

You can edit a report using the Object Browser, just like you can the module pool of a dialog application. In the Object Browser, or directly with the Menu Painter, you can create one or more separate statuses for the report. They must be of type *List* or *List in dialog box*, depending on their later use. You can set a default for the status in the Menu Painter.

This default contains a series of function codes processed by the system. The default secures the required minimum functionality of the list, such as scrolling the list or printing. These defaults are not identical to the default status, which is automatically set by the system if no custom status is called in a report. This default status belongs to the program SAPMSSY0. Do not under any circumstances change the default status to incorporate your own function codes. Additional functionality always requires a custom status.

There are two ways to create a custom status. One way is to create and manually edit a new status in the Menu Painter. Filling the status with the default simplifies this work. The second, much easier, method is to copy one of the default statuses from the program and process it. Copying is relatively easy in the Object Browser's object list. You place the cursor on the status to be copied and call the menu function *Development object → Copy*. The system then asks you to enter the missing specifications for the target object in a popup.

3.4.3   Details lists

One of the most important tasks of interactive reports is to react to the selection of a line in the list with a double-click or the F2 function key. The following short report demonstrates this principle.

```
REPORT YZZ34010.

DO 30 TIMES.
  WRITE: / 'Line', SY-INDEX.
  WRITE /.
ENDDO.

AT LINE-SELECTION.
  WRITE: / 'List level              :', SY-LSIND COLOR 4.
  WRITE: / 'Row relative            :', SY-CUROW COLOR 4.
  WRITE: / 'Column relative         :', SY-CUCOL COLOR 4.
  WRITE: / 'Absolute line number    :', SY-LILLI COLOR 4.
  WRITE: / 'Content                 :', (40)SY-LISEL COLOR 4.
```

The report first creates a list in which 30 lines of text are output, each followed by a blank line. Double-clicking on one of these lines switches to a new screen, on which some values appear. These values are the list number, the mouse pointer's position in relation to the screen, and the absolute line number and contents of the selected line. All of the information is made available by automatically filled system fields. The first list is generally called the basic list; all of the other lists are called details lists.

Even a program as short as this makes several informative experiments possible. One double-click on the details list leads to the creation of a new list. This is visible particularly in the increase in SY-LSIND value. With every double-click on the list, the value displayed increases by one; every press of the F3 function key causes a return to the previous list.

When a line is selected, the system sets several system fields. These can be queried, as shown in the example, and analyzed further along in the program. Table 3.27 shows the system fields important in interactive reporting.

Table 3.27   System fields for interactive reporting

System field	Meaning
SY-LSIND	number of the list (basic list = 0)
SY-CUROW	line position of the cursor in the last list displayed
SY-CUCOL	column position of the cursor in the last list displayed
SY-LISEL	contents of the selected line
SY-LILLI	absolute line number of the selected line
SY-LISTI	list number of the selected line
SY-PFKEY	name of the current user interface status
SY-CPAGE	first page displayed
SY-STARO	first line displayed
SY-STACO	first column displayed

Creation of a new list begins after the AT LINE-SELECTION statement. Other statements can appear after this statement that set basic settings for a new list. So you can set a new status using SET PF-STATUS; you can change the dimensions of the list and so on. Such settings are only valid for the details list, not for the basic list. For example, if a new status is set in a details list, upon returning to the basic list the old status is active again. No specific statements exist for details lists, with the exception of the TOP OF PAGE statement. This statement ensures the creation of a page header in basic lists. This event is not processed for details lists. Instead, a similar statement is used, as follows:

```
TOP OF PAGE DURING LINE-SELECTION.
```

All details lists are handled in this event. If you want to set different headings for details lists at different levels, the system field for the list level must be analyzed in TOP OF PAGE processing.

In the example above, any number of branchings can be created. In practice, however, this is neither necessary nor sensible. To stop additional branching, you must query the list level in an IF statement. Note that immediately after AT LINE-SELECTION, the value for SY-LSIND already corresponds to the new list level. If there is output, no new list level is created on the screen. To end branching after the first details list, the following modification is required:

```
AT LINE-SELECTION.
  IF SY-LSIND < 2.
    WRITE: / 'List level           :', SY-LSIND COLOR 4.
    WRITE: / 'Row relative         :', SY-CUROW COLOR 4.
    WRITE: / 'Column relative      :', SY-CUCOL COLOR 4.
    WRITE: / 'Absolute line number :', SY-LILLI COLOR 4.
    WRITE: / 'Content              :', (40)SY-LISEL COLOR 4.
  ENDIF.
```

Line selection is only possible for lines that have really been written to the list. Double-clicking after the last line causes no reaction in the report.

A selected line is made available in SY-LISEL as it was written in the list. This means that if there were an analysis, only the information that appears in the list would be available for analysis. For hypertext applications (for example, online help), this is very useful, since you can use SY-CUCOL from SY-LISEL to determine the term where the cursor is located. For other applications, on the other hand, this behavior is disadvantageous. If, for example, a data record should be selected on the basis of the information in the basic list, and information in addition to this should be displayed in the details list, this would only be possible if the complete key were to appear in the basic list and could be filtered out of the SY-LISEL value. This requires quite a bit of effort, would lead to complex lists, and would fail in multi-line list entries. You can therefore use a special statement to place additional data in a so-called hidden data area for every line of the list. This data is stored and is made available again when the line is selected. It does not appear on the screen. The use of the hidden data area requires a special command and a program structure tailored to it. The command is as follows:

HIDE *field.*

This statement places the current contents of the field into the hidden data area of the current line. The field can be a simple field, a field string or the header line of a table. You can handle any number of fields using HIDE. To enter several fields in a HIDE statement, you must use the colon variant of the command:

HIDE: *field_1, field_2, ... field_n.*

There are several statements, which reference a line in the list, that read the data hidden with HIDE back into the field. One of the commands that causes a read-back, for example, is the AT LINE-SELECTION event. The following programming example demonstrates the use of the HIDE command:

```
REPORT YZZ34020 LINE-SIZE 60.
DATA: LINE TYPE I VALUE 1.

FORMAT COLOR 4.

DO 30 TIMES.
  WRITE: / 'Line', SY-INDEX, AT SY-LINSZ ' '.
  HIDE LINE.
  WRITE: / 'Next line', AT SY-LINSZ ' '.
  HIDE LINE.
  WRITE: /.
  ADD 1 TO LINE.
ENDDO.

AT LINE-SELECTION.
  IF SY-LSIND < 2.
    WRITE: / 'Selected line:', LINE COLOR 4.
  ENDIF.
```

This report, too, makes several experiments possible. In the list, you output two related lines at a time and highlight them in color for better orientation. For each of these lines, you place the value of the LINE field in the hidden data area using HIDE. Separate the line groups with a blank line, for which there is no HIDE statement.

Selection of a line with a double-click retrieves the value for the LINE field from the hidden data area and displays it. No program statements are necessary for this; the procedure is automatically controlled by the system.

Although you have not hidden a value for the separator lines, double-clicking on one of the blank lines creates a details list and displays a value for LINE. This value, however, is always the value from before. It does not change, even when different blank lines are selected. If a line is selected for which no information has been hidden, the current field contents do not change. The execution of the event, however, is independent of the existence of data in the hidden data area. This undesirable behavior of interactive reports makes some minor modifications necessary in the program, so that the HIDE mechanism delivers accurate results. As a side effect, the display of details lists can be made dependent on data in the hidden data area, making analysis of SY-LSIND extraneous in many cases. To test this, copy the preceding program and modify the copy.

```
REPORT YZZ34030 LINE-SIZE 60.
  ...
DO 30 TIMES.
  ...
ENDDO.

CLEAR LINE.

AT LINE-SELECTION.
  IF NOT LINE IS INITIAL.
    WRITE: / 'Selected line:', LINE COLOR 4.
    CLEAR LINE.
  ENDIF.
```

This report corresponds for the most part to the previous version. The only new thing is that after list creation, the LINE field is set to its initial value with the CLEAR statement. In the statement block for line selection, no query is made for the list level any more. Instead, the LINE field is tested against the initial value. The details list is created only if the LINE field has a value that is different from the initial value. This is the case only if a line has been selected for which information for the LINE field was hidden using HIDE. After the details list is created, LINE must of course be reset to the initial value.

When analyzing data elements that originate in the hidden data area of a line, the field names must absolutely match. Errors result if several individual fields of a field string are hidden in the HIDE statement, but later the entire field string is tested against the initial value.

Since no HIDE statements are executed in the details list, the IF statement also prevents the creation of additional details lists. The various details lists or the different lines of a list can place different data fields into the hidden data area. At the AT LINE-SELECTION event, the application's actual action can be determined based on either the current field contents or the system field SY-LSIND.

In the examples presented so far, the details list always occupies the entire screen. There is an ABAP/4 statement that allows you to define windows (popups) of any size for the display of a details list. The statement is as follows:

WINDOW STARTING AT *x1 y1* **ENDING AT** *x2 y2.*

The coordinates determine the upper left (x1, y1) and lower right (x2, y2) corners. The ENDING AT clause is optional. If you leave this clause out, the dimensions of the window are automatically determined according to the current dimensions of the list. A short example for this statement follows. The changes affect only the creation of the details list:

```
AT LINE-SELECTION.
  IF NOT LINE IS INITIAL.
    WINDOW STARTING AT 5 5 ENDING AT 50 10.
    WRITE: / 'List level            :', SY-LSIND COLOR 4.
    WRITE: / 'Row relative          :', SY-CUROW COLOR 4.
    WRITE: / 'Column relative       :', SY-CUCOL COLOR 4.
    WRITE: / 'Absolute line number :', SY-LILLI COLOR 4.
    CLEAR LINE.
  ENDIF.
```

It is not mandatory that a list be created for the AT LINE-SELECTION event. Other activities, such as the call of a dialog application, are also possible. The following example demonstrates the call of a function module.

```
REPORT YZZ34040 LINE-SIZE 60 .

TABLES: TRDIR,                 " ABAP/4 programs table
        TEXTPOOL.              " Structure for language-dependent text

* internal table for language-dependent text
DATA: BEGIN OF ITEXT OCCURS 20.
  INCLUDE STRUCTURE TEXTPOOL.
DATA: END OF ITEXT.

FORMAT COLOR 4.

SELECT * FROM TRDIR
  WHERE CNAM = SY-UNAME      " current user
    AND APPL <> 'S'          " no generated programs
    AND SUBC IN ('l', 'M', 'F') . " no Includes

* output the program name
  WRITE: /(60) TRDIR-NAME.
  HIDE TRDIR.

* language-dependent text for program in Itab
  READ TEXTPOOL TRDIR-NAME INTO ITEXT LANGUAGE SY-LANGU.

* search for description
  CLEAR ITEXT.
```

```
   ITEXT-ID = 'R'.
   READ TABLE ITEXT.

* if exists, then output
   IF SY-SUBRC = 0.
     WRITE: /(60) ITEXT-ENTRY.
     HIDE TRDIR.
   ENDIF.

* separator line
   WRITE /.

ENDSELECT.

CLEAR TRDIR.

AT LINE-SELECTION.
   IF NOT TRDIR IS INITIAL.

* call editor for program, display only
   CALL FUNCTION 'EDITOR_PROGRAM'
     EXPORTING
       PROGRAM    = TRDIR-NAME
       MESSAGE    = ' '
       DISPLAY    = 'X' "      if SPACE, then changing possible
       TRDIR-INF  = TRDIR.
     CLEAR TRDIR.
   ENDIF.
```

The attributes of all of the programs that the current user has created are read from the TADIR table. The text of several of the attributes ensures that no Include files and no programs generated by the system appear in the list. The TADIR table contains only some general management information. The short description must be read separately. All of an application's language-dependent elements, such as numbered text elements, headings and even the short description, are stored separately from this management data and must be read with additional statements when needed. There is a specific variant of the READ command for this. You do not have to access tables directly. The READ command fills an internal table with all of the texts of the various types. The program's short text must be read from the internal table with a code. If a short description exists, it is also output to the list. For both lines, the entire header line of the TADIR table is placed in the hidden data area. When a line is selected, the program editor for that program is called. The DISPLAY flag ensures that the editor begins working in display mode after the call.

In addition to calling a function module, you can trigger the following functions in interactive reporting:

- provision of information for the selected record in global fields or in application-spanning areas of memory, and exiting of the report with LEAVE
- CALL TRANSACTION for calling a transaction
- SUBMIT for calling another report

- CALL FUNCTION for calling function modules
- CALL DIALOG for calling dialog modules
- CALL SCREEN for calling screens that belong to the current program

Of special interest is the last variant, due to the fact that a report, too, can have several screens. Analogous to this, you can turn on list mode in an interactive application with the statement LEAVE TO LIST-PROCESSING. This makes the boundaries between reports and dialog applications somewhat more fluid. Mixing a lot of list processing and dialog processing in a single application, however, quickly leads to incomprehensible programs.

If you want to create a screen in a report, you can use the Object Browser's object list or the navigation mechanism. In the source code, you enter the CALL SCREEN statement. After a double-click on the screen number, the system creates this screen. The programmer must enter several additional specifications in various screens.

Generally, all of the examples described above also function at the AT USER-COMMAND event, assuming this event is processed upon triggering of a custom function code. At this event, as well, a line selection is performed on the line specified by the current cursor location. However, if only one action should be executed for a line, such as always branching to a second list, it is easier for the user to select this line with a double-click than for him or her to first place the cursor on the line and then click on a pushbutton, or to search for a menu function. Analogous to this, the modification commands described below can also appear at the AT LINE-SELECTION event.

3.4.4   List modifications

Not all actions in a list require the creation of a details list. Often it is enough to edit or process lines of the current list. One example of this is the various selection lists, such as those in matchcodes. Depending on the type of list, you can mark one or more data records and transfer them into the calling program. Sometimes, this selection requires modifying entries in an existing list.

The most important command for modifying a list is the MODIFY command. It exists in several variants, with several clauses being possible for each variant. The following command should suffice to demonstrate this principle:

```
MODIFY CURRENT LINE.
```

This command always refers to the last line selected with line selection. In the basic form noted above, the contents of the SY-LISEL system field are output at the position of the line in the list. The MODIFY command can only change existing lines; it cannot add new ones. Upon successful execution, the command fills the system field SY-SUBRC with the value 0. If MODIFY could not find the line to be changed, SY-SUBRC is filled with a value unequal to 0. The error code is always dependent on whether the line to be changed was found or not. The clauses still to be described do not influence the contents of SY-SUBRC.

To process the following examples, you always need a status that can deliver four additional function codes of the form FNCx, in addition to the default function codes required for list processing. Please create this status on your own, preferably by copying and then modifying the default status STLI out of the SAPMSSY0 program. Give the new status the name STAT1. The target program YZZ34050 must already exist before you make the copy. Copying is easiest using the Object Browser. In the object list of the SAPMSSY0 program, place the cursor on the STLI status and click on the icon for *Copy* or call the menu function *Development object* → *Copy*. In the popup that appears, enter the target for the copy process, then click on the *Copy* pushbutton.

The individual function codes of the status should be available with the function keys from F5 on and with pushbuttons. You can keep copying the first program and modifying the copy accordingly for the various examples. To do this, you must mark the GUI Status point explicitly in the popup in which you select the elements to be copied. The program itself is somewhat larger, since an internal table is needed to demonstrate all of the possibilities.

```
REPORT YZZ34050.

DATA: BEGIN OF ITAB OCCURS 5,
  SELECT,
  NAME(20),
END OF ITAB.

ITAB-SELECT = ' '.
ITAB-NAME = 'iXOS Munich'.
APPEND ITAB.

ITAB-NAME = 'iXOS Leipzig'.
APPEND ITAB.

ITAB-NAME = 'iXOS Walldorf'.
APPEND ITAB.

ITAB-NAME = 'iXOS America'.
APPEND ITAB.

ITAB-NAME = 'iXOS Prague'.
APPEND ITAB.

SET PF-STATUS 'STAT1'.

LOOP AT ITAB.
  WRITE: / ITAB-SELECT, ITAB-NAME.
ENDLOOP.

AT USER-COMMAND.
  IF SY-LILLI > 1.
    CASE SY-UCOMM.
      WHEN 'FNC1'.
        SY-LISEL+30 = 'modified'.
        MODIFY CURRENT LINE.
    ENDCASE.
  ENDIF.
```

In this program, an additional text is appended to the line where the cursor is located with function code FNC1 (double-clicking does not work here!). While the original lines of the list appear highlighted in color (usually blue, depending on the system setting), the character strings added appear in the normal color (usually black).

Additional changes to the output format are easy. You expand the AT USER-COMMAND section of the first example by analyzing a second function code:

```
AT USER-COMMAND.
...
  WHEN 'FNC2'.
    MODIFY CURRENT LINE LINE FORMAT INTENSIFIED OFF.
```

The FNC2 function code turns off highlighting for the current line. Behind FORMAT, you can use all of the options for this command. In this example, they refer to the entire line, due to the second LINE. Multiple use of the term LINE in the statement may not be very elegant, but it is fully correct syntax-wise. The first LINE belongs to CURRENT; the second one specifies that FORMAT should count for the entire line. The explicit use of LINE hints that modification of individual line fields is also possible. You do this for the format using the clause

... FIELD FORMAT *field_1 format_1* ... *field_n format_n.*

You enter the names of the fields to be modified and their formats one after the other. This command, too, can be demonstrated quite easily with a third function code, which changes the color highlighting for the first two fields of the line:

```
AT USER-COMMAND.
...
WHEN 'FNC3'.
  MODIFY CURRENT LINE FIELD FORMAT ITAB-SELECT COLOR 7
                           INVERSE ON ITAB-NAME COLOR 5.
```

Field modification works only if data fields have been output in the list. The attributes of constants cannot be changed afterwards in this way. For ABAP/4, numbered text is also a type of data field, so it can also be given a new format.

To enable the modification of individual fields, the internal control logic must store the fields that were output for every line, along with their output positions. You can also use this information to assign new contents to the fields of a line. The command for this resembles the command for assigning new formats:

... FIELD VALUE *field_1* **FROM** *value_1* ... *field_n* **FROM** *value_n.*

The following lines demonstrate the use of this command. They set the ITAB-SELECT field of the current line to the value "X", thereby marking the record for eventual analysis later.

```
AT USER-COMMAND.
...
  WHEN 'FNC4'.
    MODIFY CURRENT LINE FIELD VALUE ITAB-SELECT FROM 'X'.
```

You can simplify the command somewhat by entering the new values directly into the fields to be changed. You can then leave the FROM clause out of the MODIFY statement. In the case of a single statement, as in this example, this version of the command provides no advantage. However, in a case where several fields should be changed, the MODIFY statement becomes much clearer.

```
WHEN 'FNC4'.
  ITAB-SELECT = 'X'.
  MODIFY CURRENT LINE FIELD VALUE ITAB-SELECT.
```

If the modified fields were used in a HIDE statement during creation of the list, the hidden data area is also changed. Of course, this field change affects only the values in the list or in the hidden data area. This form of assignment does not change the internal table or even a database table used for the creation of the list. This causes a new problem. The most recently used function code marks a line. This information is, of course, analyzed in practical applications. It must therefore be possible to read the current field values from the list. You cannot use SY-LISEL, because it is difficult to select individual values there. Using a special form of the READ statement, you can read current values directly from the list. This represents the counterpart to the MODIFY VALUE statement. In the form presented, the MODIFY statement works with the current line, due to the CURRENT LINE clause. Several other clauses are possible in place of this clause that extend the operational area to any lines in any of the lists that exist in the program. These clauses are possible for both READ and MODIFY. The READ statement will therefore be demonstrated with one of these alternative clauses, which can also be used in connection with the MODIFY statement. In practice, optional reading is necessary in a list more often than optional writing is. The syntax of the READ command is as follows:

READ LINE *index* **FIELD VALUE** *list_field_1* **INTO** *prog_field_1* ...
                          list_field_n **INTO** *prog_field_n*.

The list fields to be named are read from the line identified by the line number and written into program-internal fields. If you leave out the INTO *prog_field* clause, the contents of the list fields are presented in the original fields. All of the fields not named remain unchanged. In addition to reading the explicitly specified fields, all of the field contents hidden with HIDE are also read for this line. If there are no values in the hidden data area, the corresponding fields remain unchanged. The result of the READ command is therefore only really meaningful when all of the fields to be read by READ are initialized immediately before this command is executed. This has already been demonstrated for the analysis of the HIDE fields.

   The example that follows corresponds in large part to the one already used, although several changes are also necessary in the main program. An additional data field and two events must be entered. Due to the events for the title, you also need a statement to mark the beginning of the "main program." You should therefore insert the following statements between the declaration of the internal table and the first assignment to the table's header line:

```
...
DATA I TYPE I. "help field for choosing

* Basic List Heading
TOP-OF-PAGE.
  WRITE: / 'Please select'.
  SKIP.

* Details List Heading
TOP-OF-PAGE DURING LINE-SELECTION.
  WRITE: / 'You have selected:'.
  SKIP.

* Create basic list
START-OF SELECTION.
```

You need to modify the loop for list creation only slightly:

```
LOOP AT ITAB.
  WRITE : / ITAB-SELECT INPUT, " manual input possible
            ITAB-NAME.
ENDLOOP.
```

In addition, you need to modify the existing event and add a second one:

```
* commands per pushbutton
AT USER-COMMAND.

* only if cursor located in correct line
  IF SY-LILLI > 1.

    CASE SY-UCOMM.

* set selection flag
      WHEN 'FNC1'.
        MODIFY CURRENT LINE FIELD VALUE ITAB-SELECT FROM 'X'.

* reset selection flag
      WHEN 'FNC2'.
        MODIFY CURRENT LINE FIELD VALUE ITAB-SELECT FROM ' '.

* details list with all marked records
      WHEN 'FNC3'.
        IF SY-LSIND < 2.
          I = 1.
          CLEAR ITAB.

* read line I from list
          READ LINE I FIELD VALUE ITAB-SELECT ITAB-NAME.

* SY-SUBRC <> 0 → line I does not exist → end list
          WHILE SY-SUBRC = 0.
```

```
              IF ITAB-SELECT <> ' '.
                WRITE: / ITAB-NAME.
              ENDIF.

* set line counter I to next line and read it
              I = I + 1.
              CLEAR ITAB.
              READ LINE I FIELD VALUE ITAB-SELECT ITAB-NAME.
            ENDWHILE.
          ENDIF.

      ENDCASE.
    ENDIF.

* line selection with double-click
AT LINE-SELECTION.
    CLEAR ITAB.

* read flag of line at cursor location
    READ CURRENT LINE FIELD VALUE ITAB-SELECT.

* analyze and modify flag
    IF ITAB-SELECT = ' '.
      MODIFY CURRENT LINE FIELD VALUE ITAB-SELECT FROM 'X'.
    ELSE.
      MODIFY CURRENT LINE FIELD VALUE ITAB-SELECT FROM ' '.
    ENDIF.
```

Up to the setting of the status, this program is like the preceding example. The I field later assumes the function of a line counter when the list is read. The loop for creating the basic list also exhibits a modification. When the SELECT field is output, this field is assigned the INPUT format. Such a field is input-ready in the list, meaning it can be filled manually with a value by the user. This value exists only in the list; its input does not change the internal table. This behavior corresponds to field changes with MODIFY. Inputs in such a field are later read with the READ statement.

At the AT USER-COMMAND event, the flags are either set or turned off with the function codes FNC1 and FNC2. This command is nothing new; it has already been used in the preceding example. Of interest is the processing for function code FNC3. Here, all of the records of the basic list are read. All of the marked data records are written to a details list.

For reading, the command READ is used in the form already mentioned. A record counter is necessary for reading, which must be set to a starting value before the first line is accessed. The field string that contains the fields to be read by READ is also initialized before every READ. The return code of READ corresponds to that of MODIFY. So it only provides information about whether a line to be read exists or not. You cannot determine from the error code of READ whether the field to be read is in this line. The contents of ITAB-SELECT are unequal to the initial value after READ only if the field has actually been found and filled in the list with a value unequal to a blank space. Only then is the *Name* field of that line output to the details list. The details list is not displayed until all of the statements of the AT USER-COMMAND block have been processed. Therefore, all additional READ statements still read from the basic list. In more complex programs, one must always pay attention to which list is currently active, to ensure that the wrong list is not read.

After a list line has been analyzed, the line counter is incremented and the next line is read. If a line should be read after the end of the list, READ delivers a return code unequal to zero. This can serve as the criterion for termination.

In selection lists such as this, of course, you can also use the middle of the line selection to turn marking on and off. The AT LINE-SELECTION event shows the statements needed for this. First, the current line is read. Depending on the state of the flag, it is then either set or turned off. This is one of the cases in which reading the current line with the clause CURRENT LINE makes sense.

You can manually fill the fields for the selection flag of every data record with values. The sample program evaluates all contents except a blank space as a set flag. In screens in which true check boxes or radio buttons can be defined, the internal control logic ensures that marked fields are always represented by the letter X. Other applications may therefore be programmed in such a way that equality to the letter X is checked instead of inequality to a blank space. Incorrect entries by the user could then lead to undesirable application behavior. For this reason, the WRITE statement also provides an option for designing check boxes. You can test this by switching one line in the example:

```
WRITE: / ITAB-SELECT AS CHECKBOX,  " manual input possible
         ITAB-NAME.
```

Instead of the input field for any alphanumeric data, there is now a check box in the list. You can change the content of the field with a single mouse click in the field. A marked field is represented internally by an X, an unmarked field by a blank space. Changing the marking works without the statements after AT LINE-SELECTION, too. You can temporarily comment out the two MODIFY commands of this event. However, the line selection ensures that marking can be set by double-clicking on any place in the line, while check box input fields only react to a mouse click within the field.

The examples presented so far only allow you to make modifications in a line without changing the structure or length of the list in the process. Several of the uses mentioned in the beginning for interactive reporting, however, assume that the list is created from scratch when a line is selected. Double-clicking on a node in the Workbench object list does not display a details list, but rather builds the actual list (the basic list) again. Such functionality is easiest to achieve by linking a screen to embedded list processing. The screen itself is inactive during this process; it is processed in the background with SUPPRESS DIALOG. In the PAI section of the screen, a list is constructed with LEAVE TO LIST-PROCESSING. A user command or a line selection in this list triggers an event, which ends list processing using LEAVE LIST-PROCESSING. In this case, however, the screen is re-executed, meaning the list is rebuilt. At the end of this section, you will find a more extensive example that demonstrates the linking of a dialog-oriented application to list processing.

3.4.5   Function codes on the selection screen

There are only a few reasons to trigger a custom function code on the selection screen. One reason would be to set certain values for the parameters or modify the selection screen with the push of a button (display additional input fields or such). Another reason would be to set options for the layout of the list or for the execution of the program. The primary use of many low-level reports is not the display of information but rather the execution of data-related actions, such as repairing skewed data or checking data sets for consistency. Many of these reports run in two different modes, a check mode that only displays errors and a repair mode that also removes errors. You could define two pushbuttons for such reports, *Check* and *Repair*, and set a flag that would be analyzed in the report according to the function code. However, it is not exactly good programming style to branch from the selection screen into completely different lists with custom function codes.

It has already been demonstrated how custom function codes can be created and analyzed on a selection screen using additional pushbuttons. A more general, but more time-consuming, method consists of setting a custom status for the selection screen. This can occur at the INITIALIZATION event or the AT SELECTION-SCREEN OUTPUT event. You should always use a copy of the default status as the basis for a custom status, so that all of the important function codes are retained. You can find the default status of a selection screen in the RSSYSTDB program. It is called %_00.

You must, of course, process all custom function codes yourself. At the AT SELECTION-SCREEN event, the current function code is contained in the SSCRFIELDS-UCOMM field, regardless of whether the function code was created with a menu or with pushbuttons on the selection screen.

The system handles all function codes that are created by the default status of the selection screen. After the function code in question is processed, the selection screen is active again, as long as the report was not exited and there was no branching to the execution of the report. Function codes that are not processed by the system also lead to renewed processing of the selection screen. From a program-related point of view, the selection screen is the real kernel of the program, and all other functions, including the creation of the actual list, are, in the final analysis, subroutines. You start the creation and output of the list from the selection screen using the function code ONLI. To have a custom function code start list creation, you need to use a little trick, as shown in the following example.

```
REPORT YZZ34060 NO STANDARD PAGE HEADING.

TABLES SSCRFIELDS.
DATA G_UCOMM LIKE SSCRFIELDS-UCOMM.

PARAMETERS P1.

SELECTION-SCREEN SKIP 3.

SELECTION-SCREEN FUNCTION KEY 1.
SELECTION-SCREEN FUNCTION KEY 2.

SELECTION-SCREEN PUSHBUTTON 5(15) PB1 USER-COMMAND 0001.
```

```
SELECTION-SCREEN PUSHBUTTON 25(15) PB2 USER-COMMAND 0002.
SELECTION-SCREEN PUSHBUTTON 45(15) PB3 USER-COMMAND 0003.

INITIALIZATION.
  SSCRFIELDS-FUNCTXT_01 = 'Button 1'.
  SSCRFIELDS-FUNCTXT_02 = 'Button 2'.
  PB1 = 'Button 3'.
  PB2 = 'Button 4'.
  PB3 = 'Button 5'.

AT SELECTION-SCREEN.
  G-UCOMM = SSCRFIELDS-UCOMM.
  SSCRFIELDS-UCOMM = 'ONLI'.

START-OF-SELECTION.
  WRITE: / 'Triggered was Button'.
  CASE G_UCOMM.
    WHEN 'FC01'.
      WRITE '1'.
    WHEN 'FC02'.
      WRITE '2'.
    WHEN '0001'.
      WRITE '3'.
    WHEN '0002'.
      WRITE '4'.
    WHEN '0003'.
      WRITE '5'.
  ENDCASE.
```

The function code that is actually triggered is temporarily stored in a program-internal data field and analyzed in the actual report. List creation starts when SSCRFIELDS-UCOMM is filled with the function code ONLI, which is required for this. The P1 parameter is necessary because a selection screen can only be displayed if it contains at least one parameter or one selection.

3.4.6   An example

Instead of ending with exercises, this chapter ends with the development of a longer example. Since not all of the steps of program development are described in detail, creating this program is also good practice for using the development environment and the various tools.

First, you create a screen and link some simple list processing to it. This list first displays the numbers of all available color attributes. A double click on a number displays or hides several additional lines in the list, which contain examples of this color and other attributes.

In a second section, you create another screen with a single input field. For this input field, you program possible entries help that uses the screen created in the first section.

To create the entire example, follow these steps:

1. Create a module pool. You can choose any name you like that follows the existing conventions. The module pool should have a Top Include, in which you enter the following declarations:

```
DATA: BEGIN OF ITAB OCCURS 20,
   INDEX TYPE I,
   COLOR TYPE I,
   DETAIL,
   TEXT(20),
END OF ITAB.
```

```
DATA: G_INIT VALUE 'X', " Flag: first time screen started
   G_LINE TYPE I,         " uppermost displayed line of the list
   G_PAGE TYPE I,         " uppermost displayed page of the list
   G_INT TYPE I,          " help field
   G_COLOR(20).           " global field for return of line selected, for Part 2
```

2. In this module, create a screen (9100). The fullscreen of this screen should remain empty. You do not need an assignment to the OK Code field. In the course of the application, you use the number 9100 for this screen. The flow logic is shown in the following listing.

```
PROCESS BEFORE OUTPUT.
 MODULE D9100_INIT.
*
PROCESS AFTER INPUT.
 MODULE D9100_FCODE.
```

3. Create the two modules according to the following listing:

```
MODULE D9100_INIT OUTPUT.
* set status for list
  SET PF-STATUS 'STAT1'.
* structure of help table at first call
  IF G_INIT = 'X'.
* initialize internal table
    CLEAR ITAB.
    REFRESH ITAB.
* initialize global fields
    CLEAR: G_INIT, G_INT, G_LINE, G_PAGE.
* one data record for each color
    WHILE G_INT < 8.
      ITAB-INDEX = G_INT + 1.
      ITAB-COLOR = G_INT.
      ITAB-DETAIL = ' '.
      ITAB-TEXT = 'Color'.
```

```
          ITAB-TEXT+7(5) = G_INT.
          APPEND ITAB.
          ADD 1 TO G_INT.
       ENDWHILE.
     ENDIF.
* suppress input in screen
   SUPPRESS DIALOG.
 ENDMODULE.

 MODULE FCODE INPUT.
   LEAVE TO LIST-PROCESSING.
   NEW-PAGE NO-TITLE NO-HEADING.
* output every line of Itab
   LOOP AT ITAB.
     WRITE: / ITAB-TEXT INTENSIFIED OFF.
     HIDE ITAB.
* if flag set, then examples for color and attributes
     IF ITAB-DETAIL = 'X'.
       WRITE: /5 'Normal            ' COLOR = ITAB-COLOR
                                       INTENSIFIED OFF
                                       INVERSE OFF.
       HIDE ITAB.
       WRITE: /5 'Highlighted       ' COLOR = ITAB-COLOR
                                       INTENSIFIED ON
                                       INVERSE OFF.
       HIDE ITAB.
       WRITE: /5 'Inverse           ' COLOR = ITAB-COLOR
                                       INTENSIFIED OFF
                                       INVERSE ON.
       HIDE ITAB.
       WRITE: /5 'Highlighted Inverse ' COLOR = ITAB-COLOR
                                       INTENSIFIED ON
                                       INVERSE ON.
       HIDE ITAB.
       WRITE /.
     ENDIF.
   ENDLOOP.
* because LINE-SELECTION
   CLEAR ITAB.
* if list reconstructed after line selection,
* then jump to old position
   SCROLL LIST TO PAGE G_PAGE LINE G_LINE.
 ENDMODULE.
```

4. Create the status called in the INIT module, STAT1. It should have the type *List*. Fill it with the Menu Painter default. Change the function code for the F3 function key to FT03. Be sure to perform this change in the menus, too.

5. Program the following two events in the module pool, preferably in a separate Include file (MYZZxF91). You must link this Include to the INCLUDE statement in the control program:

```
AT LINE-SELECTION.
  IF NOT ITAB IS INITIAL.

* remember current position of first line displayed
    G_PAGE = SY-CPAGE.
    G_LINE = SY-STARO.

* toggle flag for detail display
    IF ITAB-DETAIL <> ' '.
      ITAB-DETAIL = ' '.
    ELSE.
      ITAB-DETAIL = 'X'.
    ENDIF.

* change data record in table
    MODIFY ITAB INDEX ITAB-INDEX.

* jump back to PBO part of screen → reconstruction of list
    LEAVE LIST-PROCESSING.
  ENDIF.

AT USER-COMMAND.
  CASE SY-UCOMM.
  WHEN 'FT03'.
    LEAVE TO SCREEN 0.

  ENDCASE.
```

6. Create a transaction that uses the 9100 screen as an initial screen. Test the application. It creates a short list with the numbers of the colors available in lists. Double-clicking on one of these lines displays four additional lines with color display examples.

7. Create a second screen (9200). In the fullscreen of this screen, create an input field for the global data field G_COLOR. The flow logic of the second screen has three module calls:

```
PROCESS BEFORE OUTPUT.
  MODULE D9200_INIT.

PROCESS AFTER INPUT.
  MODULE EXIT AT EXIT-COMMAND.

PROCESS ON VALUE-REQUEST.
  FIELD G_COLOR MODULE GET_COLOR.
```

8.   Create the modules called by the 9200 screen:

```
MODULE D9200_INIT OUTPUT.
  SET PF-STATUS 'STAT2'.
ENDMODULE.

MODULE EXIT INPUT.
  LEAVE TO SCREEN 0.
ENDMODULE.

MODULE GET_COLOR INPUT.
  G_INIT = 'X'.
  CALL SCREEN 9100 STARTING AT 5 5 ENDING AT 30 10.
ENDMODULE.
```

9.   Create the status STAT2. Give it the type *Screen*. Only one Exit function is needed in this status to be able to end the application. It is enough to assign to the F3 function key any function code not yet used in the two statuses. Set the Exit attribute for the function code in the function list.

10. Create the function code SELE in the STAT1 status. Assign it to a function key (such as F5) and a pushbutton. You can use *Select* as the text.

11. Enter the function code analysis just created in the AT USER-COMMAND event. You only need a second WHEN branch to do this.

```
WHEN 'SELE'.
  IF NOT ITAB IS INITIAL.
    G_COLOR = ITAB-TEXT.
    LEAVE TO SCREEN 0.
  ELSE.
    MESSAGE ID 'YY' TYPE 'I' NUMBER '000'.
  ENDIF.
```

12. Create a second transaction that uses the 9200 screen as an initial screen, then test the application.

Discussion

In Step 1, you declare the data needed in the program. The internal table, or more precisely the DETAIL flag, later controls the display of the additional lines with the examples of the output formats. The two fields INDEX and COLOR are, like the text, included just to simplify the program somewhat. In principle, you could also derive the information contained in them at runtime from the index (data record number) of the internal table.

Calling a list in a dialog application requires a screen. You create this in Steps 2 and 3. In the Init module, you fill the internal table with eight data records. Deleting the table before filling it is not yet necessary in the first part of the example. The reasons for this will be described later. In addition to the list being constructed, several global fields are initialized, to reach a defined basic state. These later store the current line of the list.

At the end of the Init module, you suppress dialog processing with SUPPRESS DIALOG. The application therefore begins immediately with processing of the sole PAI module. In this module, list processing is turned on and the list is built. For every line of the internal table, at least one line appears in the list. If the DETAIL flag is turned on in the internal table, four additional lines are output with the various attribute combinations. When the internal table is created, this flag is turned off, so the list receives only eight simple lines. For every line that is output, the entire data record is placed in the hidden data area with HIDE.

When the list is displayed, the user can perform two activities. Pressing the F3 function key or clicking on the corresponding icon triggers the FT03 function code. This is processed by the event AT USER-COMMAND and leads to ending of the application, since it jumps to screen 0. The default function code suggested in the Menu Painter may not be used at this point. The default function code would be analyzed by the system and would end only list processing, not the entire application. After list processing, however, the calling screen is activated again, which would immediately create the list again. Orderly exiting of the application is only possible using self-programmed analysis of a function code.

The most interesting part of the application is the AT LINE-SELECTION event. After a line selection, the data record placed in the hidden data area with HIDE is automatically retrieved in the ITAB header line, if one of the data lines of the list has been selected. The leading IF statement is responsible for recognizing this.

The display of the list on screen is controlled mainly by the DETAIL flag in the data records of the internal table. This is toggled in the table's header line. Afterwards, the data record index contained in the header line is used to update the contents of the internal table. If the index of the data record cannot be directly determined from the retrieved data, the record must be searched for in the internal table. For this reason, a unique key must definitely be stored in the hidden data area for every data record. After modification of the internal table, list processing is ended with an appropriate command. The PBO part of the 9100 screen is processed again. This naturally leads to renewed display of the list. The list is built again completely, according to the flag just set or turned off.

When a list is constructed again, it is displayed beginning with the first line. Since even this little demo list can become longer than a single screen, under certain circumstances, after double-clicking, the user would find himself or herself on a different page of the list than before line selection. To avoid this, the user should save the current line and page number in global fields at AT LINE-SELECTION. After the list is built, the statement SCROLL jumps to that line of the list.

Embedded list processing is often used to provide the user with possible entries help in which he or she can select from a certain set of values. The primary procedure can be demonstrated easily with the program just created. First, in Step 7 of the statements above, you create a screen, 9200, with an input field. The only task of this screen is to demonstrate possible entries help for a data field. Other than that, it has no real functionality. The data field that works together with this input field must be accessible from both the 9100 screen and the 9200 screen, since it is used for data transfer between the two. Screen 9200 is executed in dialog mode. It therefore needs a status that has a function code for exiting the application. You create this function code as an Exit function code in the status. In the PAI section, only a simple Exit module is required.

You implement the possible entries help using another event in the flow logic of the 9200 screen. This is processed when the F4 function key is pressed in the input field. The statements for calling possible entries help are simple, as might be expected. First, you set the flag that triggers initialization of the 9100 screen. If the input field is called several times, the 9100 screen is always called again, but the internal table ITAB is located in the application's global data area and is retained until the transaction is exited. To receive the basic form of the list every time possible entries help is started, you trigger renewed building of the help table using the G_INIT flag.

Afterwards, you call the 9100 screen with CALL. You force execution of the screen and thus of the list into a popup with the clauses STARTING AT and ENDING AT. The 9100 screen is entirely runnable. The list is displayed in the popup. A double-click presents the detailed display for a data record. F3 causes a jump back to the 9200 screen. Since the 9100 screen was called with the CALL statement, the LEAVE TO SCREEN 0 statement does not lead to the end of the entire program, but rather jumps back to the calling screen.

In the 9100 screen, or more precisely at the AT USER-COMMAND event, the only thing you still need to implement is the data transfer to the calling screen. It would be enough to fill the global data field G_COLOR immediately before LEAVE using the text from the ITAB header line, which is filled with data from the hidden text area at AT USER-COM-MAND. To give the user this capability without terminating data transfer, you incorporate an additional function code (SELE) for the data transfer in the status of screen 9100 and analyze it at the AT USER-COMMAND event. When the function code is triggered, the global field G_COLOR is filled with the value of the selected line before the jump back. The function code ends the screen only if a correct line has been selected, however. As the listing implies, the user should receive an error message if no line can be determined. Since the message class and the message in all likelihood do not exist, they will receive only an empty popup without an error message. Even if a message class and a message do exist, there will be no connection between the message text and the cause of the error.

3.5   Function modules and dialog modules

Function modules and dialog modules were mentioned in connection with the commands handled so far, and they have occasionally been used without much explanation. Function modules, in particular, are very powerful tools for modularizing applications.

You create function modules in a so-called function pool. A function pool is comprised of one or more logically linked function modules. The function pool makes global data declarations and common subroutines (form routines) available for all of the function modules contained in it. In this way, it is similar to a module pool. The contents of the data fields declared in the global data area (in the control program) or of internal tables are retained as long as the calling program is active. For this reason, this is sometimes called local memory.

Function modules resemble subroutines (forms). They encapsulate program code and have a user interface for data exchange. There are, however, considerable differences between function modules and traditional subroutines:

- Function modules must be contained in a program of a certain type, called a function pool. They can manipulate the global data of the program to which they belong. A function pool with function modules is also called a function group.

- You can call function modules from other programs using their names. It is not necessary to specify the function pool. Function modules must therefore have names that are unique system-wide.

- You can maintain function modules independently of the function pool using a separate maintenance transaction (SE37, *Development → Function Library*).

- Function modules have a predetermined and documentable user interface. If certain requirements are met, you can expand this user interface without having to change anything in existing programs from which the function module is called.

- A test environment simplifies checking and maintenance of function modules. For every module, you can store test data that allows you to check the behavior after reworking a function module.

3.5.1 Creating function modules

In keeping with the methodology followed to this point, this section describes the creation of a function group and of a simple function module. It also demonstrates the test environment. The section that follows this one discusses detailed information.

When you create a new function module, you must specify to which function pool it should belong. If no suitable function pool exists yet, you must create it. This is the same as creating a new function group. A function group contains one or more function modules. It makes available a commonly usable data area for these modules. It is the logical shell around several function modules.

As is the case with the other development objects, there are several ways to create function groups and function modules. In the end, however, all methods use the same tool, the function module editor. You can access this directly using transaction code SE37, or from the main menu of the SAP Workbench, using a pushbutton, the F8 function key or the menu function *Development → Function library*.

The simplest way to do this, again, is to use the Object Browser. The initial screen of the Object Browser contains a separate four-character input field for function groups. In this field, you enter the name of the function group. You can choose any name, although the first letter should follow the conventions already described (A–X for SAP, Y and Z for customer applications). The system creates the name of the function pool using the character string "SAPL" followed by the name of the function group. In this example, the function group name YZ31 is used. Y is preset, 3 represents the chapter, and 1 represents the first function group. You use the second letter, in this case a Z, to distinguish between users in cases where this example is executed by more than one programmer. Figure 3.41 shows the initial screen of the Object Browser at this point.

After you click on the *Display* pushbutton, the Object Browser constructs the object list for existing function groups. If the desired function group does not yet exist, the Object Browser creates this function group. Several popups appear for this, for example a Workbench Organizer popup. In one of these popups, you record a short description for the function group (see Figure 3.42).

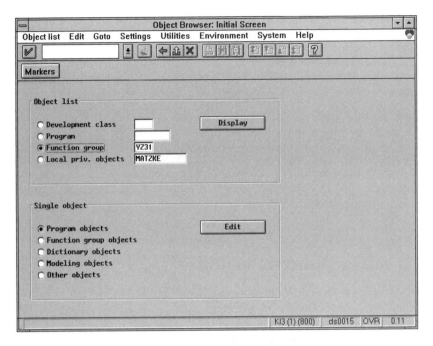

Figure 3.41   Initial screen of the Object Browser

The Object Browser now automatically creates the function pool, which contains two Include files from the beginning. Figure 3.43 shows the object list for a newly created function group. Naming of the Include files proceeds in a similar fashion to naming of module pool Include files. The first five characters consist of the letter L and the name of the function group, and the last three characters can be selected as desired. However, creating your own Include files is less often necessary when processing function groups than when processing other types of programs, since many are created by the system. These automatically created Includes end with the characters Uxx, where xx is either a two-digit number or the two characters XX.

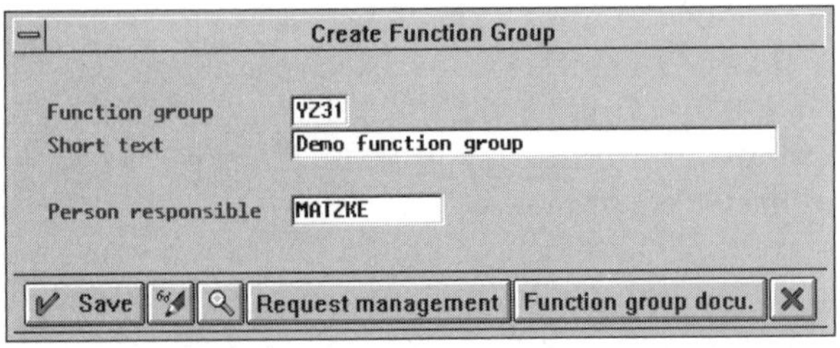

Figure 3.42   Creation of the short description for a new function group

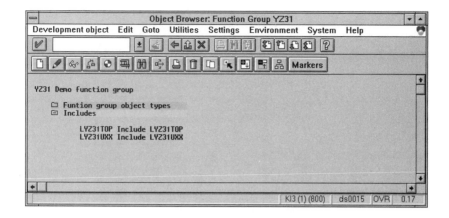

Figure 3.43 Object list of the newly created function group

The newly created function pool contains two Include files. One of these is, again, a Top Include. It contains the program header and later receives the data declarations. You can either enter these manually or create them from within the function modules using the navigation mechanism. Only during the first call of a function group in an application are all of the function group's global fields initialized. All other changes to these fields are possible only through the various function modules of the function group. The values of the global elements are retained until the calling application ends.

The second Include is used by the function pool to manage the function modules of the group. It always ends with the characters UXX. It cannot (and may not) be edited manually.

You can create the individual function modules themselves very easily from the Browser's object list. Place the cursor on the name of the function group. Then choose the menu function *Development object → Create*, press the F5 function key, or click on the corresponding icon to create a new development object. Enter the name of the function module to be created in the popup (see Figure 3.44). This popup resembles the popup used in dialog applications, although the entries are different.

Mark the *Function module* entry in the popup, and enter the name of the module in the input field. Use the name YZ31_TEST_PARAMETER for the first module to be created. Function module names must be unique in the whole R/3 System. So, although it is not required, you usually begin the names of function modules with the name of the function group. This at least avoids mistakes caused by similar-sounding names. In addition, the actual identifiers of the function module indicate its function in a unique fashion without tricks or unusual abbreviations being necessary to guarantee a unique name. The first function module demonstrates the parameter interface and its characteristics. After you confirm the input by clicking on the Create symbol in the popup, the system asks you for additional specifications for the function module (see Figure 3.45).

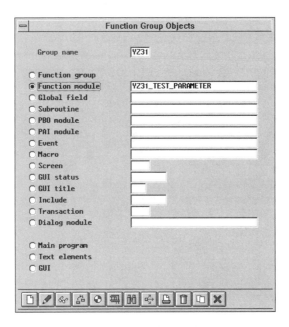

Figure 3.44   Popup for creating a function module

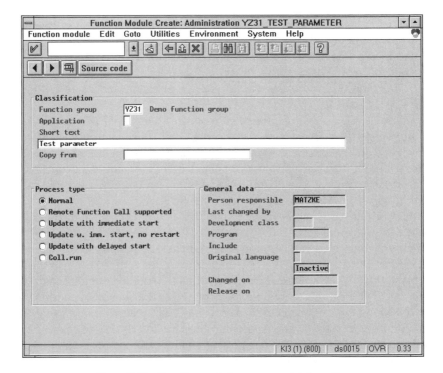

Figure 3.45   Function module management information

These specifications are the short description, the application and the process type. The short description is mandatory. The *Application* field is less important. It is not a mandatory input field and can remain empty. In the group for the process type, the *Normal* entry is marked as the default. An entry here is mandatory. The next section discusses the reasons for this. The information to be recorded in this screen corresponds in its importance to report or screen attributes. For function modules, however, it is called management information.

Save the specifications in the management screen. The system adds several status fields in the screen, for example the name of the Include field, in which the source code for the new function module will be stored later. Every function module receives its own Include file. You should never edit these files directly, for example with the default editor (SE38). In particular, you should never delete these files manually! To guarantee the consistency of the function group, you should only edit function groups using the Object Browser, and you should only edit function modules using SE37.

From the management screen, you can maintain both the parameter user interface for the module and the source code. You can access the appropriate tools with the menu functions *Goto → Imp./exp. user interface, Goto → Tab./exc. user interface* and *Goto → Function module*. Alternatively, you can access the screens for user interface maintenance with the forwards and backwards icons in the toolbar. In contrast to simple subroutines (form routines), in which you enter several specifications when you declare the subroutine to determine the user interface for data transfer, you must define the parameters of a function module in some special screens.

There are three large parameter groups: simple parameters (fields or field strings), tables and exceptions. Only simple parameters will be used in connection with this example. You maintain these with the menu function *Goto → Imp./exp. user interface*. Simple parameters are also divided into three subgroups: import parameters, export parameters and changing parameters. The third group is new in Release 3.0. You maintain all three subgroups in a common screen (see Figure 3.46). For every parameter group, there is a uniquely named section available on the screen.

In the function module, every parameter is identified by a unique name. You enter this name in the *Parameters* field. In the fields *Struct./field* and *Type*, you can specify the data type of the parameter in more detail. These specifications are optional; all parameters not declared in detail are handled as CHAR fields. You can assign a default value (constant or system field) to a parameter. If no value is assigned to the parameter when the function module is called, this default value is used. The user interface of a function module can be expanded at a later point in time. To ensure that already programmed calls of the module do not have to be changed later, you can and must identify the additional parameters as optional parameters using a flag. Parameters with default values automatically become optional parameters.

For the first test, record the parameters represented in Figure 3.46 in the parameter screen of the function module. Table 3.28 shows the settings again.

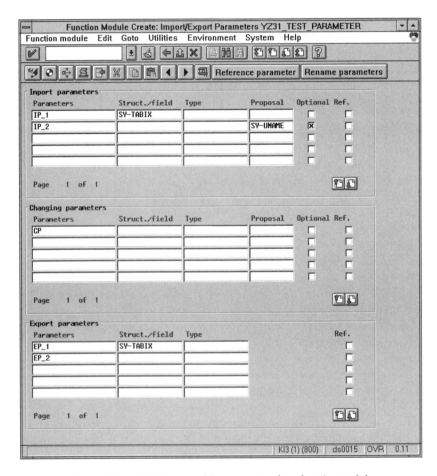

Figure 3.46   Maintenance of the parameters for a function module

Table 3.28   Parameters for the test module

Parameter type	Parameter	Structure/field	Type	Default	Optional	Reference
Import	IP_1	SY-TABIX				
Import	IP_2	SY-UNAME	X			
Changing	CP					
Export	EP_1	SY-TABIX				
Export	EP_2					

After you enter the parameters in the screen fields, save the settings. Using the menu function *Goto → Function module,* call the editor for editing the source code. Use of this editor corresponds to a large extent to use of the familiar editor SE38. There are, however,

differences in some of the pulldown menus, since they contain functions related to the
development object in question. The system starts by creating a framework for the function module that consists of the statements FUNCTION and ENDFUNCTION. The
description of the user interface is automatically inserted in this framework as a comment.
All of the parameter's properties that were set in the parameter screen emerge from the
comments for the user interface. Changes to these comments, of course, have no influence
on the design of the user interface.

You can now enter several specifications in the function module. In this example, several
manipulations of and assignments to the parameters will suffice. You will find the complete source code of the function module, including the automatically created comments,
below.

```
FUNCTION Y310_TEST_PARAMETER.
*"----------------------------------------------------------
*"*"Local User interface:
*"          IMPORTING
*"             VALUE(IP_1) LIKE SY-TABIX
*"             VALUE(IP_2) DEFAULT SY-UNAME
*"          EXPORTING
*"             VALUE(EP_1) LIKE SY-TABIX
*"             VALUE(EP_2)
*"          CHANGING
*"             VALUE(CP)
*"----------------------------------------------------------

  EP_1 = IP_1 * 5.
  EP_2 = IP_2.
  CP = CP + EP_1.

  IP_1 = 9999. " no effect on calling program

ENDFUNCTION.
```

In this example, new values are assigned to the output parameters. These new values
result directly or indirectly from the import parameters, so their analysis can be demonstrated. You can test the function module directly from the development environment, as you
can in report tests. Before you can execute function modules, however, you must activate
them. Only active function modules can be tested or executed. You can turn off activation
at any time. You call both actions from the development environment using the functions
of the *Function module* menu. Upon activation, the module is checked for correct syntax.
Modules with syntax errors cannot be activated. You do not need to reactivate the function module after every change. Once activated, a module remains active. Any changes to
the user interface or the source code become effective immediately.

After successful activation, you can call the test tool for function modules using *Utilities*
→ *Test environment*. The initial screen of the test environment (Figure 3.47) contains input
fields for all of the import parameters of the module to be tested, and these fields are filled
with the defaults declared in the user interface. The length of the input field depends on

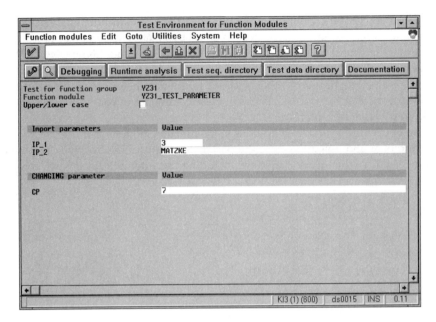

Figure 3.47   Test environment for function modules: input screen

its data type. For parameters that have no type specification, a very long input field is provided. In this case, the system deviates from the default length of 1 for data fields without a type specification.

For all of the parameters that have a default value, this value is entered on the input screen. You can, of course, overwrite this default. The test environment screens use embedded list processing with interactive elements. So you can easily modify the user interface to the interfaces of very different function modules. After you enter the test values, you start the test by pressing the F8 function key or by clicking on the corresponding icon. When processing ends, the return parameters are displayed in a second screen in the test environment (see Figure 3.48). Successful processing of the parameters by the function module is easy to replicate.

The current values of the parameters appear on the results screen. Even the two export parameters that were missing on the input screen appear on the results screen. Although in certain cases the import parameters can be filled with new values in the function module, as demonstrated in the example, this does not influence the fields in the calling program. Such new assignments are only effective within the function module. They can be used to spare local data fields. This is not, however, good programming style.

Instead of the test environment, you could also use a little application to call the function module just created. A separate report or one of the demo programs for embedded list processing would be especially suitable for this.

```
REPORT YZZ35010.
DATA:   X TYPE I VALUE 2,
```

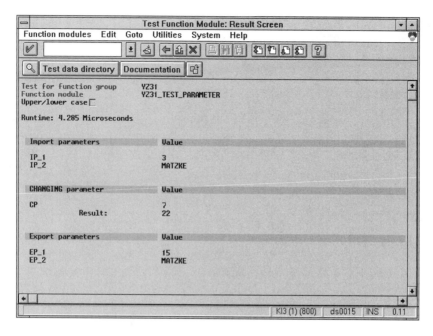

Figure 3.48 Test environment for function modules: result screen

```
      Y TYPE I VALUE 3,
      N TYPE I.
      S(20).

CALL FUNCTION 'YZ31_TEST_PARAMETER'
  EXPORTING
     IP_1 = X
     IP_2 = 'MEIER'
  IMPORTING
     EP_1 = N
     EP_2 = S
  CHANGING
     CP = Y.

WRITE:  / N,
        / S,
        / Y.
```

Of particular note here is the use of the terms import and export. Data that a function module receives, that is, imports, must be sent in the calling program, that is, exported. The function module's import parameters thus appear under the EXPORTING statement in the call, while the parameters declared in the function module as export parameters are identified by IMPORTING.

You must assign data fields as current parameters to all formal parameters that return values to the calling program. You can give constants to all parameters that only pass values to the module.

3.5.2   Function modules in detail

Function modules are used in ABAP/4 applications for logically very different tasks. Accordingly, the attributes that you can set for function modules are very different. A module's programming method must also suit its later purpose. Before the programming and use of function modules are demonstrated with some examples, let us discuss the fundamental principles.

Function type

When you create a new module, you must mark one of several available function types (see Figure 3.45, initial screen of SE37). These function types have decisive influence on the type of processing of a function module. A module given the type *Normal* is the basic form of function module. It is called from applications and executed immediately. The calling program does not continue until the function module has been processed completely. In this kind of call, the called function module must be located in the current R/3 System. A mechanism called *RFC* (Remote Function Call) makes it possible to call function modules in other systems and to execute them there, allowing different SAP systems to communicate with each other and exchange data. The systems involved can have different SAP versions and release versions. If certain prerequisites are met, it is also possible to communicate with non-SAP systems. Function modules to be called from other systems must have the type *Remote Function Call supported*.

All other function types are meant for so-called update programs. Update programs are specialized function modules that require certain specifications both when being declared and when being called later. Database changes, that is, writing data to the database, take a certain amount of time. If many tables are affected by the changes, and these changes in turn trigger other actions (for example, updating indexes or matchcodes), this time period can become so large that comfortable dialog processing is no longer possible, since the application would have to wait until the end of the write procedure. For this reason, complex database changes are not usually executed at the same time as the rest of the program, but are removed to update modules that run asynchronously. These modules are not executed until the calling program triggers a COMMIT WORK. You identify them in the call with the clause

```
.. IN UPDATE TASK.
```

When a module that has been thus identified is called, the system automatically saves the passed parameters without executing the function module. The module can thus be called more than once, using different values for the parameters. The system does not execute the update programs until it encounters a COMMIT WORK, at which time it passes the correct parameters to them. This kind of execution is very practical, since the parameters can be passed in the same way as with other function modules. You can even create and test update modules as normal function modules at first, then change them later into real update programs.

Since update programs run asynchronously to the calling application, they can, of course, not return any values. They may therefore not have any export parameters. Although they can trigger error messages if they encounter errors in processing, they cannot output these messages in the calling program; they only appear in various error logs.

The various function types for update programs differ mainly in their processing events. Update programs of the type *Update with immediate start* and *Immediate start, no restart* are executed immediately. The calling program continues, instead of waiting for the update program to end. So both processes run in parallel. This kind of updating is also called a V1 update. Since the system stores the data to be updated internally, a failed update process can usually be repeated. To prevent such an update repeat, you must use the second function type mentioned.

The last two function types, *Update with delayed start* and *Collective run*, define update programs that run in a time-delayed fashion. The starting point can be delayed until times when the system load is light. This kind of update is also called a V2 update.

For all asynchronous update programs, keep in mind that you cannot predetermine the exact update point. This makes the following case possible: a data record has been written by a transaction, but an application started afterwards cannot find the data record, because the update program has not yet run. You need to take such consequences into consideration when you program your own applications. Often, compromises are necessary between the currentness of the data and the performance of the application.

Parameters

Parameters are used to exchange data between function modules and the calling application. You identify the parameters with their names. When a function module is called, the values passed (latest parameters) are directly assigned to the named, formal parameters of the interface. The sequence of the parameters in the function module call is therefore irrelevant.

The parameters of a function module can be one of three types: simple data fields and field strings, tables, or exceptions. Simple data fields are divided into the following subgroups: import parameters, export parameters, and changing parameters. The parameters can have different properties and attributes, which are described first here. However, not all of the attributes are available for all types of parameters. You set the attributes in the parameter screen. There is one parameter screen for simple parameters and another for tables and exceptions.

You can give the formal parameters of a function module's interface a type description. In this case, the system checks at runtime whether the type and the properties of the latest parameter match the formal parameter. If this is not the case, the control logic generates a runtime error.

Parameter name
The *parameter name* identifies the parameter. You must create it in accordance with the naming conventions for data fields. To increase clarity, the parameter's type (import, export, changing, table) is often indicated with a prefix, although this is not required.

Since changing parameters are new in Release 3.0, but you need data fields that function as both import and export parameters for recursive calls, you can create import and export parameters with identical names. In this case, they must have matching data types.

Structure and Struct./field
When you declare data fields, you can use the LIKE statement to copy the data type and several other properties from existing fields or field strings. You can also describe parameters of function modules more specifically this way. To do so, enter the field to be copied or the structure in the *Struct./field* attribute. You must use a structure to describe table parameters. Therefore, on the second parameter screen, the corresponding input field is simply called *Structure*. In the comments you insert in the function module source code, you reference the type assignment for the description of the interface using the LIKE or STRUCTURE statement.

Type
Beginning with Release 3.0, type declarations are possible in ABAP/4. They can be entered directly in programs, or they can be located in so-called type pools. You can include a type pool in an application with the statement

```
TYPE-POOL type-pool.
```

If the type declaration is in the control program of a function group, you can also declare parameters using references to data types from this type pool.

Default
You can give a simple parameter a default value. This value is used if there is no explicit assignment to the parameter when the function module is called in a program. The default value can be either a constant of the data type in question, or one of the system fields (SY-...) Although you can enter a program-internal field, for example from the function group's global data area, this has no effect when the function module is executed.

Optional
Parameters for which this flag has been set do not necessarily have to be given a value when the function module is called. Their use is therefore optional. If the interface for a module that is already used in programs is later changed, and the new parameters are identified as optional, the existing calls do not have to be changed. All of the parameters with a default value automatically become optional parameters. If an assignment is missing for a mandatory parameter when a module is called, the system reacts with a runtime error.

Reference
In traditional programming languages such as C or Pascal, when parameters are passed to subroutines, they are passed either as value parameters or as reference parameters. In the case of value parameters, the value of the latest parameter is copied into a local data area, to which the formal parameter then points. If the value of the formal parameter is changed in the function module, this has no influence on the value of the latest parameter. In the case of passing by reference, the formal parameter directly points to the contents of the latest parameter. Changes to the formal parameter have a direct effect on the latest

parameter. Using the *Ref.* flag, you can determine the type of parameter passing for simple parameters in function modules. Tables are always passed as reference parameters.

Reference parameters are not necessary for function modules in ABAP/4. The concept of import and export parameters already guarantees the passing of values to the calling program. However, passing by reference saves memory and improves performance somewhat, since no copying of data is necessary. For this reason, tables have always been passed as references.

There is one peculiarity to note in the case of reference parameters, which occurs when an exception is triggered in the function module. This corresponds somewhat to the triggering of a message in screens. Processing of the function module immediately ends, and the calling program continues after the calling point. All value assignments to reference parameters become effective at the moment of assignment. They are therefore retained even if the function module ends with an exception after the assignment. Value parameters, in contrast, are passed only if the function module ends in an orderly fashion!

An explanation of the various parameter types follows the description of the attributes.

Import parameters
Import parameters are used to pass data to the function module. In the case of value parameters, import parameters can be filled again in the function module, since the value of the latest parameter does not change when an assignment is made to a value parameter. The assignment of a new value to an import reference parameter, on the other hand, triggers a runtime error, since such an assignment changes the value of the latest parameter.

In a function module call, both constants and data fields can be assigned to import parameters, regardless of whether they are value parameters or reference parameters. In comparison to methodology of other, comparable programming languages, this is unusual. In those languages, the compiler writes the constants directly into the created machine code. No memory is reserved for them in the data area, making passing by reference impossible.

For import parameters, you can set all of the attributes mentioned above.

Export parameters
Export parameters are used in function modules to return results to the calling program. The export parameters are assigned values in the function module. After the function module is processed, the contents of the export parameters are passed to the latest parameters, changing these. Export parameters can also be read and used on the right side of assignments within a function module. This only makes sense, however, once the export parameter has been assigned a correct value. Prior to that, its contents are undefined, because no data is passed from the latest parameter to the export parameter.

Export parameters are automatically optional parameters. They do not need to be analyzed. When you call a function module, you can comment out or delete any of the export parameters that are not needed. You cannot set default values for export parameters in the interface definition.

Changing parameters
Changing parameters exhibit the properties of import and export parameters. They accept the value of the latest parameter and make it available to the function module. If you

make an assignment to a changing parameter, the value is passed into the latest parameter after the function module has been processed. Just as you can for input parameters, you can use all of the attributes mentioned for changing parameters.

Table parameters

You pass internal tables to the function module using the parameter type *Table parameters*. Passing is always by reference parameter. Changes to the function module take effect immediately in the table. Beginning with Release 3.0, you may identify tables as optional, which was not possible in earlier releases. You must always create table parameters with a reference to a structure or a data type.

Exceptions

When a function module is processed, unforeseen events may occur that the calling program must be made aware of. Since a function module can be called by various applications in different contexts, it is often not possible to react appropriately to such events in function modules. For this reason, you can send error situations to the calling program using something called exceptions. You define the exceptions that are possible in the function module's interface. These are the names that describe the exceptions. No other specifications or attributes are required. Using intuitive names for exceptions (such as NOT_FOUND, RECORD_LOCKED) makes it easier for the user of the function module to analyze the exceptions. The next section describes how exceptions are handled in the program.

Exception handling

For various reasons, function modules should not always react to unexpected events themselves, but leave this to the calling program. Function modules must therefore inform the calling program in a suitable way about errors or unexpected events. This information should be as transparent as possible, and the passing mechanism for it should be flexible. It is also important to ensure that exception situations are actually processed and do not remain undetected. All of these tasks are taken on by exception handling.

The exceptions already mentioned are executed in the interface of a function module. They are available in the function module as a sort of predefined identifier. In a function module call, the programmer can decide which of the possible exceptions the function module should handle itself. A numerical value is assigned for this purpose to the exceptions to be handled. This value need not be unique. Different exceptions can have the same value. In this case, however, you can no longer distinguish in the calling program which exception was triggered. If this is not required anyway, it is also enough to enter the exceptions to be handled without value assignments behind EXCEPTIONS. The value that is returned later for these exceptions is undetermined, but unequal to zero. Exceptions that are not to be handled do not receive any values. You must either comment them out or delete them from the call.

When a function module triggers an exception that should be handled in the calling program, the function module ends, and the exception's number is placed in the SY-SUBRC field. In the calling program, this system field can then be analyzed. The assignment of a number to an exception is enough to signal to the function module that this exception is handled by the calling program. It is not possible to check whether the calling program is really reacting to the exception.

How a function module reacts to exceptions that are not analyzed by the calling program depends on the type of event in the function module. Exceptions must be triggered explicitly in the function module. They are not simply generated automatically when any problem occurs. There are two commands for this. You trigger an exception with

RAISE *exception.*

If the calling program handles this exception, handling takes place as described. If the calling program does not handle this exception, however, the system generates a runtime error. The next variant for creating exceptions is somewhat more flexible. You give the MESSAGE statement a clause, as follows:

MESSAGE ... RAISING *exception.*

The function module now no longer reacts with a runtime error to an exception that is not handled. Instead, it reacts by sending the message specified in the MESSAGE statement. If the exception is handled by the calling program, on the other hand, the process already described takes place. However, several other fields are filled in addition to SY-SUBRC. The message class relevant for the MESSAGE statement is passed to the SY-MSGID field. Analogous to this, the SY-MSGTY field is filled with the message type, and the SY-MSGNO field is filled with the actual message number. Using the WITH clause, you can pass up to four parameters to a MESSAGE-RAISING statement, which appear in the error text instead of several place holders. These parameters, if present, are passed into the system fields SY-MSGV1 through SY-MSGV4. This way, the calling program has all of the information available for calling the error message itself, if necessary.

Often you only need to check for successful execution of the function module in the calling program, without having to distinguish between the individual exceptions. In this case, it is not necessary to pass all of the exceptions individually in the module call. Using the OTHERS exception, which is predefined by the system, you can name all of the exceptions for a function module that were not individually listed in the call. You can use this exception both with and without value assignment.

It is sometimes undesirable for function modules to trigger messages with MESSAGE themselves. You can suppress this even if message sending in the module is handled with the simple MESSAGE statement without the RAISING clause. To do this, you use the ERROR_MESSAGE exception, which is also predefined, in the module call. If you set this exception, all E and A messages in the function module immediately trigger the ERROR_MESSAGE exception. All other messages are suppressed.

The following program demonstrates the use of the various exceptions in more detail. First, you create a new function module with the function type *Normal* in the function group that was used earlier. It is relatively simple. The comments in the source code illuminate the structure of the interface. You maintain the exceptions together with the table parameters in a separate screen, which you access with the menu function *Goto → Tab./exc. user interface.*

```
FUNCTION YZ31_TEST_EXCEPTION.
*"----------------------------------------------------
*"*"Local User interface:
*"      IMPORTING
*"         VALUE(a) LIKE SY-TABIX DEFAULT 1
*"      EXCEPTIONS
*"         A1
*"         A2
*"         A3
*"----------------------------------------------------
  CASE A.
    WHEN 1.
      RAISE A1.
    WHEN 2.
      MESSAGE ID 'YY' TYPE 'I' NUMBER '002' RAISING A2.
    WHEN 3.
      MESSAGE ID 'YY' TYPE 'E' NUMBER '003' RAISING A3.
    WHEN 4.
      MESSAGE ID 'YY' TYPE 'I' NUMBER '000'.
    WHEN 5.
      MESSAGE ID 'YY' TYPE 'E' NUMBER '000'.
  ENDCASE.
ENDFUNCTION.
```

Depending on the value of the import parameter, the function module triggers either an exception or an error message. The following report calls the module with several exception handling variants. The number of the exception to be triggered appears opposite the return value SY-SUBRC.

```
REPORT YZZ35020 NO STANDARD PAGE HEADING.

* combined interception of several exceptions
WRITE: / 'Combined interception' COLOR 5.
DO 3 TIMES.
  CALL FUNCTION 'YZ31_TEST_EXCEPTION'
    EXPORTING
      A = SY-INDEX
    EXCEPTIONS
      A1 A2 A3.

  WRITE: / 'Exception:', (4)SY-INDEX, 'SY-SUBRC', (4)SY-SUBRC.
ENDDO.

* selective interception of a single exception + Message in FM
WRITE: /, / 'Selective interception' COLOR 5.
DO 4 TIMES.
  CALL FUNCTION 'YZ31_TEST_EXCEPTION'
```

```
      EXPORTING
         A = SY-INDEX
      EXCEPTIONS
         A1 = 11
         A2 = 12
         A3 = 13.
   WRITE: / 'Exception:', (4)SY-INDEX, 'SY-SUBRC', (4)SY-SUBRC.
ENDDO.

* Use of OTHERS and ERROR_MESSAGE
WRITE: /, / 'OTHERS and ERROR_MESSAGE' COLOR 5.
DO 5 TIMES.
   CALL FUNCTION 'YZ31_TEST_EXCEPTION'
      EXPORTING
         A = SY-INDEX
      EXCEPTIONS
         A2 = 1
         OTHERS = 99
         ERROR_MESSAGE = 33.

   WRITE: / 'Exception:', (4)SY-INDEX, 'SY-SUBRC', (4)SY-SUBRC.
ENDDO.
```

The first DO loop triggers the three true exceptions and the type I message one after the other. The three exceptions are handled by the calling program, but no individual numbers are assigned to the exceptions. The output in the report shows that for all three exceptions, a value of 1 is returned in SY-SUBRC. This makes it possible to determine that an exception was created in the function module, but not which one. This becomes possible only when values are assigned to the exceptions, as shown in the second loop. The values assigned to the exceptions are random. Normally you would use consecutive numbers, not random values as in the example. Within the loop, the function module now also outputs a message. Because of the I type, this appears as a popup that must be confirmed. This message type does not cause the program to terminate. For this reason, a zero appears as a return value in the report.

The statements in the third loop demonstrate the clauses OTHERS and ERROR_MESSAGE. The second exception is handled separately. For it, the return value 1 appears in the report. The OTHERS statement assigns the value 99 to all exceptions that are not explicitly listed, in this case A1 and A3. ERROR_MESSAGE prevents error messages of all types from being sent. Now, neither the Info popup nor the true error message triggered by the parameter 5 appears. The latter, however, places the value of the ERROR_MESSAGE exception in the SY-SUBRC field.

There are several other characteristics of exception handling that cannot be presented in the example above, since they lead to program termination. This occurs, for example, when exceptions are triggered that the calling program does not intercept. For this reason, you should call the function module in the following form, in another report that you create yourself. Save the report before every start!

```
CALL FUNCTION 'YZ31_TEST_EXCEPTION'
  EXPORTING
    A = 1. " Insert 1 through 3 one after the other
```

Peculiarities in calling

You call function modules with the statement

CALL *function_module* ...

You must enclose the name of the function module in single quotes. It must appear in capital letters, otherwise the function module will not be found! You must list all of the parameters to be passed in the statement. In addition, you must identify the individual parameter groups using the statements EXPORTING, IMPORTING, TABLES and EXCEPTIONS. Since function module interfaces can be quite large, the ABAP/4 program editor provides a help function for inserting the entire statement. With the menu function *Edit →
Insert statement*, you can call a help function that can insert several complex statements in the source code. In a popup (Figure 3.49), it first asks for data for the object to be inserted.

In this popup, mark the *CALL FUNCTION* radio button. In the corresponding input field, you must enter the name of the module to be inserted. If you do not know the correct syntax, you can call up the possible entries help with the F4 key.

After you confirm the entry by pressing the Enter key or by clicking on the corresponding icon, the system inserts a complete command for calling the module in the source code. This call contains all of the function module's parameters. Each parameter appears on a separate line. Although all of the optional parameters are copied into the source code, they are commented out. You can activate them if necessary by removing the comment character and assigning a current parameter. For parameters with defaults, the default is entered in the assignment. Since such parameters are automatically optional, they are naturally also commented out. They need to be included in the call only if a value

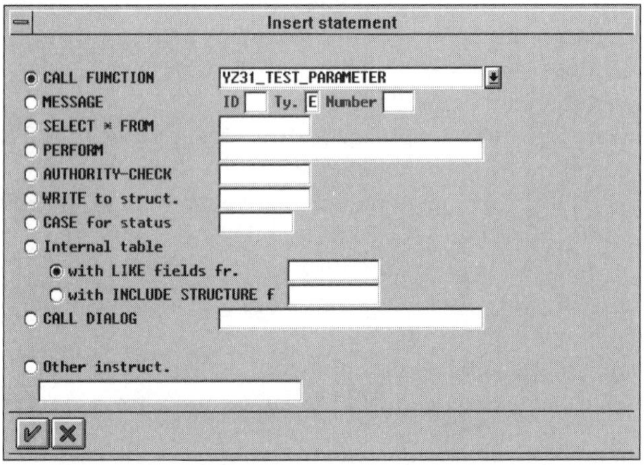

Figure 3.49   Popup for insertion of a function module

other than the default value should be passed. Lines that are commented out can remain in the source code. This makes it very easy to make changes later by removing the comment character and assigning a value.

Mandatory parameters appear in real statement lines not identified as comments. Since value assignments are still missing, however, an error would be displayed if such a program were started or if its syntax were checked separately. You must assign values to these parameters. If a parameter is missing when a function module is called, a runtime error is triggered.

All of the exceptions declared in the function module also appear in the automatically generated call. The system gives them consecutive numbers. If an exception should not be handled, it can be commented out. The programmer can easily change the assigned numbers.

Automatic commenting out sometimes results in minor errors. If all of the parameters in a parameter group are optional, the corresponding group identifier (for example, EXPORTING or TABLES) must be commented out manually. If such a statement appeared without being followed by parameters, this would cause a syntax error.

In addition to the simple call seen in the examples so far, there are several other clauses for the CALL FUNCTION statement, which call special function types or ensure a particular type of execution of the called function module. At this point, only the IN UPDATE TASK clause will be examined. It is required for calling update function modules.

Documentation

Since function modules are often created for cross-application use, documentation for the module itself, the function group as a whole and the individual parameters takes on considerable importance. A potential user should receive enough information from the documentation for the parts mentioned to use the function module. A look at the source code should be unnecessary. You should thoroughly document all function modules that are meant for cross-application use. You can call the tools for this from various places in the development environment. Here, again, the focus is on the Object Browser.

You can document a function group from the group's object list (see Figure 3.43). Place the cursor on the name of the function group and call the menu function *Edit* → *Documentation* → *Change*. The Object Browser calls a particular editor (SAP Script Editor) in which you can record detailed documentation. Although this editor also works in line-oriented fashion, it has little else in common with the program editor used elsewhere. There are fundamental differences in their usage philosophies and their actual usage (menu functions, function key layout). Using the SAP Script Editor, you can give documents certain format statements (visible in the left margin of the input area).

You can also use the function just mentioned to give individual function module documentation (Figure 3.50). To do this, you just place the cursor on the name of the function module. You can create detailed documentation in the function module editor. You can jump to documentation maintenance for a function module from just about anywhere in the function module editor by using the menu function *Goto* → *Documentation*.

This screen contains input fields for the short description of a module (identical to the title recorded in the initial screen of the function module editor) as well as all parameters and exceptions. You can enter a short description in the parameter input fields. Double-

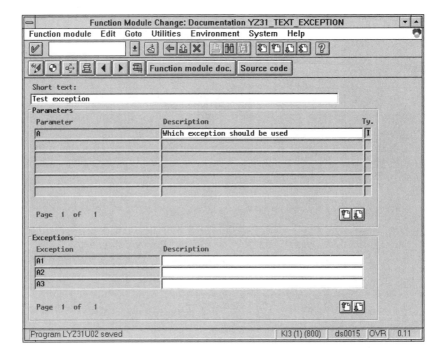

Figure 3.50   Screen for maintaining function module documentation

clicking on an input field branches to the SAP Script Editor, in which you can create documentation for this parameter. Double-clicking on the input field of the short description tion allows you to edit the entire documentation for the function module, which is also accessible from the function group's object list.

3.5.3   Examples of function modules

The examples described up to this point demonstrate some of the characteristics of function modules. This section presents some practical application examples for using function modules.

Standardized dialogs

Programs often require various standard queries. The function library of the SAP system already contains a great many such dialogs. They adhere to the requirements of the SAP Style Guide. You can and should use these function modules in custom applications, to provide the user of the SAP system with a consistent user interface. Although in the end the queries are built by a screen, implementing them as function modules offers greater flexibility. The function modules available for use are divided into different task areas. They also belong to different function groups (SPO1 through SPO6 and STAB). The following areas are distinguished:

- Confirmation prompts
- Selection of alternatives
- Input of data
- Dialogs for printing
- Display of text
- Display of tables

The simplest of the modules is POPUP_TO_CONFIRM_LOSS_OF_DATA. You use this module, for example, when you want processing of a screen to be terminated, for example by an exit function, without saving the data. You have probably encountered such queries often in your work up to this point. This function module is very easy to use. The listing shows a section from a real program.

```
...
IF ( ( FLG_ACTION = C_JA ) OR ( SY-DATAR = 'X' ) ).
  CALL FUNCTION 'POPUP_TO_CONFIRM_LOSS_OF_DATA'
    EXPORTING
      TEXTLINE1      = TEXT-015 " Do you really want to cancel?
"     TEXTLINE2      = ' '
      TITEL          = TEXT-021 " Caution!
"     START_COLUMN   = 25
"     START_ROW      = 6
    IMPORTING
      ANSWER         = L_ANSWER.

  IF L_ANSWER = 'J'.
    LEAVE TO SCREEN 0.
  ENDIF.
ELSE.
  LEAVE TO SCREEN 0.
ENDIF.
...
```

This example clearly demonstrates the use of this module. Three of the parameters are mandatory. They include a text (TEXTLINE1), the title that appears in the header of the popup (TITLE) and the return parameter (ANSWER). With the ANSWER parameter, the module returns information stating which of the two pushbuttons in the popup was used. This value is either 'J' or 'N'. In the module, the default answer is *No*, to ensure that accidental confirmation of the popup with the Enter key does not lead to program termination. Analyzing this very simple module, both its source code and its other elements (such as user interface definition and documentation), provides interesting insights into programming and strengthens knowledge already gained.

Although some other function modules make considerably more complex tools available, they also require more time-consuming programming. The considerably more complicated program that follows uses two function modules, one for entering values and one for selecting data records from a table. For simple demonstration purposes, the statements are incorporated in a report. A few minor changes can turn this report into simple possible entries help that can be used at the PROCESS ON VALUE-REQUEST event. To do this, you would move the report's source code (except the first line with the REPORT statement) to a module, or, even better, to a subroutine (form). You would then replace the output of the selected value with an assignment to the screen field. Finally, of course, you would have to remove the WRITE statements.

The report first displays a popup in which two templates can be entered, one for the name of a user and one for a development object. Examples of development objects are programs, tables or module pools. After recording these two values, the application reads all of the objects from the TADIR that correspond to the selection criteria entered and lists them in table form in a second popup. In this popup, an entry can be selected with a double-click. As a control, this entry is output in the actual report.

Because of its size, this listing is divided into several sections for explanation. You will find explanations for each source code section between the parts of the listing.

```
REPORT YZZ35030 NO STANDARD PAGE HEADING.
TABLES TADIR.

*...fields for input of search criteria
  DATA: L_NAME LIKE TADIR-OBJ_NAME,   " development object name
        L_AUTHOR LIKE TADIR-AUTHOR,   " owner of the object
        L_RETURNCODE LIKE SY-TCODE,   " return value FM
        L_FIELD_LEN TYPE I,           " help field length
        L_LINES TYPE I.               " help field line counter
```

At the beginning of the program, some data fields must be declared. In addition, of course, the table to be analyzed, TADIR, must be specified. The names of the help fields all begin with the prefix L_. This prefix is meant to identify local fields. In the "main program" of a report, this is not necessary. ABAP/4 programs, however, especially dialog-oriented applications, make intensive use of global fields. These global fields are often also read or even written to in subroutines, circumventing interfaces. Differentiating between locally and globally valid fields can considerably increase the clarity of an application.

```
*...macro for declaration of internal tables
  DEFINE DEFITAB.
    DATA: BEGIN OF &1 OCCURS &3.
      INCLUDE STRUCTURE &2.
    DATA: END OF &1.
  END-OF-DEFINITION.

*...table for input fields
  DEFITAB I_INF HELPVAL 10.

*...table for field identifiers of the list popup
  DEFITAB I_TABF HELP_VALUE 10.

*...table for data lines of the list popup
  DATA: BEGIN OF I_VALUES OCCURS 100,
```

```
   LINES(256) TYPE C,
 END OF I_VALUES.
```

In addition to the simple data fields, three different internal tables are required, which provide the function modules mentioned with data. Two of these tables are derived from Data Dictionary structures. These structures do not need to be declared with TABLES, as long as they are only used in the INCLUDE STRUCTURE statement. The names of the internal tables receive the prefix *I_* for unique identification. The description of the input fields of the first popup is constructed in the I_INF table. The corresponding function module returns the values read in this table. The two other tables define the structure of the list popup (I_TABF) and fill the table's fields with values (I_VALUES). To save coding effort, a macro is used in the declaration.

```
*...structure of the definition for the input screen
 CLEAR I_INF.
 I_INF-TABNAME    = 'TADIR'.
 I_INF-FIELDNAME  = 'OBJ_NAME'.
 I_INF-KEYWORD    = 'Development object'.
 DESCRIBE FIELD TADIR-OBJ_NAME LENGTH L_FIELD_LEN.
 I_INF-LENGTH     = L_FIELD_LEN.
 I_INF-VALUE      = '*'. " Preset
 I_INF-LOWERCASE  = ' '.
 APPEND I_INF.

 CLEAR I_INF.
 I_INF-TABNAME    = 'TADIR'.
 I_INF-FIELDNAME  = 'AUTHOR'.
 I_INF-KEYWORD    = 'Agent'.
 DESCRIBE FIELD TADIR-AUTHOR LENGTH L_FIELD_LEN.
 I_INF-LENGTH     = L_FIELD_LEN.
 I_INF-VALUE      = SY-UNAME. " Preset
 I_INF-LOWERCASE  = ' '.
 APPEND I_INF.
```

The fields of the input popup must be uniquely described by several parameters. This description replaces the definition of the fields in a screen. The specifications required are correspondingly extensive. For every screen field, a data record must be created in the I_INF table. The fields TABNAME and FIELDNAME name a field from the Data Dictionary that the function module needs to determine the correct structure specifications. These specifications are necessary for the type conversion of the value entered.

Every input field is described by an identifying prefix that must be entered in the KEYWORD field. The desired length of the input field must appear in the LENGTH field. This value should be derived from the Data Dictionary. In the case of custom modifications, it may under no circumstances exceed the length stored in the Data Dictionary. An entry in the LOWERCASE field causes upper- and lowercase to be heeded. If this field is not set, values entered are automatically converted to uppercase. The INTENSE field is set, highlighting the field name on the screen.

The VALUE field is the actual value field. The values contained there when the function module is called are displayed and edited. The function module returns the values recorded in the popup in the same field.

```
CALL FUNCTION 'HELP_GET_VALUES'
    EXPORTING
"       CUCOL        = 5
"       CUROW        = 5
        POPUP_TITLE  = 'Search terms development objects'
    IMPORTING
        RETURNCODE   = L_RETURNCODE
    TABLES
        FIELDS       = I_INF
    EXCEPTIONS
        NO-ENTRIES   = 01.

*...after correct input values in prog fields
  IF ( SY-SUBRC = 0 ) AND ( L_RETURNCODE = SPACE ).
    LOOP AT I_INF.

      CASE I_INF-FIELDNAME.
        WHEN 'OBJ_NAME'.
          L_NAME = I_INF-VALUE.
          TRANSLATE L_NAME USING '*%+_'.

        WHEN 'AUTHOR'.
          L_AUTHOR = I_INF-VALUE.
          TRANSLATE L_AUTHOR USING '*%+_'.
      ENDCASE.

    ENDLOOP.
  ELSE.
    WRITE: / 'Not a valid entry'.
    EXIT.
  ENDIF.
```

Calling the function module is relatively easy. Use the menu function *Edit → Insert statement* to insert the call into the source code. The statement need then only be supplemented with several parameters, such as the title and the previously created table with the field descriptions.

When the function module ends, both SY-SUBRC and RETURNCODE return information about the execution of FM. In the case of true errors, an exception is triggered that sets the SY-SUBRC field to a value unequal to zero. If entry is terminated at the desire of the user, a value unequal to SPACE appears in the RETURNCODE field.

After the function module has been called and has ended properly, the values recorded in the popup appear in the VALUE field of the internal table. To be able to use them in the rest of the program, they must be passed from the table fields into local fields in the program. This is done with a LOOP program loop in the I_INF table. This loop analyzes the

FIELDNAME field, to assign the value from VALUE to the correct data field in the program. After the value is passed, any wildcards are converted. The user normally uses the characters * and +. The LIKE operator of the SELECT statement, however, expects the characters % and _.

```
*...fill the table with the individual fields,
*...every field one record
*...sequence: 1st line, 1st field; 1st line, 2nd field;
*...2nd line, 1st field...
  SELECT * FROM TADIR
  WHERE OBJ_NAME LIKE L_NAME
    AND AUTHOR LIKE L_AUTHOR.

    I_VALUES = TADIR-OBJ_NAME. APPEND I_VALUES.
    I_VALUES = TADIR-PGMID.    APPEND I_VALUES.
    I_VALUES = TADIR-OBJECT.   APPEND I_VALUES.

  ENDSELECT.

  IF SY-DBCNT = 0.
    WRITE: / 'No development objects found'.
    EXIT.
  ENDIF.
```

After the search terms are read in, the search can be started in the database. The field values of the data records found must be passed to the I_VALUES table individually, and absolutely according to the structure of the list popup's table defined below. If the SELECT statement does not find any data records, the program ends.

```
*...construct selection list

*...fill the table for column identifiers
*...first, column 1 for name of the object
  I_TABF-TABNAME = 'TADIR'.
  I_TABF-FIELDNAME = 'OBJ_NAME'.
  I_TABF-SELECTFLAG = 'X'.        " selection field, is returned
  APPEND I_TABF.

*...afterwards, column 2 for object group
  I_TABF-TABNAME = 'TADIR'.
  I_TABF-FIELDNAME = 'PGMID'.
  I_TABF-SELECTFLAG = ' '.
  APPEND I_TABF.

*...finally, column 3 for object type
  I_TABF-TABNAME = 'TADIR'.
  I_TABF-FIELDNAME = 'OBJECT'.
  I_TABF-SELECTFLAG = ' '.
  APPEND I_TABF.
```

The second function module builds a popup with a list. For this, it needs to have the structure of the list passed to it. This structure must correspond to the contents of the I_VALUES table. In particular, the number of columns in the table must match the number of values written from the data record in I_VALUES, since the table's fields are later filled line by line from I_VALUES, without additional checks. Declaring the table is easy. It is simply a matter of passing the table and the field name again, so that the function module can take type specifications from the Data Dictionary. One column in the table can have a special meaning. You identify it by setting the SELECTFLAG field. When a table line is selected, the contents of this marked column are returned to the calling program.

```
*...call the function module that creates the selection list
  CALL FUNCTION 'HELP_VALUES_GET_WITH_TABLE'
"      EXPORTING
"         CUCOL                           = 0
"         CUROW                           = 0
"         DISPLAY                         = ' '
"         FIELDNAME                       = ' '
"         TABNAME                         = ' '
"         NO_MARKING_OF_CHECKVALUE        = ' '
"         TITLE_IN_VALUES_LIST            = ' '
"         TITLE                           = ' '
"         SHOW_ALL_VALUES_AT_FIRST_TIME   = ' '.
        IMPORTING
          SELECT_VALUE                    = L_NAME
        TABLES
          FIELDS                          = I_TABF
          VALUETAB                        = I_VALUES
        EXCEPTIONS
          FIELD_NOT_IN_DDIC               = 01
          MORE_THAN_ONE_SELECTFIELD       = 02
          NO_SELECTFIELD                  = 03.

  IF SY-SUBRC = 0.
    WRITE: / 'Selection:', L_NAME.
  ELSE.
    WRITE: / 'ERROR'.
  ENDIF.
```

The application ends with the call of the second function module. The module can be modified with a great number of parameters. In the standard case, however, it is enough to pass the two internal tables and assign a data field for the return value. If a line has been selected in the list, this value is output in the list.

Reading of screen fields

The example just described introduces another set of problems. Possible entries help that works according to the principle above requires the entry of values by the user. Although the user may already have entered a value in the screen that could now be used as a search term, at the PROCESS ON VALUE-REQUEST event, the values contained in the screen have not yet been passed to the program-internal fields. However, using a certain function module, help is possible here too. It allows values to be read directly from a screen, bypassing the standard passing mechanism. The actual work is taken over by the DYNP_VALUES_READ function module. It expects only a few parameters.

```
CALL FUNCTION 'DYNP_VALUES_READ'
     EXPORTING
          DYNAME                  =
          DYNUMB                  =
  "       TRANSLATE_TO_UPPER      = ' '
     TABLES
          DYNPFIELDS              =
     EXCEPTIONS
          INVALID_ABAPWORKAREA    = 01
          INVALID_DYNPROFIELD     = 02
          INVALID_DYNPRONAME      = 03
          INVALID_DYNPRONUMMER    = 04
          INVALID_REQUEST         = 05
          NO_FIELDDESCRIPTION     = 06
          UNDEFIND_ERROR          = 07.
```

The DYNUMB and DYNAME parameters are used to pass the number of the screen and the name of the program contained in this screen. The TRANSLATE_TO_UPPER flag takes care of converting the value or values read to uppercase. The table to be passed in DYNPFIELDS at first contains the name of the field or fields to be read in the FIELD-NAME fields. After successful execution of the function module, the values read appear in the FIELDVALUE fields of this table. The exact structure of the table to be passed to DYNPFIELDS can be seen in the function module's parameter interface.

3.5.4   Dialog modules

Dialog modules resemble normal dialog transactions that have been condensed and are still accessible for data exchange only through a precisely defined interface. In this way, they resemble function modules. One or more dialog modules are assigned to a module pool the way function modules are assigned to a function pool. This module pool contains the same elements as a normal dialog application, that is, a user interface, screens and modules. There is no analogy, however, to the term function group.

Except for the interface definition for a dialog module, its programming corresponds to that of a normal dialog application. For this reason, you should first create a module pool. You can also program the functionality, that is, create screens and the modules for these. Afterwards, you can call the tool for maintaining dialog modules from the basic screen of the Workbench using *Development → Programming environ. → Dialog modules* or the SE35 transaction code. There, you record the name and create the module with the

Create pushbutton. In the subsequent screen, you enter the mandatory short description, the name of the module pool and the number of the initial screen. In additional screens, you define the user interface. This procedure corresponds to the procedure for creating the user interface of function modules, although the user interface of a dialog module is simpler.

Strictly speaking, dialog modules represent only one precisely defined calling possibility for screens, which could also be executed other ways, for example with CALL SCREEN. They are therefore implemented much less often than function modules.

4 Maintenance of the Data Dictionary elements

In addition to requiring programming work *per se*, that is, writing source code, creating an ABAP/4 application often requires creating elements in the Data Dictionary. You can implement certain subtasks such as the possible entries help or maintenance modules without programming, simply by maintaining Dictionary elements. This chapter describes the Dictionary elements and their specific properties, as well as the tools for maintaining those objects. The examples, or created objects, presented in this chapter serve as the basis for other examples in this book, in particular the long demo application in Chapter 6. It is therefore a good idea to carry out all of the examples and exercises. The structure of the individual sections of this chapter corresponds largely to the structure of preceding chapters, with a practical demonstration being followed by an extensive section with theoretical explanations.

You can access the tools described below from the main menu of the ABAP/4 Workbench using the *ABAP/4 Dictionary* pushbutton, the menu function *Development →* *ABAP/4 Dictionary*, or the SE11 transaction code. The initial screen for Dictionary maintenance appears (Figure 4.1).

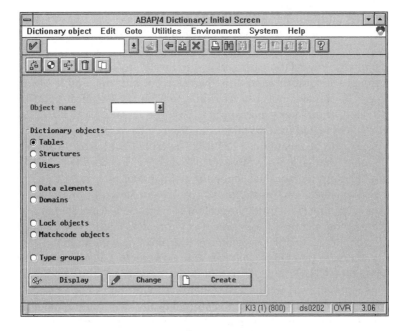

Figure 4.1   Initial screen for Dictionary maintenance

On this initial screen, in the single input field, you enter the name of the object to be edited. You must define the object's type using the radio buttons. The three pushbuttons on the screen branch to the typical editing types: Create, Change and Display. Objects of different types can have the same name. This is not true, however, of all types. Views, structures, and tables have a common name range. An object of one of these three types must have a name that is unique across all three types.

The elements created in this chapter have the character string ZZ in their names. You can replace these two characters with unique initials if desired. This allows several programmers to work in the same system without influencing each other.

4.1   Domains, data elements, tables and structures

Chapter 2 described the basic relationships between domains, data elements and tables. The same information will not be repeated here. The Dictionary elements described in this section are used to create two very simple tables. One of these tables is for storing codes for different branches of industry, and the other is for storing the language-dependent long texts for these codes.

4.1.1   Domains

Domains serve as the basis for table field definition. They represent a direct link to the database. They contain technical attributes such as the data type and the length. Beyond that, you can enter additional specifications to restrict the set of values that is predefined by data type and field length. To some extent, domains have lost their character as purely technical descriptive elements, due to automatic value checking of constants and value tables and the foreign key relationships related to this. Many domains also indirectly contain application-specific information. It is therefore not unusual, and is sometimes even necessary, to create domains not just according to a purely technical point of view, but with an eye towards their later use in applications. The reasons for this will become clear later, once you have created the two tables mentioned above.

The first domain to be created is YZZBEZ. The table field based on this should later accept an identifier, that is, a descriptive text. To create a domain, you enter the name of the domain in the input field of the Dictionary maintenance tool, mark the *Domains* radio button, and click on the *Create* pushbutton. The screen shown in Figure 4.2 appears, in which you can enter almost all of the important specifications for a domain.

As is true for almost all other development environment objects, you must enter a short description for domains. Its purpose is informational only, so its contents are not critical. Truly important are the two fields *Data type* and *Field length*. Give the new domain to be created the data type CHAR and a length of 30, as shown in Figure 4.2. To suppress the automatic conversion of field contents to uppercase, mark the *Lowercase letters* check box. Save the entries. The *Output length* field is automatically filled. In the case of other data types, other fields might be filled automatically. No additional specifications are necessary for the YZZBEZ domain.

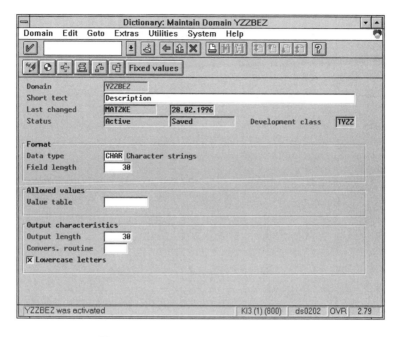

Figure 4.2   Maintenance screen for a domain

A new domain, or changes to an existing one, does not take effect until the domain has been activated. You activate a domain by selecting the appropriate menu function or a pushbutton. When you reactivate a domain that is already being used in data fields and tables after changes, all of the dependent objects (tables, data elements and so on) are also reactivated, since the new attributes must become effective for them, as well. Activation of the dependent objects can take an extremely long time, if there are many dependent elements. For this reason, when you develop a new application, you should determine the data structure in the beginning, to keep the number of later changes and related time-consuming regenerations to a minimum. There are, however, situations where step-by-step processing of domains with multiple activations is unavoidable.

You can give domains so-called fixed values. When these fixed values are entered in screens, they are automatically checked; deviating entries are not possible. To simplify input, the system creates possible entries help for domains that have value checking; this help displays the set of available values in a selection list. The second domain to be created will be given some fixed values. It should have the name YZZBRA, the data type CHAR, and a length of 1. Record and save these specifications the same way you did for the first domain. Afterwards, you can use the menu function *Goto → Fixed values* or the *Fixed values* pushbutton to jump to the input screen for fixed values. Figure 4.3 shows this screen.

The lower portion of the screen contains a multiple-line list. You record single values or ranges in this list. For every value or range, you can enter a short identifier or description in the last field of the list. This identifier appears later in the automatically created

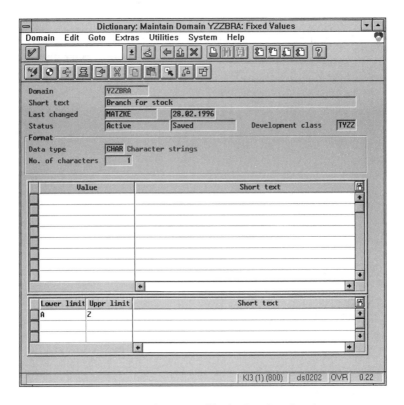

Figure 4.3   Maintenance of fixed values for a domain

possible entries help. So, in case it is later used, you should make it as meaningful as possible. The setting for the domain in Figure 4.3 ensures that later only the letters A through Z can be entered in a data field based on this domain. After entering the fixed values, activate the domain. The domains for the first two sample tables have now been created. The rest of this section describes several important attributes of the domains.

Format

When you maintain a domain, you assign it a format or data type. The data types available for domains do not correspond to either the ABAP/4 data types or the data types of the database system. Rather, they represent a middle layer from which conversion in either direction is possible. The Dictionary can easily convert these data types into the concrete data types of the database system or into ABAP/4 data types. Since the domains take over the link to the database system, or more exactly the link to individual fields of a database table, the domain data types rely on the capabilities of the database systems.

A domain's data type also determines the essential characteristics of the Dictionary field that will later be created with that domain. Some data types have, among other things, an output template for display of the value on screen. The data types available for domains are listed in Table 4.1. Instead of calling these domain data types, one usually refers to them as *external formats*. When you select the external format, you must take into consideration the length or the value range of the value that will be stored in this field later, since the various external formats (types) have different lengths and value ranges.

Table 4.1   Data types for domains, specifications for use in tables

Data type	Description	Template (see footnotes)	Number of chars	Decimal places/default	Output length/ default
ACCP	update period YYYYMM	___.__	6		any/6
CHAR	character string		<= 255		any/number of characters
CLNT	client		3		3
CUKY	currency key, reported by CURR fields		5		5
CURR	currency field, stored as DEC	a, b	<= 17	<= number of characters/2	any/number of characters + separator + plus or minus sign
DATS	date field (YYYYMMDD), stored as CHAR(8)	__.__.____	8		10
DEC	calculation or amount field with decimal point and plus or minus sign	a	<= 17		any/number of characters + separator + plus or minus sign
FLTP	floating point number with 8-byte precision		16	16	any/22 + plus or minus sign
INT1	1-byte integer, decimal number <= 254		3		any/3
INT2	2-byte integer, only for length field before LCHR or LRAW		5		any/5 + plus or minus sign
INT4	4-byte integer, decimal number with plus or minus sign		10		any/10 + plus or minus sign
LANG	language identifier		1		1

Table 4.1 continued   Data types for domains, specifications for use in tables

Data type	Description	Template (see footnotes)	Number of chars	Decimal places/default	Output length/ default
LCHR	long character string, requires preceding INT2 field		> 255		any/number of characters
LRAW	long byte sequence, requires preceding INT2 field		> 255		any/number of characters
NUMC	character string consisting only of numbers		any		any/number of characters
PREC	precision of a QUAN field				
QUAN	quantity field, points to a unit of measure field with the format UNIT	*a*	<= 17	<= number of characters	any/number of characters + separator + plus or minus sign
RAW	uninterpreted sequence of bytes		any		any/2* number of characters
TIMS	time field (HHMMSS), stored as CHAR(6)	__:__:__	6		any/8
UNIT	unit of measure key for QUAN fields		2 or 3		number of characters
VARC	long character string, no longer supported starting with Rel. 3.0		any		any

a   Decimal points and thousands points are set by the system.
b   Number of decimal places depends on the currency.

Some data types have a prescribed length; for other types you can select the field length within certain boundaries. In either case, the screen's input check makes an entry in the *Field length* field mandatory, even if the field length is automatically set or corrected by the system to a predefined value later, when the values are saved or the Enter key is pressed.

All of the data types used in domains are later copied by the Data Dictionary onto the ABAP/4 data types. In the process, different external formats may be converted into the same ABAP/4 data type. If you want a program-internal data field to accept the contents of a table field, you must give it the type and length into which the external data type will be converted. The easiest way to do this is to declare the data field with the help of the LIKE statement. In case you cannot use this statement, Table 4.2 provides some information about the conversion of external data types into ABAP/4 types.

Table 4.2   Representation of external formats in ABAP/4 (n = places, m = places after the decimal point, s = 1 for plus or minus sign, otherwise 0)

External data type	Representation in ABAP/4
ACCP	N(6)
CHAR n	C(n)
CLNT	C(3)
CUKY	C(5)
CURR n, m, s	P((n+2)/2) DECIMALS m (NO-SIGN)
DATS	D(8)
DEC n, m, s	P((n+2)/2) DECIMALS m (NO-SIGN)
FLTP	F(8)
INT1	I
INT2	I
INT4	I
LANG	C(1)
LCHR	C(n)
LRAW	X(n)
NUMC n	N(n)
PREC	
QUAN n, m, s	P((n+2)/2) DECIMALS m (NO-SIGN)
RAW n	X(n)
TIMS	T(6)
UNIT	C(n)
VARC n	C(n)

Valid values

You can check fields for valid input when values are entered in screens. One way to do this is to use corresponding statements in the flow logic. It is also possible, however, to perform an automatic check against a predefined set of values. As a side effect, possible entries help is available for all fields subject to automatic checks, which display the valid set of values. This checking mechanism is of particular importance for certain maintenance modules provided by the system (for example, the transactions SM30, SM31). You can maintain table contents using these tools without having to write separate programs to do so. These maintenance tools are used mainly in Customizing, where automatic checks ensure a minimum level of data integrity.

Among other things, automatic checks require some settings in the domain that define the set of values to be used for checking. You can define fixed values for this, or you can specify a value table. This value table must have a key field that is based on the domain in question. When entries are made later, only those values are allowed that are contained in the corresponding field in the value table. Just specifying a value table, however, is not enough for a check. You must also define items called foreign keys. Since this topic is very complex, it is explained in detail in Section 4.1.5.

You edit the fixed values for a domain in a separate screen, as already demonstrated. On the basic screen for domain maintenance, there is an input field available for the value table. A table may only be the value table for a single domain. If the table entered in the *Value table* field is already the value table for another domain, this results in an error message during activation.

Output attributes

In the *Output characteristics* field group, you specify attributes that have influence on the display of the field in a list or a screen. Several data types accept decimal numbers. In the *Decimal places* field, you can specify how many decimal places should be allowed. For some external formats, such as FLTP for floating point numbers, this value is predefined, while for others it can be selected as desired. If a place should be reserved for a plus or minus sign, you must mark the *Sign* field. The number of places necessary for the output of a value may differ from the field length, depending on the internal representation of the value as well as the places required for decimal places and a plus or minus sign. The output length is automatically calculated by the system, although it is not always necessarily updated. You can also set the output length manually. If the value in the *Output length* field differs from the calculated length, this usually results in a warning. If necessary, then, you can select an output length that differs from the true length. It may be useful, for example, in the case of very long CHAR fields, to select an output length that is smaller than the length of the database field. Several standard tools such as the Data Browser (transaction SE16) and the two tools for table maintenance (SM30 and SM31) access the specifications in the Dictionary in order to create output lists or maintenance screens. These tools would try to display very long fields in their original length on the screen, which could lead to a very cluttered or confusing screen. By setting a shorter output length in the domain for such fields, you can minimize this kind of undesirable side effect.

Conversion exits were already mentioned in the section on reports, specifically in the section about the variants of the WRITE command. They are function modules that convert the value of a field before output or after input. A conversion exit can be specified for any domain. The variable part of the name of a conversion exit is five characters long and can be entered in the *Convers. routine* field. Such conversion routines are rarely used, however. Much more important is the last flag, *Lowercase letters*. This flag is normally not active. In this state, it causes the automatic conversion of all letters into uppercase. This attribute is especially important for labels. When the flag is activated, no conversions take place, meaning the characters are saved the same way they are entered. Conversion into uppercase precedes the transfer of the field to the database; it has an effect on the screen display already.

4.1.2   Data elements

After the data elements have been declared, they can be created. The data elements retrieve the technical specifications from a domain and supplement them with business information or program-specific information. Data elements and domains have separate name ranges. They can therefore have identical names. Since domains and data elements are often clearly assigned to each other, identical names in this case increase clarity.

You create data elements similar to the way you create domains, on the basic screen of the Dictionary Maintenance tool. After you enter the name in the input field and mark the *Data elements* field, you can click on the *Create* pushbutton. The maintenance screen for data elements appears (Figure 4.4).

As usual, you must first enter the mandatory short description. Creating a data element actually consists of assigning a domain. You enter its name in the input field provided. In

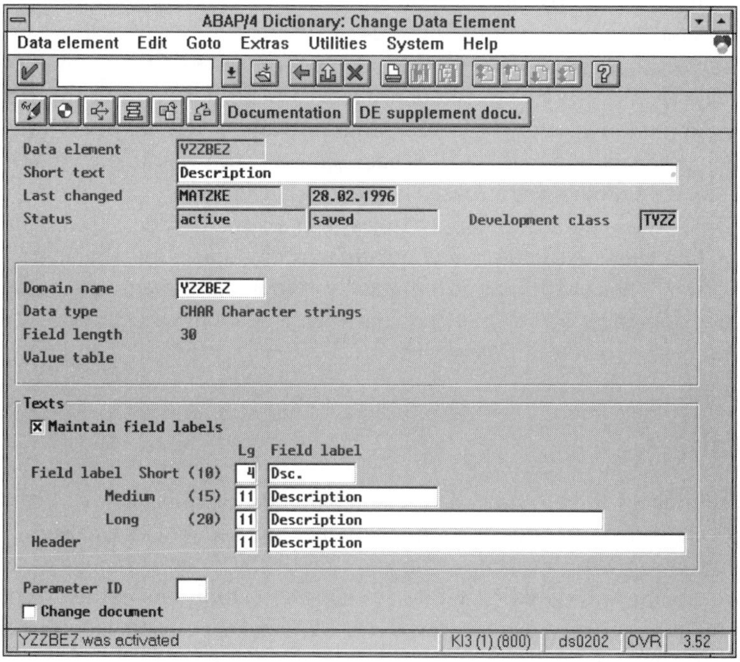

Figure 4.4   Maintenance of a data element

the *Texts* box, you now define the identifiers for the data element. These identifiers appear as key fields in screens or column headings in automatically generated lists. They must therefore be correct and as meaningful as possible. In the end, it is the short description and the field identifiers that decide how the field is interpreted in applications. They indicate which information should be stored in the corresponding table field. Text maintenance is only necessary or successful if the *Maintain field labels* flag is active, which is the default setting. You do not need field identifiers for data elements that should not appear in screens. In this case, you must turn off the flag. Note that this is only possible starting with Release 3.0.

After entering the identifiers, you activate the data element. As is the case with domains, changes to data elements do not take effect until activation. If the data element is already being used, all of the dependent objects are automatically activated, as well.

Once you have successfully created the YZZBEZ data element, repeat the process for the YZZBRA data element. Link it to the YZZBRA domain and give it the identifier *Branch*.

Two additional input fields appear in the lower portion of the maintenance screen that can have considerable importance in professional applications. The SAP system provides several procedures for exchanging data across applications using global memory areas. One of these uses Get/Set parameters. Such a parameter contains a unique, three-character identifier. Specific ABAP/4 statements (SET PARAMETER ..., GET PARAMETER ...) write a value into such a parameter or read a value from it. The contents of a parameter are retained during a user's entire session, that is, from logon to logoff. You can assign such a parameter to screen fields as an attribute. When the screen is processed, the field is then automatically filled with the contents of the parameter, or the value of the field is written into the parameter. This can minimize tedious input in various transactions. For example, the system stores the name of one of the programs you have edited in such a parameter. When you call one of the various maintenance tools directly, for example the Screen Painter or the Menu Painter, the input field for the program name is automatically filled.

If such a parameter is assigned to a data element, this parameter is automatically assigned to any screen field that is based on that data element.

The SAP system is able to log data changes selectively. A specific transaction must be used for this, to create so-called change document objects and include some other functions in programs. These functions automatically recognize changes to a data record and create a change document for it. Only changes to data fields in which the *Change document* flag is set are taken into account, however.

4.1.3 Tables

After preparing all of the required data elements and domains, you can create a table. Since the special types of pool and cluster tables mentioned in Chapter 2 are being replaced step-by-step with transparent tables, only the latter table type is described here. Unlike data elements and domains, tables are not only definitions in the Data Dictionary, but are objects that actually exist in the database. For this reason, additional steps are required for creating tables. Demonstrating these steps is the focus of the section that follows.

Table structure

First, of course, you must define the structure of the table. For this, you enter the table name (YZZB) in the basic Dictionary maintenance screen, mark the *Tables* radio button, and click on the *Create* pushbutton again. A screen appears in which you must maintain the table's data fields, along with several other attributes.

As usual, you must first enter the short description. You can select any text you desire, but it should indicate the table's task, which is to accept valid branches. You must also enter a value in the *Delivery class* field. The contents of this field are relatively meaningless in relation to the examples described here. In productive SAP applications, however, the delivery class influences whether and to what extent entries from other systems can be imported into this table. For YZZB and the table to be created after it, YZZBT, you can use delivery class C (Customizing table).

It has already been mentioned repeatedly that special maintenance programs can be generated for tables. This is only possible, however, if the *Tab. Maint. Allowed* flag is set. Since both of the tables, YZZB and YZZBT, should be maintained later with such tools, you should set this flag for both tables. This flag does not affect the processing of tables in dialog applications you program yourself.

After this preparatory work, you can determine the data structure. A step loop area is available in the lower section of the screen for this; it allows you to define several fields in a single process. Enter the name of the field to be created in the *Field name* column. Aside from the length, you should follow the same conventions as for naming program-internal data fields. Field names must, of course, be unique within a table. If the field is to be a key field, mark the *Key* flag. The key fields must appear at the beginning of the table. To describe the attributes of the data field, specify a data element in the third input-ready column.

One note at this point: beginning with Release 3.0C, you can enter a data type directly instead of referencing a data element. This makes sense in the case of help fields that will never appear in a screen or a report, since for such fields you cannot maintain headings, identifiers, or foreign key relationships. Direct entry of data types is not possible until you have changed the maintenance mode for the table fields using the menu function *Edit* → *Direct type entry*. This capability will not be used in this example, however.

You want the first table, YZZB, to accept only two fields. The SAP system can have multiple clients. The development objects created, no matter whether they are programs, tables or other elements, are valid throughout the entire system. This means that, in tables that should receive client-related data, a field must be available to receive the client. The Data Dictionary processes this field automatically when the table is accessed. It is not necessary to analyze this field in any way in applications. In client-dependent tables, however, it must always be created as the first field in the table. This field is always called MANDT. It is a key field that is based on the data element of the same name, MANDT. This data element is already contained in the standard SAP system. It cannot and may not be edited.

The second field of the table is the BRANCHE field. It, too, should be a key field and use the data element YZZBRA. After you enter the values and press the Enter key or save the entries, the system figures out several important specifications based on the data elements and fills the remaining columns of the table definition with these. The maintenance screen should now look something like the one in Figure 4.5.

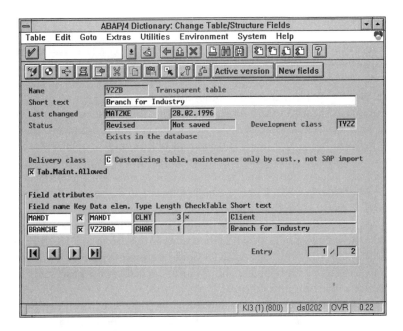

Figure 4.5   Maintenance of the data fields of a database table

Unit and currency fields

Table fields that contain currency amounts or quantity specifications (CURR and QUAN types) are handled in a special way. Specifications for currencies and units of measure are created in central tables (for example, TCURC and T006), and a key is assigned for the currency or the unit of measure that is unique system-wide. These specifications are used to describe in more detail fields with currency amounts or units of measure. You must therefore assign an additional field called a reference field to every field of type CURR or QUAN, in which a currency or unit key is available at an application's runtime. This field can be in the same table, or it can be in a different table. When such a field is displayed in a screen, the system determines the currency or unit key and formats the field accordingly. You assign the reference field in a popup that appears in the table structure maintenance screen when you double-click on a field name. The input fields for the reference table and the reference field are only input-ready for fields of the types named.

Technical settings

Relational database systems do not create tables randomly in bulk memory. Instead, they attempt to optimize space requirements and access speeds. To this end, several database systems (Oracle and Informix) expect the programmer to make certain specifications. These and several other specifications belong to what are called the technical settings of a table. You record these in a second screen, which you access either by clicking on the *Technical settings* pushbutton or by using the menu function *Goto* → *Technical settings*. In some cases, for example if you try to activate a table without technical settings, the system automatically jumps to this screen. The specifications in this screen are necessary only so that the database system can optimize table access. Technical settings have no effect on the main functionality of the table, only on table access performance. They are non-critical in terms of an application's functionality.

Since valid values may differ depending on the database system used, it is best to use the possible entries help to find an appropriate entry.

Three of the fields are particularly important to maintain. The first, *Data class*, provides information about the access frequency. In the example, APPL2 is selected for Customizing data, which is rarely accessed. The second field, *Size category*, tells the database the number of data records to expect. It can then reserve consecutive memory space for the table. Since our example uses only a few data records, the lowest value will be entirely sufficient. The third required specification concerns the buffer type. The *Not buffered* selection is marked as the default. You can retain this selection.

Some additional information is required for buffering. The SAP system can hold entire tables or selected portions of them in an internal buffer and thus speed up access to the data. Buffering is only useful if a transaction performs multiple read accesses of a data record. The effectiveness of buffering diminishes if write procedures occur. When a record of the database table is read, additional records are automatically read and placed in the buffer according to the buffering type set. If complete buffering has been selected, the table is either loaded into the buffer in its entirety or, if there is insufficient memory space, not at all. This buffering type is only recommended for very small tables up to about 30 kbytes in size.

In generic buffering, all of the data records with the same key are buffered. You must name the key fields that should be analyzed for buffering. A maximum of 32 characters are recognized. This type of buffering is useful, for example, for language-dependent tables. If a table is to undergo generic buffering, the sequence of the key fields must be optimized accordingly. The front portions of the key should be as consistent as possible for the records to be read subsequently, so that the buffer does not always have to be refilled. In practice, this means, for example, that in the case of language-dependent tables, the field with the language key should follow immediately after the client field.

In individual buffering, the data records read are stored in a buffer. This type of buffering is only worthwhile if there are a lot of read accesses to relatively few data records using entirely different keys.

After editing the technical settings, you can save them. Pressing the F3 function key or clicking on the corresponding icon takes you back to the central table maintenance screen, where you then activate the table. Activating the table marks the table as active in the Data Dictionary and creates it as a real table in the database.

After you have successfully edited the YZZB table, you can create the second table, YZZBT. It should accept a descriptive text for every branch, which can be maintained separately for every logon language. Table 4.3 shows the fields and data elements to be included in the table.

Table 4.3   Structure of the YZZBT table

Field name	Key	Data element
MANDT	X	MANDT
SPRACHE	X	SPRAS
BRANCHE	X	YZZBRA
BEZEICH		YZZBEZ

The SPRAS data element and the MANDT data element are predefined elements in the standard SAP system. For tables with language-dependent text, use of these data elements and of a language field based on them is mandatory. The language field must of course belong to the key, but it is not necessary that it appear in second place, directly after the client. As you did for the YZZB table, you need to maintain the technical settings for this table. You can use the same values. After that, activate the table. Two tables are now available for processing.

Foreign key definition

Although the two tables are not identical, they are tightly linked logically. In a later application, the user should be able to record a value in the YZZB table and enter the corresponding description in YZZBT at the same time. This should not happen with a dialog transaction that you have written yourself, but rather with the table maintenance provided by the system. To this end, you will later need to generate a maintenance module for the YZZB table. In order for this module to be able to link the two tables correctly, you must create a so-called foreign key. A foreign key defines table dependencies. It is automatically analyzed by various tools. The theoretical concepts for foreign keys are discussed in a separate section. This section will only demonstrate how the two tables, YZZB and YZZBT, are linked to each other with a foreign key.

The two tables are linked using the BRANCHE data field. The texts in YZZBT are supposed to be assigned to a branch and thus to a data record from YZZB. The actual link is created using the domain of the database field.

The text table is the subordinate table. It should contain only texts for branches that already exist in YZZB. For this reason, you should enter a value table in addition to the fixed values in the YBRANCHE domain. This value table is YZZB. One way to enter the value table, of course, is to call up the domain from the basic Dictionary maintenance screen. However, as in program maintenance, there is a polished navigation mechanism available in Dictionary maintenance. Double-clicking on the name of the data element in the table structure's field list jumps directly to the maintenance screen of this data element. From there, you double-click on the name of the domain to maintain it. To guard against erroneous entries, the maintenance transactions called at first work in display mode only. To actually edit one of the objects, you must click on a pushbutton or select a menu function to turn on change mode.

Regardless of how you maintain the domain, you must enter the YZZB table in the *Value table* field. Afterwards, you activate the domain. Entering the value table does not yet influence the checking of the domain. It only determines against which table checks should be made. The check itself is not executed until a foreign key relationship is later defined for the table field to be checked.

Adding a value table can be one of the reasons to re-edit an active domain. Since the domain itself is used in the value table, there is a circular dependency. The value table cannot be entered in the domain until the YZZBRA table exists. This, in turn, cannot be created until the YZZBRA domain exists.

An asterisk now appears in the *CheckTable* column on the BRANCHE field row in the field list of the YZZBT table. This asterisk means that a value table exists for the underlying domain, but no foreign key has yet been defined. You now create this by placing the cursor in the BRANCHE field row and calling the menu function *Goto → Foreign key*. Alternatively, you can use the F8 function key or a pushbutton. Since no foreign key exists yet, a popup appears, which you can use to create a default for the foreign key. Confirm this popup by clicking on the *Yes* pushbutton.

The definition of the foreign key now appears in a second popup (Figure 4.6). The default is determined by the system based on the labels and domains of the field for which the foreign key is to be created. Mark the *Check required* flag in the *Screen check* box, if it has not already been set automatically. In the *Semantic attributes* group, mark the *Key fields of a text table* radio button. This selection is crucial to ensure that the maintenance modules created later automatically analyze the language field of the YZZBT table. You can now insert

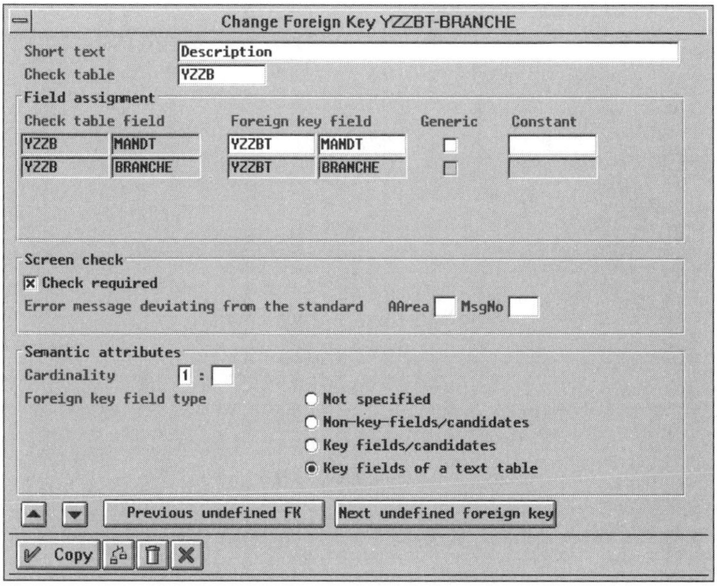

Figure 4.6   Default for creating a new foreign key

the foreign key definition into the table definition by clicking on the *Copy* pushbutton. Now, instead of the asterisk, the name of the table against which the field should be checked appears in the *CheckTable* column. Finally, activate the table.

Generated table maintenance

The definition of the foreign key sets the stage for creating the maintenance module for the YZZB table. Maintenance modules are created from the basic table maintenance screen. You access this by selecting the menu function *Environment → Gen. maint. dialog,* which is only active and executable if the table is being edited in change mode. Beginning with Release 3.0 of the SAP system, the table maintenance generator is a relatively complex tool. In contrast to the tool in previous release versions, it does not generate a module pool with a simple screen, but rather an entire function group. This can be manually edited later and modified to the specific desires of the user. After making changes to the table, you can regenerate selected parts of the function group, while manual additions are retained in certain circumstances.

Only a few entries in the table maintenance generator screen (Figure 4.7) are necessary to generate a simple maintenance module for the YZZB table and the corresponding text.

In the *Function group* field, you enter the name of a function group in which all of the generated objects for maintaining the table should be created. In the example, use the

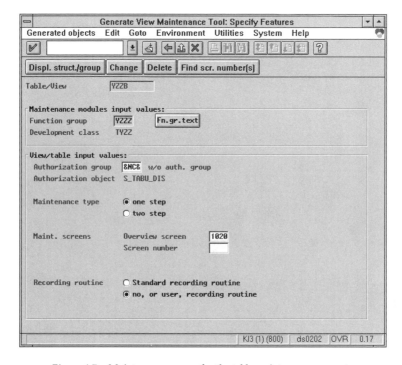

Figure 4.7   Maintenance screen for the table maintenance generator

name YZZB. Mark the *one step* radio button for the *Maintenance type* field. For the screen number of the maintenance screen, use 1020. The only field for which no generally valid statement can be made at this point concerning its contents is the *Authorization group* field. A maintenance module for table maintenance must be assigned an authorization group that allows only a certain group of users to use this tool. Authorizations and the problems associated with them have not yet been discussed. Every user of the SAP system has authorizations that allow him or her to access certain elements of the system. Several authorizations can be combined into authorization groups using intermediate stages. Which groups these are, which authorizations a user is given with regard to a group, and which tasks he or she can execute with them can differ from system to system. It is highly probable that the possible entries help for the authorization group will offer the entry &NC&, which stands for *W/o auth. group*. If this entry is not available, or if it causes problems later, you will need to consult your system administrator to find a suitable authorization group or to create one.

After entering all of the values, you can generate the maintenance module by clicking on the *Create* pushbutton or selecting the menu function *Generated objects* → *Create*. A message in the status bar on the screen provides information about the success of the job's execution. Afterwards, you can call the table maintenance module just generated directly from the table maintenance generator screen. Simply enter the transaction code /nSM31 in the OK field. This ends the current application and calls the basic table maintenance screen (Figure 4.8).

On this screen, you just enter the name of the table to be maintained (maximum of five characters) and select the editing type *Maintain* with the pushbutton. The transaction then calls the maintenance functions required for editing. As long as these have not been manually changed, they display the contents of the table in list form. In the case of empty tables, an empty screen without input fields appears. Select the menu function *Edit* → *New*

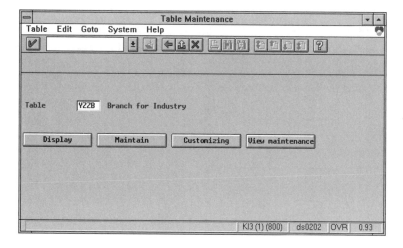

Figure 4.8   Basic screen of table maintenance

entries or click on the *New entries* pushbutton to display a list in which the new data records can be recorded. Figure 4.9 shows the screen after three data records have been entered. After data entry, you must save the changes.

The maintenance screen provides possible entries help for the BRANCHEN input field. After you call up the possible entries help (using F4 or the icon to the right of the input field), a popup appears that identifies the valid range of values.

Both the SM30 transaction and the SM31 transaction require that you enter the name of the table to be edited in their initial screens. Since both tools are used mainly in Customizing, you can use a parameter transaction to jump directly to the table's editing screen. You can enter this transaction in a menu, which allows you to maintain a very specific table without additional entries. The following example describes its use with SM30. If you are executing this example on an SAP system with a release prior to 3.0, you must generate a maintenance view for the two tables for this. You will find notes on this in the subsection on peculiarities of Release 2.2.

Start by creating a new transaction, which you should give the name YZZB for the sake of clarity. In the subsequent popup, select the transaction type *Parameter transaction*. The popup that follows (Figure 4.10) has a structure that is somewhat more complex than that of the one for editing simple dialog transactions.

A parameter transaction can either call a transaction, or directly call a screen from a module pool. The latter possibility is of interest if no transaction exists yet for the module pool or the program, or if the transaction should be started with a different screen. In the case at hand, an existing transaction should be called: mark the *Transaction* radio button and enter the transaction code to be executed in the input field next to it. Since you want to jump directly into table maintenance, you will want to skip the initial screen of transaction SM30. To do so, mark the *Skip initial screen* flag under the transaction code input field. To ensure that the called transaction can work correctly, it must, of course, somehow

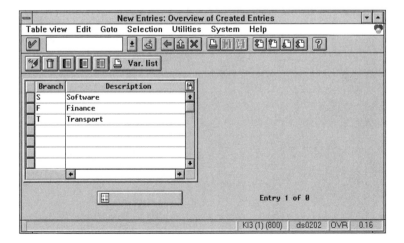

Figure 4.9   Recording of new data records using table maintenance

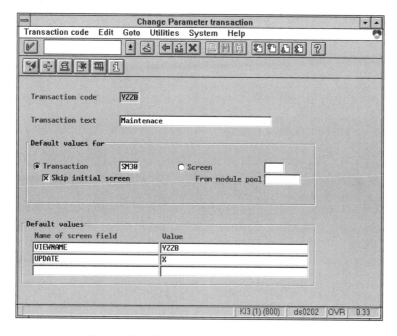

Figure 4.10   Creation of a parameter transaction

be given the values that would otherwise be entered on the initial screen. This is exactly why you use the parameter transaction. In the lower third of the popup, there are input fields in which you can enter the parameters to be passed. In the left-hand column, you enter the name of one of the screen fields from the transaction's initial screen, and in the right-hand column you enter the value to be passed. The developer of a parameter transaction must know the transaction to be called exactly, or at least the structure of the initial screen. It is not possible to create a correct parameter transaction without this information. You obtain this information either by reading the corresponding documentation or by analyzing the source code of the application to be called.

After you have entered the parameters as shown in Figure 4.10, you can save the new transaction and execute it immediately.

Include structures and append structures

Editing table definitions in the Dictionary is relatively simple. You can ascertain the use of most of the available menu functions from their names or simply by trying them. Several details of the attributes of tables will supplement the information presented so far.

If you want to expand tables with new fields, you usually do this by inserting the new fields in the field list. If possible, you should always append fields to the end of the table. That makes it easier for the database to adjust the structure of the database table. In the table maintenance screen, there is a menu function available for appending new table fields: *Edit → New fields*.

New fields should not be appended directly to the original table in every case, however. Two other possibilities are also available: the Include structure and the Append structure. Include structures are used to insert existing table definitions in other tables. This allows you to reuse large definitions and can save a lot of coding work. If a substructure should be used in several places, an Include structure simplifies the changes, which then need only be maintained in one place. Includes are also available in earlier releases.

When you define a table, you insert an existing table or structure into the current table using the menu function *Extras → Substructure → Insert substructure*. In the table, the term .INCLUDE appears as the field name, and the name of the inserted table appears instead of the data element. You enter the name of the object to be inserted in a small popup (see Figure 4.11), in which you can also enter a name suffix.

Generally, this field can remain empty. However, if problems should arise with duplicate field names when the Include is inserted, you can fix these with a suffix. You append this character string to the names of all of the fields inserted with the Include. This eliminates ambiguities; but field names change, and this must be taken into account when you program applications that access such tables.

Includes have another important task related to customer modifications. Occasionally, applications must be modified to meet the specific needs of a customer. To do this, it is often necessary to give tables additional fields. If new SAP software that includes the modified table is imported into a system that has been modified this way (because SAP, too, has continued developing the application), the changes would usually be overwritten. Special maintenance tools, however, make it possible to incorporate customer modifications and avoid loss of data during such upgrades. This task is simplified if the fields appended by the customer are moved into an Include. During the upgrade, then, only the Include must be reinserted.

Beginning with Release 3.0, the problem just described can be solved more elegantly using Append structures. An Append structure is a table structure that contains a reference to a superordinate table in its management data. When the superordinate table, which need not itself contain a reference to the Append structure, is activated, all of the Append structures are automatically assigned to the superordinate table. Since the subordinate structures automatically append themselves to the superordinate table, even if their structure is changed by an SAP upgrade, no manual comparison is necessary. Similar to Includes, Append structures are created in table maintenance with the menu function *Goto → Append structures ....*

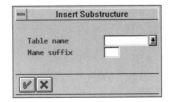

Figure 4.11   Insertion of an Include structure in a table definition

Indexes

Searches in tables can be greatly accelerated with appropriate indexing. An index contains selected fields of a database system table, by which the data records are always sorted. With appropriate procedures such as a binary search, the search for a data record can proceed rapidly. In the index, a pointer references the place in the database table where the data record belonging to the index term can be found. The database system uses indexes automatically. When a table is accessed, for example with SELECT ... WHERE, the database system searches for an index that matches the WHERE clause. If it finds one, it uses it. If not, a sequential search takes place in the database table. The database system automatically updates the indexes when data records are inserted or deleted.

For every database table, the system creates a so-called *primary index*, which contains all of the key fields. Beyond that, the programmer as well as the user of the SAP system can create additional, *secondary indexes*. This is done from the main table maintenance screen using the *Indexes* pushbutton or the menu function *Goto* → *Indexes*. Starting with Release 3.0, an index is identified by the table name and a three-character identifier. During maintenance of an index from within table maintenance, the name of the table is of course fixed. You simply need to enter the three-character index identifier in the little popup (Figure 4.12).

The index identifier serves to differentiate among several indexes in the maintenance tools. Since indexes are used automatically by the database system, it is not necessary, or not possible, to reference a specific index in programs.

After you enter an index and confirm the entry with Enter, you can edit the index. Figure 4.13 shows the corresponding screen.

Of course, you must first enter a short description. The *Unique index* flag determines if entries in the index table must be unique. If this flag is set, the database checks not only the uniqueness of the table's key fields but also the uniqueness with regard to the index file. This means that a data record might not be accepted in a table, although it might seem acceptable based on the values in its key fields. For secondary indexes, this setting seldom makes sense. In fact, it is rather dangerous, since such an additional data check could interfere with the functionality of existing applications.

In the screen's step loop area, you now enter the table fields that should be used to build the index. You call up possible entries help with the *Choose fields* pushbutton or the menu function *Edit* → *Choose fields*. In the possible entries help, you can mark all of the fields to be copied using mouse clicks and copy them into the index definition in a single

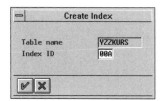

Figure 4.12   Selection of the index to be processed

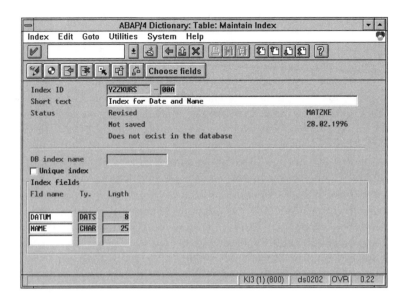

Figure 4.13   Maintenance of an index

process. When you use the possible entries help, the system copies all of the marked fields into the field list of the index in the sequence in which they appear in the help. The sequence of the fields in the index can have a lot of influence on its operation. In this case, you should either enter the fields manually, or you should select them one by one in the desired sequence using multiple calls to the possible entries help.

After entering the fields, you must activate the index. During activation, the index is also created in the database. Successful activation also ends the editing of an index.

Secondary indexes should be tailored specifically for runtime-critical search processes. This means that the sequence of the fields in a WHERE clause and the index fields must be coordinated. The first index field should already make an extensive selection possible. It should therefore be a field whose contents often change. In the WHERE clause, the fields must be listed in the sequence in which they appear in the index definition. An index can only be analyzed to the extent that valid fields (from the index's point of view) appear in the WHERE clause.

An example of cooperation between the index and the WHERE clause follows. A table is given, with the fields CUSTNR (key field), NAME, FIRST_NAME, STREET, CITY and ZIP. In case there will be many searches by name and city, a secondary index should be constructed using NAME and CITY. The WHERE clause should then contain the fields in exactly this order:

```
...
WHERE NAME = ...
  AND CITY = ...
...
```

A WHERE clause structured like this would be able to use the index very efficiently to find the data records with the desired names and then, if several entries were found, could also find the city, again using the index. If the sequence of the fields in the WHERE clause were reversed, most likely no index could be used. On the other hand, if the index were constructed from the three field names NAME, FIRST_NAME and CITY, you could use the index only up to the NAME field in the search. In the data records identified this way, you would then have to perform a sequential search for the desired city, since there is no value in the WHERE clause for the FIRST_NAME index field.

Database utility

The so-called *database utility* is available in many maintenance tools. You can access it using the menu function *Utilities* → *Database utility*. The Dictionary tools edit only the logical definitions of the various objects. In many cases, however, these must still be physically created in the database. For example, after the structure of a table has been defined, it must also be created as a real table in the database system, so that data can actually be stored. The Dictionary itself simply makes available the description of the table from the point of view of the SAP system. Creating and deleting objects in the database is accomplished with the database utility. When the utility is called from the Dictionary tools, several parameters, such as the name of the object, are pre-filled. The user can select various activities (Create, Change, Convert) and different execution modes (for example, online or batch processing) in the database utility. Some maintenance functions, particularly those for creating new objects, call the database utility automatically. If manual use of the database utility becomes necessary, the activation logs of the various elements indicate this. The *Convert* function, which must be called for tables whose structure has been changed, is especially important. During the conversion process, the old data is also transferred into the new table structure.

If you want to delete Dictionary objects that exist in the database, you must first delete the object from the database. Currently, you must call the database utility manually to do this.

Delivery class

The tables in the SAP system contain very different information. Some accept the user's transaction data, while others modify the R/3 System to meet the actual demands of the user in Customizing. Other tables deliver data that the SAP system requires for its work, such as authorizations, currencies and so on; several applications are even directly controlled by the entries in some tables. Just as varied as the tasks of the tables are the reasons and methods for modifying their contents. When the SAP software is installed, many of the tables are filled with default values. Later deliveries of corrections or new release versions, or the copying of clients, might have to overwrite these contents. In the process, changes to or deletions of user-specific settings must be avoided. Changes to system tables by the user must also be prevented, because they could jeopardize the functionality of the entire system. The individual tables are therefore assigned a certain attribute, called the *Delivery class*. This attribute determines who may update the contents in this table and in which form it was delivered by SAP. Table 4.4 lists the different delivery classes.

Table 4.4   Delivery classes

Delivery class	Description
A	application table
C	customizing table
E	general system table
G	protected table
L	temporary data
S	SAP system table
W	table for system operation

Application tables accept the data that is created by the various business applications. Such tables are always delivered empty by SAP. Only the customer inserts contents. Customizing tables are used for modifying the system to meet customer needs. Although defaults are delivered for such tables when the R/3 System is initially installed, only the customer later maintains them. These table contents are never overwritten by SAP upgrades. Protected tables resemble the Customizing tables, except that an SAP upgrade can add values, although it cannot change any existing values. Tables for temporary data resemble application tables in their behavior. They are delivered empty and are never filled with values by SAP. The difference between them and the application tables is that while the contents of application tables can be copied when a client's data is copied, the contents of temporary tables cannot. General system tables have a name range for customers. This name range is not affected by SAP upgrades, but entries in the SAP name range can be changed. SAP system tables, in contrast, may only be maintained by SAP. They are delivered in a filled state. While the system tables of classes E and S accept information of a more static nature, the tables for system operation (class W) contain data that is indirectly changed by various transactions. They contain data that the R/3 System needs to maintain its functionality, for example the descriptions of Dictionary elements or the source code for programs. The contents of these tables are not subject to any special protection.

Release 2.2

Several Dictionary tools have been reworked to a great extent for Release 3.0, meaning that several of the editing steps in the examples described so far are different. The main relationships between the individual elements and the necessary steps are the same, however. It would be excessive at this point to re-execute and completely describe the example for Release 2.2, although the major differences will be listed.

Transactions SM30 and SM31, which you use to maintain the contents of tables, have a similar interface, but they are based on a different principle than the same transactions in

Release 3.0. In Release 3.0, the prerequisite for the work of both transactions is the generation of a large function group with the table maintenance generator. This function group, or the function modules and screens contained therein, is used by both transactions. Up to and including Release 2.2, however, both transactions work entirely independently of each other. For SM31, you must create a so-called table screen when you maintain the table definition. Behind this function is hidden the automatic generation of a simple screen with flow logic. The flow logic uses the variant of the LOOP command for database tables described in Chapter 3. Since the name of the table to be processed is incorporated in the name of the generated module pool, the name of the table to be maintained this way may be no more than five characters long. The maintenance screen comprises only the fields of a table. No foreign key relationships are analyzed, and therefore no dependent tables are included either, such as those for language-dependent text.

Up to and including Release 2.2, somewhat easier-to-use maintenance is only possible using so-called view maintenance (SM30). With this transaction, as the name implies, you can maintain views. For a table to be edited with SM30, you must first create a view. In this case, you do not do this manually with the Dictionary maintenance tool. First you must make an entry in the TVDIR table that describes the modules to be created in more detail. Several of the parameters required (function group, screen numbers) resemble those that must be entered in the table maintenance generator in Release 3.0. Afterwards, you generate the required modules and the views using the RSVIEWGN report. Only then can you maintain the table contents using SM30.

Another difference in the use of the Dictionary tools is manifest in the database utility. In versions prior to Release 3.0, it is not called automatically, but must be manually started.

4.1.4   Structures

Dictionary structures basically consist of the declaration of a field string in the Dictionary. This structure has a name and a field list, like a table. However, no database table is created for a structure. The maintenance tool closely resembles that for editing tables, although several database-related functions are missing.

In programs, structures are declared like tables, using TABLES. They can be used in a program like a field string, meaning it is possible to assign data to them. Structures combine the advantages of a field string (common handling of several logically related data fields) with the advantages of a Dictionary element (foreign key checking, field identifiers, simple passing in screens).

If fields from several tables are maintained in one screen, a structure that contains all of the fields to be maintained makes programming a lot easier in comparison to the direct use of the table. When the screen is edited, all of the required fields can be inserted into the screen's fullscreen in a single process. In the application, such a structure simplifies data handling. For one thing, it makes the program clearer, since you are always working with a single structure to access the screen data. The passing of data to check routines or update programs is also clearer, since you only have to use a single parameter.

4.1.5   Foreign key relationships

Dependencies exist between the various tables in a database. The relational database concept is designed to store information in tables with as little redundancy as possible and to link the tables to each other using common keys. When a database is created, this assignment is at first made on a purely logical level. Beyond that, the SAP system's Data Dictionary allows you to create physical dependencies using so-called foreign keys. These foreign keys can perform several tasks, depending on their actual definition:

- Document the table relationships and thus the data model
- Provide table linking information for other tools
- Perform value checks in screens

Foreign keys are defined in a table for one table field at a time. They indicate how the contents of this field are dependent on the contents of another field in a superordinate table (also called a check table). The table that contains the foreign key is also called the foreign key table, and the field for which the foreign key has been created, that is, the field to be checked, is called the check field. The foreign key can contain other fields in addition to the check field, which are called foreign key fields.

A simple example of foreign keys is provided by the tables YZZB and YZZBT, which were defined earlier. Both of these tables contain the BRANCHE field. Since only supplemental text for the data records of YZZB should appear in the YZZBT table, only those values may be entered in the YZZBT-BRANCHE field that are contained in the YZZB-BRANCHE field. For this reason, a foreign key was defined in the YZZBT table. The YZZBT table is thus the foreign key table, and the YZZBT-BRANCHE field is the check field. The YZZB table is the check table for the foreign key.

In order for a foreign key to be able to perform its task, it must contain some important information:

- Which table is the check table?
- Against which field in the check table should the check be done?
- Should additional fields be considered, to restrict the set of values from the check table?
- What type of dependency on the check table should exist?

The system determines some of the required information when a foreign key is created. Several other specifications must be manually entered. You edit foreign keys in a popup, which was already shown in Figure 4.6. The individual aspects of foreign key definition require some more explanation.

Check table and check table field

When you want to check a field, you must specify clearly against which field of which table the check should be performed. These two properties of a foreign key cannot be selected as desired. They are determined by the domain on which the table to be checked is based. It is possible to enter a value table in the attributes of a domain. This value table is then suggested as the default check table when a foreign key is defined. In the check table, the system searches for a field from this table that is based on the same domain. It then checks against that field.

You can overwrite the default for the check table. However, you can only select a table that is directly or indirectly linked to the actual value table of the domain through foreign key relationships. You enter the new table name in the corresponding input field in the foreign key popup. After you press Enter, the foreign key fields and the assignment defaults are updated. In this case, the value and the check table are different.

Key fields

During the definition of a foreign key, the system attempts to find corresponding fields for all of the check table's key fields in the foreign key table (the subordinate table). For this, the domains of the check table's key fields are analyzed. Fields of the foreign key table that are based on the same domain are incorporated in the foreign key. If no suitable fields exist in the foreign key table, the system indicates that the foreign key cannot be specified completely.

When the contents of a field from a foreign key table are later checked, the system takes the current values from the foreign key fields of the foreign key table and uses them to build the key for the check table. Afterwards, only the data records of the check table identified with the key are used for checking.

To minimize the effects of this far-reaching limitation on the set of values, you can reverse the field assignments to check table key fields by marking the *Generic* flag in the foreign key popup. The contents of this field are then no longer used to select data records in the check table during a foreign key check.

Dependency

You can maintain so-called semantic attributes for foreign keys. These provide information about the type of dependency between the foreign key fields and the check table. They have no importance where the actual data check in the screen is concerned. They are, however, used to build so-called aggregates (views, possible entries help and so on).

The cardinality determines how many dependent records can exist for a check table record. It is specified in the form n:m. If n has a value of 1, this means that there should be one record in the check table for every record in the foreign key table. A value of C, on the other hand, indicates that there are also records in the foreign key table for which there is no record in the check table. The value for m specifies how many records may exist in the dependent table for every check table record. In this case, 1 represents exactly one, C represents at most one, N represents at least one, and CN represents any number.

The degree of dependency determines whether the foreign key fields, which do not have to be key fields in the foreign key table, uniquely identify the data records in the check table or not. Of particular importance here is the *Key fields of a text table* radio button. It says that, except for an additional language field, the foreign key fields of the foreign key table correspond exactly to the key fields of the check table, and that they are key fields themselves.

4.2 Views

Views represent a glimpse into one or more tables. Views are often used to link the information from several tables together without complicated queries or programs, or to give certain users a view of only selected fields. Views are often used in Customizing or implemented for special tasks. Many views are generated automatically. Since views do not have as important a role in general programming as tables or screens do, this section only demonstrates the creation of a simple view. Some background information on views can be found in Chapter 2.

As is the case for tables and structures, there is a separate radio button in Dictionary maintenance for editing views. Since views can be used similar to the way tables are used, in particular because they can be incorporated into applications with the TABLES statement, a name must be used that has not already been given to a table or a structure. It is easiest to give a name that indicates that this is a view. This is just a recommendation, however, not a requirement. The names of many of the views delivered by SAP, for example, begin with the letter V. Often, the name of the primary table used in the view appears in the name, as well. For this example, it seems appropriate to use the name YVZZB. Enter this name in the basic Dictionary maintenance screen, mark the *Views* radio button, and click on the *Create* pushbutton. The basic screen for view maintenance (Figure 4.14) appears.

In addition to the short description, you must specify the view type and the primary table as a minimum. Possible entries help (F4) is available for the type. The different types of views were already described in Chapter 2. Of particular importance here are the customizing view and the database view. To demonstrate the tool, enter the type D for database views or select it from the possible entries help. The primary table is the YZZB

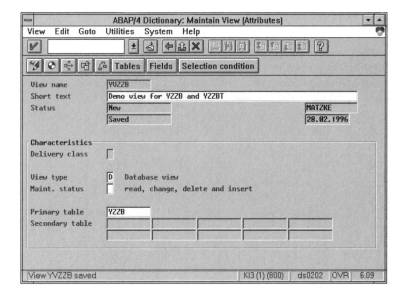

Figure 4.14   View maintenance

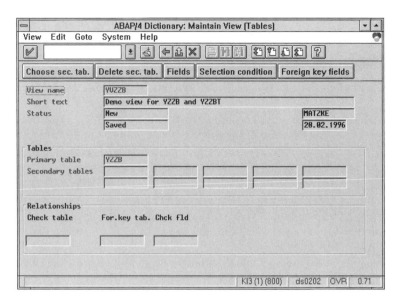

Figure 4.15   Maintenance of secondary tables of the view

table. Save the specifications in the screen. If necessary, you can add additional tables, so-called secondary tables, to the view. To do so, click on the *Tables* pushbutton or select the menu function *Goto → Tables*.

The corresponding screen (Figure 4.15) does not have any active input fields. To add tables, you must call up a popup, using the *Choose sec. tab.* pushbutton or the menu function *Edit → Choose sec. tab.*, that displays all of the available table names (Figure 4.16).

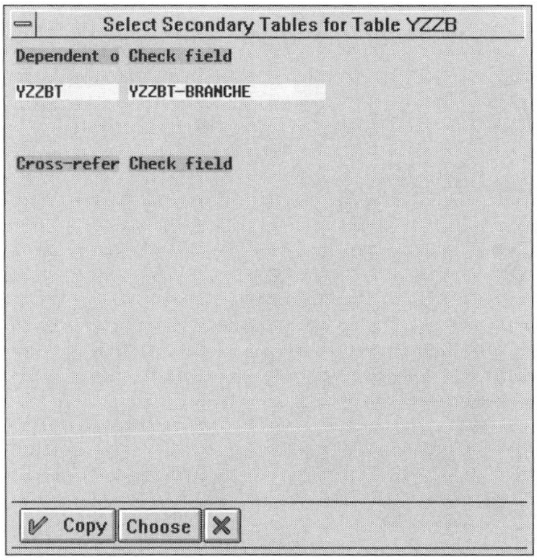

Figure 4.16   Selection of secondary tables

Which tables can be used as secondary tables is determined by existing foreign key relationships. This takes place in both directions. A primary table can have both dependent tables and referenced tables. Dependent tables have fields that reference the current table (the primary table) with foreign keys. The current table is thus the check table for dependent tables. Tables that the primary table itself references with foreign keys are referenced tables.

For the YZZB table, there is only a single dependent table, YZZBT. This table is passed as a secondary table. For this, you first mark it with a double-click. Then you click on the *Copy* pushbutton, which inserts the secondary table in the view definition. After all of the required tables have been passed, you can select the fields that should appear in the view. To do this, on the basic view maintenance screen (see Figure 4.14), you click on the *Fields* pushbutton or select the menu function *Goto → Fields*. A field list appears in the now processed screen in which the key fields of the primary table have already been entered as default values. In this screen, you place the cursor on the table name and click on the *Fields* pushbutton. You can then mark the desired fields in a popup. You can also delete a selection. If you know the table and field names, you can also edit the field list directly by manually entering the field name. Figure 4.17 shows the field list of the view after the most important fields have been incorporated.

After selecting the view fields, you save the specifications. When you return to the basic view maintenance screen, you activate the view. This makes it usable in applications. You can use database views to change table data only if no more than one table is

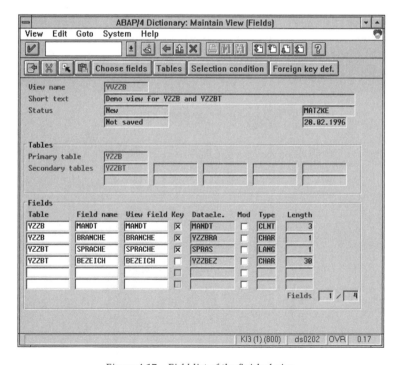

Figure 4.17   Field list of the finished view

contained in the view. In this example, this requirement is not met, so you can only read the data with the view. The letter R, automatically set in the *Maint. status* field, indicates the view's Read Only status. If you also want to be able to maintain data using views you have defined that contain several tables, you must use type C (customizing view).

Database views (type D) are implemented as views of the database system, so, like tables, they must be created in the database with the database utility after they have been defined. While this happens automatically during activation in Release 3.0, in older release versions the database tool must be called manually.

4.3   Matchcodes

Matchcodes belong to possible entries help, which has already been mentioned in various places. Using matchcodes, you can search for a data record's key field with other, non-key fields. Matchcodes are generated automatically by the system according to several specifications from the programmer. To use a matchcode in an application, you simply enter it in the attributes of a screen field.

Matchcodes consist of two parts. The actual search procedure is controlled with a so-called matchcode ID. This determines which database fields can be used for the search. When a matchcode is used, a matchcode ID displays on the screen as a popup with its own input fields, in which the user can enter the search terms. One or more matchcode IDs constitute a matchcode object. When a matchcode is executed, the matchcode object presents the user with all of the available matchcode IDs in a selection list. The matchcode object determines the table field to be searched for. This field is valid for all of the matchcode IDs.

In this section, you will create a simple matchcode that searches for a value for the BRANCHE field of the YZZB table, using the identifier. Since matchcodes have a separate name range, you can give it the name YZZB. Matchcode names may be a maximum of four characters long. You enter the name in the input field on the basic Dictionary maintenance screen, and mark the *Matchcode objects* radio button. Afterwards, you click on the *Create* pushbutton. In the subsequent screen (Figure 4.18), you maintain the basic properties of the matchcode object. In addition to the short description, this includes the name of the primary table.

The primary table contains the data field that should be found with the matchcode. If the primary table is linked to additional tables with foreign keys, their contents can be searched, as well. These tables must be included as secondary tables in the matchcode object. As with views, you do this using the *Tables* pushbutton or the menu function Goto → *Tables*. In this screen, you then call up a popup using the *Choose sec. tab.* pushbutton or the menu function *Edit → Choose sec. tab*. You can select secondary tables in this popup. The entire procedure corresponds to that for editing views.

You must expressly name all of the table fields to be used later in the search, regardless of which matchcode ID they will be used in. You must include them in the matchcode object's field list, the way you do for the definition of views. The key fields of the tables involved are automatically passed to the field string. To complete the example, you therefore only still need to pass the BEZEICH field from the YZZBT table. A matchcode returns

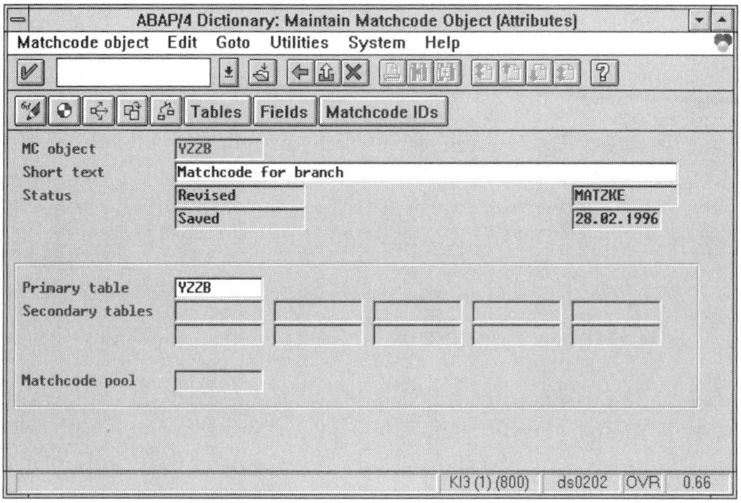

Figure 4.18   Maintaining the properties of a matchcode

the contents of exactly one table field to the screen field with which it has been linked. You can determine which field this is by marking the *SrchFiel* column. The corresponding fields are check boxes rather than radio buttons, so you can select several lines of the field list and thus several table fields. Of course, when the specifications are checked or stored, an error is displayed in this case. It is the responsibility of the programmer to select the right search field. The system does not check later to see whether a matchcode returns a value that matches the screen field to which it was assigned. In the example, the BRANCHE field is the search field. The matchcode's field list can be seen in Figure 4.19.

With the creation of the field list, the definition of the matchcode object is finished. It just represents the frame or the basis for the matchcode ID or IDs, of which you will now create one. To do so, save the field list and return to the basic matchcode maintenance screen (attributes screen, Figure 4.18). There, you activate the matchcode object. Afterwards, you can call up the tool for maintaining a single matchcode ID by clicking on the *Matchcode IDs* pushbutton or selecting the menu function *Goto → Matchcode IDs*. Immediately after you have selected this function, you must specify a unique code (SAP matchcode) or a number (customer matchcode) in a small popup. In the matchcode object, this code is a unique identifier for a matchcode ID. It appears later, when you are working with the finished matchcode, in a popup where you select one of the matchcode IDs for the search using exactly this code. For this example, you can use the number 1. After you confirm the entry in the popup, the screen for editing the matchcode ID appears. As usual, you first record a short description. This appears at the application's runtime in the matchcode object's selection list. It must therefore be as meaningful as possible and factually correct.

Afterwards, you select from the tables declared in the matchcode object those tables for which input fields should be provided in the ID. To do this, you click on the *Choose sec. tab.* pushbutton or choose the menu function *Edit → Choose sec. tab.* In a second process, you

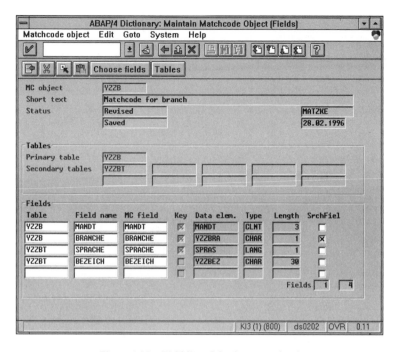

Figure 4.19 Field list of the demo matchcode

then pass the actual table fields to the ID's field list (*Fields* pushbutton, then *Choose fields*). The sequence of the fields in the field list determines the sequence of the input fields in the matchcode popup at runtime. It also determines the sequence of the input fields in the selection list in which the data records found for the selection are made available. For this reason, several menu functions allow you to delete or move entries in the field list.

The structure of the field list of the matchcode ID differs from that of the matchcode object. With additional attributes, it is possible within a certain scope to influence the attributes of the input fields in later popups. In particular, you can turn on the Get/Set parameter mechanism. You can also determine the position of the input fields. For the example, all of the fields are inserted in the matchcode ID. The client field appears automatically in the field list, but is later not displayed on the matchcode's entry popup (see Figure 4.20).

Save the field list. Afterwards, you must activate the matchcode ID, so that the matchcode is ready for use. You can do a preliminary test from the attributes screen of the matchcode object using the menu function *Utilities* → *Matchcode data* → *Display*.

When you define the matchcode ID, you must specify an activation type. This activation type has considerable influence on the technical implementation of the matchcode in the system. Some of the matchcode types originated in the SAP product R/2, which did not at first work with relational databases. Matchcodes are therefore not necessarily just simple search programs. Occasionally, there are extensive data sets hidden behind a matchcode that must be maintained in parallel to the actual application data.

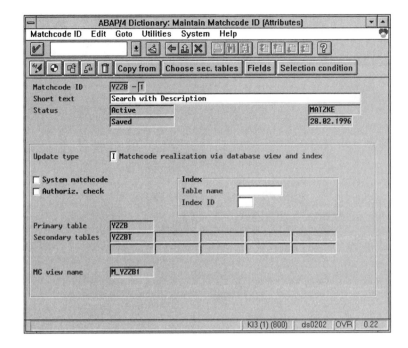

Figure 4.20   Matchcode ID

The activation type used so far, I, creates a matchcode that is implemented as a database view. In addition, a program is generated that reads the desired information using this view. This matchcode always accesses the current data in the database. This matchcode type is currently the default matchcode type.

In several modules of the SAP system, a so-called classification is performed, in which, for any tables, additional sort criteria can be recorded and given values. The customer, too, can create this classification. The matchcode type K makes it possible to use such classification data to search for a data record. Using a classification, however, requires well-grounded knowledge of this tool. It also requires rather extensive programming work. For this reason, classification and the matchcodes for it are not discussed here.

The other three matchcode types constitute a separate data set that must be updated again and again in parallel to the actual data. This data area contains only those fields that should be searched with a matchcode. In addition, indexes may exist that can accelerate the search. This data set can and must be updated continuously. This is also called the structure of matchcode data. There are three different methods available for this. In matchcode type A, the data is updated with a utility that works asynchronously to the rest of the application. This kind of matchcode is therefore mainly suited for searching in data sets that are rarely updated. In matchcode type S, the data is updated synchronously to the changes in the actual database tables. This updating is controlled by the Data Dictionary, or, more precisely, the database interface. In the final method, an application program can update the matchcodes of type P itself by calling an automatically generated function module.

4.4   Lock objects

With lock objects, a program can block access to selected data records or to several tables. The actual lock is set or released by a call of one of the function modules generated by the system. The locking functionality does not use the services of the database system, but is implemented in the Dictionary using SAP mechanisms. The required function modules are structured according to the definition of a lock object in the Dictionary. During the call, the key values of the data records to be locked are passed to these function modules as parameters. When a lock object is defined, therefore, two particular processes are necessary. First you must specify the tables that should be locked together. Then, you can select the fields needed as a lock argument for these tables. This process resembles the process for defining views and matchcodes.

The following example describes the definition of a common lock object for the two tables YZZB and YZZBT. In case these two tables will not be maintained as already demonstrated using the automatically generated maintenance modules, but rather using a dialog application that you have programmed yourself, you must use lock objects to protect the just-processed data records against concurrent processing by someone else.

To start, enter the name of the lock object in the basic Dictionary maintenance screen, mark the *Lock objects* radio button, then click on the *Create* pushbutton. The name of the lock object should begin with an E, according to SAP's recommendations. You can choose the rest of the name as desired, but usually one uses the name of the primary table. The name of the lock object for this example, then, is EYZZB.

After creating the lock object, you must enter a short description and the name of the primary table. Using the *Tables* pushbutton or the menu function *Goto → Tables*, you call up a screen in which you can select additional secondary tables, as for views and matchcodes. Again, the system determines the valid tables based on the foreign key relationships. For the YZZB table, therefore, only the YZZBT table can be selected as a secondary table.

Using the *Fields* or *Lock arguments* pushbuttons, you can jump from any of the various screens into a screen where you can select all of the fields to be used later to determine the data records to lock. This step resembles field selection for views and matchcodes. The labels of the tables involved (MANDT, BRANCHE and SPRACHE) are automatically inserted into the field list. Other fields are not necessary for this example.

From the field selection screen, you must still specify the lock mode for the individual tables. For this, you use a pushbutton or a menu function (*Lock mode*) again. Figure 4.21 shows the corresponding screen.

This lock mode determines if and how several users can access the locked data records. *Shared* mode (code S) allows simultaneous read access by several users. Access is not blocked until a user attempts to modify the data. *Exclusive* mode (code E, default) locks the specified data records immediately and completely for all other users. The locking user can lock again, however. This so-called cumulative locking is excluded by the mode with the code X. The user can then only lock the data record a single time, that is, in a single mode.

After entering all of the attributes, you activate the lock object. Two function modules are created whose names consist of the prefix ENQUEUE_ (lock) or DEQUEUE_ (release,

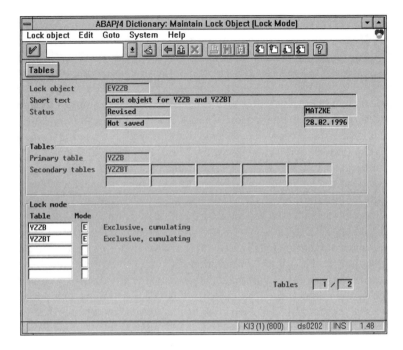

Figure 4.21   Lock object

unlock) and the name of the lock object. The two function modules for this example are therefore called ENQUEUE_EYZZB and DEQUEUE_EYZZB. These function modules have several general parameters and several parameters that are dependent on the lock arguments of the lock object. The following listing shows the call of this module, as it might be inserted in the program editor using the function *Edit → Insert statement*.

```
CALL FUNCTION 'ENQUEUE_EYZZB'
     EXPORTING
"        MANDT          = SY-MANDT
"        BRANCHE        = ' '
"        SPRACHE        = ' '
"        X_BRANCHE      = ' '
"        X_SPRACHE      = ' '
"        _SCOPE         = '2'
"        _WAIT          = ' '
     EXCEPTIONS
     FOREIGN_LOCK   = 01
     SYSTEM_FAILURE = 02.
```

All of the parameters of the function module have default values. For this reason, they are at first automatically commented out in the inserted statement template. The default values are entered in the inserted statement template. If the defaults differ from the required values, enter the correct value and remove the comment character.

The first parameters of both function modules are always the lock arguments. Their names correspond to those of the table fields. One X parameter follows every lock argument except MANDT. This parameter determines how the actual lock argument will be analyzed by the function module. If both the lock argument and the X field are filled with a blank space, there is a generic lock. An "X" in the X field, on the other hand, ensures that the contents of the lock argument are analyzed in the form in which it was passed, that is, they must really contain blank spaces.

All of the subsequent parameters are parameters that are generated for every lock module. The contents of the _SCOPE parameter determine how a set lock is handled in update modules. The valid values and their effects are shown in Table 4.5.

Table 4.5   Transfer of locks

Value	Effect
1	Locks are not passed to the update program.
2	The lock is passed to an update program. The dialog that set this lock loses its influence on the lock.
3	The lock is first passed to the update program. It must later be released in both the update program and the dialog.

If a lock fails, for example because the data record or records to be locked are already locked, the function module usually terminates immediately with an exception. However, if the _WAIT parameter contains an "X", the module makes additional lock attempts after a short waiting period. The number of lock attempts and the maximum waiting period are determined by parameters in the system profile. These parameters can only be changed by the system administrator at operating system level.

A lock function module returns status information in the system field SY-SUBRC. A value of 0 means the execution was successful. If the lock could not be set because one or more records are already locked by other applications or users, the module returns the value of the FOREIGN_LOCK exception. In this case, the name of the locking user can be determined from the system field SY-MSGV1. System errors, on the other hand, are reported by the SYSTEM_FAILURE exception. Function modules that belong to the lock objects with the lock mode "X" have a third exception, as well: OWN_LOCK. This exception is triggered if the same process has already requested a lock that overlaps the current lock request.

If the defaults are used for the parameters of the lock module, the entire table is locked.

The function modules for releasing do not trigger any exceptions. Their interface is therefore also somewhat simpler, as the following listing shows.

```
CALL FUNCTION 'DEQUEUE_EYZZB'
    EXPORTING
"      MANDT           = SY-MANDT
"      BRANCHE         = ' '
"      SPRACHE         = ' '
"      X_BRANCHE       = ' '
"      X_SPRAS         = ' '
"      _SCOPE          = '3'
"      _SYNCHRON       = ' '.
```

In this case, in addition to the parameters already described, there is also the parameter _SYNCHRON. If it is given a value of "X", the module waits until the lock has actually been released. Generally, this module works asynchronously.

4.5   Type groups

The *Type groups* selection is new in Release 3.0. It does not fit into the scheme of the Dictionary objects already described, since there are no database-specific objects hidden behind the type groups, just certain program statements. User-specific data types or constants are declared in a type group, also called a type pool. You use the statements TYPES and CONSTANTS for this. You can insert type groups in an application using the following statement:

TYPE-POOLS type_group.

Afterwards, all of the type group's declarations are available in the program. Type groups should be assigned to a development class. SAP therefore recommends that you build the name of a type group using the name of the development class and one or two additional letters. The names of the elements declared in a type group must start with the name of the type group and an underscore (_).

4.6   Exercises

1   If logging on in a different language is possible in your system, test the general table maintenance for the two tables using different languages.

2   Create the tables YZZAKT and YZZKURS, along with the necessary data elements and domains (domain name = data element name). Take the structure of the table from the overview that follows (Tables 4.6 and 4.7). The NAME field of the YZZKURS table should have a foreign key relationship to the NAME field of the YZZAKT table, that is, YZZAKT is the value table for the YZZAKTIE domain. For the KURS field of the YZZKURS table, enter the YZZAKT-WAEHR field as the reference field. The required input fields will become accessible after a double-click on the field name. Give both tables delivery class A. You do not need to generate the modules for general table maintenance.

Table 4.6   Structure of the YZZAKT table

Field name	Key	Data element	Type	Length	Check table	Short text
MANDT	X	MANDT	CLNT	3	*	client
NAME	X	YZZAKT	CHAR	25		stock name
BRANCHE		YZZBRA	CHAR	1	*	branch identifier
WAEHR		WAERS	CUKY	5	TCURC	currency key

Table 4.7   Structure of the YZZKURS table

Field name	Key	Data element	Type	Length	Check table	Short text
MANDT	X	MANDT	CLNT	3	*	client
NAME	X	YZZAKT	CHAR	25	YZZAKT	stock name
DATUM	X	YZZDATUM	DATS	8		date
KURS		YZZKURS	CURR	8		share price

5 Development environment utilities

The creation of an ABAP/4 application is a complex task that requires a multitude of tools. Several utilities simplify the work. This chapter demonstrates the most important utilities in detail.

5.1 Workbench Organizer

The entire R/3 System is a very complex application on which several hundred developers are working simultaneously at times. Development must be coordinated and brought to the customer in a functional state. This task is handled by several tools that are combined under the term *Workbench Organizer*. Some of these tools work in the R/3 System, while others work at operating system level. Although setting up the Workbench Organizer is a large task, it does not fall into the task area of a programmer. This chapter therefore describes only those parts of the Workbench Organizer with which the developer comes into contact on a daily basis.

The Workbench Organizer has also undergone extensive modification for Release 3.0. Although the tool familiar from previous release versions is still available, it only implements a subset of the new functionality.

5.1.1 Tasks

Just as an application can lock a table against outside access, the developer must be able to lock the elements currently being worked on against access from third parties. This lock differs from that for tables in that it often remains in place for a longer period of time, occasionally several weeks. During this time, usually only the developer who has placed the lock on this object can edit the object. The first task of the Workbench Organizer, then, is to assign objects to be edited to a developer and to prevent access by other developers. Another task consists of logging edits to objects. All of the objects to be edited and their editors are recorded in special system tables. This way, one can determine when and by whom an object was edited.

All developments must be tested and later transported to the customer or into your own live system. Development and testing in one and the same system are practically impossible, at least at SAP. Testing requires that the applications be in a defined state, or more importantly, a state that remains unchanged for a period of time. This means that no development should take place during testing. For this reason, a system group is available for development. Finished development projects are transported (physically copied) from the development system into a so-called consolidation system, where they are tested. Lists are maintained in the Workbench Organizer for the various developers and projects with all of the objects edited. After a development is finished, the objects edited are determined based on these lists, making selective transport of the edited objects possible.

Transport of new developments to customers is handled in a similar fashion. Except in the case of entirely new installations, not all of the objects are transported to the customer, only those that have changed since the last delivery. This functionality, too, is made possible by analysis of the Workbench Organizer's logs.

5.1.2   Principle

When a user wants to create a new object or edit an existing one, the system requires that he or she create a so-called request. Alternatively, he or she can specify an existing request. Hidden behind such a request is a list that includes every element to be edited. Such a request is given a descriptive identifier and is assigned to one developer (in rare cases to several). A development object contained in such a request cannot be included in any other request. This ensures that only the owner (or owners) of the request can edit the object in question. Each developer may create any number of such requests. This makes it possible to distinguish between different development projects. After a development is finished, the request is released. This means that the objects contained therein are no longer locked. The list of objects that were edited in this request remains intact, but it is no longer analyzed when potential locks are determined. Depending on the type of system, the objects edited and the system configuration, the edited elements may also be exported. This means that all of the data records from the system tables that describe the development objects contained in the request are written to a file at operating system level. The structure of this file is independent of the operating system. It can be brought to a different system and imported there. This is how development objects are transported to other systems. This also means that development objects that have not been recorded in such a request cannot be transported.

5.1.3   Terms

Several terms used in connection with the Workbench Organizer will be described here. Beginning with Release 3.0, the functions of the Workbench Organizer are controlled with the SE09 transaction. The transaction used previously, SE01, is still available for special needs. The two transactions use different terms for the same objects. The following list includes both the terms from Version 3.0 and the terms from older release versions.

Task

A task is the smallest physical organization unit in the Workbench Organizer. It is used to register the edited objects. Tasks are identified by a unique number. One or more tasks are assigned to a request. Whenever the Workbench Organizer wants to register a new object to be edited, although the programmer must enter the number of the request, the information is stored in a task within this request. A task thus corresponds in principle to the already mentioned list.

The Workbench Organizer distinguishes tasks using different types. The type is generally of no interest to the user of the Workbench Organizer. This type of distinction is necessary, because one system can contain development objects with different statuses that require individual handling. A task can only ever possess objects that have the same status. The different types of tasks (also called attributes of tasks) are listed in Table 5.1. Generally, the Workbench Organizer creates tasks automatically and also assigns the type.

Table 5.1   Attributes of tasks

Task type	Description
Not assigned	Newly created tasks without contents.
Development/correction	Contains only objects that were newly created in the current system (originals).
Repair	Contains only objects that were created in other systems and were transported into the current system (copies).

Request

A request is a logical management unit that combines all of the tasks for a self-contained development task. It can contain one or more tasks of different types and with different owners. The request determines the type and method of passing to other systems for all of the objects of the tasks it contains. Requests are generally created automatically, with one task always being created and submitted to the new request.

To register an object in the Workbench Organizer, the programmer specifies the request to which the object should be assigned. The Workbench Organizer then automatically determines the actual task in which the object will be registered, based on the user and the status of the object. If no appropriate task exists, it automatically creates one.

Requests also have a type, which is determined by the transport attributes of the objects contained in it, or, more precisely, the transport attributes of the first object to be included (see Table 5.2). All of the objects to be registered later in the course of development must have the same transport attributes. If this is not the case, the object cannot be registered in this request. The Workbench Organizer then creates a new request.

Table 5.2   Attributes of a request

Request Type	Description
Not assigned	Empty request
Transportable	Request with objects that can be exported into a non-SAP system
Local	Request with objects that cannot be exported from the system

If a single request contains tasks from different developers, all of the developers can edit all of the objects in this request.

Local private objects

New objects to be created can be assigned the status *Local object*. Such objects are edited outside the Workbench Organizer. They cannot be protected against editing by third parties using the mechanisms of the Workbench Organizer, and they cannot be transported. The only possibility for protection consists of locking the object during direct editing with the maintenance tool being used. This lock is not set by the Workbench Organizer; it is just a normal database lock.

Development class

A complex ABAP/4 application consists of many different development objects. The development class is the common generic term for all of the elements of an application. This development class determines the transport attributes of the objects it contains, in particular the target system for an eventual export. If you enter the development class as an object in the Workbench (transaction SE80), the Workbench's Object Browser displays all of the development objects for the development class.

Before a development is started, a development class should be created. Only users with certain authorizations can do this. Setup can be done in Customizing or with general table maintenance, SM31. The table to be maintained is TDEVC. Beginning with Release 3.0, transport paths are not determined directly, but rather by specification of a transport layer that contains the source system and the target system. This transport layer is maintained in the DEVL table.

Original and copy

Development of applications takes place in a development system from where the development objects are distributed. This procedure takes place periodically, to fix errors or to make new functionality available. Permanent changes to a development object are therefore possible only in the system from which the delivery is done. For every development object, therefore, a note is made about the system in which the object was created. This system is also called the original system of the object, and the object in this system is called the original. All other systems to which SAP upgrades are delivered, including customer systems, contain only copies of the object.

Repair

This term is no longer used in Release 3.0. A development object can be either an original or a copy in a system. Sooner or later, changes to copies are overwritten by transports from the original system. They are, however, sometimes necessary to fix errors. The term repair is used for both the procedure itself and the object in the Workbench Organizer where the object list is maintained for the repaired (edited) objects. Beginning with Release 3.0, repairs are called tasks with the repair attribute. Repairs are only transported in exceptional cases. They can therefore be released either with or without a transport request.

Correction

This term, too, originates from releases prior to Release 3.0. In contrast to repairs, corrections record objects that are originals in the system in question. Beginning with Release 3.0, corrections are called tasks with the development/correction attribute. Since new development projects are passed to other systems for the reasons already mentioned, corrections can only be released to a transport request.

Transport request

In releases up to and including Release 2.2, the term transport request is a synonym for a transportable request. A transport request is automatically created by the system, although several specifications such as the target system and one of the three transport types must be entered manually. Transport requests are divided into three subtypes:

- Transports to the consolidation system
- Transports with change authorization (move)
- Transports without change authorization

In Release 3.0, a request corresponds to a transport into the consolidation system.

5.1.4   The Workbench Organizer in practice, Release 3.0

This section demonstrates the procedures for creating a new object in an SAP development system. The names of the objects involved follow the conventions for SAP development, not those for customer objects. This example is only meant to be a demonstration. You cannot replicate it in this form in your own system. As a rule, you should never create transportable objects in your system and actually transport them unless you are certain about the potential effects on your system.

A report, RFFMAEBL, is to be created. A report with this name is created using the transaction SE38 or the Workbench. In the program editor's attributes screen, a short description and the program type are entered. These steps are identical to those for creating the "Hello World" program in Chapter 3. When the specifications on the attributes screen are saved, the first Workbench Organizer popup appears (see Figure 5.1). Up to now, this popup was usually ended by clicking on the *Local object* pushbutton, which meant the object was created outside the Workbench Organizer.

If the object should be created with the Workbench Organizer, a development class (in this case, FMBS) must be entered in this popup. This causes the transport attributes of this class (target system) to be copied for the new object. Afterwards, the popup is ended with the Save pushbutton. The Workbench Organizer recognizes that the new object must be included in a request. It therefore asks for the request number in a second popup (Figure 5.2).

Clicking on the *Own requests* pushbutton displays as possible entries help the own requests available whose attributes allow the inclusion of the current object. The last number edited may be inserted automatically as the default in the input field for the request number. With the *Create request* pushbutton, a new request is created. In this case,

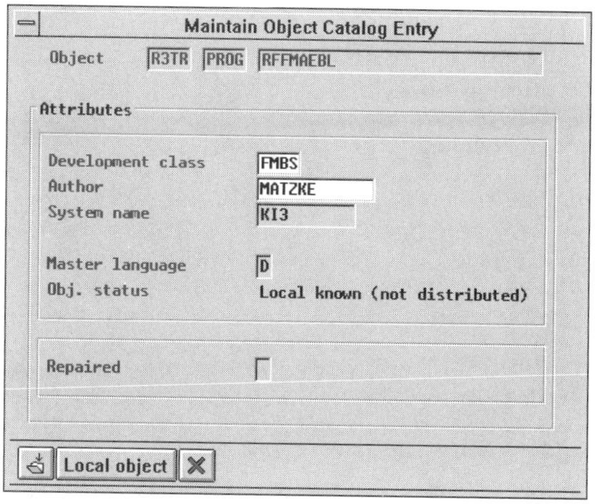

Figure 5.1   *Assignment of a development class*

a short description must be recorded in a third popup. After saving the third popup, you return to the second, in which you finally create the request with the Enter key or with the corresponding pushbutton (green check mark). If necessary, it is possible to include additional objects in this request.

When development ends, the request must be released. The *Workbench Organizer,* which should not be confused with the actual Workbench, is used for this. It is accessible with the transaction code SE09 or with the menu function *Overview → Workbench Organizer* from the program development main menu. Figure 5.3 shows this tool's interface.

All requests and tasks can be maintained from the basic screen of the Workbench Organizer. The right-hand side of the screen shows an overview of all of the current user's transports. If the system has been incorporated in a so-called transport group, transports from other systems are included in this overview.

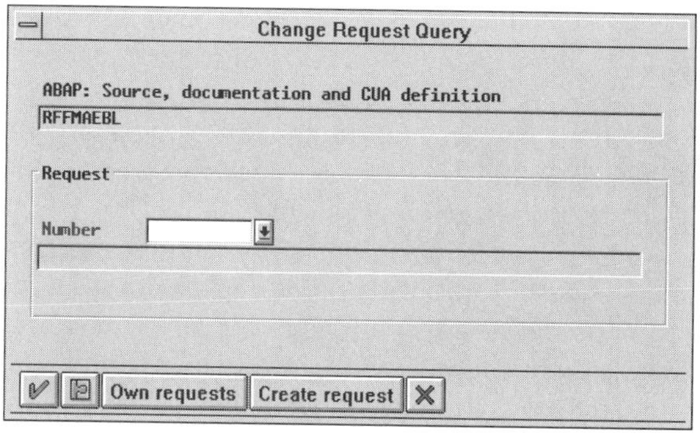

Figure 5.2   *Search for a request number*

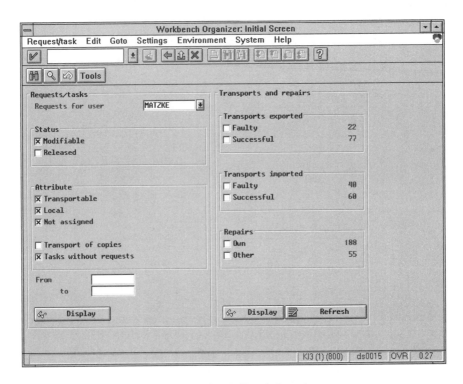

Figure 5.3   The Workbench Organizer

On the left-hand side of the screen, you first select the tasks and requests to be edited using their attributes. After you click on the *Display* pushbutton, all of the tasks and requests that correspond to the marked attributes are displayed in a second screen (Figure 5.4).

Some of the selection possibilities, the attributes, have already been explained. The two fields *Transport of copies* and *Tasks without requests* enable the management of objects that were created with the earlier transaction, SE01. Transport of copies means transport requests without change authorizations. Tasks without change requests are corrections or repairs that are not yet assigned to a request. The two fields *Modifiable* and *Released* make it possible to differentiate between released, that is, finished, requests and those that can still be edited.

To be able to release the just-created request, it is necessary to mark at least the *Modifiable* and *Transportable* fields. After the *Display* key is pressed, the transaction builds a new screen that contains an interactive report (see Figure 5.4).

Double-clicking on the folder icon in front of the request number displays all of the tasks belonging to that request. Additional double-clicking on the folder icons of the tasks displays their contents. To release a request, all of the tasks must first be released. To do this, you place the cursor on the number of the task to be released and click on the *Release* pushbutton. Released tasks are highlighted in a different color. Afterwards, you repeat the process for the request. After a task has been released, its object list (the list of objects to be edited) is copied into a list that is assigned to the request. This maintains the locking

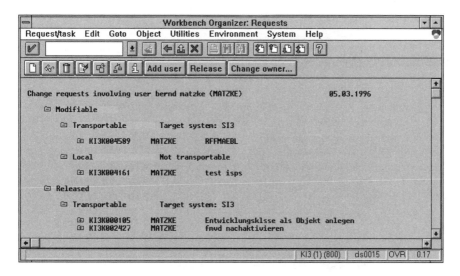

Figure 5.4   Overview of tasks and requests

effect until the request has also been released. After the request has been released, the object can be edited by another user.

Various errors may appear during export from the system and import into another system. The system therefore creates a log, which can be viewed using the menu function *Goto → Logs → Transport log*.

The detail screen for the tasks and requests provides several other possibilities for editing. With the *Change owner ...* pushbutton, the marked object can be given a new owner. Only the owner can release a request or a task. This function is useful for ensuring that the tasks or requests can continue to be edited by other employees when their owners are absent. This function can also be executed with foreign objects, meaning you can also retrieve the objects of other employees.

If changing the owner does not seem sensible, you can assign additional employees to a request instead. To do so, you mark the request using the cursor, then click on the *Add user* pushbutton. The name of the additional employee can then be entered in a popup. A separate task is then created for this employee.

5.1.5   Release 2.2

The process is similar in principle for all versions. While in Release 3.0 a task is immediately assigned to a request, or if necessary a new request is even created, in releases prior to Release 3.0, tasks (called corrections or repairs) are created as separate objects. This, too, can be demonstrated with an example. The starting point is another new report. This is created using the SE38 transaction. When the attributes are saved, the Workbench Organizer popup appears again (Figure 5.5). It resembles the one in Release 3.0. Entry of the development class is required in this case, as well.

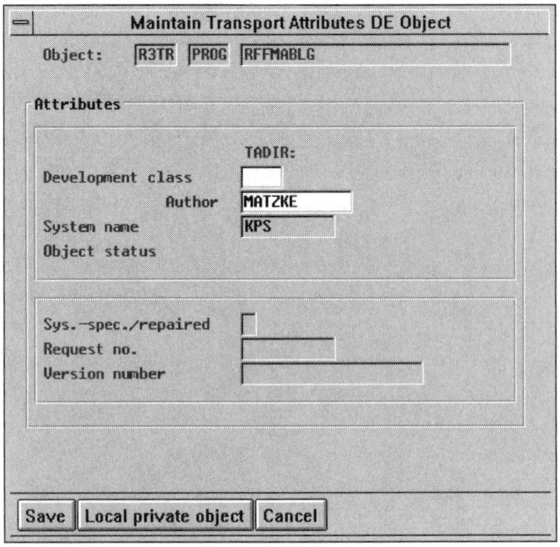

```
 ┌──────────────────────────────────────────────────────────┐
 │ ▭ │        Maintain Transport Attributes DE Object          │
 │      Object:   [R3TR] [PROG] [RFFMABLG]                       │
 │    ┌─Attributes──────────────────────────────────────────┐ │
 │    │                           TADIR:                       │ │
 │    │   Development class      [    ]                        │ │
 │    │            Author        [MATZKE]                      │ │
 │    │   System name            [KPS]                         │ │
 │    │   Object status                                        │ │
 │    │                                                        │ │
 │    │   Sys.-spec./repaired    [ ]                           │ │
 │    │   Request no.            [        ]                    │ │
 │    │   Version number         [          ]                  │ │
 │    └────────────────────────────────────────────────────┘ │
 │   [ Save ][ Local private object ][ Cancel ]                │
 └──────────────────────────────────────────────────────────┘
```

Figure 5.5   Workbench Organizer popup in Release 2.2

After the specifications are saved, the Workbench Organizer asks for a correction number. A correction corresponds to a task in Release 3.0. If corrections already exist, possible entries help can be called with the *Find correction* pushbutton. This is rather complicated to use; a description follows later. With the *New correction* pushbutton, the Workbench Organizer is asked to create a new correction. A short description must be recorded for this new correction in another screen. The specifications in this screen are saved, and the screen is ended with the F3 function key or the corresponding symbol or menu functions. The previous popup becomes active again, in which the correction number and the just-recorded description are now visible. Figure 5.6 shows the popup in this state.

Now the popup can be saved with the *Edit* key. At that moment, the object to be edited is registered in the correction. After development is finished, the correction must be released. You call the SE01 transaction for this, or you call the menu function *Maintenance*

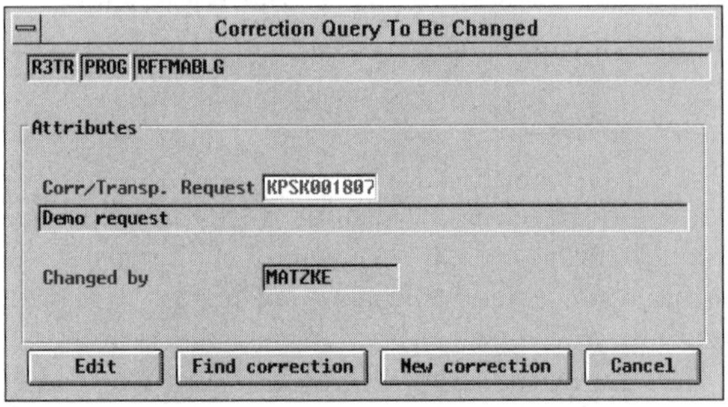

```
 ┌──────────────────────────────────────────────────────────┐
 │ ▭ │          Correction Query To Be Changed                 │
 │  [R3TR] [PROG] [RFFMABLG]                                    │
 │    ┌─Attributes──────────────────────────────────────────┐ │
 │    │                                                        │ │
 │    │  Corr/Transp. Request  [KPSK001807]                    │ │
 │    │  [Demo request]                                        │ │
 │    │                                                        │ │
 │    │  Changed by            [MATZKE]                        │ │
 │    └────────────────────────────────────────────────────┘ │
 │   [ Edit ][ Find correction ][ New correction ][ Cancel ]   │
 └──────────────────────────────────────────────────────────┘
```

Figure 5.6   Newly created correction

→ *Corrections* from the main menu of the development environment. The initial screen of the SE01 transaction appears, which is somewhat comparable in meaning to Figure 5.3. In this screen, the type of the object to be edited (transport, correction or repair) is determined with three radio buttons. The appropriate number is entered in the input field. The *Change* pushbutton then calls the tool for maintaining the object in question. A screen appears for the correction to be released that corresponds to the one in which the short description was entered when the correction was created. Now, however, several new functions are available.

Release takes place by way of a pushbutton with the same name. Since corrections must be released to transports, the Workbench Organizer asks in a popup if a new transport request should be created or if the correction should be released to an existing transport request. This way, several corrections that are destined for the same target system can be transported together. After asking for a new transport request, the system starts a special editor and waits for correction documentation to be entered. Generally, it is sufficient to save the outline text and exit the editor. The number of the created transport request is entered in a field on the screen for corrections (Figure 5.7). This number must be recorded if you want to avoid using the search function.

After the correction is released, the transport request just created must be released. To do this, you mark the *Transport request* radio button on the basic screen of the SE01 transaction, and you enter the correct transport number in the input field. After the *Change key* is pressed, the screen for editing transport requests is displayed (Figure 5.8).

In this screen, you select the transport type (release to the consolidation system in this case) and enter the target system. Transports to the consolidation system are transports of original objects into a system that is used for consolidation and for testing development projects. Such transports are only possible for objects in whose development class the current system is entered as the source system, and the target system entered in the transport request is entered as the consolidation system. The transport type *Transport without change*

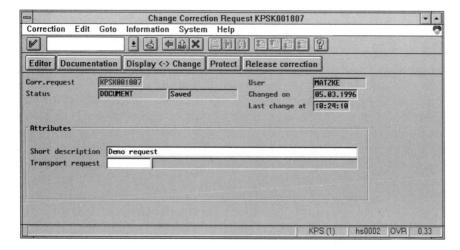

Figure 5.7   Release of a correction

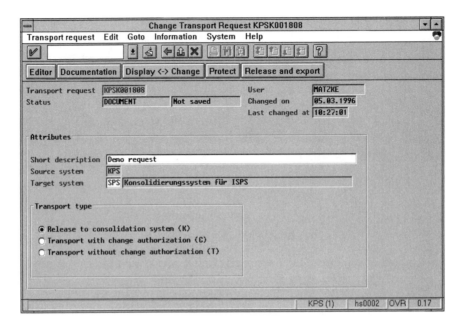

Figure 5.8   Editing of a transport request

authorization is required for all other transport paths. It enables the transport of objects to any target system. The only exception is the transport of originals from the development system into the consolidation system. Since the development system is the only system in which an object can be an original, usually only copies are transported in transports without change authorization. This transport type is therefore also called transport of copies. For example, further transports of maintenance levels or patches from a customer's test system into the customer's live system are transports of copies. The last transport type, *Transport with change authorization*, is a so-called move. In such transports, originals are moved from one system into the other. This type of transport is required mainly in complex development systems.

After the two values have been input and saved, the transport can be released. A short text in the form of an embedded report tells whether the release was successful or encountered problems. From the transport request's editing screen, you can display the log of the export and, if necessary, also the log of the import into the target system, using the menu function *Information* → *Transport log*.

Returning to the basic screen of the SE01 transaction, the *Find* pushbutton calls a search tool (Figure 5.9). You have to fill some fields with search patterns; some fields are filled with default values by the system.

If the search function is called from the basic screen, the radio button currently selected determines which objects (transport, correction, or repair) will be searched for. All default entries can be overwritten. You start the search with the *Execute* pushbutton. The result is a list that contains the numbers and short texts. Double-clicking on a number calls up the maintenance tool for the selected element.

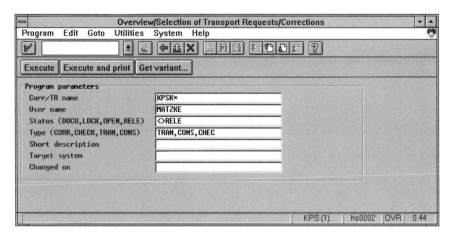

Figure 5.9   Search for objects of the Workbench Organizer

5.2   The debugger

Debuggers greatly simplify the search for errors during program development. The ABAP/4 development environment has such a tool, of course. You can use it to process an application step by step at source code level.

There are three different ways to start the debugger. In the main menu of the SE38 transaction (the ABAP/4 program editor), you can use a pushbutton, *Debugging*, or a menu function, *Program → Execute → Debugging*. This function processes the report entered in the input field in debug mode. Since direct processing is possible only for reports, it follows that you can only call the debugger directly for this type of program. Release 2.2 has this variant, as well, although the pushbutton and the menu function have different names there.

If you want to run dialog programs with the debugger, you can call it with a special command in the OK field. Enter the character string "/h" and press the Enter key. A text in the status bar notes that debug mode is turned on. The debugger processes the next action that results in the processing of a command, that is, all of those that end data entry on the screen and begin executing the PAI section. Instead of the next screen, the interface of the debugger appears. This command can, of course, be used in reports, too. However, for this program type, this is only useful on the selection screen or after the display of a details list in interactive reporting, since for simple reports the list is not displayed until the entire program has been processed.

Neither of the methods for calling the debugger mentioned so far allows you to specifically choose a starting point. Directly placing one or more stopping points (breakpoints) in the program makes such a choice possible. There are, in turn, several different variants for defining a breakpoint. You can enter the following statement in the program:

```
BREAK-POINT.
```

When this statement is reached, the debugger is activated. This statement may not, of course, be contained in live applications, but only in applications in the development phase. A somewhat weakened variant of this statement is:

BREAK *user*.

This breakpoint becomes effective only if the name of the current user matches the argument in the BREAK statement. All other users can execute the program without interruptions. You can use as many of these statements as you want.

Breakpoints cannot only be set using hard-coded program statements; they can also be set dynamically in the editor or in the debugger. A menu function, *Utilities → Breakpoints → Set*, is available in the program editor, and in some editor modes there is also a corresponding pushbutton. This sets a breakpoint in the line in which the cursor is located. This variant, too, can be used as often as desired. Breakpoints set this way, however, are only retained for a single session. In the debugger, you set or delete breakpoints with a double-click in front of the first character on a program line. Beginning with Release 3.0, these are identified by an icon (a stop sign). Older release versions use a lowercase "b".

Some special types of breakpoints are analyzed dynamically. They are not linked to specific line numbers but rather to events. Triggering events are a jump into a subroutine, reaching a selected command, a change to a value in a data field, and recognition of a value unequal to 0 in SY-SUBRC. You can determine the settings for this only in the debugger, using the menu function *Breakpoint → Breakpoint at*.

When you jump to the debugger, it first appears in preferred mode. Figure 5.10 shows this screen. In the middle area, there is an excerpt of the program currently being processed. The statement to be executed next is identified with a greater-than sign (>). On the uppermost line of the work area, that is, directly below the pushbutton bar, some status information and seven pushbuttons reduced to minimal width appear. Below the program area, several input fields are displayed in which the contents of data fields can be displayed.

The debugger can work in different display modes. These modes differ mainly in the program-related information they display. The preferred mode, which is active when you first jump into the editor, is the one that allows data fields to be displayed. The commands for continued program processing available in these modes are almost identical.

Before describing the debugger's different display modes, this section will describe commands generally available in all modes. With a few exceptions, they are available with pushbuttons, in the interest of simple use. For all pushbuttons, of course, there are also menu functions, whose use is much more time consuming, however. Efficient work requires the use of pushbuttons or function keys. The functions described here are also available in older release versions, but they cannot necessarily be called the same way there.

Using the *Single step* key (F5), you process the statement marked by the > character. This includes branching into subroutines or function modules, which can also be processed statement by statement. The *Execute* key (F6), on the other hand, executes the marked command without branching into modularization units. With *Continue* (F8), you end step-by-step processing, meaning the program runs to the next breakpoint or until the end of the program. With *Return* (F7), you can end the processing of a subroutine or function

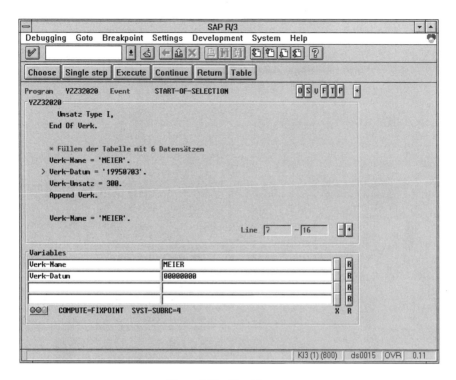

Figure 5.10   The debugger

module. The debugger processes the subroutine in its entirety and then stops again in the superordinate program, that is, at the statement after the subroutine call. The last key, *Table* (Shift-F2, only accessible in the default mode) triggers a function that can also be reached with one of the small pushbuttons on the screen. It switches the display mode to the display of internal tables. Next to the default mode, this is the display mode most often used. For this reason, you can access it not only using the pushbutton on the screen, which is very difficult to select because of its small size, but also with a function key and with the additional, easy-to-use pushbutton. Other display modes contain the *Program* pushbutton (Shift-F1), with which you can return to the default mode.

To test an application, test data is often created that is changed by the application. Since every screen change in an application triggers a Commit Work and consequently the writing of database changes, the test data must be created again after every run of the debugger. To avoid this, you can trigger a rollback of the database using the menu function *Debugging → Database → Rollback.*

In the upper right-hand corner of the screen's work area, next to the six pushbuttons for selecting the display mode, there is an additional, small pushbutton identified with a plus or minus sign (+ or -). This key enlarges the source code display area to the entire screen area or returns it to the normal state (source code with additional information, depending on the display mode).

A total of six display modes are available that can be activated at any time with the small pushbuttons in the upper right-hand corner of the screen or with several menu functions. Under certain circumstances, additional functions are available in these modes. The display modes and any special functions they contain are described below. The identifiers used for the modes correspond to the letters on the small pushbuttons.

V mode (variables)

This mode is the default mode already mentioned. In addition to the source code, it contains four pairs of fields for displaying the contents of data fields (simple fields or field strings, including table header lines). You enter the name of the data field in a field on the left, and the current contents of the field then appear in the field on the right. Field strings are interpreted as fields of type C. The field contents are updated during PAI processing of the debugger screen. After manually entering a field name in the left column, you must press the Enter key for the field contents to appear. You can also select fields to be displayed by double-clicking in the source code. They are automatically entered in the next empty field in the display area. If all fields are filled, the lowermost entry is overwritten.

In this mode, you can not only analyze field contents, but also change them in a more permanent way. To do this, you enter the new value in the right-hand column, which is actually also an input field, and then click on the small pushbutton marked R (Replace) to the right of the input field.

T mode (tables)

This mode is the next most often used, after the default mode. It displays the contents of an internal table. In this mode, only a few lines of the source code are available (see Figure 5.11). It is thus less suitable for following the program flow.

Since the screen is often not wide enough to display all of the fields, there are four pushbuttons available for moving the displayed table contents horizontally (one column right or left; first or last column). The data records are displayed in the sequence in which they appear in the table. For orientation, the data record number appears in front of the data record. The first line of the table display includes the header line. It is identified by the character string ">>>>>>".

Internal tables are displayed in almost the same way in debuggers of older release versions, too. In Release 3.0, several elements are added. Two input fields next to those for the table name allow you to enter a data record number to jump to and to choose a display type for the internal table. Underneath these three fields, another input field appears that extends across the entire width of the window. The column headings appear in this field. By overwriting the column names, you can change the sequence of the displayed columns. With the four additional pushbuttons under the table area, you can add new columns, delete existing columns and change individual field values.

F mode (fields)

In this mode, all of the information for a particular field is displayed, not just its contents. In this mode, you can select a field as a *watchpoint*. The program stops every time a value

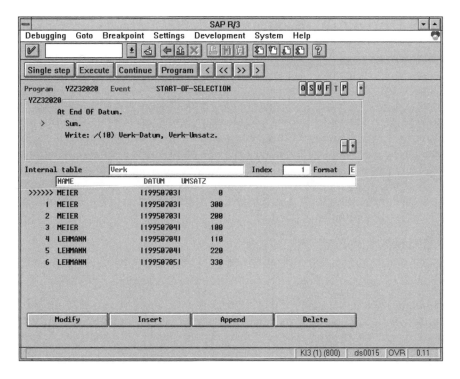

Figure 5.11   Display of internal tables in the debugger

is assigned to this field. This mode is interesting in connection with the SY-... system fields. If you enter SYST as the field name, the contents of all system fields are displayed.

O mode (overview)

In this mode, the debugger displays the structure of the current programs with modules, events and subroutines.

S mode (stack)

This mode displays the call sequence of the various subroutines and function modules, as well as of the events.

P mode (program)

In this mode, the debugger displays all of the programs that are required to execute the current program.

5.3   Authorization concept

Authorizations are extremely important for protecting programs and data from outside access and should therefore be used in custom development, too. Authorizations are based on a rather complicated system, however, and the maintenance of authorizations for different users is quite time consuming. Every additional authorization increases the time needed for maintenance and the likelihood of problems. For these reasons, it is best to use already existing authorizations whenever possible in custom applications. Because customer applications are limited in most cases to additions to existing SAP applications, this is usually possible. Even if you need to create custom authorizations, you can often use ready-made elements called authorization objects. When including authorization checks in custom applications, a distinction is made between three methods, each of which requires a different level of effort:

• Using existing authorizations

• Creating and using new authorizations based on existing authorization objects

• Creating new authorization objects and deriving authorizations from these

To maintain various elements of the authorization system, you need certain authorizations, which of course not every user may possess for reasons of system security. Checks within authorization maintenance are organized in such a way that the tasks can be divided into several subsections and assigned to different users. The tasks described below do not necessarily belong to the task area of every developer; they are to be executed by a system administrator. Depending on your actual authorizations in the system, you may or may not be able to execute the example. If you cannot, the explanations accompanying the screens should at least give you an overview of the elements of the authorization system.

The example explains the entire process, beginning with the creation of an authorization field all the way to insertion of an authorization in a user master record, based on an authorization for the demo program in Chapter 6. This description corresponds to the three points listed above, although it handles them in the opposite sequence.

5.3.1   Authorization classes, fields, and objects

An authorization object is a template for an authorization. The authorization object contains fields that must be filled with values later in the authorization. An authorization object is therefore remotely comparable to a type declaration. Several authorization objects for one application group (for example, Financial Accounting or Materials Management) constitute an authorization class. This is used only for logically grouping authorization objects, to increase clarity.

Only fields that are contained in one of three special Dictionary structures can be included in authorization objects. You edit these structures, however, using the tools for maintaining authorization objects, meaning that you do not have to edit them directly using Dictionary maintenance. To increase clarity, different structures are used for the authorization objects of the SAP Basis tools, SAP applications and customer applications.

These structures have the name AUTHA for application development fields, AUTHB for Basis tool fields and ZAUTHCUST for the fields of authorizations created by the customer. While AUTHA and AUTHB are always available, ZAUTHCUST must be created when needed by copying the AUTHC structure. If the ZAUTHCUST structure does not yet exist in your system, you can create it by copying the AUTHC structure. You do this with the Dictionary maintenance transaction (SE11). Without this structure, you cannot replicate the following examples in your system.

To create several authorization objects, up to three different steps are required:

- Define the authorization fields.
- Create an authorization class.
- Create authorization objects.

You can access the tools needed for these tasks from the main menu of the development environment, using the menu functions *Development* → *Other tools* → *Authorization obj.* → *Fields* (transaction code SU20) or *Development* → *Other tools* → *Authorization obj.* → *Obj.* (transaction code SU21).

First, you create an authorization field using the SU20 transaction or the menu function mentioned above. On the initial screen of this transaction (Figure 5.12), click on one of the three available pushbuttons to select the desired category for the new authorization fields.

The system checks whether the selection matches the current system type. After a correct selection, the available authorization fields for the group in question are displayed in a list. Using pushbuttons or menu functions, you can now add new fields or edit existing ones. During creation, the system asks for only two specifications in a popup (Figure 5.13).

The specifications that the system asks for are the name of the authorization field, which you can select as desired according to the naming conventions, and the name of the data element, which determines the attributes of the authorization field. In this example, YZZAKTIE should be the name, and YZZAKT should be the data element. The three display fields in the popup are not updated with the properties of the data element until the specifications are saved. The specifications also appear in a list. You can create additional fields this way, too, of course. For the example, however, this one field is enough.

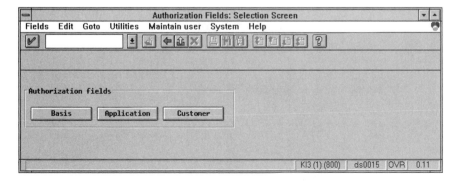

Figure 5.12   Creating authorization fields

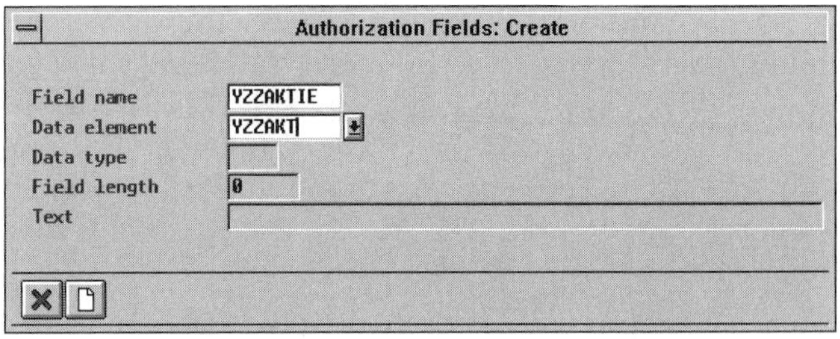

Figure 5.13   Defining a new authorization field

In the second step, you create a new authorization class. The method here basically corresponds to the method for creating a new field. First start the SU21 transaction, either by directly entering the transaction code or by using the appropriate menu function. Although the menu function is called *Objects* instead of *Classes*, a list of all the authorization classes appears. With a pushbutton or a menu function, you can create a new class. You enter the specifications for the new class (identifier and description) in a popup (Figure 5.14).

After you create the class, it appears in the list of available classes. You can edit the objects in a class by double-clicking on the class name in that list or by clicking on the *List objects* pushbutton. These objects are also displayed in a list, to which you can add new objects by using a menu function or a pushbutton. The popup for defining an authorization object requires the specification of an object name and a short description. If necessary, you can also change the authorization class. In addition to these specifications, you can enter up to 10 authorization fields in the lower area of the popup (Figure 5.15).

For technical reasons concerning the system in which the examples for this book were created, the naming conventions could not be followed for the authorization object. Instead of the intended name, Y_ZZAKT, D_ZZAKT had to be used. In your own system, you should use Y_ZZAKT instead.

Once you have defined the authorization object, the first part of the required maintenance work for authorizations is completed.

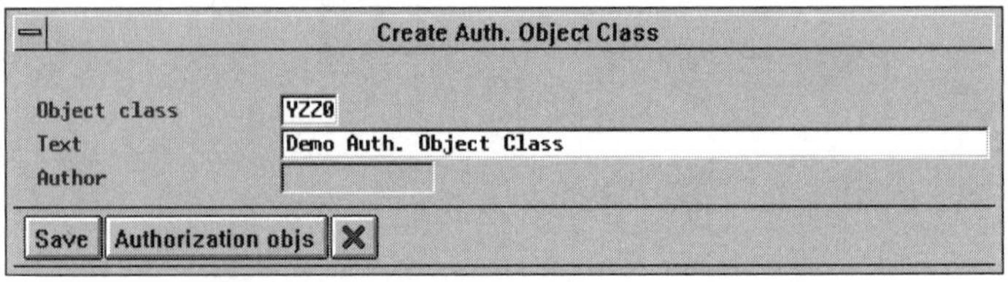

Figure 5.14   Creating an authorization class

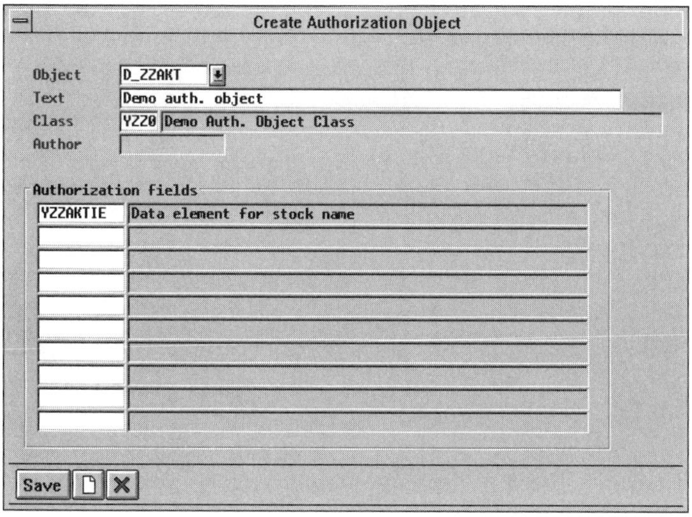

Figure 5.15   Creating an authorization object

5.3.2   Authorizations

The authorization object can now be used to define an authorization. An authorization is an instance of an authorization object. It is given its own name, and it contains all of the fields of the authorization object, although values can be assigned to the fields. The authorization check is later carried out against these values.

There are various methods for calling up authorization maintenance. In the various screens of the SU20 and SU21 transactions, there is a menu called *Maintain users* with three functions, *Authorization, Profiles* and *Users*. This same menu is also contained in the system administration area menu, which you can activate from the basic menu of the SAP system (S000 area menu) by choosing *Tools → Administration*. The transaction codes for the three menu functions are SU01 (user), SU02 (profile) and SU03 (authorizations).

To create an authorization, you call the appropriate transaction. A list appears with all of the available authorization classes. However, only the textual description is displayed, not the actual identifier. Since the list is sorted alphabetically according to this short description, the sequence of the entries is different in comparison to the list in the SU21 transaction. The line "Authorization class demo" appears in the first third of the list. Double-clicking on this entry branches to a list in which all of the authorization objects for this class appear. This list, too, contains only the short descriptions. However, you can display the actual identifier with the *Technical name* pushbutton. All of the authorizations derived from an authorization object are visible in a third list, which you display by double-clicking on the name of the authorization object. In the example, this list is still empty. With the *Create* pushbutton or the menu function *Authorization → Create*, you create an authorization. A popup appears in which you must enter the authorization identifier and a short description. Since an authorization contains actual values and thus enables or

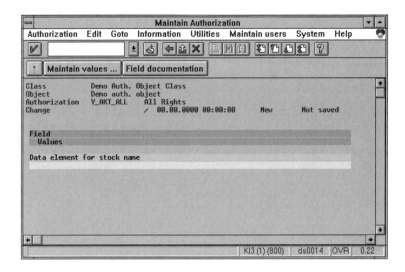

Figure 5.16   Maintaining an authorization

disables specifically defined actions, it should have a meaningful name. Give the first authorization the name Y_AKT_ALL. Enter any short description you desire.

The authorization created this way now appears in the list (Figure 5.16), but it is still empty. Next is the assignment of values, which is done with the *Maintain values…* push-button, the menu function *Goto → Maintain values…* or a double-click on the name of the authorization. In the popup that is now active (Figure 5.17), you can enter one or more individual values or value pairs.

Figure 5.17   Assignment of values to an authorization

After determining the field values, you must save the authorization and activate it. The values entered do not take effect until after activation. The status of an authorization (edited, active) is identified by some text in the list with the authorizations. Sometimes, the authorizations for maintenance and activation are split between two different administrators, meaning changes made by one must be confirmed by a second person before they become effective. When a transaction is edited, therefore, two versions are stored, the one that is currently valid for the user, and a maintenance version. Only after activation does the maintenance version become the current version. To make it easier for the activating administrator to execute his or her control function, the system displays the current version and the maintenance version opposite each other during activation. Only after the *Activate...* function has been executed again does activation finally take place.

You can create any number of authorizations with different field values for one authorization object. To determine the actual authorizations for a user, you must store the authorization in that user's master record. You cannot do this directly; you must use an intermediate step known as profiles. A profile combines one or more logically related authorizations, simplifying the maintenance of user data. Direct assignment of an authorization to a user master record is not possible.

To create a profile, you call the SU02 transaction or the menu function *Maintain users* → *Profiles*. The basic screen of this transaction provides an input field that enables you to preselect the profiles to be edited in the following list. You can also skip this basic screen without entering a value by pressing the Enter key, causing all of the available profiles to appear in the list. You can create a new profile, similar to authorization objects or classes, using the *Create* pushbutton. You must then enter the profile's identifier (Y_AKT_PROALL) and a short description in a popup.

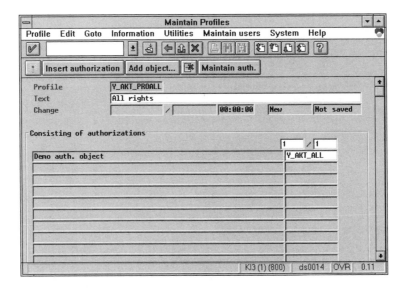

Figure 5.18   Creating a profile

In this popup, you must also choose between a single profile and a composite profile. A single profile contains authorizations, while a composite profile contains other profiles. For this example, you should create a single profile.

A screen now appears for the new profile, with a relatively large step loop area (Figure 5.18), which consists only of output fields, however. In this loop area, you list the profile's authorizations. Inserting authorizations is only possible using a particular function that you call using the *Insert authorization* pushbutton or the menu function *Edit* → *Insert authorization*. This function allows you to select an authorization with possible entries help. It displays the list with all the authorization classes, from which you select one by double-clicking on it. Another list appears containing all of the authorizations for all of the authorization objects of this class. You can now select one of these authorizations, which is then entered in the profile.

Like changes to an authorization, changes to a profile do not take effect until after activation. In this case, too, the active version and the maintenance version are first displayed, then actually activated once the intention to activate has been confirmed.

After you have created the profile, you can store it in the user's user master record. You can, of course, create a new user (or have one created) to test the authorizations, or you can insert the new authorization into your own user master record. To provide a better overview, the following demonstration starts with a new user master record for an imaginary user, DEMO.

You maintain a user master record with the SU01 transaction or the menu function *Maintain users* → *Users*. In the single input field of this transaction, you enter the name of the user to be created or changed, then click on the *Create* pushbutton or the *Change* pushbutton. In the subsequent screen, you can enter the profile Y_AKT_PROALL in the step loop area, then save the data. The changes take effect the next time the corresponding user logs on to the system.

6 An example

With the help of a small example, this chapter demonstrates the basic programming technique for creating a dialog application. The focus is not on the use of the individual tools or the activities for creating the application, but rather on the program structure and the description of the tasks of the individual program elements.

The example calculates share prices for stocks. The stocks for which share prices are to be recorded are maintained in the YZZAKT table. The share prices appear in a separate table, YZZKURS. Both tables were already created in Chapter 4. The tables YZZB and YZZBT, which were also used before, are used again here. Figure 6.1 shows the relationships between the tables. An entity relationship diagram is used for this, as is done often at SAP.

The table maintenance already generated should suffice for editing YZZB and YZZBT. Below, separate programs are created for YZZAKT and YZZKURS only. The application for YZZAKT should allow the creation, change, display, and deletion of data records. Deletion is implemented as a subfunction of the Change program branch. It is based on the concept with two screens, which has been mentioned several times already. The second application allows the creation or display of share price data for all of the data records maintained in YZZAKT. Since share prices can be maintained only for stocks for which a data record exists in YZZAKT, the example must begin with the application for YZZAKT.

6.1 Program structure

An application consists of one or more screens, which are called one after another. Each screen, together with the statements in the flow logic, performs a precisely defined subtask. The transition from one screen to another indicates that one subtask has ended and another is to be executed. Each screen thus represents a state within the application. The

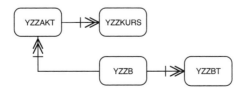

Figure 6.1   Relationships between the tables in the demo application

first task when creating an application is therefore to divide the action to be executed into subtasks, assign these to the various screens and determine under which conditions and triggered by which actions the various screens should be processed. For YZZAKT, determining subtasks is relatively easy. There are only two, as follows:

- Select a data record.
- Process a data record.

Each of these tasks is passed to a screen. For more complex applications, it may be necessary to further subdivide the tasks named above and increase the number of screens. To keep this example simple, however, two screens are enough.

After you have determined the number and tasks of the screens, you must define the transitions possible from one screen to another. It only makes sense to have such transitions in the PAI section of a screen. This section is not processed, however, until the user has triggered a function in the screen. So you must decide which functions and function codes should be available in a screen and what results they should have. Both the basic requirements in the SAP Style Guide and application-specific requirements play a role here. The SAP Style Guide, for example, requires that the following commands have the same reaction anywhere in the system: *Back* (F3 function key), *Cancel* (F12 function key) and *Exit* (F15 function key). It may not make sense to have all of these commands in every screen, but when one of these commands is used, the application's reaction should be predictable for the user.

The navigation structure of the demo application is shown in Figure 6.2. This graphic requires an explanation. It is unusual to write separate applications for each of the subtasks Create, Change, Display, and Delete. Instead, in a single application, the system branches to different program sections based on the transaction code. For this reason, the basic screen of an application often provides several menu items that allow you to switch from one basic functionality of the application to another. These function codes lead to a new call of the application with a corresponding transaction code. Furthermore, the application's basic screen must contain at least one opportunity for exiting.

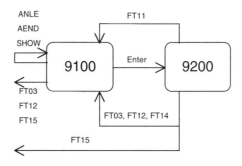

Figure 6.2   Navigation among the screens

The Enter key is used to reach the edit screen from the basic screen after entry of the selection criteria. This characteristic, too, is implemented the same way throughout the system, to ensure that when a transaction is called with CALL TRANSACTION, the AND SUBMIT FIRST SCREEN clause functions correctly.

On the actual edit screen, the Enter key usually leads to checking of the entered data and possibly to the call of another data entry screen. Since this example does not have another screen, pressing the Enter key on the edit screen always leads back to the edit screen. Saving data ends an editing procedure. It is not necessary to remain in the edit screen after saving; it is possible to return to the application's basic screen.

Leaving the edit screen without checking or saving data must also be possible. The functions *Back*, *Cancel*, and *Exit*, which were already mentioned, are available for this. Although in the basic screen each of these three functions leads to the exiting of the application, the Style Guide requires that they function differently in an edit screen. The *Cancel* function should, if possible, return to the previous screen. If data has been entered in the current screen, the user must be notified of the possible loss of data. The user should be given the opportunity to stop the *Cancel* function. The *Back* function should also return to the previous screen, with the user being able to save changed data. Saving should also be possible in the case of the *Exit* function; this function, however, should not only exit the current screen – it should exit the entire application.

If a data record is to be deleted, it does not make sense to check the current data in the screen. Deleting can therefore take place in the Exit module, with a confirmation prompt also being required, of course. After the deletion of a record, one should return to the basic screen.

6.2 Program 1: YZZAKT

A description of a program's structure is a prerequisite for analysis of its source code. Since an application does not consist only of the actual source code, but includes additional elements, these elements are described here.

- The application can be called with any of three dialog transactions: *YZZI* for creating (Insert), *YZZU* for changing (Update), and *YZZS* for displaying (Show). All three execute the 9100 screen of the SAPMYZZA module pool.

- A parameter, YZN, has been defined in the TPARA table for the table field YZZAKT-NAME. This table contains all of the Get/Set parameters. Transaction SM31 is used to maintain it.

- Screen 9100 contains the YZZAKT-NAME field as a mandatory input field. Since such a field does not accept a value that consists only of blank spaces, you ensure that no data records can be created without names. This field has been linked to the YZN parameter, and the Get/Set mechanism has been activated.

- Screen 9200 is shown in Figure 6.3. This figure also shows the field names of the screen fields. In this screen, only the two fields YZZAKT-BRANCHE and YZZAKT-WAEHR are input fields. All of the others are display fields. The 2-*dimens.* attribute has also been set for some of these.

- Both screens store the function code in the FCODE field.

- There are two statuses, STAT_G for the basic screen (9100) and STAT_A for the working screen (9200). Figure 6.2 already shows the function codes needed in this status and their types. All of the function codes whose graphs lead to the left of or down from a screen are Exit function codes. All others are simple function codes. The assignment of the function codes to the icons in the toolbar is preset by their task. Only one pushbutton, for the delete function code FT14, is defined.

- There is a lock module for the YZZAKT table.

The starting point for the analysis of an application is the screens and their flow logic. The following listing shows the flow logic of the 9100 screen.

```
PROCESS BEFORE OUTPUT.
  MODULE D9100_INIT.

PROCESS AFTER INPUT.
  MODULE D9100_EXIT AT EXIT-COMMAND.

  FIELD YZZAKT-NAME
    MODULE D9100_READ_RECORD.

MODULE D9100_USER_COMMAND.
```

All of the initializations are to take place in the D9100_INIT module. Such a module can be found in almost all screens. Additional activities in the PBO section are not necessary.

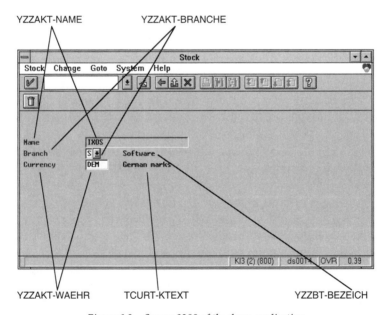

Figure 6.3   Screen 9200 of the demo application

Even the PAI section contains nothing special. Analysis of the Exit function code requires one module; analysis of the rest of the function codes requires a second one. Since the data record to be processed is to be read in the 9100 screen, a corresponding third module is needed.

The D9100_INIT module has a very simple structure. First, depending on the transaction code, a heading is set. This consists of a fixed text "Stock &" which includes a variable parameter. The wording of the variable part, which is programmed as a numbered text element here, is inserted as a comment behind the statement.

```
MODULE D9100_INIT OUTPUT.

*...set the titlebar of the window
  CASE SY-TCODE.

  WHEN 'YZZI'.
    SET TITLEBAR '001' WITH TEXT-001. " Create
  WHEN 'YZZU'.
    SET TITLEBAR '001' WITH TEXT-002. " Change
  WHEN 'YZZS'.
    SET TITLEBAR '001' WITH TEXT-003. " Display

  ENDCASE.

*...set status for basic screen
  SET PF-STATUS 'STAT_G'.

*...delete table header line
  CLEAR YZZAKT.

ENDMODULE.                          " D9100_INIT OUTPUT
```

After the heading is set, the status is set, to ensure the availability of the function code. As insurance, the YZZAKT header line is also initialized. This ensures that an empty data record is always available when new data records are created in the 9200 screen. If initialization were left out, in some cases, during the creation of a new data record in the 9200 screen, the contents of the screen last processed might appear. The YZZAKT-NAME field, however, is always set to the most current value as a result of the Get/Set parameter.

The PAI module D9100_EXIT INPUT is also very simple. The only thing of note is the handling of the screen's function code. The FCODE field, which is used for the function code, is a global data field. If no function code has been assigned to the Enter key (not possible before Release 3.0), pressing this key does not lead to overwriting of the field contents of FCODE. This field would then still contain the previously valid function code. In many applications that have not been redeveloped or completely reworked for Release 3.0, the function code is saved in a second field, and the actual field for the function code is deleted. Although the example was developed using Release 3.0, this programming technique is used here. This enables problem-free execution of the application using older release versions, as well.

```
MODULE D9100_EXIT INPUT.

*...save and delete function code field, see text
  G_FCODE = FCODE.
  CLEAR FCODE.

  CASE G_FCODE.

*...three function codes branch into other transactions
  WHEN 'ANLE'.
    LEAVE TO TRANSACTION 'YZZI'.
  WHEN 'AEND'.
    LEAVE TO TRANSACTION 'YZZU'.
  WHEN 'SHOW'.
    LEAVE TO TRANSACTION 'YZZS'.

  ENDCASE.

*...if no branching, exit program
  LEAVE TO SCREEN 0.

ENDMODULE.                           " D9100_EXIT INPUT
```

The Exit module must concentrate on analyzing the three function codes ANLE, AEND and SHOW, since different handling is required for each. All of the other Exit function codes should exit the application. Therefore, after the CASE statement, only a jump to screen 0 is required. Since the LEAVE TO SCREEN statement is not available in releases prior to Release 3.0, in older systems it should be replaced with the following two statements:

```
SET SCREEN 0.
LEAVE SCREEN.
```

Even easier than the Exit module is the module for analyzing the normal function code. The 9100 screen has only the Enter key. Its use should enable processing of the selected data record. Since this occurs in the 9200 screen, the only thing that needs to be programmed in the corresponding module is the jump to the 9200 screen.

```
MODULE D9100_USER_COMMAND INPUT.

  G_CODE = FCODE.
  CLEAR FCODE.

*...if Enter key pressed, process data record
  IF G_FCODE = ' '.
    LEAVE TO SCREEN 9200.
  ENDIF.

ENDMODULE.                           " D9100_USER_COMMAND INPUT
```

The true functionality of the screen is contained in the D9100_READ_RECORD module, where the record to be processed is made available. It is necessary to distinguish whether a new record is to be created or an existing one is to be edited. This distinction is necessary because the functionality of the create and change transactions may not be mixed up. The first thing the module tries is to read the data record based on the keyword entered in the screen. Then the SELECT statement's return code undergoes analysis based on the transaction code. If the data record has been successfully read, it is protected against unauthorized access through the call of the lock module.

Messages are triggered in the module if the result of the SELECT statement does not fit the current transaction code. As a result of this, the screen is processed again, that is, the D9100_USER_COMMAND module is not executed.

```
MODULE D9100_READ_RECORD INPUT.

* ....try to read the desired record
  SELECT SINGLE * FROM YZZAKT
    WHERE NAME = YZZAKT-NAME.

*... SY-SUBRC provides information if record found
  IF SY-SUBRC = 0.

*.... for Create transaction, no record may exist yet
    IF SY-TCODE = 'YZZI'.

*...... Text: Stock & already exists!
      MESSAGE E001 WITH YZZAKT-NAME.
    ENDIF.

*...lock record
    CALL FUNCTION 'ENQUEUE_EYAKT'
      EXPORTING
*       MANDT           = SY-MANDT
        NAME            = YZZAKT-NAME
*       X_NAME          = ' '
*       _SCOPE          = '2'
*       _WAIT           = ' '
      EXCEPTIONS
        FOREIGN_LOCK    = 1
        SYSTEM-FAILURE  = 2
        OTHERS          = 3.

    IF SY-SUBRC <> 0.

*........Text: Record cannot be locked!
      MESSAGE E005.
    ENDIF.

*...Record does not exist
  ELSE.

*......For Change and Display the record must exist
    IF SY-TCODE = 'YZZU' OR SY-TCODE = 'YZZS'.
```

```
*........Text: Stock & does not yet exist!
      MESSAGE E002 WITH YZZAKT-NAME.
    ENDIF.
  ENDIF.
ENDMODULE.                     " D9100_READ_RECORD INPUT
```

The 9200 screen takes over all maintenance tasks for the data record selected in the 9100 screen. This includes checking the input values and saving the data. Due to the more extensive tasks of the Exit function codes and the differentiated handling required for them, the source code for this module is somewhat larger. This can already be seen in the flow logic.

```
PROCESS BEFORE OUTPUT.
  MODULE D9200_INIT.
  MODULE D9200_READ_INFO.
*
PROCESS AFTER INPUT.
  MODULE D9200_EXIT AT EXIT-COMMAND.

*...recognize data changes
  CHAIN.
    FIELD: YZZAKT-BRANCHE
           YZZAKT-WAEHR.
    MODULE D9200_DATA_CHANGED ON CHAIN-REQUEST.
  ENDCHAIN.

*...check branch
  FIELD YZZAKT-BRANCHE MODULE D9200_BRANCHE_CHECK.

  MODULE D9200_USER_COMMAND.
```

An INIT module is required again, to set the status and modify it, if necessary. In the YZZAKT table, the WAEHR and BRANCHE fields are just abbreviations. It is often useful for the user to see long text for these identifiers. The fields needed for this are already provided in the screen. They must, of course, be filled with values before the screen is displayed. This task has been moved to a second PBO module.

The first thing required in the PAI section is the analysis of the Exit function code. In the subsequent CHAIN chain, all of the input fields of the screen are checked for possible input. If data changes have taken place, a corresponding flag must be set that influences the confirmation prompts during an exit. Since more than one field should be linked to a module, the CHAIN statement is needed for linking. It would also be possible to program two separate module calls, as shown here:

```
FIELD YZZAKT-BRANCHE
  MODULE D9200_DATA_CHANGED ON CHAIN-REQUEST.

FIELD YZZAKT-WAEHR
  MODULE D9200_DATA_CHANGED ON CHAIN-REQUEST.
```

A valid data range is defined in the domain on which the YZZAKT-BRANCHE data field is based. The automatic field checks test the contents of the screen field against this value range only. If there should be an additional restriction of the valid values for the entries maintained in the YZZB table, another check module (D9200_BRANCHE_CHECK) is needed. In the end, the normal function codes, of which there are still several in this screen, must be processed.

Because of the different reactions of the application to the function keys F3, F12 and F15, the two modules for function code processing must interact. For this reason, the other four modules will be described first.

In the Init module, two new activities are required in addition to the tasks described for the 9100 screen. First, the screen should be modified dynamically. In the display transaction, for example, all of the fields must be converted into pure output fields. In the other transactions, only the YZZAKT-NAME field must be locked against input. In the 9200 screen, it is displayed for information only. Of course, changes to the key must not be allowed after selection and locking of a data record.

```
MODULE D9200_INIT OUTPUT.

*...set screen fields to inactive
*...for Display, all, otherwise only the name
  LOOP AT SCREEN.
    IF SCREEN-NAME = 'YZZAKT-NAME'
      OR SY-TCODE = 'YZZS'.
        SCREEN-INPUT = OFF.
        MODIFY SCREEN.
    ENDIF.
  ENDLOOP.

*...for Display transaction, set Save function to inactive
  CLEAR I_FCODE.
  REFRESH I_FCODE.
  IF SY-TCODE = 'YZZS'.
    I_FCODE-FCODE = 'FT11'.
    APPEND I_FCODE.
  ENDIF.

*...for all transactions except Change
*...deactivate delete code
  IF SY-TCODE <> 'YZZU'.
    I_FCODE-FCODE = 'FT14'.
    APPEND I_FCODE.
  ENDIF.

*...set status for Change screen
  SET PF-STATUS 'STAT_A' EXCLUDING I_FCODE.

*...initialize global flags
  G_EXIT          = FALSE.
```

```
  G_DELETE        = FALSE.
  G_EXIT_MODULE = FALSE.

ENDMODULE.                              " D9200_INIT OUTPUT
```

The second new task consists of deactivating function codes that are not needed. To this end, an internal table is filled with the function codes. This table is passed to the system when the status is set by the EXCLUDING clause. The 9200 screen contains several flags that regulate the behavior of the application. Some of these flags are reset after every run of the PBO section. The need for this procedure will become clear later, when the two function code modules are examined.

The module for reading the two identifiers for branch and currency is so simple that it requires no further explanation.

```
MODULE D9200_READ_INFO OUTPUT.

*...prepare branch identifier
  SELECT SINGLE = FROM YZZBT
  WHERE BRANCHE = YZZAKT-BRANCHE AND
    SPRACHE = SY-LANGU.

*...delete old contents if search unsuccessful
  IF SY-SUBRC <> 0.
    CLEAR YZZBT.
  ENDIF.

*    provide currency identifier
  SELECT SINGLE * FROM TCURT
  WHERE WAERS = YZZAKT-WAEHR AND
    SPRAS = SY-LANGU.

*...delete old contents if search unsuccessful
  IF SY-SUERC <> 0.
    CLEAR TCURT.
  ENDIF.

ENDMODULE.                              " D9200_READ_INFO OUTPUT
```

The case is similar for the two PAI modules.

```
MODULE D9200_DATA_CHANGED INPUT.

*...SY-DATAR is always re-initialized,
*...so it must be saved
  IF SY-DATAR = TRUE.
    G_CHANGED = TRUE.
  ENDIF.

ENDMODULE.                              " D9200_DATA_CHANGED INPUT
```

The DATA_CHANGED module just sets a global flag. This flag must, of course, also be retained if the screen is reprocessed after a change in data is recognized, for example because there was a mistake or because the Enter key was pressed. This flag may therefore not be initialized in the PBO section!

The D9200_BRANCHE_CHECK module is so simple that additional description is not necessary.

```
MODULE D9200_BRANCHE_CHECK INPUT.

  SELECT SINGLE * FROM YZZB
  WHERE BRANCHE = YZZAKT-BRANCHE.

  IF SY-SUBRC <> 0.

*...Text: Branche & not maintained!
    MESSAGE E006 WITH YZZAKT-BRANCHE.
ENDIF.

ENDMODULE.                              " D9200_BRANCHE_CHECK INPUT
```

The screen's two function code modules, on the other hand, are quite complex. The source code of the Exit module comes first. This module makes intensive use of several subroutines, since some functions are needed in both the Exit module and the User-Command module. Moving these functions to subroutines is therefore an attractive option.

```
MODULE 9200_EXIT INPUT.

  G_FCODE = FCODE.
  CLEAR FCODE.
  G_EXIT_MODULE = TRUE.

*...handle Delete separately, since independent of data changes
  IF G_FCODE = 'FT14'.
    PERFORM D9200_DELETE_QUESTION.
  ELSE.

*......if data changed, confirmation prompt
  IF G_CHANGED = TRUE OR
    SY-DATAR = TRUE.

*........set G_CHANGED, so that content enables correct
*........analysis in first run, too
    G_CHANGED = TRUE.

*......if necessary, execute confirmation prompt and set Exit flag
    PERFORM D9200_CHECK_SAVE.

*......if Exit without save desired,
*......jump back directly to EXIT module
```

```
    IF G_EXIT = TRUE AND
       G_SAVE = FALSE.
       G_CHANGED = FALSE.

*......unlock record, then jump back
         PERFORM D9200_DEQUEUE.
         PERFORM D9200_NAVIGATE.
       ENDIF.

    ELSE.

*.......if no data changed,
*.......set G_EXIT due to analysis in D9200_NAVIGATE
       G_EXIT = TRUE.

*......unlock record, then jump back
       PERFORM D9200_DEQUEUE.
       PERFORM D9200_NAVIGATE.
     ENDIF.
   ENDIF.

ENDMODULE.                                    " D9200_EXIT INPUT
```

The function code is saved again in a second field, and the field linked to the screen is initialized. A flag is used to indicate that the Exit module has been called. Not all Exit function codes necessarily lead to exiting the application. If the processing of the screen continues, it must be made easy to recognize in the User-Command module that the Exit module has been executed.

After the flag is set, the system checks whether the data record should be deleted. If this is the case, the user must confirm this desire in a popup. For all other Exit codes, checking for data changes follows. If an Exit function code was already triggered in the first run-through of screen processing, the G_CHANGED flag cannot be set yet. Therefore, it is necessary to test both SY-DATAR and G_CHANGED in the Exit module. In order for all additional checks to be able to access G_CHANGED the same way, this flag may be set.

Depending on the Exit code, the user should be given the opportunity to cancel the procedure or at least to save the input data before the screen ends, if data was changed. This behavior is controlled by the two flags G_EXIT and G_SAVE. The execution of the confirmation prompt and the analysis of the results is taken over by the D9200_CHECK-SAVE subroutine. It is called without parameters and sets the two flags mentioned. If the screen should be exited without saving, the data record to be processed is unlocked directly in the Exit module and the screen is exited. These two functions, too, are executed by subroutines. The two functions are executed without additional queries if an Exit code (other than FT14) is triggered but no data was changed in the screen.

The two function codes F3 and F15 should allow changed data to be saved. The current contents of the screen fields are not yet available in the Exit module, however. Field checks also have not yet been performed. For this reason, if data must be saved, the function codes linked to these two function keys may not exit the screen directly in the Exit module. Instead, only the various flags may be set and the program continued. For this reason, after the Exit module is executed, the two check modules and the User-Command module are executed, if necessary. The User-Command module is somewhat smaller, since the actual functionality has been moved to the subroutines. The function code is saved in a second field again. This is only necessary if the Exit module was not run through. In this case, it is not necessary to call the D9200_CHECK_SAVE subroutine.

```
MODULE D9200_USER_COMMAND INPUT.

*...if FCODE already reset in the EXIT module
   IF G_EXIT_MODULE = FALSE.
     G_FCODE = FCODE.
     CLEAR FCODE.

*...Determine if data must be saved and screen may be
*...exited. Query only necessary if EXIT module was not effective.
     PERFORM D9200_CHECK_SAVE.

   ENDIF.

*...save data
   PERFORM D9200_SAVE.

*...jump back, target depends on function code
   PERFORM D9200_NAVIGATE.

ENDMODULE. " D9200_USER_COMMAND INPUT
```

The two subroutines D9200_SAVE and D9200_NAVIGATE are run through in any case, even if the Enter key is pressed. However, since the two flags G_EXIT and G_SAVE, which are set according to the function code in D9200_CHECK_SAVE, are analyzed in these routines, running through these routines is not the same as exiting the application. The following listing shows the last routine mentioned.

```
FORM D9200_CHECK_SAVE.
   CASE G_FCODE.

*......ENTER key
*......→ only data check
     WHEN ' '.
       G_SAVE = FALSE.
       G_EXIT = FALSE.

*......F3 = BACK
*......→ opportunity to save in case of data change
     WHEN 'FT03'.
       PERFORM D9200_SAVE_QUESTION.
```

```
*......F11 = SAVE
*......→ absolutely save and exit the screen
    WHEN 'FT11'.
      G_SAVE = TRUE.
      G_EXIT = TRUE.

*......F12 = CANCEL
*......→ only note possible loss of data
    WHEN 'FT12'.
      PERFORM D9200_CANCEL_QUESTION.

*......F15 = EXIT
*......→ opportunity to save in case of data change
    WHEN 'FT15'.
      PERFORM D9200_SAVE_QUESTION.

  ENDCASE.

ENDFORM.                                   " D9200_CHECK_SAVE
```

Depending on the function code, either the global flags are set or the confirmation prompt is executed. These have been moved into separate subroutines to increase clarity. The actual query is executed by a call of a function module delivered by SAP. Depending on the query results, the global fields are set.

```
FORM D0200_SAVE_QUESTION.
DATA: L_ANSWER.

*...query only necessary if data was changed
  IF G_CHANGED = TRUE.

    CALL FUNCTION 'POPUP_TO_CONFIRM_STEP'
      EXPORTING
*         DEFAULTOPTION = 'Y'

*.........Text: Data will be lost!
          TEXTLINE1 = TEXT-012

*.........Text: Save first?
          TEXTLINE2       = TEXT-013
          TITEL           = TEXT-010
*         START_COLUMN    = 25
*         START_ROW       = 6
      IMPORTING
          ANSWER          =     L_ANSWER
      EXCEPTIONS
          OTHERS          = 1.

    CASE L_ANSWER.
```

```
*........save and exit
        WHEN JA.
          G_SAVE = TRUE.
          G_EXIT = TRUE.

*........exit without saving
        WHEN NEIN.
          G_SAVE = FALSE.
          G_EXIT = TRUE.

*........cancel the function → screen is not ended
        WHEN ABBRUCH.
          G_SAVE = FALSE.
          G_EXIT = FALSE.

    ENDCASE.

*...if data not changed, then exit
*...always possible
  ELSE.
    G_SAVE = FALSE.
    G_EXIT = TRUE.
  ENDIF.

ENDFORM.                                 " D9200_SAVE_QUESTION
```

The POPUP_TO_CONFIRM_STEP module gives the user three possible options: *Yes, No* and
Cancel. Viewed in light of the reason for the query, these answers mean *Exit with Save, Exit
without save* and *Do not exit screen*. In contrast, the POPUP_TO_CONFIRM_LOSS_OF_DATA
module only provides the selections *Yes* and *No*, which in the application mean *Exit without
Save* and *Do not exit screen*.

```
FORM D9200_CANCEL_QUESTION.
DATA: L_ANSWER.

  CALL FUNCTION 'POPUP_TO_CONFIRM_LOSS_OF_DATA'
    EXPORTING
      TEXTLINE1       = TEXT-011 " Cancel anyway?
*      TEXTLINE2       = ' '.
      TITEL           = TEXT-010 " Caution
*      START_COLUMN    = 25
*      START_ROW       = 6
    IMPORTING
      ANSWER          = L_ANSWER
    EXCEPTIONS
      OTHERS          = 1.

*...if Cancel anyway, then set EXIT flag
  IF L_ANSWER = JA.
```

```
    G_EXIT = TRUE.
    G_SAVE = FALSE.

*...otherwise turn off EXIT flag
  ELSE.
    G_EXIT = FALSE.
  ENDIF.

ENDFORM.                              " D9200_CANCEL_QUESTION
```

The confirmation prompt that appears when a data record is deleted is similar to the
one just presented, except for the text. However, in this case, the G_DELETE flag is set, signaling to the D9200_SAVE routine that the data record from YZZAKT and all of the share
price data from YZZKURS should not be saved but rather deleted.

```
FORM D9200_DELETE_QUESTION.
DATA: L_ANSWER.

  CALL FUNCTION 'POPUP_TO_CONFIRM_STEP'
    EXPORTING
      DEFAULTOPTION = 'N'

*........Text: data record with all subsequent records
      TEXTLINE1     = TEXT-021

*........Text: Are you sure about deleting?
      TEXTLINE2     = TEXT-022

*........Text: DELETE
      TITEL         = TEXT-023
*     START_COLUMN  = 25
*     START_ROW     = 6
    IMPORTING
      ANSWER        = L_ANSWER
    EXCEPTIONS
      OTHERS        = 1.

  IF L_ANSWER = JA.
    G_DELETE  = TRUE.
    G_EXIT    = TRUE.

  ELSE.

*...not absolutely necessary, just for safety's sake
    G_DELETE  = FALSE.
    G_EXIT    = FALSE.
  ENDIF.

ENDFORM.                              " D9200_DELETE_QUESTION
```

Because of these two basically different tasks, D9200_SAVE is now somewhat larger again.

```
FORM D9200_SAVE.

  IF G_SAVE = TRUE.

    MODIFY YZZAKT.

*......test status of database operation
    IF SY-SUBRC <> 0.

*......Text: Error during Save of the data record!
      MESSAGE E003.
    ELSE.

*......Text: Data saved for &.
      MESSAGE S004 WITH YZZAKT-NAME.
    ENDIF.

*......unlock data record
    PERFORM D9200_DEQUEUE.

*......write changes
    COMMIT WORK.

*......reset data change flag
    G_CHANGED = FALSE.

  ENDIF.

  IF G_DELETE = TRUE.
    DELETE FROM YZZKURS
      WHERE NAME = YZZAKT-NAME.

    DELETE FROM YZZAKT
      WHERE NAME = YZZAKT-NAME.

    COMMIT WORK.
    G_EXIT = TRUE.
  ENDIF.

ENDFORM.                           " D9200_SAVE
```

In contrast, the function of D9200_NAVIGATE is clear, making any description unnecessary.

```
FORM D9200_NAVIGATE.
  IF G_EXIT = TRUE.
    CASE G_FCODE.

*......F3 = BACK
*......→ return to previous screen
      WHEN 'FT03'.
```

```
        LEAVE TO SCREEN 9100.
*......F11 = SAVE
*......→ return to previous screen
      WHEN 'FT11'.
        LEAVE TO SCREEN 9100.

*......F12 = CANCEL
*......→ return to previous screen
      WHEN 'FT12'.
        LEAVE TO SCREEN 9100.

*......F14 = DELETE
*......→ return to previous screen
      WHEN 'FT14'.
        LEAVE TO SCREEN 9100.

*......F15 = EXIT
*......→ exit the entire application
      WHEN 'FT15'.
        LEAVE PROGRAM.

    ENDCASE.

  ENDIF.

ENDFORM.                                " D9200_NAVIGATE
```

For the sake of completeness, the global database declarations and the subroutine for releasing the database lock are also listed here.

```
PROGRAM SAPMYZZA MESSAGE-ID YZ.

TABLES:
  YZZAKT,
  YZZKURS,
  YZZB,
  YZZBT,
  TCURT
.  " TABLES

CONSTANTS:
  TRUE        VALUE 'X',
  FALSE       VALUE ' ',
  JA          VALUE 'J',
  NEIN        VALUE 'N',
  ABBRUCH     VALUE 'A',
  ON TYPE I   VALUE 1,
  OFF TYPE I  VALUE 0
.  " CONSTANTS
```

```
DATA:
  FCODE          LIKE SY-UCOMM,
  G_FCODE        LIKE FCODE,
  G_CHANGED      LIKE FALSE VALUE FALSE,
  G_SAVE         LIKE FALSE VALUE FALSE,
  G_EXIT         LIKE FALSE VALUE FALSE,
  G_DELETE       LIKE FALSE VALUE FALSE,
  G_EXIT_MODULE  LIKE FALSE VALUE FALSE,
  BEGIN OF I_FCODE OCCURS 5,
    FCODE LIKE SY-UCOMM,
  END OF I_FCODE
  .            " DATA

FORM D9200_DEQUEUE.

  CALL FUNCTION 'DEQUEUE_EYAKT'
       EXPORTING
*         MANDT      = SY-MANDT
          NAME       = YZZAKT-NAME
*         X_NAME     = ' '
*         _SCOPE     = '3'
*         _SYNCHRON  = ' '
       EXCEPTIONS
          OTHERS     = 1.

ENDFORM.                              " D9200_DEQUEUE
```

6.3 Program 2: YZZKURS

After the detailed description presented for the first application, it should be no problem for you to create the second application yourself. Its structure is very similar to that of the application just described. This results in very similar source code, too.

In the first screen, a date is entered. In the second screen, for every stock maintained in the YZZAKT table, the share price for this day is recorded, or, if one already exists, it is edited. Data record deletion and pure display are not provided for. That is why there is only a single dialog transaction, YZZK.

For the processing of share price data, an internal table is created whose structure corresponds to that of the YZZKURS table. For every stock from YZZAKT, a data record is appended to this table and given an existing share price, if one exists. In the edit screen, this table is processed with a step loop. Figure 6.4 shows the layout of this screen.

You can begin by copying the existing module pool SAPMYZZA, along with all of its elements. You could call the target SAPMYZZK, for example. When copying, make sure that all of the elements (statuses, Includes) are actually copied. A popup appears during

*YZZKURS-DATUM   *YZZKURS-NAME   G_DATUM   *YZZKURS-KURS

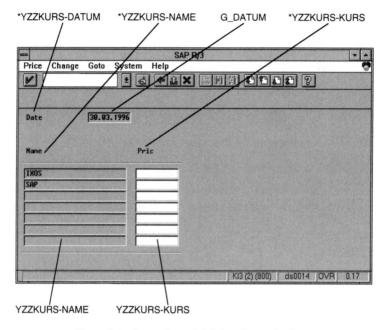

YZZKURS-NAME   YZZKURS-KURS

Figure 6.4   Screen for maintaining share price data

the copy process in which you must select all of the elements to be copied. You can then remove all of the source code elements from the copy and program them from scratch after editing the screens. You should try to program this second application yourself. You can use the source code of the first application and some of the examples from the preceding chapters. For help in case of problems, you will find the complete source code in Chapter 9.

7 Tips and potential pitfalls

7.1 Tips

7.1.1 Creating screen fields

Screen fields should always be created with a Dictionary reference. This ensures simple translation. The *Attributes* popup contains several specifications for the current Dictionary reference. The key field and the input screen belonging to it can easily belong to different tables, or it may be that only the key field has a Dictionary reference, to make a translatable text available, while the input screen refers to any program-internal field. It is also possible for screens to create Dictionary structures that contain all of the fields needed in the screen.

7.1.2 Side effects of function codes

The function code in a screen is often stored in a global field in the module pool, which is used for this purpose by several screens. Problems can occur if the PAI section of the screen calls another screen with CALL, for example as a popup. After returning from the object called with CALL, the contents of the function code's global field are most likely different than before. This can lead to problems if this field must be analyzed again in the PAI section after the call with CALL. You can avoid such problems by moving all analyses of a screen's function code into a subroutine and copying the function code at the beginning of the subroutine into a local field in this screen. Then, only the local field is used for analysis.

7.1.3 Field checks

Field checks are only necessary when data needs to be saved or analyzed in subsequent screens. It is therefore advisable to test the OK code in the modules responsible for field checks and perform the checks only if these OK codes are actually performing saves. This avoids unnecessary field checks, for example, when a supplemental popup is called that returns to the main screen anyway.

If a module pool is used for several transactions, the transaction code should be tested in addition to the function code, so that field checks can also be suppressed in the case of transactions that are purely display transactions.

7.1.4   Field specification for SELECT-OPTIONS

The correct syntax for the SELECT-OPTIONS command is

SELECT-OPTIONS *selection* **FOR** *field.*

This means that a selection is created for the specified field. The name of the field is important for the following reasons:

1   The specified field determines the format of the field on the selection screen, especially the field length.

2   If the selection is used in a CHECK command in the following form:

CHECK *selection.*

the command automatically checks the selection that was filled when the report started against the field from the SELECT-OPTIONS command. This can be, for example, a table field from a table that is read in a loop.

If, on the other hand, the selection is used with the IN operator in a SELECT statement or in an IF statement, the field name is of no interest if the comparison field is explicitly specified. However, if the shortened form is used, such as

IF *selection.*

the field specified in the SELECT-OPTIONS statement is used again.

7.1.5   Structures

Structures do not store any data in a database table, but they are automatically a header line, which they can use to store data. They can link a structure to screen fields, too, without having to derive a field string from the structure.

7.1.6   Unlocking

Sometimes (network problems, client failure), some elements can no longer be edited. For the SAP system, they are apparently still being edited, since their editing did not end in an orderly fashion. Since they are locked for editing, accessing them again to change them is not possible. The message "User xyz is already editing abc" appears.

To be able to continue working, you must release the lock. You do this with the menu function *Tools → Administration → Monitoring → Lock entries*. In the subsequent screen, you can enter restricting search terms. Afterwards, a list appears showing the current lock entries, which you can mark, then delete using the *Delete* pushbutton.

7.1.7   Formal parameters and offset specifications

You can access individual characters or character groups of a field using offset and length specifications. To edit the formal parameters of a form routine using offsets, however, either you must copy the contents to a local variable for editing and transfer them back into the formal parameter afterwards, or you must use a field symbol that points to the parameter. You can access the field symbol using offset and length specifications.

7.1.8   Scope of validity for fields

Modules do not represent a separate scope of validity for fields. This means that no fields may be defined in modules that already exist in the main program. Fields specified in modules are also valid outside the module.

If a field is defined using DATA in a FORM routine, it is only available until the END-FORM of the routine in question has been reached. If another routine is called from that routine, the field is not usable there.

If a field is defined using LOCAL in a FORM routine, the current contents of the field, which must already exist, are saved internally and not retrieved until the routine is exited. So you always work directly with the globally defined field. This sometimes has different contents, regardless of the program block in which the LOCAL appears, and these contents are valid even when another routine is called!

7.1.9   Function keys

On subscreens such as popups for list selection, pushbuttons are displayed along the lower edge. These pushbuttons are defined in the user interface for this subscreen the way pushbuttons are usually defined in normal screens.

The size of the popups is often determined dynamically, that is, depending on the width of the data line to be displayed. It is possible that the width of the popup is insufficient to accommodate all of the pushbuttons. In this case, although they are activated, they are not visible. It is therefore helpful to display the function key layout with the right mouse button, in case important functions that should be available in the popup are not accessible. The mouse pointer must be located inside the popup for this. When you design the interface, you should define the most important pushbuttons first, so that they appear as far to the left as possible.

7.1.10   Pushbuttons

The function codes of pushbuttons and those of the Menu Painter are managed separately, even when the same function code is involved. This means that a pushbutton as well as a function key can trigger the same function code, but with a different function type. These function codes are sometimes handled differently in the flow logic, although the function code in question is apparently the same! This error can also occur in the case of two push-buttons in a screen, that is, several keys with the same function code and different function types. Function types are only visible in interface or screen maintenance; when a program is debugged they remain undetected.

7.1.11   Syntax check

The syntax of a function group's function pool is checked completely. *All* of the functions of a function group can be locked by syntax errors in other program sections or Includes, even if a function is called whose code is not being worked on. The only remedy is for new program code to be free of syntax errors when it is saved, which is not to say that it must also operate error-free.

7.1.12   Return to initial screen of a transaction

Many programs have a basic screen in which key values are entered, after which the program branches to actual processing. This basic screen is always displayed after the actual edit screen is exited. You accomplish this in the PAI section of the edit screen using one of two methods. In one method, you specify the subsequent screen explicitly, for example using:

```
SET SCREEN 100.
LEAVE SCREEN.
```

In this case, the transaction is not exited, meaning global data and so on remain intact.
    The second method consists of starting the transaction again:

```
LEAVE TO TRANSACTION SY-TCODE.
```

In this case, everything is initialized again, database locks are released and so on. This often circumvents problems with update modules and the like.

7.1.13   Screen modification

You can modify the appearance of a screen by looping in the automatically generated SCREEN table (input, hide, ...). Using the ACTIVE attribute for a field, you can eliminate the field entirely from the screen. All of the fields located under this field move up, and boxes are automatically resized.

7.1.14   Pushbuttons in selection screens

In selection screens, you can create any number of pushbuttons in the screen area and one or two pushbuttons in the toolbar. Even if they are declared, pushbuttons appear on the screen only if at least one selection or one parameter exists.
    The function codes delivered by the pushbuttons must be analyzed, for example at the AT-SELECTION-SCREEN event. The problem, of course, is that only selected function codes branch to list creation (START-OF-SELECTION). All other function codes just cause a return to the selection screen. So, if a pushbutton should start the report, usually after a certain flag is set, the function code is analyzed with SSCRFIELDS-UCOMM in AT-SELECTION-SCREEN, then the function code that triggers the jump to list processing, usually "ONLI", is placed into SSCRFIELDS-UCOMM.

```
CASE SSCRFIELDS-UCOMM.

  WHEN 'TEST'.
    G_CHANGE = ' '.
    SSCRFIELDS-UCOMM = 'ONLI'.

  WHEN 'COPY'.
    G_CHANGE = 'X'.
    SSCRFIELDS-UCOMM = 'ONLI'.

ENDCASE.
```

7.1.15   Input readiness on basic screens

Many screens are structured in such a way that the key values are entered in an initial
screen, and data for these is then edited in a subsequent screen. If the key values entered
do not match any records, all of the input fields for the key must become active again. This
means that the read and check routines and a FIELD statement for all of the key fields
must appear in a CHAIN chain. If reading takes place directly in the OK-CODE module,
this module must be executed in the CHAIN chain.

```
PROCESS AFTER INPUT.
CHAIN.
  FIELD: TAB-A, TAB-B, TAB-C.
  MODULE OKCODE.
ENDCHAIN.
```

7.2   Tricks

7.2.1   Function parameters (Release Versions prior to 3.0)

Up to and including Release 2.2, function modules had only import and export parameters. Input parameters are read in the module, but no data is returned upon exiting. Export
parameters, on the other hand, are used for data return, but not to pass data to the function module. So if a function module should read the contents of a parameter, change
them, then pass them back, both an import parameter and an export parameter must be
created, to which the same field is assigned when the module is called, as shown in the
following example:

```
CALL FUNCTION 'UPPER_CASE'
  IMPORTING
    IP_WORD = L_WORD
  EXPORTING
    OP_WORD = L_WORD.
```

Beginning with Release 3.0, a CHANGING parameter may be used for this purpose.

7.2.2   Screens

To create additional values for a screen for which there is no room on the screen, you use subsequent screens. To insure the clarity of such a sequence of screens, the subsequent screens are often displayed as (multiply nested) subscreens. To spare the user having to run through all of the screens one by one when the final screen is exited, you can pass the exiting function code through all of the subscreens from back to front. For example:

```
SCREEN 400:
...
CALL SCREEN 500 STARTING AT 10 10.
* Subscreen 500 is called and processed.
* Exiting occurs, for example, with the DATU (copy data)
* and EABB (cancel) function codes
* The function code is stored in the global field FCODE,
* which is not deleted in Screen 500

IF FCODE = 'DATU'.
  CLEAR FCODE. "only in first subscreen
  SET SCREEN 0.
  LEAVE SCREEN.
ENDIF.
...

SCREEN 500:
...
IF FCODE = 'DATU'.
  SET SCREEN 0.
  LEAVE SCREEN.
ENDIF.
...
```

The results of these statements are as follows. The calling screen, 400, from whose flow logic the lines above originate, is the first subscreen called from a basic screen. Screen 500 is called and processed, also as a subscreen. The function keys "Copy data" (function code DATU) and "Cancel" (EABB) should be available in this screen. The "Copy data" key should trigger a return to the basic screen, exiting all subscreens in one pass. For this reason, FCODE is not deleted in the 500 screen, but is instead passed to the 400 screen. There, FCODE is analyzed immediately after the CALL SCREEN statement, and that screen is also exited. To prevent any undesirable side effects from occurring in the calling basic screen, FCODE is initialized beforehand.

   If a cancel should be performed across several levels, the statements are copied by analogy from the 400 screen to all other screens. The initialization of FCODE may then, of course, only occur in the screen that was called from the basic screen.

7.2.3   Simple output of character fields

Many test reports list table contents, usually key fields of type C or N. This means that all of the fields to be output must be recorded in the output statement. This procedure can be simplified assuming the fields to be output are really only C and N fields. First you create a field string that contains all of the fields of the table to be output. You then insert an empty field between each of these fields, for example:

```
DATA: BEGIN OF F_TEST,
  NAME LIKE TAB-NAME,
  SPACE1
  FIRST_NAME LIKE TAB-FIRST_NAME,
  SPACE2
  BIRTHDAY LIKE TAB-BIRTHDAY,
END OF F_TEST.
```

In the program, you then assign the contents to the field string in the SELECT loop using MOVE-CORRESPONDING, and you output the field string using

```
WRITE / F_TEST.
```

Since the field string as a whole is handled by the system as a C field, the display is then correct. Conversions based specifically on data types, for example conversion functions controlled by the data element, do not work in this case.

7.3   Potential pitfalls

7.3.1   String comparisons using CA (Contains any) and NA (Not any)

Strings have a predefined length. If the comparison pattern of a character string comparison is not specified as a string constant but as a field, the pattern must have exactly the same length as the field, meaning it must fill it completely. Otherwise, the following problem arises: the positions not occupied are filled with blank spaces, as are any unoccupied positions of the string to be checked. The comparison then returns TRUE, since blank spaces are contained in both strings. Of course, this behavior is undesirable, and the error is also difficult to uncover.

7.3.2   Passing data from screens

When a screen is exited, the data just entered is not valid until after an AT EXIT-COMMAND statement. Until that time, the old values still appear in the screen fields. This means that saving data is not possible in EXIT-COMMAND modules!

Therefore, AT EXIT-COMMAND modules are only suitable for exiting processing WITHOUT saving data. You can, however, determine in the AT EXIT-COMMAND module whether data has been changed by using the system variable SY-DATAR, which contains an "X" in this case. A confirmation prompt can then at least indicate the impending loss of data. This field, however, is reinitialized every time PBO is run through and is filled only if data has been changed in the current run-through.

Even in the help request modules, the screen fields are not easily accessible. In some cases, reading can take place directly from the screen using Basis function modules (see Chapter 3, Function Modules).

7.3.3   Initializing screen fields

Screen fields can be initialized in PBO modules. In the case of transactions that create new data records, it is desirable to empty the fields every time the screen is called, so that the new values can be recorded. Otherwise, if the second screen (the actual edit screen) were canceled after data input, the screen fields might still contain values from previous transactions. In this particular case, however, the initializations may not take place in the PBO modules of the second screen; they must instead take place during branching from the first screen. Otherwise, the fields would be initialized again every time an error message was generated in the second screen, because E messages cause complete reprocessing of the screen.

A second method would be to use a flag, which would be set during the first call after initialization of the screen fields and would be turned off after every LEAVE. Initialization could then take place in the PBO modules. But this only shifts the problem, since the flag would have to be correctly monitored and edited at all jumping points in and out.

7.3.4   SELECT INTO

Generally, records found with the SELECT command are made available in the work area (header line) of the table searched and can be analyzed there. After a SELECT–ENDSELECT loop, what appears in the table's header line is the last record found, not the last record of the table. This is useful for checking if records exist when you know only part of the key. No processing takes place in the SELECT–ENDSELECT loop; the header record is not processed until the loop is exited.

Behavior is different than that described here if the INTO TABLE Itab clause or INTO work area clause is used. In this case, the header line of the table that was searched is definitely empty! The results appear either in the field string or in the table that was specified behind INTO. The header line of the internal record is empty at first, too. Only the work area can be used immediately; after ENDSELECT, it contains the last record read.

If you are working with an internal table, either you must fill the internal table's header line as a precautionary measure using

```
READ Itab INDEX 1.
```

or you must process the table in a loop.

7.3.5   READ in internal tables

You can use READ in an internal table to read a record with any key. You must, however, fill non-search fields with a blank space. You do this with the command

MOVE SPACE TO *field_string*.

Initialization using

CLEAR *field_string*.

does not always have the desired result, since in this case several fields (depending on their type) are filled not with blank spaces but with other characters, which are automatically used for searching. Usually, no records are found this way!

7.3.6   Incorrect structure for form routines

In form routines, you can assign a structure, using the keyword STRUCTURE (or some other constructs), to a field string that is passed as a parameter. This makes it possible to access individual fields of the field string by name. This structure assignment has no type checking function. The only thing checked when form routines are called is the length of the parameter. The actual parameter may not be shorter than the field string specified as the structure. So it is possible to specify a completely incorrect structure. This is then simply laid over the real data. If the structure and the field string do not match, this can lead to incorrect interpretation of the data, as shown in the following example.

```
REPORT BMPRIV20.
DATA: BEGIN OF S1,
  A(5) TYPE C,
  B(10) TYPE C,
END OF S1.

DATA: BEGIN OF S2,
  A(10) TYPE C,
  B(3) TYPE C,
END OF S2.

S1-A = 'aaaaa'.
S1-B = '1234567890'.

PERFORM F1 USING S1.
WRITE /.
WRITE /.
PERFORM F2 USING S1.

FORM F1 USING P STRUCTURE S1.
  WRITE / P-A.
  WRITE / P-B.
ENDFORM.
```

```
FORM F2 USING P STRUCTURE S2.
  WRITE / P-A.
  WRITE / P-B.
ENDFORM.
```

This report creates the following output:

aaaaa
1234567890

aaaaa12345
678

7.3.7 Global data

Global data is only global in the program where it has been declared. For example, if a function module is called from a module pool, its module pool may contain a data element that has the same name as a data element in the calling module pool, although the two may have different contents.

7.3.8 LOCAL

The LOCAL statement is used in form routines. It ensures that the contents of a global field are rescued in internal intermediate memory and saved later when the routine ends. Within the routine, therefore, the field can be used as desired. Problems occur if the LOCAL variable is also passed as a parameter due to poor programming or by accident.

```
REPORT BMPRIV04.

DATA V1(10) TYPE C.
V1 = 'A'.
WRITE: / 'before:  ', V1.
PERFORM TEST USING V1.
WRITE: / 'after:   ', V1.
FORM TEST USING V2.
LOCAL V1.
  V1 = 'B'.
  WRITE: / 'test 1 ', V1.
  V2 = V1.
ENDFORM
```

The contents of the global field V1 are changed in the FORM routine, because V1 is passed to the routine as a reference parameter with the name V2. This behavior is desired. When the routine is exited, however, the LOCAL statement causes the old contents to be placed back into V1. You can avoid such side effects by using the DATA statement instead of LOCAL, which is also better programming style (a truly local variable).

7.3.9   Deleting views

When views are created that are to be used later with the SM30 transaction, an entry is required in the TVDIR file. This entry ensures that some screens are generated for view maintenance. If the view is later deleted, this entry must also be deleted from the TVDIR file.

7.3.10   Scope of validity of function goups

Function groups, or their internal data areas, are only valid within the boundaries of the calling program. Multiple calls of a function group from different programs can create different instances, and thereby data areas, of a function group. The following example demonstrates this.

Function group 1 contains the functions A and B, and function group 2 contains the function C. Within A, C is called, and from there, B is called. Three data areas are created, since a new instance of the function group 1 is created for the call of B from C. So, if B stores data in global data of the function group, this is not available in A. In this case, data must be passed using memory (for example, with EXPORT and IMPORT).

7.3.11   External performs

If external subroutines are called, the command interpreter processes the declaration part of the external program. If the external routine accesses global variables, the global variables that are valid are always those of the program in which the subroutine is located, not those of the calling program.

7.3.12   SY-DATAR

The system variable SY-DATAR is automatically set to "X" when data is entered in a screen. This variable is reset every time the screen is run through (even if, for example, a cancel is stopped in an EXIT module by a confirmation prompt), and the screen is processed from the beginning again. In this case, SY-DATAR is reset although changes have been made and not yet saved.

7.3.13   Parameters and selections during report calls

If a report is called from a screen with the SUBMIT statement, no check is performed to see if all of the report's parameters or selections are actually filled. There is also no check to see if all of the parameters or selections entered in the call really exist in the report. Typographical errors result in values not being passed to the report.

7.3.14   Data declarations in modules

Modules do not constitute a complete, separate unit in terms of the scope of validity of data fields. Fields that are declared in a module from a module pool are globally valid at the time of the declaration. In the case of multiple calls of the module, this means that the declaration and therefore also the assignment of an initial value are only carried out the first time. This is also the case if the screen to which the module belongs is exited and then called again. If by accident a field is declared in a module that is to be used as a counting variable for loops or something like that, this field must be set to its initial value with a statement. If the initial value is not assigned until the declaration, this may have undesirable consequences.

8 Quick reference

The complete reference for all ABAP/4 commands is about the size of this book. Since the availability and scope of functionality of many commands depends on the release version of the system, and you can call up appropriate documentation at any time using the system's online help, this chapter contains only an inventory of the ABAP/4 commands and a short description. That should be enough to allow you to recognize the power of the language and to gain an overview of the commands and their variants.

8.1 Description of the meta symbols

The command syntax is described with a meta language in this chapter. Even using this tool, it is not always possible to represent the syntax in a clear manner, as it is very complex in places. In particular, there are often ambiguities when it comes to the valid combinations of the various clauses and parameters and their number. When in doubt, you should turn to the written description in this chapter or the online help in the R/3 System.

The following syntax conventions are used in the command descriptions:

Bold: elements of the command, which must be entered exactly in this form.

Italics: place holders for other elements such as field names.

Normal font: meta symbols, described in Table 8.1.

Table 8.1 Meta symbols used, in order of priority

Symbol	Meaning
[]	Optional parameters and clauses are enclosed in square brackets. These elements may be used a maximum of one time.
{}	Elements enclosed in curly braces may be used one or more times.
|	The pipe symbol indicates an alternative. You may use either the element that appears before the pipe symbol or the element that appears after the pipe symbol, but not both.
...	Ellipses (three dots) indicate that you can repeat the last element as many times as you like.

8.2   Command overview

ADD *value* **TO** *field.*

The contents of *value* (field or constant) are added to *field*, and the result is stored in *field*.

ADD *field_1* **THEN** *field_2* **UNTIL** *field_z* **GIVING** *field.*

The contents of the fields *field_1* through *field_z* are added, and the result is stored in *field*. *field_1* is the first and *field_z* is the last in a series of fields with identical distances. In addition, all of the fields must have the same type and the same length. The distance from each other is determined by the distance between *field_1* and *field_2*.

ADD *field_1* **THEN** *field_2* **UNTIL** *field_z* **TO** *field.*

Builds a sum like the preceding variant does. The result is added to the current contents of *field*.

ADD *field_1* **THEN** *field_2* **UNTIL** *field_z*
  ACCORDING TO *sel* **GIVING** *field.*

The addition and assignment are the same as in variant 2. In the addition, only those fields are used whose index is specified by the selection table *sel*. The first field has the index 1. The selection table must have been created with SELECT-OPTIONS or RANGES.

ADD *field_1* **FROM** *start* **TO** *end* **GIVING** *field.*

The *field_1* field is the first in a series of fields of the same type and same length that follow one after another. The *start* and *end* values specify the index of the first and the last field to be summed. The result is stored in *field*.

ADD-CORRESPONDING *field_string_1* **TO** *field_string_2.*

Only those fields are taken into consideration whose names appear in both *field_string_1* and *field_string_2*. The contents of the fields in *field_string_1* are added to the fields with the same names from *field_string_2*.

APPEND *Itab* [**SORTED BY** *field* | **SORTED BY** (*field_name*)].

A new data set is appended to the internal table *Itab*. The data is taken from the header line of the internal table. There are no restrictions with regard to the number of data records in the table.

   The SORTED BY *field* clause sorts the new data record into the table according to the contents of *field*, in descending order. The SORTED BY clause limits the number of data records in the table. If the number of records reaches the value of the OCCURS parameter, the last data record is lost if the new data record is inserted ahead of it. The sort field can be specified dynamically. The parameter for SORTED BY contains the name of the sort field. The dynamic parameter must appear in parentheses. You can restrict the sort field by specifying offset and length.

APPEND *field_string* **TO** *Itab*
  [**SORTED BY** *field* | **SORTED BY** (*field_name*)].

Like APPEND ITAB. The data to be appended, however, is taken from *field_string*.

ASSIGN [*field* | (*field_name*)] **TO** *<field_symbol>*
  [**TYPE** *type*]
  [**DECIMALS** *decimal_pl*].

The field symbol shows the contents of field. Without the clauses, the attributes of *field* (type, length, conversion exit) are copied. These attributes can be overwritten using the TYPE clause or the DECIMALS clause. If the source field is specified directly, offset and length specifications can be used. The length specification (*) causes monitoring of the field length during assignments. The field can also be specified dynamically, although no length and offset specifications may then be used. If the field name is specified dynamically, the field is searched for at several levels (local data area, global data area, TABLES name range, external name range).

ASSIGN LOCAL COPY OF [*field* | (*field_name*)] **TO** *<field_symbol>*
  [**TYPE** *type*]
  [**DECIMALS** *decimal_pl*].

Like ASSIGN *field* TO ..., although a copy of the field is created on the data stack beforehand. Assignments to the field symbol thus do not change the contents of the original field.

ASSIGN TABLE FIELD (*field_name*) **TO** *<field_symbol>*.

Like ASSIGN *field_name*, although the field is only searched for in the TABLES name range.

ASSIGN COMPONENT *value* **OF STRUCTURE** *field_string* **TO** *<field_symbol>*
  [**TYPE** *type*]
  [**DECIMALS** *decimal_pl*].

If *value* is of type C, or if *value* corresponds to a structure that does not contain any internal tables, *value* is viewed as the name of a component of *field_string*. Otherwise, *value* is viewed as an index (initial value 1). The component of the field string identified this way is assigned to the field symbol. With the TYPE or DECIMALS clause, you can overwrite the automatic type assignment.

AT LINE-SELECTION.

This is an event. The statement block belonging to it is always processed when a valid line in the list is selected (double-clicking with the mouse or triggering the PICK function code, usually with F2).

AT USER-COMMAND.

The statement block for this event is processed when the user triggers a function or makes an entry in the OK Code field. However, it only operates for function codes that are not intercepted by the system.

AT PFn.

This event is processed when a function key has been pressed that is filled with the function code PFn, where n is a numerical value between 00 and 99.

AT NEW *field.* **... ENDAT.**

This statement is only useful in a LOOP program loop in an internal table or in an EXTRACT data set. *field* is a subfield of the internal table or of the data set. The statements between AT NEW and ENDAT are executed when the contents of *field* or of a field that appears before *field* in the definition of the structure changes. The current data record is compared to the data record processed in the previous loop iteration. The start of a new group is recognized.

AT END OF *field.* **... ENDAT.**

Like AT NEW, although the comparison is made between the current data record and the subsequent data record. This way, the end of a group is recognized.

AT FIRST. ... ENDAT.

This statement is used only in a LOOP program loop. The statements of this block are executed before the first loop iteration.

AT LAST. ... ENDAT.

This statement is used only in a LOOP program loop. The statements of this block are executed after the last loop iteration.

AT *field_group* [**WITH** *field_group_1*]. **... ENDAT.**

This statement is used only in a LOOP program loop in an EXTRACT data set. The statement block is executed only if the current data record belongs to *field_group*, that is, was created with EXTRACT *field_group*. The WITH clause also ensures that the statement block is only executed if a data record follows the current record that was created with EXTRACT *field_group_1*.

AT SELECTION-SCREEN ON [*parameter* | *selection*].

This is an event that is used only in reports with selection screens. It is processed after data entry on the selection screen. If an error message is triggered in the statement block, only the specified parameter or the selection becomes input-ready.

AT SELECTION-SCREEN ON BLOCK *block.*

This is an event that is used only in reports with selection screens. It is processed after data entry on the selection screen. If an error message is triggered in the statement block, only the input fields of the specified block become input-ready.

AT SELECTION-SCREEN ON END OF *selection.*

This is an event that is used only in reports with selection screens. For every selection, a second selection screen can be displayed in which several data records or intervals of the selection table can be recorded. The event is processed after data entry in this second screen ends. Since at this event all of the values entered in the selection table are available, they can be checked here. The error message does not, however, make the second screen input-ready!

AT SELECTION-SCREEN ON HELP REQUEST FOR
  [*parameter* | *selection-LOW* | *selection-HIGH*].

This event expects either the name of a parameter or the name of a selection as a clause. In the latter case, the actual input field must be specified with the LOW clause or the HIGH clause after the name of the selection. The event is processed when the cursor is located in the named field on a selection screen and the F1 function key (help) is pressed.

AT SELECTION-SCREEN OUTPUT.

This event is processed immediately before output of the selection screen.

AT SELECTION-SCREEN ON RADIOBUTTON GROUP *radio_button_group*.

This is an event that is used only in reports with selection screens. It is processed after data entry on the selection screen. If an error message is triggered in the statement block, only the radio buttons belonging to *radio_button_group* become input-ready.

AT SELECTION-SCREEN ON VALUE-REQUEST FOR
[*parameter* | *selection-LOW* | *selection-HIGH*].

This event awaits either the name of a parameter or the name of a selection as a clause. In the latter case, the actual input field must be specified behind the name of the selection with the LOW or the HIGH clause. The event is processed when the cursor is located in the named field on a selection screen and the F4 function key (possible entries help) is pressed. At the selection screen's runtime, the symbol for possible entries help is displayed to the right of the input field.

AUTHORITY-CHECK OBJECT *object*
  ID *name* **FIELD** *value*
  . . .
  [**ID** *name* **DUMMY**].

This statement checks existing authorizations. *object* is the name of the authorization object. You use *name* to specify the authorization fields of the authorization object. After this command is executed, SY-SUBRC provides information about whether the current contents of the specified authorization fields match *value*. If so, the user has the required authorization. A maximum of 10 authorization fields can be passed to the command as parameters. If no checking is desired for a field, checking can be turned off with the ID *name* DUMMY.

BACK.

After TOP-OF-PAGE processing, positions the cursor in list processing on the first line of the current page. When used together with the RESERVE statement, the cursor is positioned on the first line output after RESERVE.

BREAK *name*.

If the program is executed in dialog mode, processing of the program is interrupted and the debugger is turned on, assuming the current user has the specified name. This way, in the development phase, you can insert custom user interruptions that do not affect the work of other users. In batch or update mode, there is no interruption, just a syslog message.

BREAK-POINT.

Mandatory interruption point, assuming the program is being executed in dialog mode. Program processing is interrupted, and the debugger is turned on. In batch or update mode, there is no interruption, just a syslog message.

BREAK-POINT *field*.

Like BREAK-POINT, although the contents of *field* are also copied into any syslog message that is displayed.

```
CALL FUNCTION  function
   [EXPORTING   parameter = value ... ]
   [IMPORTING   parameter = field ... ]
   [TABLES      parameter = Itab ... ]
   [CHANGING    parameter = field ... ]
   [EXCEPTIONS  [exception = value ... ]
               [OTHERS = value ]
               [ERROR_MESSAGE = value ]].
```

The function module *function* is called. The name can be either a character string constant, which must be enclosed in single quotes, or a field that contains the name.

The values to be passed to the function module are listed after EXPORTING. After IMPORTING, the fields for the return values are listed. Internal tables are listed after TABLES. Using CHANGING, you declare combined import/export parameters. The exceptions to be handled by the calling function module must be listed after EXCEPTIONS.

```
CALL FUNCTION  function STARTING NEW TASK task-name
   [DESTINATION dest]
   [PERFORMING  subroutine ON END OF TASK ]
   [EXPORTING   parameter = value ... ]
   [TABLES      parameter = Itab ... ]
   [EXCEPTIONS  exception = value [MESSAGE field ]].
```

The function module is started asynchronously in a new session (or, if DESTINATION is used, in a different system). The calling program continues its work without waiting for the end of the called function module. Returning values from the called function module is thus not possible using the parameters of the function module, but it can, if necessary, be accomplished with a subroutine named PERFORMING. An error created during establishment of the link to a distant system is called an exception. These must be intercepted with EXCEPTIONS. With the MESSAGE clause, you can name a field in which the system places an explanatory text when an error occurs. In this type of call, all of the systems involved must be working with R/3 Systems of at least Release 3.0.

```
CALL FUNCTION  function IN UPDATE TASK
  [EXPORTING    parameter = value ... ]
  [TABLES       parameter = Itab ... ].
```

The function module is not executed at once, but is just presented for processing. The values passed are automatically temporarily stored. Not until a COMMIT WORK is the module actually executed, using the temporarily stored values.

```
CALL FUNCTION  function DESTINATION dest
  [EXPORTING    parameter = value ... ]
  [IMPORTING    parameter = field ... ]
  [TABLES       parameter = Itab ... ]
  [CHANGING     parameter = field ... ]
  [EXCEPTIONS  [exception = value ... ]
               [OTHERS = value]
               [ERROR_MESSAGE = value ]
               [MESSAGE field]].
```

The specified function module is called in the *dest* system and executed. This type of execution is called a *Remote Function Call* (RFC). *dest* can be a character string constant or a field that contains the name of the system to be called. The calling program waits for processing to end and can therefore also accept return values. Exceptions are handled like normal function modules, but special handling of several link-related exceptions using MESSAGE is also possible.

```
CALL FUNCTION  function IN BACKGROUND TASK
  [DESTINATION dest],
  [EXPORTING    parameter = value ... ]
  [TABLES       parameter = Itab ... ].
```

The function module is reserved for asynchronous updating. The values passed are temporarily stored. If necessary, execution can later also take place on a different system with the DESTINATION clause.

```
CALL CUSTOMER-FUNCTION identifier
  [EXPORTING    parameter = value ,... ]
  [IMPORTING    parameter = field, ... ]
  [TABLES       parameter = Itab, ... ]
  [CHANGING     parameter = field, ... ]
  [EXCEPTIONS  [ exception = value ... ]
               [ OTHERS = value ]
               [ ERROR_MESSAGE = value ]].
```

SAP provides something called Customer Exits to allow customers to easily expand existing applications. These are function modules that are delivered empty and can be completed by the customer. The interface, the call event and the actual name are set by SAP. *identifier* is a three-character string constant consisting only of numbers or a field with the corresponding contents.

CALL SCREEN *screen* [**STARTING AT** *x1 y1* [**ENDING AT** *x2 y2*]].

The *screen* screen of the current main program is called. After the end of screen processing, the program continues with the statement after the CALL statement. If necessary, the called screen can be positioned on the screen using STARTING AT. It then appears as a popup. The size is determined either implicitly through the actual area of the screen used (*Used* attribute) or explicitly through the ENDING AT parameter.

CALL TRANSACTION *transaction*
   [**AND SKIP FIRST SCREEN**]
   [**USING** *Itab* [**MODE** *mode*]
                [**UPDATE** *update*]
                [**MESSAGES INTO** *message_table*]].

The specified transaction is called. After the called transaction ends, the current program continues with the statement after the CALL statement. The name of the transaction can be specified as either a character string constant or a field with the corresponding contents. The clause AND SKIP FIRST SCREEN skips the first screen of the called transaction, assuming all of the input fields there have been given valid values using appropriate mechanisms (for example, Get/Set parameters).

The USING clause passes to the called transaction a table with screens in batch input format. In this case, the behavior of the transaction can be modified with several additional parameters (see Table 8.2).

Table 8.2   Clauses for batch processing

Clause	Parameter	Result
MODE	A	display screens
	E	display screen only in case of error
	N	do not display screen
UPDATE	A	asynchronous update
	S	synchronous update

Since error messages cannot be displayed on the screen during batch processing, it is possible to collect them in an existing internal table with the command clause MESSAGES INTO. This table must have the BDCMSGCOLL structure. Such a structure is defined in the Dictionary.

CALL METHOD OF *object method*
  [**=** *field*]
  [**EXPORTING** *parameter* **=** *field* ...]
  [**NO FLUSH**].

The specified method of the OLE object *object* is called. If necessary, the return value of the method can be stored in a data field with the first clause. If parameters are to be passed to the method, this is possible in similar fashion to the calls of function modules with EXPORTING. Several successive OLE calls are buffered by the system and passed together when a non-OLE statement is executed. With the NO FLUSH clause, continued buffering is possible. The OLE calls are then not executed until the FREE command.

CALL *C-function* [**ID** *identifier* **FIELD** *value* ...].

Call of an SAP kernel system function. This function can and should only be used by SAP.

CASE *field*.

Case distinction. The CASE statement introduces a complex statement block. This block is closed with ENDCASE. Within the block, the contents of *field* can be compared with *value* using the statement WHEN *value*. If there is a match, the statements up to the next WHEN branch are executed. A statement block for all other values can be introduced by the statement WHEN OTHERS, which must be entered as the last WHEN branch.

CHECK *logical_expression*.

This statement checks the logical expression. If the value is true, processing continues with the next statement. If not, the reaction depends on the type of the current statement block. In loops, the program jumps to the beginning of the loop and starts the next loop iteration. In modularization units (subroutines, modules, function modules or events), the program jumps out of the modularization unit.

CHECK *selection*.

The specified selection is checked. The table header line or field string against which the check is made is already specified when the selection table is declared. If the check criterion is not met, the current statement block is exited or started again.

CHECK SELECT-OPTIONS.

This statement is used only after a GET event when logical databases are being processed. A check is made for the database table specified after GET. This kind of check is made unnecessary by so-called *dynamic selections*.

CLEAR *field* [**WITH NULL**].

The field is set to a type-dependent initial value. The WITH NULL clause, on the other hand, causes the field to be filled with a NULL sign.

CLOSE DATASET *filename*.

The specified file is closed. This command is only needed if the file will be opened several times in a row in an application. In the command, *filename* can be either a character string constant or a field with the corresponding contents.

CLOSE CURSOR *cursor*.

The database cursor, *cursor*, is closed. This command is only needed if the cursor will be used more than once to read from database records.

CNT (*field*)

The CNT statement is not a true ABAP/4 statement. It is a field that is automatically created and filled. Analysis of the field contents makes sense only in a LOOP program loop in a sorted extract data set. In addition, the sort key must include *field*. After a control footer, CNT returns the number of different values in *field*.

COLLECT *Itab*.

A new data record is appended to the internal table *Itab*, or it is added to an existing entry with the identical key. The data is taken from the header line *Itab* of the internal table. In this case, the key consists of all of the fields that are not numerical fields, that is, whose type is unequal to I, F, or P. If COLLECT finds a record in the internal table whose key matches that of the data record to be inserted, the values of all of the numerical fields of the new record are added to those of the existing record. In this case, no new record is inserted in the internal table. There are no restrictions with regard to the maximum number of records in the table.

COLLECT *field_string* **INTO** *Itab*.

Like COLLECT Itab, but the data is taken from *field_string*.

COMMIT WORK [**AND WAIT**].

With this statement, all database changes are finally written. All update routines (PER-FORM ON COMMIT, CALL FUNCTION IN UPDATE TASK) and reserved background processing (CALL FUNCTION IN BACKGROUND TASK) are executed. Database locks are released. All of the actions confirmed by COMMIT WORK are called a logical unit of work (LUW).

One exception is the call of COMMIT WORK in dialog applications that have been called with CALL DIALOG. There, the only thing that happens is that database locks are released. The true Commit, that is, the confirmation of database changes and the execution of update routines, is not executed until after a COMMIT WORK in the calling program.

The AND WAIT clause causes the application to wait for the ending of all update procedures.

COMMUNICATION ...

The many variants of the COMMUNICATION statement enable the communication of several programs based on the CPI-C protocol (CPI-C: Common Programming Interface-Communication). The following variants exist:

... **INIT DESTINATION** *dest* **ID** *ident* [**RETURNCODE** *ret*].

Establishment of the link to the *dest* system. The identification number for the link is returned in *ident*. If necessary, the return code can be passed to an expressly named field, *ret*, with the RETURNCODE clause. Usually, the return code is available in SY-SUBRC.

... ALLOCATE ID *ident* [**RETURNCODE** *ret*].

The initialized link is set up.

... ACCEPT ID *ident* [**RETURNCODE** *ret*].

With this variant, a requested link is accepted and initialized.

... SEND ID *ident* **BUFFER** *buffer*
    [**RETURNCODE** *ret* , **LENGTH** *length*].

The contents of *buffer* are sent to the opposite side. With the LENGTH clause, you can specify the length of the characters to be transmitted.

... RECEIVE ID *ident* **BUFFER** *buffer* **DATAINFO** *I* **STATUSINFO** *S*
    [**RETURNCODE** *ret*]
    [**LENGTH** *length*]
    [**RECEIVED** *number*].

Data sent from the opposite side is received and stored in *buffer*. The fields *info* and *status* provide information about the transmission. With the LENGTH clause, you can restrict the number of characters to be read. With the RECEIVED clause, you can determine the number of lines actually read.

... DEALLOCATE ID *ident*.

The link is closed and broken down.

COMPUTE *field* **=** *expression*.

The (arithmetic) result of an expression is calculated and stored in *field*. You can leave out the COMPUTE statement, resulting in the short form:

field **=** *expression*.

CONCATENATE *value*, **...** **INTO** *field*
    [**SEPARATED BY** *separator*].

All of the values (field contents or constants) are interpreted as character strings and combined into a single character string. Any trailing blank spaces are ignored. The result is stored in *field*. With SEPARATED BY, you can define a character string to be inserted as the separator between the individual elements.

CONDENSE *field* [**NO-GAPS**].

The contents of *field* are interpreted as a character string, regardless of the actual type. Several blank spaces in a row are combined into a single one, or they are suppressed entirely (NO-GAPS). The result is available in *field*.

CONSTANTS *field*[(*length*)]
    [**TYPE** *type* | **LIKE** *like-field*] **VALUE** *value*.

Declaration of a data field, *field*, with constant contents, which must be assigned using VALUE. The constant's type can be determined by the value assigned, by a type specification or by derivation from an existing field.

CONSTANTS: BEGIN OF *field_string,* **...** **END OF** *field_string.*

Declaration of a field string with constant contents. When the subfield is declared, a value must be assigned to every single field of the field string with VALUE.

CONTINUE.

This statement is used only in loops. It causes a jump to the beginning of the loop and the start of the next iteration.

CONTROLS *name* **TYPE** *control-type.*
CONTROLS *name* **TYPE TABLEVIEW USING SCREEN** *screen_number.*

With the CONTROLS statement, you define an object for displaying data visually. The object's type is determined by *control-type.*

   This type is not one of the standard data types, but rather the name of an element programmed by SAP.

   Currently, only the so-called table view is available, which can be considered a further development of step loops. For the declaration of a table view, the CONTROL statement must be supplemented with additional parameters, so that at the moment only the special form of the CONTROL statement shown above can be used.

CONVERT DATE *date* **INTO INVERTED-DATE** *field.*

The *date* (field contents or fixed value) is inverted (9's complement of the internal representation), and the result is stored in *field.* This conversion causes the most recent date to have the numerically smallest value, which can be helpful when sorting by date.

CONVERT INVERTED-DATE *date* **INTO DATE** *field.*

Converts an inverted date into the original value.

CREATE OBJECT *object class* [**LANGUAGE** *language*].

Creates an OLE2 object that can be processed with other commands.

DATA *field*[(*length*)]
   [**TYPE** *type* | **LIKE** *like-field*]
   [**TYPE** *type* **OCCURS** *roll_area* [**WITH HEADER LINE**] |
     LIKE *like-field* **OCCURS** *roll-area* [**WITH HEADER LINE**]]
   [**TYPE LINE OF** *Itab-type* | **LIKE LINE OF** *Itab*]
   [**VALUE** *value*]
   [**DECIMALS** *decimal_places*].

Declaration of a data field *field.* You can determine the type and other properties with various clauses, assuming you do not want to use the default values. You determine the size of the data field by specifying *length.* This value must be enclosed in parentheses and must appear without separators immediately after the field name. TYPE gives the field the predefined or user-defined type. LIKE copies the attributes of an existing field. With VALUE, you can assign a value in the declaration. For fields of type P, you can determine the number of decimal places using DECIMALS. The two LINE OF clauses create a field string instead of a simple data field. This field string's structure corresponds to the specified type or the structure of the specified table. The two OCCURS clauses, on the other hand, declare an internal table without a header line. The structure of this table corresponds to the specified type or the structure. For either of these two table declaration variants, you can also create a header line for the table using the WITH HEADER LINE clause. The *roll_area* parameter in the declaration of internal tables indicates how many data records of the internal table should be held in main memory before they are moved to the hard disk swap area.

```
DATA: BEGIN OF field_string,
  (field ...),
END OF field_string.
```

This statement declares a field string. The subfields of the field string must be declared between BEGIN OF *field_string* and END OF *field_string*; you can use the clauses described for DATA here. Separate the individual declarations from one another with a comma.

```
DATA: BEGIN OF Itab OCCURS roll_area,
  (field ...),
END OF Itab [ VALID BETWEEN field_1 AND field_2 ].
```

With this statement, you declare an internal table and the header line belonging to it. The *roll_area* parameter indicates the number of data records to be stored in main memory. Data records are not moved to the hard disk swap area until this number is exceeded. The fields of the table are declared just like those of field string. With the VALID BETWEEN clause, you determine two table fields that the PROVIDE command uses to form a scope of validity.

```
DATA: BEGIN OF COMMON PART name,
  (field ...),
END OF COMMON PART.
```

This statement defines a data block in the global memory area. This data block can be used by several programs at once, if it is declared in all of the programs with the same name and the same structure. In practice, you declare a common part in a separate file, which you include in all of the programs that are to use the common part with an INCLUDE statement. If only one common part is to be used, you can leave out the name. You declare the structure the same way you do for field strings. Simply put, a common part is a field string that can be used across program boundaries.

```
DEFINE macro_name. ... END-OF-DEFINITION.
```

You use DEFINE to define macros, which consist of ABAP/4 statements. You end the definition of the macro with END-OF-DEFINITION. You can use the position parameters &1 through &9 in the macro. A macro call is replaced by the statements of the macro definition at a program's translation time (before the first execution).

```
DELETE FROM table | (field) WHERE condition [CLIENT SPECIFIED].
```

Deleting data records from a database table. All of the data records identified with the WHERE condition are deleted. The name of the table can be either entered as a constant in the statement or passed in a data field. As the default, deleting takes place in the current client only. Using the CLIENT SPECIFIED clause, you can turn off automatic client handling. The client must then be processed like any other table field in the selection condition.

```
DELETE table | *table | (field)
  [CLIENT SPECIFIED]
  [FROM work_area].
```

This statement deletes a single data record from the specified table. The name of the table can, in turn, be passed either statically in the statement or dynamically in a data field. The complete key of the data record to be deleted must be passed in the table's header record or in an explicitly specified work area (FROM ...). If the table name is dynamically passed, specification of a work area is mandatory. The contents of the work area are transferred character by character into the key fields of the table, therefore the work area must be able to accept all of the key fields. This requires that the key values in the work area appear in the sequence and length decided on in the Data Dictionary for the table in question. The internal structure of the work area can, however, differ from the structure of the table. This means that the work area does not absolutely have to be a field string, but can also be a long-enough data field of type C or N. With the CLIENT SPECIFIED clause, you can turn off automatic client handling.

```
DELETE table | (field) FROM TABLE Itab [CLIENT SPECIFIED].
```

All of the data records whose key matches one of the data records of the internal table *Itab* are deleted from the specified database table. The data records of the internal table must meet the same requirements as the work area in the previously described version of the DELETE statement. With the CLIENT SPECIFIED clause, you can turn off automatic client handling. You can pass the name of the database table statically or dynamically.

```
DELETE table | *table VERSION table_name.
```

This variant enables dynamic passing of the table name in the *table_name* field, although there are several restrictions with regard to the name. Since the other versions of the DELETE statement now also enable dynamic name passing, this variant of the command is only still supported for compatibility reasons and should not be used for new development.

```
DELETE Itab [INDEX index].
```

Deletion of a data record from an internal table. Without the clause, this statement only makes sense in a LOOP program loop in the table, where it deletes the current record. The INDEX clause makes it possible to delete a specific record outside of loops, assuming you know its data record number. You can use several variants of the READ command, for example, to determine what it is. The count begins with 1.

```
DELETE FROM DATABASE table(area) ID key
  [CLIENT field].
```

Deletion of a so-called data cluster from the table and the area (both constants). The cluster is identified by a key that is specified as a constant or as the contents of a field.

DELETE DATASET *filename*.

Deletion of the specified file at operating system level. This is not a table, but usually a file in non-SAP format, such as text files or binary files from other systems.

DESCRIBE FIELD *field*
   [**LENGTH** *result*]
   [**TYPE** *result*]
   [**TYPE** *type* **COMPONENTS** *number*]
   [**OUTPUT-LENGTH** *result*]
   [**DECIMALS** *result*]
   [**EDIT MASK** *result*].

This statement determines one or more attributes of a field and places them in the *result* field. You must use at least one clause. If you use several clauses at the same time, of course, you need different fields for the results.

DESCRIBE TABLE *Itab* **LINES** *lines*.

Places the number of the data records of the internal table Itab into lines.

DESCRIBE TABLE *Itab* **OCCURS** *roll_area*.

Places the OCCURS parameter specified in the declaration of the internal table into *roll_area*.

DESCRIBE DISTANCE BETWEEN *field_1* **AND** *field_2* **INTO** *distance*.

Places the distance in bytes between the fields *field_1* and *field_2* into *distance*.

DESCRIBE LIST [**INDEX** *index*] **NUMBER OF LINES** *lines*.

This command writes the number of list lines into the *lines* field. If necessary, you can specify the list level using INDEX, to access a different list than the one currently being displayed.

DESCRIBE LIST [**INDEX** *index*] **NUMBER OF PAGES** *pages*.

This command writes the number of pages in the list into the pages field. If necessary, you can specify the list level using INDEX, to access a different list than the one currently being displayed.

DESCRIBE LIST [**INDEX** *index*] **LINE** *line* **PAGE** *page*.

This command delivers the page number on which the specified line is to be found. In this case, too, you can specify the list level with INDEX, to access a different list than the one currently being displayed.

DESCRIBE LIST [**INDEX** *index*] **PAGE** *page*
   [**LINE-SIZE** *result*]
   [**LINE-COUNT** *result*]

```
[ LINES      result ]
[ FIRST-LINE result ]
[ TOP-LINES  result ]
[ TITLE-LINES result ]
[ HEAD-LINES result ]
[ END-LINES  result ].
```

The various clauses for this command provide information about the layout of a selected page in a list. If you use several clauses at the same time, of course, you need different fields for the results. The return values of the individual clauses are shown in Table 8.3.

Table 8.3   Clauses for the DESCRIBE LIST PAGE command

Clause	Returns
LINE-SIZE	line length
LINE-COUNT	number of lines allowed
LINES	number of lines output
FIRST-LINE	absolute line number of the first line of the page
TOP-LINES	number of lines output in the page header (title + column headings)
TITLE-LINES	number of lines output as title
HEAD-LINES	number of lines output as column headings
END-LINES	number of footers reserved for page end

DIVIDE *field* **BY** *divisor*.

The value in *field* is divided by *divisor*. The result appears in *field*. The divisor can be a constant or a field.

DIVIDE-CORRESPONDING *field_string_1* **BY** *field_string_2*.

Fields with matching names are searched for in both field strings. If such a field exists, its contents in *field_string_1* are divided by the contents of the field with the same name in *field_string_2*. Afterwards, the result appears in the field of *field_string_1*.

DO. ... **ENDDO.**

Infinite loop. The statements between DO and ENDDO are repeated until the loop is exited with EXIT, STOP, or REJECT.

DO VARYING *field* **FROM** *start* **NEXT** *difference*. ... **ENDDO.**

This infinite loop is also processed until it is exited with EXIT, STOP, or REJECT. In each loop iteration, *field* receives a new value. The first value results from the contents of *start*. The next field is always determined by adding the distance between *start* and *difference* to the memory address of the current field. If a value is assigned to *field*, this change also takes effect at the place in main memory where the current contents of *field* were read. Several VARYING clauses can be combined in one DO statement.

DO *n* **TIMES. ... ENDDO.**

The loop is iterated *n* times.

DO *n* **TIMES VARYING** *field* **FROM** *start* **NEXT** *difference*. ... **ENDDO.**

Combination of the VARYING clause with a predefined number of loop iterations.

EDITOR-CALL FOR *Itab* [**TITLE** *title*] [**DISPLAY-MODE**].

The internal table *Itab*, which may consist only of fields of type C, and which may be a maximum of 72 characters wide, is loaded into the program editor and can be edited there. After the editor command *Back* (F3) or *Save* (F11), the changes are saved in the internal table. Using TITLE, you can set a title. The DISPLAY-MODE clause prevents editing of the table and allows it to be displayed only.

EDITOR-CALL FOR REPORT *program* [**DISPLAY-MODE**].

The specified program is loaded into the program editor and can be edited there. The DISPLAY-MODE clause puts the editor into display mode, in which no editing of the program is possible.

END-OF-PAGE.

Event. The accompanying statement block is executed if the END-OF-PAGE area of a page is reached during output, or if the RESERVE statement does not find the required number of empty lines available. This event does not take effect if the default setting of LINE-COUNT (0) is used, or in the case of NEW-PAGE.

END-OF-SELECTION.

The statement block of this event is executed after all of the statements of the actual selection section of a report have been executed. This is the case, for example, when all of the data records of a logical database have been read.

EXEC SQL [**PERFORMING** *subroutine*]. ... **ENDEXEC.**

A so-called Native SQL statement appears between EXEC and ENDEXEC. This statement is handed directly to the database. It must, therefore, take into account any peculiarities of the database system used. Data exchange between ABAP/4 and Native SQL takes place with ABAP/4 data fields, which are preceded by a colon in the SQL statement. Using PER-FORMING, you can define an ABAP/4 subroutine that is executed once for every data record that the SQL statement returns. Native SQL statements are not always portable. They should therefore be used as a last resort only.

EXIT.

Exits a processing section. The exact reaction depends on the position of the statement in the program. If the statement appears in a loop, only the loop is exited. Within a modularization unit (subroutines, statement block of an event), but outside a loop, an EXIT leads to the ending of the processing unit. Within a report, EXIT ends processing and leads to the display of the list created so far.

EXIT FROM STEP-LOOP.

This statement refers to the screen loops. The corresponding loop is exited, meaning no more data records are placed into or read from the screen's step loop area.

EXIT FROM SQL.

This statement ends Native SQL processing started with EXEC SQL PERFORMING.

EXPORT [*field*] [*Itab*] [**FROM** *source_field*]
  TO DATABASE *table(area)* **ID** *key* [**CLIENT** *client*].

Fields or internal tables are written into a database table, *table*. They are stored there in a so-called area. Several objects may be stored together under a common key. With the CLIENT clause, data can be stored in a different data record than the data record of the current client. With the FROM clause, which must be specified separately for every field, a field with a different name can be created in the table.

EXPORT *field* | *Itab* [**FROM** *source_field*] **TO MEMORY**
  [**ID** *key*].

Fields or internal tables are written into a global memory area, where they can be read by other applications. This makes data exchange possible across applications. With the FROM clause, you can store an object under a different name. With the ID clause, you can give the stored objects an identifier with which they can later be read in again. The EXPORT command overwrites. In the case of repeated exports, all of the existing objects with the same identifier are deleted.

EXTRACT *field_group*.

The current contents of the fields defined in *field_group* are written into the extract data set of a program. If a HEADER field group has been declared, its field contents are placed in front as the key.

FETCH NEXT CURSOR *cursor* **INTO** *field_string*.

Reads the next data record from a data set determined with OPEN CURSOR. The result is stored in *field_string*.

FIELD-GROUPS *field_group*.

This statement declares a so-called field group. This is the combination of several existing fields into one object that is similar to a field string, with which they have nothing in common functionality-wise, however. Field groups are used only in connection with extract data sets.

FIELD-SYMBOLS <*field_symbol*>
  [**STRUCTURE** *table* **DEFAULT** *field*] |
  [**TYPE** *type*] |

```
[TYPE LINE OF type] |
[LIKE field] |
[LIKE LINE OF field_string] |
[TYPE ANY].
```

This command declares a field symbol. The angled braces in which the name of the field symbol appears belong to the command. They are mandatory. A field symbol is a pointer that is later assigned to a data field with the ASSIGN command.

The field symbol's type is not determined until assignment. With the STRUCTURE clause, you create a field symbol that can point to a complete structure defined in the Data Dictionary. You can access the individual fields of the structure later using *<field_symbol>-field_name*. You must provide a work area, *field*, for such field symbols, and its size must correspond to the size of the Dictionary structure. The other clauses determine the field symbol's type. This type is checked during an ASSIGN.

```
FORM subroutine
   [TABLES Itab
      [STRUCTURE structure | TYPE type | LIKE field_string] ...]
   [USING [parameter | VALUE(parameter)] [typing]...]
   [CHANGING [parameter | VALUE(parameter)] [typing]...].
```

This statement defines a subroutine. It ends with the statement ENDFORM. Both internal tables as well as fields and field strings can be passed as parameters to the subroutine. The assignment of the current parameters to the formal parameters takes place according to the sequence of the parameters during the call of the subroutine. To distinguish the parameters, you need one of the TABLES clauses for internal tables, and USING or CHANGING for field parameters. Parameters are handled mainly as reference parameters; it is the VALUE clause that forces them to be handled as value parameters. You can give all parameters additional type specifications. At runtime, the system checks if the current parameter has the required type. For space reasons, the possible statements for typing are listed in Table 8.4.

Table 8.4 Clauses available for typing parameters

Statement	Effect
... STRUCTURE field_string	The parameter corresponds to the structure of *field_string*.
... TYPE type	The parameter has the specified type.
... TYPE LINE OF Itab	The parameter has the structure of a data record of the table *Itab*, which has no header line.
... LIKE field	The parameter has the attributes and the type of *field*.
... LIKE LINE OF Itab	The parameter has the structure of the internal table *Itab*.
... TYPE TABLE	The current parameter must be a table without a header line.
... TYPE ANY	Every type is allowed.

FORMAT
  [**COLOR** [*color* | **OFF**]]
  [**INTENSIFIED** [**OFF**]]
  [**INVERSE** [**OFF**]]
  [**INPUT** [**OFF**]]
  [**HOTSPOT** [**OFF**]]
  [**RESET**].

Sets the output parameters. The new values take effect starting with the next WRITE statement. When new processing events are entered, several of the settings are reset to default values.

FREE *Itab* | *table*.

The memory space needed to process the internal table *Itab* or the database table *table* is released.

FREE MEMORY [**ID** key].

The global memory area is deleted. The basic form without any clauses deletes everything, including data that has been given a key. Targeted deleting of individual groups of data requires the specification of the key.

FREE OBJECT *object*.

The OLE object *object* is released.

GET *table* [**LATE**].

Event. This statement is only usable in reports that work with a logical database. The next data record from *table* is made available in the header line of the same name. At the same time, the contents of all tables that appear above the table in the hierarchy are retrieved. The LATE clause causes processing after all of the subordinate tables have been read.

GET CURSOR FIELD *field*
  [**OFFSET** *offset*] [**LINE** *line*] [**VALUE** *value*] [**LENGTH** *length*].

This command delivers the name of the field where the cursor is currently located. Beyond that, the clauses provide the offset of the cursor within the field, the number of any step loop line or the absolute list line, the current value, or the output length of the field. This command can be used in dialog processing as well as in interactive reporting.

GET CURSOR LINE *line*
  [**OFFSET** *offset*] [**VALUE** *value*] [**LENGTH** *length*].

This command delivers the number of the list line or the step loop line in which the cursor is located. The clauses only work in list processing. They provide the offset of the cursor in the line, the contents, or the length of the entire line.

GET PARAMETER ID *parameter_name* **FIELD** *field*.

The parameter with the specified name is read from global memory and placed into the specified field. The parameter name can be specified as the contents of a field or as a constant.

`GET TIME` [`FIELD` *field*].

The field SY-UZEIT is filled with the current time. In addition, SY-DATUM is reset. If the FIELD clause is used, the system fields are not updated. Instead, the current time is just written into *field*.

`GET RUN TIME FIELD` *field*.

The first call of GET RUN TIME initializes *field*. Every additional call fills *field* with the runtime of the application that has elapsed since the first call. The unit of measure is microseconds.

`GET PROPERTY OF` *object attribute* = *field* [`NO FLUSH`].

An attribute of an OLE object is read and placed into the specified field. The NO FLUSH clause causes several OLE statements to be combined with the goal of combined execution.

`HIDE` *field*.

The contents of *field* are placed in a hidden memory area and linked to the number of the current line. The hidden contents are reactivated by line selections in interactive reporting.

`IF` *logical_expression*.

The logical expression is analyzed. If it is true, the statements immediately following it, up to the next ELSE, ELSEIF or ENDIF, are executed. If it is not true, the next ELSEIF expression is analyzed or continued after an ELSE statement.

```
IMPORT [field | Itab] [TO target_field]
  FROM DATABASE table(area)
  ID key | MAJOR-ID maid MINOR-ID miid
  [CLIENT client].
```

Data fields or internal tables are imported from one area of a specific table. These values must have been exported with EXPORT TO DATABASE. Using the TO clause, which you must specify separately for every field or table, you can store values that have been read in other fields. The key can be either split into two parts according to the ID or specified with MAJOR-ID and MINOR-ID. If the table is client-dependent, the client number can also be passed using CLIENT.

```
IMPORT DIRECTORY INTO Itab
  FROM DATABASE table(area)
  ID key.
```

This statement delivers a list of the objects that have been stored with a certain key in the area in question in the specified table.

`IMPORT` [*field* | *Itab*] [`TO` *target_field*] `FROM MEMORY` [`ID` *key*].

You use this statement to read objects from global memory that were stored there with EXPORT. Using the clause TO, you can store values in other fields.

INCLUDE *Include-file*.

Include-file contains the ABAP/4 source code. These statements are included in the current program. The program behaves as though the statements were written directly in the actual program. Several other programs can incorporate the same Include file.

INCLUDE STRUCTURE *field_string*.

This statement only makes sense within a BEGIN OF REC ... END OF REC statement. It inserts the structure of the specified field string into the declaration.

INFOTYPES *nnnn*
   [**NAME** *name*]
   [**OCCURS** *roll_area*]
   [**MODE** *mode*]
   [**VALID FROM** *start* **TO** *end*].

A so-called infotype is defined. Described simply, an infotype is an internal table that is similar to a database table. Infotypes are used only rarely, in certain applications.

INITIALIZATION.

This is an event in reporting. The specified event is processed once at the beginning of the report, immediately after creation of the parameters.

INSERT INTO *table* | (*name_field*)
  VALUES *work_area* [**CLIENT SPECIFIED**].

This is an Open SQL statement. With this statement, a data record is inserted into a database table. The data is taken from *work_area* according to the structure of the table. The work area itself can be unstructured, but it must contain all of the data in the correct sequence and length. The name of the table can be passed as a constant using a field with the corresponding contents. The data record is inserted only if no data record with the same key exists either in the table or in any UNIQUE index. You can turn off automatic client handling with CLIENT SPECIFIED. You must then provide the MANDT field with data, just like you do any other key field in the program.

INSERT *table* | *table | (*name_field*)
  [**FROM** *work_area*]
  [**CLIENT SPECIFIED**].

This statement inserts a data record in a database table. The name of the table can be passed as a constant using a field with the corresponding contents. The data is taken either from the header line of the table or from *work_area*, which can be unstructured, as described for the preceding variant. In this variant of the command, too, the data record must have a unique key with regard to the table and all UNIQUE indexes. The CLIENT SPECIFIED clause turns off automatic client handling.

INSERT *table* | (**name_field**) **FROM TABLE** *Itab*
  [**ACCEPTING DUPLICATE KEYS**]
  [**CLIENT SPECIFIED**].

With this Open SQL statement, you can insert several data records into a database table. You can pass the name of the table as a constant using a field with the corresponding contents. The data records to be inserted are taken from the internal table Itab. The structure of this table must meet the same requirements as the work area described for the two preceding variants. The ACCEPTING clause avoids a runtime error if an attempt is made to insert data records with identical keys. The CLIENT SPECIFIED clause turns off automatic client handling.

INSERT [*work_area* **INTO**] *Itab* [**INDEX** *index*].

With this command, you insert a data record into an internal table. The data is taken either from an explicitly specified work area or from the header line of the table. You use the INDEX clause to specify the position where it should be inserted. The first data record has the index 1. In a LOOP program loop in the table, you can leave out the index specification. The new data record is then inserted ahead of the current data record.

INSERT *field_1 field_2* ... **INTO** *field_group*.

With this statement, you add data fields to a field group declared earlier with FIELD-GROUPS. There is no data transport associated with this procedure; it simply determines which data fields should belong to the field group. Although this statement is identified in SAP documentation as an operational statement, not a declarative one, it nevertheless performs a task comparable to a declaration.

INSERT REPORT *program* **FROM** *Itab*.

Inserts a program into the global program set. The source code is read from the internal table Itab.

INSERT TEXTPOOL *program* **FROM** *Itab* **LANGUAGE** *language*.

Inserts text elements for the program into the program set in the specified language. The text elements are taken from an internal table.

LEAVE.

This statement ends an application (transaction, dialog, report) called with CALL and continues with the statement after the CALL statement.

LEAVE LIST-PROCESSING.

Ends list processing embedded in a dialog and started with LEAVE TO LIST-PROCESSING.

LEAVE PROGRAM.

Exits the current program.

LEAVE SCREEN.

Ends processing of the current screen and executes the screen entered in the screen attributes or previously set with SET SCREEN.

LEAVE TO LIST-PROCESSING
  [**AND RETURN TO SCREEN** *screen_number*].

In a dialog application, temporarily activates list processing. After list processing ends, the PBO section of the current screen is executed, or that of the screen specified with RETURN TO SCREEN.

LEAVE TO SCREEN *screen_number*.

Ends processing of the current screen and executes the screen with the specified number.

LEAVE TO TRANSACTION *transaction_code*
  [**AND SKIP FIRST SCREEN**].

Ends the current transaction and starts a new transaction in its place. The SKIP clause ensures that the first screen of the called transaction is not processed on screen, if all of the input fields for this screen are provided with valid values using appropriate mechanisms.

LOCAL *field*.

This statement is only possible within subroutines, that is, after a FORM statement. It rescues the current contents of *field* and recreates them after the subroutine is exited. Within the subroutine, the global field can thus be handled like a local data field. Assignments to this field are possible, but they have no effect outside the subroutine.

LOOP.

Loop in all data records of the extract data set. The data is made available in the fields of each field group.

LOOP AT *Itab*
  [**INTO** *work_area*]
  [**FROM** *start*]
  [**TO** *end*]
  [**WHERE** *condition*].

Loop in an internal table. The data records are provided one after the other in the header line of the table or in the work area specified with INTO. The clauses FROM and TO limit the loop iterations to the pertinent data records. The count begins with 1. The WHERE clause makes it possible to select the data records to be processed in the loop according to a logical condition.

LOOP AT SCREEN.

This statement makes sense only in the PBO module of a screen. It makes the description of the fields of the current screen available in the predefined header line SCREEN. SCREEN can be processed like an internal table. Changes to the header line are written into the internal table SCREEN with MODIFY and take effect when the screen is output. The form of the structure depends on the release version.

LOOP AT *table*.

This statement is outdated and is supported for compatibility reasons only. It allows record-by-record processing of certain database tables.

MESSAGE *TNNN*[(*class*)]
  [**WITH** *P1* ... *P4*]
  [**RAISING** *exception*].

The message NNN with the message type T is output. In the message text, up to four place holders represented by the character & can be replaced with the parameters P1 through P4. The message class is usually set in the REPORT or PROGRAM statement. To deviate from that specification, the message class must appear in parentheses behind the message number. In function modules, the RAISING clause causes an exception to be triggered. In this case, the message is displayed only if the exception is not handled by the calling program.

MESSAGE ID *class* **TYPE** *type* **NUMBER** *number*
  [**WITH** *P1* ... *P4*]
  [**RAISING** *exception*].

This statement corresponds to the preceding one, except that you specify the three values for identifying the message (class, type and number) separately. In this form of the statement, you can also set these values dynamically.

MODIFY *table* | **table* | (*table_name*)
  [**FROM** *work_area*]
  [**CLIENT SPECIFIED**].

Modification or insertion of a data record into a database table. You can specify its name either statically or dynamically. The data is taken from the header line of the table or from the explicitly specified work area. The data record is identified by the contents of the key fields. The CLIENT SPECIFIED clause turns off automatic handling of the client field. This field can or must then also be filled with a correct value, just like all other fields. This makes it possible to edit client-specific tables across client boundaries. The MODIFY command recognizes by itself whether an existing data record must be modified or a new data record must be appended. Since this check can have a negative effect on performance, MODIFY should be used only if no clear decision can be made between INSERT and UPDATE in the program.

MODIFY *table* | (*table_name*) **FROM TABLE** *Itab*
  [**CLIENT SPECIFIED**].

This command works like the preceding version of the MODIFY command. However, the data is taken from an internal table, so that several data records can be modified with a single command.

MODIFY *table* | **table* **VERSION** *name_field*.

This command is outdated. It allows dynamic specification of a table name. Its operation corresponds in all other ways to that of the first form of the MODIFY command.

MODIFY *Itab* [**FROM** *work_area*].

Changes the current data record of an internal table in a LOOP program loop. This command is only usable for changing. Inserting new data records, as is done with the MODIFY command for database tables, is not possible! The data is taken either from the header line of the table or from a work area specified with the FROM clause.

MODIFY *Itab* **INDEX** *index* [**FROM** *work_area*].

This command changes an internal table's data record specified by an index. It can therefore also be useful to implement it outside LOOP program loops. The index can, for example, be determined during a preceding READ statement.

MODIFY LINE *i*
   [**INDEX** *index*]
   [**LINE FORMAT** *formats* ...]
   [**FIELD VALUE** {*target_field* **FROM** *source_field*} ...]
   [**FIELD FORMAT** {*field formats* ...}].

This command only makes sense in list processing. It modifies the line *i* in the current list or in the list at the *index* list level. With the LINE FORMAT clause, you assign one or more formats to the line. The formats correspond to those for the FORMAT command. With FIELD VALUE, you assign a new value to a field that has been written into the list. This is effective immediately in the list. FIELD FORMAT makes targeted assignment of formats to a selected field possible.

MODIFY LINE *i* **OF CURRENT PAGE** | **OF PAGE** *page*
   [**LINE FORMAT** *formats* ...]
   [**FIELD VALUE** {*target_field* **FROM** *source_field*} ...]
   [**FIELD FORMAT** {*field formats* ...}].

This command changes the specified line of the current list. List counting takes place in a page that is specified with OF PAGE. Using OF CURRENT PAGE instead of OF PAGE selects the current page. Lines in other lists cannot be changed.

MODIFY CURRENT LINE
   [**LINE FORMAT** *formats* ...]
   [**FIELD VALUE** {*target_field* **FROM** *source_field*} ...]
   [**FIELD FORMAT** {*field formats* ...}].

Changes the formats of the current line (the last line read using line selection or READ LINE). The clauses correspond to those of the two preceding variants.

MODULE *module_name* [**INPUT** | **OUTPUT**].

Definition of a module that can be called in the flow logic of a screen. The module must be closed with ENDMODULE. In the PBO phase of a screen, only those modules are searched for and executed that have the OUTPUT clause. In the PAI phase, only modules without a clause or with the INPUT clause are operative.

MOVE *source_field*[+*offset*][(*length*)] **TO** *target_field*[+*offset*][(*length*)]
   [**PERCENTAGE** *percentage* [**RIGHT**]].

Transfers the contents of the source field to the target field. Both in the source and in the target, static or dynamic specifications can appear for an offset within the field and for a length. The statement can also copy complex data structures and tables. A period always serves as the decimal point.

The PERCENTAGE clause expects fields of type C as source field and target field. It transfers the part of the characters specified with *percentage* from the source field to the target field.

MOVE-CORRESPONDING `source` **TO** `target`.

This statement copies all of the fields from the field string *source* to the fields with the same name in the field string *target*. Fields that do not exist in *target* are ignored.

MULTIPLY `field` **BY** `factor`.

The contents of *field* are multiplied by *factor*, and the result is stored in *field*. You can specify *factor* statically or dynamically.

MULTIPLY-CORRESPONDING `field_string_1` **BY** `field_string_2`.

This command creates and executes a simple MULTIPLY BY statement for all fields that are contained in both *field_string_1* and *field_string_2*. The fields in *field_string_1* serve as source and target fields; the factor is taken from *field_string_2*.

NEW-LINE [`NO SCROLLING`].

This statement is only useful in list processing. It executes a line feed. The clause NO SCROLLING defines the subsequent output line as non-scrollable. Its position does not change when the list is scrolled. This characteristic is very helpful, for example, for column headings and the like.

NEW-PAGE [`options` [`options`]].

NEW-PAGE starts a new page in list processing. Empty pages cannot be created, because this command is only effective in connection with actual output in the list. Numerous clauses control the remaining structure of the list. The clauses for this command are shown in Table 8.5.

Table 8.5   Clauses for the NEW-PAGE command

Clause	Description
NO-TITLE	No output of title lines, beginning with the next page.
WITH-TITLE	Output of the title line.
NO-HEADING	No more output of column headings.
WITH-HEADING	Output of column headings.
LINE-COUNT *line_number*	New number (amount) of lines, beginning with the next page.

Table 8.5 continued   Clauses for the NEW-PAGE command

Clause	Description
LINE-SIZE *column_number*	New line length, beginning with the next page.
PRINT ON [*secondary clauses*]	Interpret all subsequent output as print statements. About 25 differentiating secondary clauses are possible.
PRINT OFF	End the print control started with PRINT ON.

ON CHANGE OF *field* [**OR** *field_2*]. ... **ENDON**.

This statement is used in SELECT loops or in GET processing blocks. It has the effect that the statements enclosed by ON and ENDON are executed only if the contents of *field* change in comparison to the preceding execution of the command. With the OR clause, you can define any number of additional fields that also trigger processing of the statements.

OPEN DATASET *filename*
  [**FOR OUTPUT** | **FOR INPUT** | **FOR APPENDING**]
  [**IN BINARY MODE** | **IN TEXT MODE**]
  [**AT POSITION**]
  [**TYPE** *attribute*]
  [**MESSAGE** *text_field*]
  [**FILTER** *command*].

The specified file is opened. This is a file at operating system level. The filename can or must therefore satisfy the requirements of the operating system and possibly contain drive and directory path specifications. The three FOR clauses determine what action is to occur: reading from the file, writing to the file or appending data to the end of the file. The IN TEXT MODE clause causes read procedures always to read a whole line. The end of a line is recognized by an (operating-system-dependent) end-of-line character. In write procedures, this end-of-line character is appended automatically after every write procedure. The IN BINARY MODE clause (default) ensures that all transforming of data is suppressed. With AT POSITION, you can specify any position in the file as the starting position. You use TYPE to pass operating-system-dependent attributes to the system. The use of the MESSAGE option places an error message delivered by the operating system into the specified field, in case the opening of the file fails. The *command* field in the FILTER clause specifies an operating system command with which the data to be processed is handled.

OPEN CURSOR [**WITH HOLD**] *cursor* **FOR** *SELECT-statement*.

The database cursor for the table specified in the SELECT statement is opened. The cursor must be of type CURSOR, that is, it must be declared with TYPE CURSOR.

OVERLAY *field_1* **WITH** *field_2* [**ONLY** *field_3*].

The contents of *field_2* are transferred character by character into *field_1*, although only for those positions in *field_1* where there is a blank space. With ONLY, you can define an alternative set of characters that should be overwritten in *field_1*. All of the fields involved are handled as character fields (type C), regardless of their actual type.

PACK *source_field* **TO** *target_field*.

The contents of the source field are packed and stored in the target field.

PARAMETERS *parameter* [*clauses*].

In list processing, you declare parameters that appear on the selection screen. Numerous clauses allow targeted setting of the parameter's attributes. The clauses possible are shown in Table 8.6.

Table 8.6   Clauses for the PARAMETERS statement

Clause	Description
DEFAULT *value*	The parameter is filled with a default value before display on the selection screen.
TYPE type	The parameter field receives the data type specified.
DECIMALS *decimal_places*	Gives the number of decimal places for parameters of type P.
LIKE *field*	The attributes of the parameter field are derived from an existing field.
MEMORY ID *G/S-parameter*	The parameter field on the selection screen is linked to a Get/Set parameter.
MATCHCODE OBJECT *matchcode*	A matchcode is linked to the parameter field of the selection screen.
MODIF ID *modification_group*	The parameter field on the selection screen receives the specified modification group as an attribute.
NO-DISPLAY	The parameter does not appear on the selection screen. The value for the parameter is transferred only in a SUBMIT.
LOWER CASE	No automatic conversion into uppercase.
OBLIGATORY	Input on the selection screen is mandatory for this parameter.
AS CHECKBOX	The parameter appears as a check box.
RADIOBUTTON GROUP *radi*	The parameter appears as a radio button in the specified group.
FOR TABLE *table*	Assignment of a database-specific parameter to a table (only in the access program of a logical database).
AS MATCHCODE STRUCTURE	Database-specific parameter for selection using matchcodes.
VALUE-REQUEST	Only for database-specific parameters. Input help can be assigned to the parameter with the event AT SELECTION SCREEN ON VALUE-REQUEST.
HELP-REQUEST	Only for database-specific parameters. Custom help can be assigned to the parameter with the event AT SELECTION SCREEN ON HELP-REQUEST.

```
PERFORM [subroutine | index_field]
  [(program) |
  IN PROGRAM program |
  OF subroutine_n ... | ON COMMIT]
  [TABLES Itab_n ...]
  [USING parameter_n]
  [CHANGING parameter_n]
  [IF FOUND].
```

The specified subroutine, defined with FORM, is called. With the clauses TABLES, USING and CHANGING, internal tables or field parameters are passed as current parameters.

Using the clauses (program) or IN PROGRAM, you can call subroutines from other programs. In the case of IN PROGRAM, you can also pass the program and subroutine names dynamically. IF FOUND suppresses any runtime errors that might be generated if the external subroutine called is not available. With OF, you can address the subroutine to be called with an index. The names of the subroutines in question appear after OF. No name appears after PERFORM. Instead, PERFORM is followed by a data field that must contain a valid index.

The ON COMMIT clause causes the subroutine not to be executed until a COMMIT WORK. Parameter passing is not possible in this case. The data must be stored in program-internal fields or in global memory until the update event.

```
POSITION column.
```

The column position for the next output is set in the list output.

```
PRINT-CONTROL [clauses].
```

With the clauses, you can set various settings for the print format of the subsequent output lines. There are numerous clauses, which are listed in Table 8.7.

Table 8.7   Clauses for the PRINT-CONTROL command

Clause	Description
CPI	Specifies the number of characters per inch.
LPI	Specifies the number of lines per inch.
SIZE	Specifies the font size.
COLOR	Specifies the output color for color-capable printers (BLACK, RED, BLUE, GREEN, YELLOW or PINK).
LEFT MARGIN	Sets the left margin.
FONT	Specifies the font type.
FUNCTION	Addresses a function directly.
LINE	Specifies the output line that the PRINT-CONTROL should affect.
POSITION	Specifies the column in the output line, determined by LINE, that PRINT-CONTROL should affect.

PRINT-CONTROL INDEX-LINE *field*.

Output of the contents of *field* as an invisible index line.

PROVIDE { *field* ... **FROM** *Itab*} **BETWEEN** *start* **AND** *end*. ...
ENDPROVIDE.

All of the contents of the specified fields of the internal tables are prepared according to ranges. Afterwards, the statements between PROVIDE and ENDPROVIDE are executed for every range.

PUT *table*.

This statement is only usable in the access program of a logical database. It triggers the GET event in the applicable report. Afterwards, all PUT subroutines of all subordinate tables are executed, assuming GET events exist for these tables in the report.

RAISE *exception*.

This command triggers an exception in a function module. If this exception is not handled in the calling program, the system generates a runtime error.

RANGES *selection_table* **FOR** *field*.

A selection table is defined for the specified field. The structure of the table corresponds to that of selection tables created by SELECT-OPTIONS. The table can be used in the program like a selection. Tables defined with RANGES, also called range tables, do not appear on selection screens, however, but must be filled manually in the program with values for a valid selection.

READ TABLE *Itab* [**INTO** *work_area*]
  [**WITH KEY** {*field* = *key_value*} | = *key* | *key*
    [**BINARY SEARCH**] |
    INDEX *index*]
  [**COMPARING** {*fields*} | **ALL FIELDS**]
  [**TRANSPORTING** {*fields*} | **NO FIELDS**].

This statement reads a data record from an internal table. The result is made available either in the table header line or in a work area named with INTO. All fields are transferred, as long as no selection is specified with TRANSPORTING. If it is just a matter of finding a data record (existence check or index determination), you can save processing time by using TRANSPORTING NO FIELDS to suppress the transfer of values.

The data record to be read can be selected various ways. You can specify the data record number using INDEX. You can define a search key using the various WITH KEY clauses, either field by field or by specifying a work area with several key values. In connection with WITH KEY, you can speed up the search using the BINARY SEARCH clause, if the table is presorted according to the key used. In this case, the statement executes a binary search instead of a sequential search. The standard form of the READ command (without a WITH KEY clause) awaits the key in the header line of the internal table. In this case, the key consists of all of the fields of the header line that are not type I, F or P, and whose contents are not equal to blank spaces.

The COMPARING clause leads to an additional comparison between the fields of the record read and the header line. It does not prevent the transfer of the record; it just sets the system field SY-SUBRC. This is helpful for checking non-key fields.

READ LINE *line_number*
  [**INDEX** *list*]
  [**FIELD VALUE** {*source_field* **INTO** *target_field*}]
  [**OF CURRENT PAGE** | **OF PAGE** *page*].

A line identified by the line number is read from a list. Without clauses, the line count is global. The two PAGE clauses cause page-related line counting; reading is done either on the current page or on the explicitly specified page. Reading occurs in the current list, if no list level is selected with the INDEX clause. The FIELD VALUE clause causes the field contents of the list line to be provided not in the source fields but rather in other, expressly specified program-internal fields.

READ CURRENT LINE
  [**FIELD VALUE** {*source_field* **INTO** *target_field*}].

The current line of the list (selected by line selection or READ LINE *line*) is read again. You can use FIELD VALUE to store the fields read in fields other than the original fields.

READ REPORT *program* **INTO** *Itab*.

The source code of the specified program is read into the internal table *Itab*. In protected systems, this command delivers the source code for non-SAP programs only.

READ TEXTPOOL *program* **INTO** *Itab* **LANGUAGE** *language*.

This statement reads the text elements of a program of the specified language into an internal table.

READ DATASET *filename* **INTO** *field* [**LENGTH** *length*].

A data record from an operating system file opened with OPEN is read and provided in the specified field. If the file was opened in binary mode, characters are read until the target field is filled. The structure of the target field should therefore correspond to the structure of the data stored. If the file was opened in text mode, one line is read. Characters are lost if the length of the target field is smaller than the length of the line read. With the LENGTH clause, the number of characters actually read can be made available in the *length* field.

READ TABLE *database_table*.

This command is outdated. Its task (reading a record in a database table) has since been taken over by the SELECT statement.

REFRESH CONTROL *control* **FROM SCREEN** *screen*.

The element *control*, defined with the statement CONTROLS, is reinitialized in the specified screen.

REFRESH *Itab*.

The internal table *Itab* is reset; all of the data records contained in it are deleted. The header line, however, remains unchanged.

REFRESH *Itab* **FROM TABLE** *database_table*.

This command is outdated and should no longer be used. Use SELECT INTO Itab instead.

REFRESH SCREEN.

This command redisplays the current screen after receipt of an RFC event. This has the same effect as pressing the Enter key.

REJECT *[database_table]*.

This command ends processing of the current data record from the current database table. Processing continues with the next record. Explicit specification of a filename causes the next data record of the specified table to be processed. This type of call is useful, for example, in GET processing for logical databases. The specified table must be at the same or a higher hierarchical level than the current table.

REPLACE *pattern_1* **WITH** *pattern_2* **INTO** *field* **[LENGTH** *length*].

This command executes character string processing. All of the fields involved are handled as fields of type C, regardless of their actual types. In the target field, *field*, the first instance of *pattern_1* is replaced by *pattern_2*. Trailing blank spaces are included! To prevent this, you must use the LENGTH clause, which allows you to specify the relevant length of the search pattern, *pattern_1*.

REPORT *program_name*
    [**NO STANDARD PAGE HEADING**]
    [**LINE-SIZE** *number_of_columns*]
    [**LINE-COUNT** *number_of_lines*[(*footer_lines*)]]
    [**MESSAGE-ID** *message_class*]
    [**DEFINING DATABASE** *logical_database*].

This introduces a report. The possible clauses determine various characteristics of the report. With NO STANDARD PAGE HEADING, you can turn off output of the default page header. The LINE-SIZE clause determines the width of the list in characters. The maximum value is 255. If this clause is left out, the page width of the report is determined at runtime based on the current window size. This can have an effect on the structure of the list! With LINE-COUNT, you can specify the page length and the area to be reserved for any footer lines. The default value for footer lines is 0. If the page length is not specified, page breaks can only be triggered with the NEW-PAGE command. If messages are to be output in the report, you can set the name of a message class with MESSAGE-ID. A message class is required for the simplified form of the MESSAGE command.

The DEFINING DATABASE clause is necessary only in the access programs of a logical database. Since these programs are automatically generated, you do not generally have to enter this clause manually.

RESERVE *number_of_lines* **LINES**.

This statement causes a page break in list processing, if the specified number of lines is no longer available on the current page.

`ROLLBACK WORK.`

All of the changes to the database since the last COMMIT WORK are reversed.

```
SCROLL LIST [INDEX index]
   [LINE line] TO FIRST PAGE |
   [LINE line] TO LAST PAGE |
   [LINE line] TO PAGE page |
   [LINE line] TO COLUMN column |
   [pages PAGES] FORWARD |
   [pages PAGES] BACKWARD |
   [BY characters PLACES] LEFT |
   [BY characters PLACES] RIGHT.
```

With this command, program-controlled scrolling of the current section of the list can be performed in list processing. The SCROLL command is only complete if it is used with one of the clauses (TO FIRST PAGE ... RIGHT). The effects of these clauses are visible in their names.

Besides the mandatory clauses, there are also optional supplements. With the INDEX clause, you specify the number of the list (list level). The other clauses specify the direction and scope of scrolling. With LINE, you specify the line on the target page where positioning should take place. In the case of the FORWARD and BACKWARD clauses, PAGES determines the number of pages that the section should be moved. Analogous to this, in the case of horizontal scrolling with LEFT and RIGHT, the BY PLACES clause defines the number of characters that the section should be moved.

```
SEARCH [ field | Itab ] FOR character_string
   [ABBREVIATED]
   [STARTING AT start]
   [ENDING AT end]
   [AND MARK].
```

The specified field or internal table (the entire table except for the header line) is searched for the specified character string. The character string can contain the wildcard, asterisk (*), as a place holder for any characters either at the beginning or at the end. With the ABBREVIATED clause, the command also finds the search pattern even if the characters to be searched for are separated from one another by other characters in the search field. With STARTING and ENDING, you can restrict the search to a specified area. For internal tables, these clauses specify the lines in which to search. The AND MARK clause converts the found character string in the search field or in the internal table into uppercase.

All of the fields involved, in particular the data records of the internal table, are handled as fields of type C.

```
SELECT [[SINGLE [FOR UPDATE]] | [DISTINCT]] field_list
   [ [INTO (field, ...) |
          work_area |
```

```
         TABLE Itab [PACKAGE SIZE number_of_records]] |
     [APPENDING TABLE Itab[PACKAGE SIZE number_of_records] ] ]
  FROM table | (name_field)
     [CLIENT SPECIFIED] [BYPASSING BUFFER] [UP TO n ROWS]
  [WHERE condition]
  [GROUP BY field_list]
  [ORDER BY field_list | PRIMARY KEY].
```

The SELECT statement is used to read data records from database tables. It consists of several clauses, which determine the behavior of the statement. The functionality of the SELECT statement is largely dependent on the current release version. In its basic form, the SELECT statement is a loop statement that must be closed with the ENDSELECT statement.

The specifications of the SELECT clause specify the type of output data (single record or data set), as well as the fields to be returned. With the SINGLE clause, you compel the return of an individual record. This record must be uniquely identified by the WHERE clause. The optional clause FOR UPDATE locks this record against processing by third parties. The ENDSELECT statement must be left out for this clause. The DISTINCT clause causes identical output records to be suppressed. The SELECT clause requires the specification of a field list that contains all of the fields to be returned. This field list can consist of an asterisk as the symbol for all fields, a list of fields or aggregate expressions.

The INTO clause determines the target for the data records read. Depending on the field list of the SELECT clause, this can be a work area (a field string), a list of individual fields or an internal table. The target is flushed before it is overwritten. In connection with internal tables, using the APPENDING clause instead of the INTO clause appends data to the internal table. No ENDSELECT is needed when transferring a selection result, unless a maximum number of data records to be written into the internal table has been predefined with PACKAGE SIZE. In that case, looping ends when all of the data records have been read.

In addition to the SELECT clause, the FROM clause is also mandatory. It determines from which table the data should be read. The table name can be passed statically or dynamically. Three optional clauses determine details of the selection procedure. Their association with the FROM clause is not necessarily logical; rather, their assignment is a historical necessity. CLIENT SPECIFIED turns off automatic client handling. The client field must then be analyzed manually. The BYPASSING BUFFER clause triggers direct reading from the database; any buffers are ignored. With UP TO n ROWS, you determine how many data records should be returned.

The WHERE clause contains the logical condition according to which data records are selected from the table.

With GROUP BY, you can combine data records that have identical attributes into groups. The field list of this statement must correspond to the field list of the SELECT clause.

The ORDER BY clause sorts the data records to be output according to the specified field list or according to the key, if the clause PRIMARY KEY is used instead of the field list.

SELECT-OPTIONS *selection* **FOR** *field*.

This statement only makes sense in reports. It declares a selection table. This table can be filled with values by the user in the selection screen of a report. You can modify the characteristics of the selection with a multitude of different parameters (see Table 8.8).

Table 8.8   Clauses for the SELECT-OPTIONS statement

Clause	Effect
DEFAULT...	Set default value(s).
MEMORY ID	Global parameter as default value.
MATCHCODE OBJECT	Left field on the selection screen with matchcode.
MODIF ID	Assignment of a modification group for the attribute SCREEN-GROUP1 to the screen fields of a selection.
NO-DISPLAY	Selection does not appear on the selection screen.
LOWER CASE	Distinction between uppercase and lowercase.
OBLIGATORY	Entry mandatory.
NO-EXTENSION	Only one line can be entered.
NO DATABASE SELECTION	Selection is not used in logical databases.
VALUE REQUEST	Allow custom-programmed value help.
HELP REQUEST	Allow custom-programmed help.

SELECTION-SCREEN `clause`.

The SELECTION-SCREEN statement is used to design the selection screen. It therefore makes sense only in reports. The statement requires the use of one of the clauses shown in Table 8.9.

Table 8.9   Clauses for the SELECTION-SCREEN command

Clause	Effect
BEGIN OF LINE	All elements declared subsequently are arranged in a line.
END OF LINE	End of the declaration of a line.
SKIP	Insertion of blank lines.
ULINE	Underlining of a line.
POSITION	Positioning of an element.
COMMENT	Output of static text.
PUSHBUTTON	Creation of a pushbutton on the selection screen.

Table 8.9 continued   Clauses for the SELECTION-SCREEN command

Clause	Effect
BEGIN OF BLOCK	Beginning of a block, which can be given a box.
END OF BLOCK	End of the declaration of a block.
FUNCTION KEY	Declaration of a pushbutton in the pushbutton bar.
BEGIN OF VERSION	Beginning of a declaration of a version of a selection screen.
END OF VERSION	End of a version declaration.
EXCLUDE	Excluding of elements from a version of a selection screen.
DYNAMIC SELECTIONS FOR TABLE	Declaration of additional limitations.

SET PF-STATUS *status*
  [**EXCLUDING** *function_code* | *Itab*].

Sets a status of the current user interface. With the EXCLUDING clause, you can deactivate selected function codes from this status. You may pass a single status to be deactivated as a constant. Several deactivations require the passing of the corresponding function codes as an internal table.

SET TITLEBAR *title_name* [**WITH** *parameter* ...].

Sets the heading of the current window. The title is maintained separately from the source code with a separate tool and is identified with a three-place identifier. In the title, plain or numbered place holders (&, &1–&9) can appear that are replaced by the parameters of the WITH clause.

SET SCREEN *screen_number*.

Sets the number of the screen that should be executed after processing ends for the current screen. A value of 0 for the subsequent screen leads to program exiting. The statement is used only in dialog applications.

SET CURSOR
  FIELD *field_name* [**OFFSET** *offset* | **LINE** *line*] |
  LINE *line* [**OFFSET** *offset*] |
  column line.

The cursor is placed in a certain location. The three clauses possible specify the type of positioning. The FIELD clause requires as a parameter a field that contains the name of the field on which the cursor should be placed. The OFFSET clause allows you to specify a character position within the field. In lists or step loops, you must also set the desired line with the LINE clause, since field names are ambiguous in this case.

When used as the primary clause, LINE positions the cursor on the specified line of a list or a step loop. In this case, too, you can use an offset for positioning within the line.

In screens, the cursor can be placed in any location by the direct specification of a line and a column.

SET PARAMETER ID *parameter* **FIELD** *field*.

Fills the global parameter *parameter* with the contents of *field*.

SET LANGUAGE *language*.

When this command is executed, language-dependent elements are output in the new language from that point on. The statement's effect is restricted to the current program.

SET COUNTRY *country*.

With this statement, you change the country identifier, which affects the display of the decimal point and the date. This statement takes effect across program boundaries.

SET BLANK LINES [**ON** | **OFF**].

With this statement, you determine whether or not blank lines should be suppressed during output. The default setting is SET BLANK LINES OFF.

SET MARGIN *column* [*line*].

This statement is useful only in reporting. After this command, printouts occur starting only at the specified line and column, that is, this statement creates an additional margin.

SET USER-COMMAND *field*.

This statement is useful only in reporting. The specified field contains a function code that is temporarily stored. In the next list display, processing is immediately executed for this function code, as though it had been triggered by the user.

SET LEFT SCROLL-BOUNDARY [**COLUMN** *column*].

This statement fixes in place on the screen all of the columns to the left of the current column or to the left of the position specified with COLUMN. Horizontal scrolling of the screen contents does not affect the columns fixed this way.

SET EXTENDED CHECK [**ON** | **OFF**].

This statement has no function during program processing. It is only analyzed by the syntax check of the editor or the check transaction SLIN. With SET EXTENDED CHECK OFF, you turn off expanded syntax checking. With SET EXTENDED CHECK ON, you turn it on again.

SET PROPERTY OF *object property* = *field* [**NO FLUSH**].

This statement is used to process OLE objects. The attribute of an object created with DATA and initialized with CREATE is set to the specified value. The NO FLUSH clause gathers OLE requests in a buffer, where they remain until the buffer is emptied with FREE.

```
SHIFT character_string [BY n PLACES | UP TO pattern]
   [CIRCULAR | RIGHT | LEFT] |
   [LEFT DELETING LEADING pattern] |
   [RIGHT DELETING TRAILING pattern].
```

This statement is used to edit character strings. In its basic form, the contents of the character string are shifted one character to the left, meaning the first character is lost. With the BY clause, you can shift by more than one character. The clause UP TO causes a search for the pattern in the character string to be edited, and, if it is found, the shift is performed up to that pattern. All three variants can be given other clauses, which influence the direction of rotation. The LEFT clause is the default, so it can be left out. CIRCULAR causes a rotation of the contents, meaning the characters are not lost, but are instead appended to the right of the character string. RIGHT causes rotation to the right. The two DELETING clauses shift the contents of the character string until one of the characters of *pattern* appears in the first or last position.

All of the fields involved are handled as character strings, regardless of their actual types.

```
SKIP [lines | TO LINE line].
```

This statement is useful only in list processing. In its basic form, it causes the output of a blank line. As an option, you can set the number of blank lines to be inserted. Positioning on an absolute line is also possible.

```
SORT [DESCENDING | ASCENDING] [BY field_list | BY field_group].
```

The basic form of this statement sorts the extract data set according to the fields of the HEADER field group. With the clauses, you can determine the sorting sequence (ASCENDING or DESCENDING), as well as select a different sort key (field list or field group). All of the fields involved, however, must be defined in the HEADER field group.

```
SORT Itab [DESCENDING | ASCENDING] [BY field_list].
```

With this statement, you sort an internal table. All of the fields that are not numerical fields or tables serve as sort keys. You can specify the sort key for each field list, if desired. You can also determine the sorting sequence with ASCENDING and DESCENDING.

```
SPLIT character_string AT separator_sequence
   INTO [TABLE Itab | field_list].
```

This statement splits a character string according to the separator sequence. The separator sequence is used in its entire, that is, defined, length. This includes trailing blank spaces if the separator sequence was filled with too few characters! The subfields are stored either in the fields of the field list or in a separate data record of the internal table. If more subfields are created during the split than there are fields available in the field list, the last field accepts all subfields.

```
START-OF-SELECTION.
```

This list processing event is processed immediately before the first access of a table. It thus introduces the "main program" of a report. When a report starts, this kind of event is automatically triggered.

STATICS.

This command is a variant of the DATA statement. It is used to create so-called static variables in subroutines (performs). It can be used with the same clauses as the DATA statement. The difference between its data fields and those created by DATA is the life-span of the declared data fields. The fields are not destroyed when the subroutine in which they were defined is exited. They remain intact, as do their values. Their scope of validity, however, is restricted to the subroutine in which they were created.

STOP.

Ends data selection and outputs the list. After STOP, the END-OF-SELECTION event is processed.

SUBMIT *report clauses*.

This statement starts a report. There are about two dozen clauses you can use to set almost all of the important parameters for the called report. A selection of the most important clauses appears in Table 8.10.

Table 8.10   Important clauses of the SUBMIT command

Clause	Effect
VIA SELECTION-SCREEN	The selection screen of the called report is displayed.
AND RETURN	After the end of processing, return to the calling report.
USING SELECTION-SET	Execution of the report with a variant.
WITH	Filling of parameters and selections.

SUBTRACT *field_1* **FROM** *field_2*.

The contents of *field_1* are subtracted from *field_2*. The result is stored in *field_2*.

SUBTRACT-CORRESPONDING *field_string_1* **FROM** *field_string_2*.

Only those fields are considered whose name appears in both *field_string_1* and *field_string_2*. The contents of the fields in *field_string_1* are subtracted from the fields of *field_string_2* with the same names.

SUM.

In a LOOP step loop, after group processing, the subtotals of all numerical fields (types F, I, and P) are made available in the header line of the internal table.

SUMMING *field*.

This statement is useful only in reporting. An internal total field with the name SUM_*field_name* is created for the specified field. Every time the original field is output with WRITE, its current contents are added to the totals field. At any event, for example even after END-OF-SELECTION, the current total is available.

SUPPRESS DIALOG.

This statement makes sense only in a PBO module of a screen. It suppresses output of the screen on the screen, preventing data entry by the user. The flow logic commands, however, are executed.

TABLES *database_table.*

The specified table or view is declared in the program. A field string with the same name is created as a work area (header line). The specified object must exist in the Dictionary and be activated.

TOP-OF-PAGE [**DURING LINE-SELECTION**].

This event is processed in reporting at the beginning of the output of a new page. In its basic form, the statement is responsible only for the basic list (first list level). For the page headers of all details lists, the statement TOP-OF-PAGE DURING LINE-SELECTION is processed.

TRANSFER *field* **TO** *filename* [**LENGTH** *length*].

The contents of *field* are written into the specified file. If the file does not yet exist, the TRANSFER command attempts to create it. The form of output depends on the mode in which the file is created (see OPEN). You can restrict the number of characters to be written by specifying an output length (optional).

TRANSLATE *character_string*
   TO UPPER CASE |
   TO LOWER CASE |
   USING *pattern* |
   FROM CODE PAGE *character_set_1* **TO CODE PAGE** *character_set_2* |
   FROM NUMBER FORMAT *format_1* **TO NUMBER FORMAT** *format_2.*

The contents of the character string are converted, after which the result reappears in *character_string*. In addition to conversion into upper- or lowercase, individual characters can be translated into others with USING. The translation is defined in *pattern*. In this parameter (field or constant), the character to be replaced and the new character appear one after the other in pairs.

With the FROM CODE PAGE clause and the TO CODE PAGE clause, the transformation occurs based on a translation table in which various character sets or code tables can be maintained with the SPAD transaction. The clauses FROM NUMBER FORMAT and TO NUMBER FORMAT transform numbers between different system-dependent displays.

TYPES *type.*

The TYPES statement defines user-specific data types. Its parameters correspond to those of the DATA statement, meaning that fields, field strings and internal tables can be defined. To be able to use the types defined with TYPES, you must create a data field using DATA ... TYPE.

ULINE [**AT** [*/position(length)*]].

In its basic form, this statement creates a continuous underline. With a format specification, you can define both the starting position and the length of the output underline.

UNPACK *source* **TO** *target*.

The packed contents of the source field are unpacked and placed into the target field. Depending on the length of *target*, it is either filled with leading zeros or truncated.

UPDATE *table* **SET** *assignment* ...
  [**WHERE** *condition*]
  [**CLIENT SPECIFIED**].

You use this statement to update individual fields of a table. The assignment of the new value takes place in the form *table_field = value*. The value can be a field or the result of an arithmetic expression, in which only addition or subtraction is possible, however. You can restrict the set of data records to be updated by using the WHERE clause. Without the WHERE clause, all of the data records are modified. With the CLIENT SPECIFIED clause, automatic client handling is turned off, meaning that the client field must be manually given correct sort criteria. In an UPDATE statement, you can use the colon mechanism to link together several substatements. The WHERE clause and the CLIENT clause, respectively, count as only one of the substatements.

UPDATE *table* | ******table* | (*table_name*)
  [**FROM** *field_string*] | [**FROM TABLE** *Itab*]
  [**CLIENT SPECIFIED**].

In its basic form (without the FROM TABLE clause), this statement modifies exactly one data record of the database table. The new data, including the key fields, which must uniquely identify the data record to be modified, are taken from the header line or from the specified work area. With the CLIENT SPECIFIED clause, you can turn off automatic client handling.

The new data can also be taken from an internal table, which you include in the UPDATE statement with the FROM TABLE clause.

WHILE *logical_expression*
  [**VARY** *field* **FROM** *field_a* **NEXT** *field_b*].

The statements between WHILE and ENDWHILE are executed until the analysis of the logical expression returns the value for true. The same statements are possible in the logical expression as are possible for IF.

The VARY clause enables a value assignment to *field* in the WHILE loop. In the first iteration, *field* receives the value of *field_a*, in the second that of *field_b*. In further iterations, the new field contents are taken from the field whose address is the result of the addition of the distance between *field_a* and *field_b* to the respective last field.

WINDOW STARTING AT *x1 y1* [**ENDING AT** *x2 y2*].

The current list is displayed in a popup. The values *x1* and *y1* specify the upper left corner of the popup in the current window. The lower right corner is identical to that of the current window or is specified with the ENDING AT clause.

```
WRITE [AT /position(output_length)] field
   [display_option]
   [output_format]
   [AS CHECKBOX] | [AS SYMBOL].
```

The WRITE statement is used only in list display. It writes the contents of a field into the output list. The output takes place according to the field's type in the default output length. You can use the AT clause to position the output in a line and limit its length. A multitude of clauses and parameters allow the output appearance to be modified. The display options (see Table 8.11) influence the display of the value, while the output formats enable the setting of color and intensity. These output formats correspond to the parameters of the FORMAT command.

Table 8.11   Display options for the WRITE command

Display option	Effect
NO-ZERO	Suppress leading zeros.
NO-SIGN	Do not output a plus or minus sign.
DD/MM/YY	Represent date according to the template.
MM/DD/YY	Represent date according to the template.
DD/MM/YYYY	Represent date according to the template.
MM/DD/YYYY	Represent date according to the template.
DDMMYY	Represent date according to the template.
MMDDYY	Represent date according to the template.
YYMMDD	Represent date according to the template.
CURRENCY	Display according to the currency.
DECIMALS	Number of decimal places to display.
ROUND	Rounds a P field.
UNIT	Display according to the unit of measure.
EXPONENT	Output as exponential number with the predefined exponent.
USING EDIT MASK	Use the formatting template.
USING NO EDIT MASK	Do not execute the conversion routine from the Dictionary.
UNDER	Output exactly below another field.
NO-GAP	Suppress separators (blank spaces) after output.
LEFT-JUSTIFIED	Align to the left in the output field.
CENTERED	Center in the output field.
RIGHT-JUSTIFIED	Align to the right in the output field.

```
WRITE field | (field_name) TO target[+offset(length)]
  [display_option]
  [INDEX data_record_number].
```

The WRITE TO statement writes its output not to the screen list, but rather into another field. You can specify an offset within the field for the target, and you can specify the length of the area to be overwritten. The characters to be passed can be processed with several of the display options from Table 8.11. It is also possible to write directly into a data record of an internal table, which must be identified with the data record number.

8.3   System fields

The system fields fill the system with current values at runtime. Some of these fields are of considerable importance in the applications, because they provide information about the status of the system. Others are used only for communication between various basic programs and are of no interest to application developers. This subsection describes the meaning of the most important system fields, organized by topic area and notes on their use.

When debugging an application, you can display the system fields either individually by entering their full name, or together, as a list. In the latter variant, you must select the debugger mode for field display (*Goto → Fields*). Enter SY or SYST as the field name. When you press the Enter key, all of the system fields appear. They are managed internally as elements of the field string SY or SYST (the names are synonymous).

8.3.1   Miscellaneous

This group contains fields that are not easily assigned to one topic area or another. This does not mean that these fields are not important. Several of the fields of this group are the most-used system fields of all!

SY-ABCDE

This field contains the alphabet used in uppercase letters. It can be used to check correct input, although that is seldom done this way in practice.

SY-DATAR

This field is initialized before the execution of a screen. After editing, but before execution of the first PAI module, the field is set to "X" if data has been changed in the screen. This allows data changes to be recognized in Exit modules and confirmation prompts to be performed, if necessary.

SY-DBCNT

After a database operation, this field contains the number of elements processed or found. This field is often used, for example, in connection with a SELECT statement, to determine whether 0, 1 or several data records exist for a certain search term. You can also use the COUNT clause in the SELECT statement for this, which also places its result in this system variable.

SY-FDPOS

Various commands for character string processing and operators in logical statements (for example, CP, CS and so on) fill this field with the position of the character string found. The field contents of SY-FDPOS can be used to make replacements in the character string or to extract a substring.

SY-LANGU

When the user logs on, this field is filled with the abbreviation for the current language. Many system-internal tools determine the correct language-dependent text and messages based on this field. This field must be analyzed in applications that create language-dependent tables themselves, for example those that contain written descriptions for a data record.

SY-MANDT

When used, this field is filled with the current client number. Analysis is seldom required, since client fields are automatically handled by the system. It may be useful, however, to lock or release certain applications in particular clients by querying this field, for example in the test phase.

SY-SUBRC

This is the most often used system field. After execution of many statements, it contains a value that provides information about the correct execution of the command. Examples of this are the OPEN SQL statements and the call of function modules.

SY-UNAME

When the user logs on to the system, this field is filled with the user's logon name. This name is used by authorization checking, for example, to determine the current authorization profile of the user. In applications, the field is often used in a data record to store the name of the last user to change that data record.

8.3.2   Flow control

SY-DYNGR

In the attributes of a screen, a value can be maintained for something known as a screen group. This attribute is optional. It is used relatively rarely. During processing of a screen, the value of the screen group attribute is held in the SY-DYNGR field.

SY-DYNNR

During processing of a screen, this field contains the number of the current screen. This value is used quite often, to execute the statements that refer specifically to a certain screen in modules that are used by several screens. This may be, for example, for setting a status or for deactivating function codes depending on the screen number.

SY-INDEX

Loop iterations (LOOP, DO, SELECT ...) are counted in this field. The value is occasionally used in a loop to create a consecutive number or simply to count actions. This value is current only within the loop in question. Outside the loop the value is undefined.

SY-LOOPC

This field contains the number of lines of a step loop that are visible on the screen. The contents are valid only within the scope of validity of a LOOP–ENDLOOP loop in the flow logic (that is, also within the modules and subroutines called from there).

SY-PFKEY

This field contains the name of the current status of the user interface. Analysis of this field is seldom required.

SY-REPID

The name of the current program is stored in this field.

SY-STEPL

In a LOOP–ENDLOOP loop in the flow logic, the number of the step loop line currently being processed is placed in this field. Like SY-LOOPC, the value is valid only within the loop. Analysis is required only in special cases.

SY-TCODE

When a transaction is executed, the transaction code is placed in this field. Since applications are often called with different transactions, this field is often used to select a concrete action within an application (for example, Create, Change, Display) or to select a value range for authorization checking.

SY-UCOMM

When a function code is triggered, it is placed in the SY-UCOMM field. Since the function code is also analyzed by other fields, such as the OK Code field of a screen, there is no read access to SY-UCOMM. Often, however, program-internal data fields that should accept a function code are derived from SY-UCOMM using LIKE.

8.3.3 Internal tables

Several system fields are set during processing of internal tables, too. These fields mainly provide information about the size and state of the table. Two of these fields are used quite often.

SY-TABIX

This field contains the number of the current data record of the most recently processed internal table. This field is updated, for example, when a data record is searched for with the READ statement. If this data record should be written back to the table after a modification, the MODIFY command requires the specification of the data record number.

SY-TFILL

This field is valid only in a LOOP program loop in an internal table. It contains the number of the data records in the internal table.

8.3.4 Text and messages

Certain system fields can be used to access certain text or properties of messages. Although this is done relatively rarely in applications, it is sometimes helpful to use these fields when debugging an application.

SY-MSGID

This field contains the message ID of the last message triggered.

SY-MSGNO

This field contains the number of the last message triggered.

SY-MSGTY

This field contains the type (E, I, W, S, A) of the last message triggered.

SY-MSGV1 to SY-MSGV4

These four fields contain the character strings that were used to replace the place holders in a message text.

SY-TITLE

This field contains the title of an application.

SY-ULINE

The system stores the character used for underlining in this field.

SY-VLINE

The system stores the character used for vertical bars in this field.

8.3.5   Time and date

Date and time specifications are used very often, for example to log the time a data record was changed. Accordingly, several of these fields are used quite often.

SY-DATUM

This field accepts the current date.

SY-DAYST

This field is set when daylight savings time is active.

SY-FDAYW

This field contains the number of the weekday according to the factory calendar.

SY-TZONE

The difference in seconds between the current time and Greenwich Mean Time (GMT) is stored in this field.

SY-UZEIT

In this field, the system stores the current time.

8.3.6   Screen and list design

Generally, the tools provided by the system for output layout are sufficient. In order for these tools to be able to work correctly, however, they need some information about the current status of the list or the screen. These values are stored in system fields and can in certain cases also be of interest in custom applications.

SY-COLNO

When a list is output, the column (character position within a line) is stored in this field.

SY-CPAGE

Current page number.

SY-CUCOL, SY-CUROW

Current cursor position.

SY-LINCT

This field contains the number of lines in a list.

SY-LINNO

This field contains the current line number during the creation of an output list.

SY-LINSZ

The system stores the usable line length of the list in this field. This value is the result either of the list width set with LINE-SIZE or of the current window size, if no value has been set for the page width. It is conceivable that the formatting of a list could be modified to fit the available space, that is, the output length of very wide fields could be shortened or fields could be hidden entirely. This only makes sense, however, if the list is mainly designed to be output on screen, since the formatting in printed lists is predefined in much detail.

SY-MACOL, SY-MAROW

With the SET MARGIN statement, you can define an empty area on the left and upper sides that is not printed on. The measurements of this area (left margin and upper margin) are available in these two fields.

SY-PAGNO

When a list is being output, this field contains the number of the current page.

SY-SCOLS, SY-SROWS

The system stores the measurements of the screen in these two fields. These values are updated when the user changes the size of the screen. These values could be used to adjust the structure of a list to the screen size.

8.3.7   Window

The fields of the window group provide information about the size and position of a window, as well as the position of the cursor.

SY-WINX1, SY-WINY1

The upper left corner of the window, relative to the superordinate window.

SY-WINX2, SY-WINY2

The lower right corner of the window, relative to the superordinate window.

SY-WINCO, SY-WINRO

Position of the cursor in the window.

8.3.8   Interactive reporting

In interactive reporting, the transfer of information takes place not only with the hidden data area (see the HIDE command), but also with several system fields. However, these fields provide only supplementary information that is useful only in special cases.

SY-LILLI

After a line selection, this field contains the absolute number of the list line selected.

SY-LISEL

After a line selection, this field contains the contents of the selected line. Since the assignment to the individual fields is lost, it is seldom useful to analyze the contents of this field.

SY-LSIND

This field is of considerable importance. It contains the list level. The basic list has the value 0, the first details list has the value 1 and so on. This field is used at various AT events to select the program branch required to build the list.

SY-STACO, SY-STARO

These two fields contain the coordinates of the first character displayed in the list, or, put a different way, the number of the first row in the window and the number of the first column displayed. These fields have an initial value of 1. This value changes if the list is scrolled. If branching into other lists occurs, then these fields receive the corresponding values for the last list displayed, not for the current list.

8.3.9   System-related fields

These fields, which provide information about the current R/3 System, are of no interest for most applications. Analysis is required only in very special cases, such as when Native SQL statements are used.

SY-DBSYS

This field contains the identifier of the database system.

SY-HOST

This field contains the name of the computer on which the R/3 System is running. This name is identical to the system name that is displayed in the status bar.

SY-OPSYS

The name of the operating system is stored in this field.

SY-SAPRL

This field contains the identifier of the system's release version.

SY-SYSID

This field provides the name of the R/3 System. This value is also displayed in the status bar.

9 Listings

What follows are the listings for the second sample application mentioned in Chapter 6.

9.1 Flow logic for the initial screen

```
PROCESS BEFORE OUTPUT.
  MODULE D9100_INIT.
*
PROCESS AFTER INPUT.
  MODULE D9100_EXIT AT EXIT-COMMAND.
  MODULE D9100_READ_DATA.
  MODULE D9100_USER_COMMAND.
```

9.2 Flow logic for the edit screen

```
PROCESS BEFORE OUTPUT.
  MODULE D9200_INIT.

  LOOP.
    MODULE D9200_FILL_LINE.
  ENDLOOP.

*
PROCESS AFTER INPUT.
  MODULE D9200_EXIT AT EXIT-COMMAND.

  LOOP.
    FIELD YZZKURS-KURS
      MODULE D9200_DATA_CHANGED ON REQUEST.

    FIELD YZZKURS-KURS
      MODULE D9200_MODIFY_ITAB.
  ENDLOOP.

  MODULE D9200_USER_COMMAND.
```

9.3   Global declarations

```
PROGRAM SAPMYZZK MESSAGE-ID YZ.

TABLES:
  YZZAKT,
  YZZKURS,
  *YZZSKURS
  .      "tables

CONSTANTS:
  TRUE          VALUE 'X',
  FALSE         VALUE ' ',
  JA            VALUE 'J',
  NEIN          VALUE 'N',
  ABBRUCH       VALUE 'A',
  ON     TYPE I VALUE 1,
  OFF    TYPE I VALUE 0
  .      "constants

DATA:
  FCODE         LIKE SY-UCOMM,
  G_FCODE       LIKE FCODE,
  G_DATUM       LIKE YZZKURS-DATUM,
  G_LOOP_LINES  TYPE I,
  I             TYPE I,
  G_ITAB_OFFSET TYPE I,
  G_TABLEN      TYPE I,
  G_CHANGED LIKE FALSE VALUE FALSE,
  G_SAVE    LIKE FALSE VALUE FALSE,
  G_EXIT    LIKE FALSE VALUE FALSE,
  G_EXIT_MODULE LIKE FALSE VALUE FALSE,

  I_AKTIEN LIKE YZZAKT OCCURS 20,   " Itab for stocks
  F_AKTIEN LIKE LINE OF I_AKTIEN,   " Header line for I_AKTIEN

  I_KURSE  LIKE YZZKURS OCCURS 20,  " Itab for share prices
  F_KURSE  LIKE LINE OF I_KURSE     " Header line for I_KURSE
  .      " data
```

9.4   PBO modules

```
MODULE D9100_INIT OUTPUT.
  SET PF-STATUS 'STAT_G'.
  YZZKURS-DATUM = SY-DATUM.
ENDMODULE.                          " D9100_INIT OUTPUT
```

```
MODULE D9200_INIT OUTPUT.
  SET PF-STATUS 'STAT_A'.

*...remember number of data records in Itab
  DESCRIBE TABLE I_KURSE LINES G_TABLEN.

*...initialize global fields
  G_EXIT        = FALSE.
  G_EXIT_MODULE = FALSE.

ENDMODULE.                              " D9200_INIT  OUTPUT MODULE


D9200_FILL_LINE OUTPUT.

*...remember number of loop lines in screen
  G_LOOP_LINES = SY-LOOPC.

*...determine index for Itab
  I = G_ITAB_OFFSET + SY-STEPL - 1.

*...transfer data record from Itab into screen fields
  READ TABLE I_KURSE INDEX I INTO YZZKURS.
ENDMODULE.                              " D9200_FILL_LINE OUTPUT
```

9.5   PAI modules

```
MODULE D9100_EXIT INPUT.
  LEAVE TO SCREEN 0.
ENDMODULE.                              " D9100_EXIT INPUT


MODULE D9100_READ_DATA INPUT.

*...fill Itab for share prices
  PERFORM D9100_READ_DATA.
ENDMODULE.                              " D9100_READ_DATA INPUT

MODULE D9100_USER_COMMAND INPUT.
  G_FCODE = FCODE.
  CLEAR FCODE.

*...if ENTER key pressed, process data
  IF G_FCODE = ' '.

*..... G_ITAB_OFFSET: first data record to display in loop
    G_ITAB_OFFSET = 1.
    LEAVE TO SCREEN 9200.
  ENDIF.
ENDMODULE.                              " D9100_USER_COMMAND INPUT
```

```
MODULE D9200_EXIT INPUT.
  G_FCODE = FCODE.
  CLEAR FCODE.
  G_EXIT_MODULE = TRUE.

*...if data changed, then confirmation prompt
  IF G_CHANGED = TRUE OR
     SY-DATAR = TRUE.

*...set G_CHANGED, so that correct analysis
*...is possible in first iteration, too
    G_CHANGED = TRUE.

*.....if necessary, perform confirmation prompt
*.....and set EXIT flag
    PERFORM D9200_CHECK_SAVE.

*.....if exit without save desired,
*.....then jump directly back to EXIT module
    IF G_EXIT = TRUE AND
      G_SAVE = FALSE.
      G_CHANGED = FALSE.

*.......unlock record, then jump back
        PERFORM D9200_DEQUEUE.
        PERFORM D9200_NAVIGATE.
    ENDIF.
  ELSE.

*.....if no data changed
*.....set G_EXIT because of analysis in D9200_NAVIGATE
    G_EXIT = TRUE.

*.....unlock record, then jump back according to function code
    PERFORM D9200_DEQUEUE.
    PERFORM D9200_NAVIGATE.
  ENDIF.
ENDMODULE.                              " D9200_EXIT INPUT


MODULE D9200_DATA_CHANGED INPUT.

*...SY-DATAR is always reinitialized,
*...so it must be saved
  IF SY-DATAR = TRUE.
    G_CHANGED = TRUE.
  ENDIF.
ENDMODULE.
```

```
MODULE D9200_MODIFY_ITAB INPUT.
  IF YZZKURS-KURS < 0.
    MESSAGE E010.   " Enter correct share price!
  ENDIF.

*...convert number of step loop line in table index
  I = G_ITAB_OFFSET + SY-STEPL - 1.

*...read data from screen fields
  MOVE-CORRESPONDING YZZKURS TO F_KURSE.

*...update Itab
  MODIFY I_KURSE INDEX I FROM F_KURSE.
ENDMODULE                                  " D9200_MODIFY_ITAB INPUT


MODULE D9200_USER_COMMAND INPUT.

*...In case of FT03 and FT15, reset FCODE
*...in the EXIT module already
  IF G_EXIT_MODULE = FALSE.
    G_FCODE = FCODE.
    CLEAR FCODE.

*.....determine if data must be saved and if
*.....screen may be exited. Query only necessary
*.....if EXIT module was not effective
    PERFORM D9200_CHECK_SAVE.
  ENDIF.

*...in the module, only movement in the step loop,
*...all other functions in Performs
  CASE G_FCODE.

*.....back to first line
    WHEN 'FT21'.
      G_ITAB_OFFSET = 1.

*.....one page up
    WHEN 'FT22'.
      G_ITAB_OFFSET = G_ITAB_OFFSET - G_LOOP_LINES.

*.....one page down
    WHEN 'FT23'.
      G_ITAB_OFFSET = G_ITAB_OFFSET + G_LOOP_LINES.

*.....to last page
    WHEN 'FT24'.
      G_ITAB_OFFSET = G_TABLEN - G_LOOP_LINES + 1.
```

```
   WHEN OTHERS.
      PERFORM D9200_SAVE.
      PERFORM D9200_NAVIGATE.
   ENDCASE.

*...at most up to the last line
   I = G_TABLEN - G_LOOP_LINES + 1.
   IF G_ITAB_OFFSET > I.
     G_ITAB_OFFSET = I.
   ENDIF.

 *...at most to the first line
   IF G_ITAB_OFFSET < 1.
     G_ITAB_OFFSET = 1.
   ENDIF.
ENDMODULE.                           " D9200_USER_COMMAND  INPUT
```

9.6   Subroutines

```
FORM D9100_READ_DATA.
RANGES R_AKT FOR YZZKURS-NAME.

*...save data from the 9100 screen, since
*...header line is changed
   G_DATUM = YZZKURS-DATUM.
   CLEAR: I_AKTIEN, F_AKTIEN.
   REFRESH I_AKTIEN.

*...read and temporarily store all stocks
   SELECT * FROM YZZAKT
   INTO TABLE I_AKTIEN.

*...build RANGES table
   R_AKT-SIGN = 'I'.
   R_AKT-OPTION = 'EQ'.
   LOOP AT I_AKTIEN INTO F_AKTIEN.
     R_AKT-LOW = F_AKTIEN-NAME.
     APPEND R_AKT.
   ENDLOOP.

   CLEAR: I_KURSE, F_KURSE.
   REFRESH I_KURSE.

*...read share prices for all valid stocks
   SELECT * FROM YZZKURS
   INTO TABLE I_KURSE
   WHERE DATUM = G_DATUM AND
        NAME IN R_AKT.
```

```
*...lock table for share prices
   CALL FUNCTION 'ENQUEUE_EYKURS'
      EXPORTING
           MANDT            = SY-MANDT
*          NAME             = ' '
           DATUM            = G_DATUM
*          X_NAME           = ' '
*          X_DATUM          = ' '
*          _SCOPE           = '2'
*          _WAIT            = ' '
      EXCEPTIONS
           FOREIGN_LOCK     = 1
           SYSTEM_FAILURE   = 2
           OTHERS           = 3.

   IF SY-SUBRC <> 0.
      MESSAGE E005.                         " Record cannot be locked!
   ENDIF.

   LOOP AT I_AKTIEN INTO F_AKTIEN.

*.....test if entries exist in YZZKURS for
*.....all records from YZZAKT, if not,
*.....then append a record
      READ TABLE I_KURSE INTO F_KURSE
         WITH KEY NAME = F_AKTIEN-NAME.

      IF SY-SUBRC <> 0.
         CLEAR F_KURSE.
         MOVE-CORRESPONDING F_AKTIEN TO F_KURSE.
         F_KURSE-DATUM = G_DATUM.
         APPEND F_KURSE TO I_KURSE.

      ELSE.
         F_KURSE-DATUM = G_DATUM.
         MODIFY I_KURSE INDEX SY-TABIX FROM F_KURSE .
      ENDIF.

   ENDLOOP.
ENDFORM.                                    " D9100_READ_DATA


FORM D9200_CHECK_SAVE.
   CASE G_FCODE.

*.....ENTER key -> data check only
      WHEN ' '.
         G_SAVE = FALSE.
         G_EXIT = FALSE.
```

```
*.....F3 = BACK
*.....-> opportunity to save if data changed
     WHEN 'FT03'.
       PERFORM D9200_SAVE_QUESTION.

*.....Fll = SAVE
*......-> unconditionally save and exit the screen
     WHEN 'FT11'.
       G_SAVE = TRUE.
       G_EXIT = TRUE.

*.....F12 = CANCEL
*......-> just point out possible loss of data
     WHEN 'FT12'.
       PERFORM D9200_CANCEL_QUESTION.

*.....F15 = EXIT
*......-> opportunity to save if data changed
     WHEN 'FT15'.
       PERFORM D9200_SAVE_QUESTION.

  ENDCASE.
ENDFORM.                              " D9200_CHECK_SAVE


FORM D9200_SAVE.
  IF G_SAVE = TRUE.
    MODIFY YZZKURS FROM TABLE I_KURSE.

*.....test status of database operation
    IF SY-SUBRC <> 0.
      ROLLBACK WORK.

*.......Text: Error during save!
      MESSAGE E013.
    ELSE.

*.......Text: Data for & saved.
      MESSAGE S004 WITH G_DATUM.
    ENDIF.

*.....release database lock
    PERFORM D9200_DEQUEUE.

*.....write changes
    COMMIT WORK.

*.....reset data change flag
    G_CHANGED = FALSE.
```

```
    ENDIF.
ENDFORM.                                        " D9200_SAVE

FORM D9200_NAVIGATE.
  IF G_EXIT = TRUE.
    CASE G_FCODE.

*.......F3 = BACK
*.......-> return to previous screen
      WHEN 'FT03'.
        LEAVE TO SCREEN 9100.

*.......F11 = SAVE
*.......-> return to previous screen
      WHEN 'FT11'.
        LEAVE TO SCREEN 9100.

*.......F12 = CANCEL
*.......-> return to previous screen
      WHEN 'FT12'.
        LEAVE TO SCREEN 9100.

*.......F15 = EXIT
*.......-> exit the entire application
      WHEN 'FT15'.
        LEAVE PROGRAM.

    ENDCASE.
  ENDIF.
ENDFORM.                                        " D9200_NAVIGATE


FORM D9200_DEQUEUE.
  CALL FUNCTION 'DEQUEUE_EYKURS'
    EXPORTING
        MANDT      = SY-MANDT
*       NAME       = ' '
        DATUM      = G_DATUM
*       X_NAME     = ' '
*       X_DATUM    = ' '
*       _SCOPE     = '3'
*       _SYNCHRON  = ' '
    EXCEPTIONS
        OTHERS = 1.
ENDFORM.                                        " D9200_DEQUEUE


FORM D9200_SAVE_QUESTION.
DATA: L_ANSWER.
```

```
*...query only necessary if data was changed
   IF G_CHANGED = TRUE.
    `CALL FUNCTION 'POPUP_TO_CONFIRM_STEP'
       EXPORTING
*            DEFAULTOPTION  = 'Y'

*..........Text: Data will be lost!
           TEXTLINE1      = TEXT-012

*..........Text: Save first?
           TEXTLINE2      = TEXT-013
           TITEL          = TEXT-010
*          START_COLUMN   = 25
*          START_ROW      = 6
       IMPORTING
           ANSWER         = L_ANSWER
       EXCEPTIONS
           OTHERS         = 1.
     CASE L_ANSWER.

*.......save and exit
       WHEN JA.
         G_SAVE = TRUE.
         G_EXIT = TRUE.

*.......exit without saving
       WHEN NEIN.
         G_SAVE = FALSE.
         G_EXIT = TRUE.

*.......cancel the function -> screen is not exited
       WHEN ABBRUCH.
         G_SAVE = FALSE.
         G_EXIT = FALSE.
     ENDCASE.

*...if data not changed, then always possible to exit
   ELSE.
     G_SAVE = FALSE.
     G_EXIT = TRUE.
   ENDIF.
ENDFORM.                              " D9200_SAVE_QUESTION


FORM D9200_CANCEL_QUESTION.
DATA: L_ANSWER.

   CALL FUNCTION 'POPUP_TO_CONFIRM_LOSS_OF_DATA'
     EXPORTING
```

```
*...........Text: Confirm cancel?
        TEXTLINE1     = TEXT-011
*       TEXTLINE2     = ' '
*...........Text: Caution
        TITEL         = TEXT-010
*       START_COLUMN  = 25
*       START_ROW     = 6
   IMPORTING
     ANSWER           = L_ANSWER
   EXCEPTIONS
     OTHERS           = 1.

     *...if cancel confirmed, then set EXIT flag
   IF L_ANSWER = JA.
     G_EXIT = TRUE.
     G_SAVE = FALSE.

*...otherwise reset EXIT flag
   ELSE.
     G_EXIT = FALSE.
   ENDIF.
ENDFORM.                                " D9200_CANCEL_QUESTION
```

10 The Disk

The accompanying disk contains almost all of the development objects (programs, tables, data elements and so on) presented in the book. The corresponding files are provided in an SAP-specific format that makes it possible to import the objects into an SAP system. There are no other uses for these files and thus for the disk. The source code for the programs is also not directly accessible. Technically, the files on the disk are equivalent to a patch. In this section, you will find notes about using the disk in your SAP system.

Importing a patch is a very low-level task. If your SAP system is correctly set up, all you need to do is copy several files into existing directories and call several system commands. However, if your system's configuration differs even minimally from the standard, problems may arise. Please review the following important notes before you import the sample programs into your system:

- You import the examples into your system at your own risk. Neither the publisher nor the author shall be held liable for damages of any kind.
- Neither the author nor the publisher can guarantee that the disk can be installed without problems on your system. Support from the author or the publisher is not possible.
- The disk and the programs contained on it are not products of SAP. Therefore, you will not receive support from SAP should you encounter problems related to this disk.
- The objects contained on the disk are within the customer naming range. If objects with the same names already exist in your system, they will be overwritten! You will find an object list for the import files at the end of this section.

All of the examples were created in SAP Version 3.0. Since several of the programs use commands that are not available prior to Version 3.0, not all examples can run on older versions. Many users still work with older systems, so a subset of the sample programs has been transported into a 2.2E system, modified there, and also made available as a file. You will find two directories on the disk that are meant for import into a Version 2.2 system (*K001611.KPS* and *R001611.KPS*), and in the directory *REL30*, you will find the corresponding files for a 3.0 system (*K002693.KI3* and *R002693.KI3*).

Several conditions must be met for you to be able to import a patch into your system:

- You must be able to log on to the system as system administrator. The system administrator works with the user name *<sid>adm*, where *<sid>* is the system ID in lowercase letters.
- The Workbench Organizer must be correctly set up. This means, among other things, that a directory called */usr/sap/trans* must exist at system level, with the subdirectories *bin, buffer, data, cofiles, exe, log, sapnames* and *tmp*, and that the program RDDIMPDP is planned as a periodic background job in the SAP system.

- There should be no open conversion requests in the target system. This means that the TBATG table must be empty (you can check this with SM31).

- The programs *tp* and *R3trans* exist at operating-system level in every SAP system. These programs are available in different versions. For import into a 3.0 system, the programs mentioned should be at least version 3.0B, and for import into a 2.2 system, they should be version 2.1M.

To import the examples, activities are required both at operating-system level and in the SAP system. You begin at operating-system level. All instructions refer to UNIX-compatible operating systems.

- Mount the disk. The commands necessary for this depend on the operating system.

- You must execute all of the following activities as the user *<sid>adm*. If necessary, log on again!

- Version 3.0: Copy the file R002693.KI3 from the disk into the directory */usr/sap/trans/data*, and copy the file K002693.KI3 into the directory */usr/sap/trans/cofiles*.

- Version 2.2: Copy the file R001611.KPS from the disk into the directory */usr/sap/trans/data*, and copy the file K001611.KPS into the directory */usr/sap/trans/cofiles*.

- Change to the directory */usr/sap/trans/bin*.

- Version 3.0: Execute the following two commands one after the other:
  ```
  tp addtobuffer KI3K002693 <SID>
  tp import KI3K002693 <SID> u4
  ```
  For *<SID>*, insert the name of your SAP system in uppercase.

- Version 2.2: Execute the following two commands one after the other:
  ```
  tp addtobuffer KPSK001611 <SID>
  tp import KPSK001611 <SID> u4
  ```
  For *<SID>*, insert the name of your SAP system in uppercase.

Execute the activities that follow in the SAP system:

- Call the SE01 transaction. Enter the name of the transport job in the input field (Version 3.0: KI3K002693; Version 2.2: KPSK001611). Display the transport job by pressing the *Display* key. Check the status of the import by using the menu function *Information →* *Transport log*. Only entries with an error status of 0 or 4 may appear. Greater error numbers indicate serious problems during the import. In that case, you must fix the errors and re-execute the import. You do this by calling the command
  ```
  tp import KI3K002693 <SID> u14
  ```
  or
  ```
  tp import KPSK001611 <SID> u14
  ```
  at operating-system level. Do not execute the next steps until the import has run successfully.

- Execute the RDDBATP1 program. This program creates the imported tables in the database. Check this program's log.

- Version 2.0: As the user DDIC, create the TYZZ development class. Use the SM31 transaction for the TDEVC table to do so.

Object list transport KI3K002693

Program ID	Object type	Object name
R3TR	DEVC	TYZZ
R3TR	DOMA	YZZAKT
R3TR	DOMA	YZZBEZ
R3TR	DOMA	YZZBRA
R3TR	DOMA	YZZDATUM
R3TR	DOMA	YZZKURS
R3TR	DTEL	YCB
R3TR	DTEL	YEF1
R3TR	DTEL	YEF2
R3TR	DTEL	YRB
R3TR	DTEL	YSL1
R3TR	DTEL	YSL2
R3TR	DTEL	YSL3
R3TR	DTEL	YZZAKT
R3TR	DTEL	YZZBEZ
R3TR	DTEL	YZZBRA
R3TR	DTEL	YZZDATUM
R3TR	DTEL	YZZKURS
R3TR	ENQU	EYAKT
R3TR	ENQU	EYKURS
R3TR	ENQU	EYZZB
R3TR	FUGR	YZ31
R3TR	LDBA	YAK
R3TR	MCOB	YZZB
R3TR	MSAG	YZ
R3TR	PARA	YZN
R3TR	PROG	MYZZ1I91
R3TR	PROG	MYZZ1O01
R3TR	PROG	MYZZ1O91

Program ID	Object type	Object name
R3TR	PROG	MYZZ1TOP
R3TR	PROG	MYZZ2I91
R3TR	PROG	MYZZ2O91
R3TR	PROG	MYZZ2TOP
R3TR	PROG	MYZZ3I91
R3TR	PROG	MYZZ3O91
R3TR	PROG	MYZZ3TOP
R3TR	PROG	MYZZ4I91
R3TR	PROG	MYZZ4O91
R3TR	PROG	MYZZ4TOP
R3TR	PROG	MYZZ5I91
R3TR	PROG	MYZZ5O91
R3TR	PROG	MYZZ5TOP
R3TR	PROG	MYZZ6F91
R3TR	PROG	MYZZ6I91
R3TR	PROG	MYZZ6I92
R3TR	PROG	MYZZ6O91
R3TR	PROG	MYZZ6O92
R3TR	PROG	MYZZ6TOP
R3TR	PROG	MYZZAF01
R3TR	PROG	MYZZAI01
R3TR	PROG	MYZZAO01
R3TR	PROG	MYZZATOP
R3TR	PROG	MYZZKF01
R3TR	PROG	MYZZKI01
R3TR	PROG	MYZZKO01
R3TR	PROG	MYZZKTOP
R3TR	PROG	SAPMYZZ1
R3TR	PROG	SAPMYZZ2
R3TR	PROG	SAPMYZZ3

Program ID	Object type	Object name
R3TR	PROG	SAPMYZZ4
R3TR	PROG	SAPMYZZ5
R3TR	PROG	SAPMYZZ6
R3TR	PROG	SAPMYZZA
R3TR	PROG	SAPMYZZK
R3TR	PROG	YZZ31010
R3TR	PROG	YZZ31020
R3TR	PROG	YZZ31030
R3TR	PROG	YZZ31040
R3TR	PROG	YZZ31050
R3TR	PROG	YZZ31060
R3TR	PROG	YZZ31070
R3TR	PROG	YZZ31080
R3TR	PROG	YZZ31090
R3TR	PROG	YZZ31100
R3TR	PROG	YZZ31110
R3TR	PROG	YZZ31120
R3TR	PROG	YZZ31130
R3TR	PROG	YZZ31140
R3TR	PROG	YZZ31150
R3TR	PROG	YZZ31160
R3TR	PROG	YZZ31170
R3TR	PROG	YZZ31180
R3TR	PROG	YZZ32010
R3TR	PROG	YZZ32020
R3TR	PROG	YZZ32030
R3TR	PROG	YZZ32040
R3TR	PROG	YZZ32050
R3TR	PROG	YZZ32060
R3TR	PROG	YZZ32070

Program ID	Object type	Object name
R3TR	PROG	YZZ32080
R3TR	PROG	YZZ32090
R3TR	PROG	YZZ32100
R3TR	PROG	YZZ32110
R3TR	PROG	YZZ32120
R3TR	PROG	YZZ32130
R3TR	PROG	YZZ32140
R3TR	PROG	YZZ34010
R3TR	PROG	YZZ34020
R3TR	PROG	YZZ34030
R3TR	PROG	YZZ34040
R3TR	PROG	YZZ34050
R3TR	PROG	YZZ34051
R3TR	PROG	YZZ34060
R3TR	PROG	YZZ35010
R3TR	PROG	YZZ35020
R3TR	PROG	YZZ35030
R3TR	TABL	YDEMO
R3TR	TABL	YZZAKT
R3TR	TABL	YZZB
R3TR	TABL	YZZBT
R3TR	TABL	YZZKURS
R3TR	TRAN	YZZ1
R3TR	TRAN	YZZ2
R3TR	TRAN	YZZ3
R3TR	TRAN	YZZ4
R3TR	TRAN	YZZ5
R3TR	TRAN	YZZ6
R3TR	TRAN	YZZB
R3TR	TRAN	YZZI

Program ID	Object type	Object name
R3TR	TRAN	YZZK
R3TR	TRAN	YZZS
R3TR	TRAN	YZZU
R3TR	VIEW	YVZZB

Object list transport KPSK001611

Program ID	Object type	Object name
R3TR	DOMA	YZZAKT
R3TR	DOMA	YZZBEZ
R3TR	DOMA	YZZBRA
R3TR	DOMA	YZZDATUM
R3TR	DOMA	YZZKURS
R3TR	DTEL	YCB
R3TR	DTEL	YEF1
R3TR	DTEL	YEF2
R3TR	DTEL	YRB
R3TR	DTEL	YSL1
R3TR	DTEL	YSL2
R3TR	DTEL	YSL3
R3TR	DTEL	YZZAKT
R3TR	DTEL	YZZBEZ
R3TR	DTEL	YZZBRA
R3TR	DTEL	YZZDATUM
R3TR	DTEL	YZZKURS
R3TR	ENQU	EYAKT
R3TR	ENQU	EYKURS
R3TR	ENQU	EYZZB
R3TR	FUGR	YZ31
R3TR	LDBA	YAK
R3TR	MSAG	YZ
R3TR	PARA	YZN

Program ID	Object type	Object name
R3TR	PROG	MYZZ1I91
R3TR	PROG	MYZZ1O01
R3TR	PROG	MYZZ1O91
R3TR	PROG	MYZZ1TOP
R3TR	PROG	MYZZ2I91
R3TR	PROG	MYZZ2O91
R3TR	PROG	MYZZ2TOP
R3TR	PROG	MYZZ3I91
R3TR	PROG	MYZZ3O91
R3TR	PROG	MYZZ3TOP
R3TR	PROG	MYZZ4I91
R3TR	PROG	MYZZ4O91
R3TR	PROG	MYZZ4TOP
R3TR	PROG	MYZZ5I91
R3TR	PROG	MYZZ5O91
R3TR	PROG	MYZZ5TOP
R3TR	PROG	MYZZ6F91
R3TR	PROG	MYZZ6I91
R3TR	PROG	MYZZ6I92
R3TR	PROG	MYZZ6O91
R3TR	PROG	MYZZ6O92
R3TR	PROG	MYZZ6TOP
R3TR	PROG	MYZZAF01
R3TR	PROG	MYZZAI01
R3TR	PROG	MYZZAO01
R3TR	PROG	MYZZATOP
R3TR	PROG	MYZZKF01
R3TR	PROG	MYZZKI01
R3TR	PROG	MYZZKO01
R3TR	PROG	MYZZKTOP
R3TR	PROG	SAPMYZZ1
R3TR	PROG	SAPMYZZ2

Program ID	Object type	Object name
R3TR	PROG	SAPMYZZ3
R3TR	PROG	SAPMYZZ4
R3TR	PROG	SAPMYZZ5
R3TR	PROG	SAPMYZZ6
R3TR	PROG	SAPMYZZA
R3TR	PROG	SAPMYZZK
R3TR	PROG	YZZ31010
R3TR	PROG	YZZ31020
R3TR	PROG	YZZ31030
R3TR	PROG	YZZ31040
R3TR	PROG	YZZ31050
R3TR	PROG	YZZ31060
R3TR	PROG	YZZ31070
R3TR	PROG	YZZ31080
R3TR	PROG	YZZ31090
R3TR	PROG	YZZ31100
R3TR	PROG	YZZ31110
R3TR	PROG	YZZ31120
R3TR	PROG	YZZ31130
R3TR	PROG	YZZ31140
R3TR	PROG	YZZ31150
R3TR	PROG	YZZ31160
R3TR	PROG	YZZ31170
R3TR	PROG	YZZ31180
R3TR	PROG	YZZ32010
R3TR	PROG	YZZ32020
R3TR	PROG	YZZ32030
R3TR	PROG	YZZ32040
R3TR	PROG	YZZ32050
R3TR	PROG	YZZ32060
R3TR	PROG	YZZ32070
R3TR	PROG	YZZ32080

Program ID	Object type	Object name
R3TR	PROG	YZZ32090
R3TR	PROG	YZZ32100
R3TR	PROG	YZZ32110
R3TR	PROG	YZZ32120
R3TR	PROG	YZZ32130
R3TR	PROG	YZZ32140
R3TR	PROG	YZZ34010
R3TR	PROG	YZZ34020
R3TR	PROG	YZZ34030
R3TR	PROG	YZZ34040
R3TR	PROG	YZZ34050
R3TR	PROG	YZZ34051
R3TR	PROG	YZZ34060
R3TR	PROG	YZZ35010
R3TR	PROG	YZZ35020
R3TR	PROG	YZZ35030
R3TR	TABL	YDEMO
R3TR	TABL	YZZAKT
R3TR	TABL	YZZB
R3TR	TABL	YZZBT
R3TR	TABL	YZZKURS
R3TR	TRAN	YZZ1
R3TR	TRAN	YZZ2
R3TR	TRAN	YZZ3
R3TR	TRAN	YZZ4
R3TR	TRAN	YZZ5
R3TR	TRAN	YZZ6
R3TR	TRAN	YZZB
R3TR	TRAN	YZZI
R3TR	TRAN	YZZK
R3TR	TRAN	YZZS
R3TR	TRAN	YZZU
R3TR	VIEW	YVZZB

Bibliography

[1] Buck-Emden R. and Galimow J. (1996). *SAP R/3 System: A Client/Server Technology*. Harlow: Addison Wesley Longman.

Additional resources

The online help of the SAP system.

Training materials for the following SAP courses:

BC170   ABAP/4 Programming Basics

BC175   List Programming Techniques

BC185   Programming Logical Databases

BC190   Dialog-oriented List Programming

BC220   Dialog Programming Basics

BC230   Additional Dialog Programming Techniques

Index